People

OSON'S

SOAP

SINGER

SINGER

BALLY

CARTER'S

EVERYTHING VINTAGE

PRICE GUIDE TO COLLECTABLES IN AUSTRALIA & NEW ZEALAND

2006
1st EDITION

PUBLISHED BY JOHN FURPHY PTY LTD

CARTER'S

EVERYTHING

VINTAGE

**Price Guide to Collectables
in Australia and New Zealand**

2006
1st Edition

Pricing in this publication is supplied by the contributor listed with the item and is based solely on the contributor's experience in their market.

Although some editing occurs, all items and descriptions are supplied by the dealers identified with the items and are not owned or provided by John Furphy Pty Ltd trading as CARTER'S Antiques & Collectables Price Guide.

This publication may not be reproduced in whole or part without prior written permission from the publishers. All advertisements are covered by copyright and may not be reproduced without prior written permission.

Publisher's Copyright - John Furphy Pty Ltd trading as CARTER'S Antiques & Collectables Price Guide.

CARTER'S Publications
The Most Comprehensive and Accurate Information

John Furphy Pty Ltd
Trading as
CARTER'S Antiques & Collectables Price Guide

PO Box 7246, BAULKHAM HILLS BC NSW 2153, AUSTRALIA

37/9 Hoyle Avenue, CASTLE HILL NSW 2154, AUSTRALIA

Toll Free Ph: 1800 670 630   Ph: (02) 8850 4600

Fax: 02 8850 4100   ABN: 37 005 508 789

Email: info@carters.com.au   Web: www.carters.com.au

ISBN 1-876079-16-9

CONTENTS

Advertiser's Index — 4

Acknowledgements — 5

Introduction — 6

Forward — 7 – 8

Advertising — 18 – 37
Beer, Wine & Spirits | Calendars | Ceramics | Coca Cola | Display Figures | Ephemera | Labels | Mannequins | Packaged Goods | Signs | Tins | Other

Art — 38 – 47
Artefacts - Australian Aboriginal | Artefacts - New Guinean | Oil Paintings | Posters | Prints | Sculpture - Animals | Sculpture - Busts/Heads | Sculpture - Figures/Groups | Sculpture - Other | Other

Ceramics — 48 – 150
Aboriginalware | Allover Floral/Chintz | Arabia | Australian Studio Pottery | Aynsley | Bailey, Lorna | Bakewells | Belleek | Bendigo Pottery | Beswick | Beswick - Beatrix Potter | Bing & Grondahl | Bisque | Bjorn Winblad | Blue & White | Bosson's | Boyd, Guy | Boyd, Kevin | Boyd, Martin | Boyd, Merric | Brownie Downing | Burleigh Ware | Carlton Ware | Clarice Cliff | Coalport | Cornishware | Crown Devon | Crown Lynn | Denby | Dennis China | Diana Pottery | Ellis | Lorenz | German | Goebel | Goebel - Hummel | Goldscheider | Gouda | Grimwades | Kalmar | Lilliput Lane | Limoges | Lladro | Maling | Masons | McLaren, Gus | MCP Mingay | Moon, Milton | Moorcroft | Neil Douglas | Other Australian Ceramics | Other New Zealand | Pates Pottery | Poole | Remued | Ridgways | Royal Albert | Royal Copenhagen | Royal Doulton - Bunnykins | Royal Doulton - Character Jugs | Royal Doulton - Figurines | Royal Doulton - Other | Royal Doulton - Series Ware | Royal Dux | Royal Winton | Royal Worcester | Seccombe, Grace | Shelley | Shorter & Son | Studio Anna | Susie Cooper | Sylvac | Tunstall | Villeroy & Boch | Wade | Wedgwood | Wembley | Other

Costume & Dressing Accessories — 151 – 165
Belts | Buckles | Clothing - Men's | Clothing - Women's | Compacts | Dressing Accessories | Hairpins & Slides | Handbags & Purses | Headwear | Parasols & Umbrellas | Scent Bottles | Shoes | Sunglasses | Other Dressing Accessories

Costume Jewellery — 166 – 174
1950's | 1960's | 1970's | 1980's | 1990's | Lea Stein

Dolls & Accessories — 175 – 178
Barbie | Bisque | Celluloid | Composition | Doll Prams | Dolls Houses | Fabric | Other Dolls | Pedigree | Teddy Bears | Other Stuffed Toys

Entertainment — 179 – 191
Computer Games | Gramophones | Movie Related | Music Related | Musical Boxes & Automata | Musical Instruments | Phonographs | Radios | Records & CDs - Beatles | Records & CDs - Other Artists | Sound Equipment | Television | Other Music Accessories

Furniture — 192 – 209
American | Art Deco Style | Australian - Fler & Tessa | Australian - Grant Featherston | Australian - Other Designers | Australian - Parker | English | European | Metal, Glass & Plastic | Scandinavian Designers | Scandinavian Style | Other Furniture

Glass — 210 – 233
American | Bottles | Carnival | English - Whitefriars | English 20th Century | European | New Zealand | Scandinavian - Holmgaard | Scandinavian - Kosta | Scandinavian - Other | Venetian - Antonio de Ros | Venetian - Archimede Seguso | Venetian - Dino Martens | Venetian - Other Designers | Other Glass

Horology — 234 – 242
Clocks - Novelty | Clocks - Other | Clocks - Wall | Watches - Pocket | Watches - Wrist

Household and Workshop — 243 – 260
Architectural | Garage Equipment | Home Appliances - Fans | Home Appliances - Heaters | Home Appliances - Jugs | Home Appliances - Other | Home Appliances - Toasters | Kitchenalia - Anodized | Kitchenalia - Bakelite & Plastic | Kitchenalia - Knives and Other Implements | Kitchenalia - Pots & Pans | Kitchenalia - Storage Containers | Kitchenalia - Other |

Machinery | Miscellaneous | Rugs & Carpets | Scales | Soft Furnishings & Wallpaper | Stoves | Telephones | Tools | Other

Industry Science & Technology   **261 – 262**
Devices & Viewers | Eye Glasses | Globes - Terrestial & Celestial | Medical Instruments | Microscopes | Pharmacy Items | Taxidermy | Other - Medical | Other Scientific Instruments & Equipment

Jewellery   **263 – 268**
Bracelets/Bangles | Brooches | Earrings | General | Georg Jensen | Necklaces/Chains | Pendants/ Lockets | Rings

Lighting   **269 – 280**
Art Deco | Candelabra/Candlesticks | Ceiling Lights | Chandeliers | Lamps - Barsony | Lamps - Ceramic | Lamps - Kerosene | Lamps - Table & Desk | Lamps - Other | Modern Classics | Venetian Glass

Memorabilia   **281 – 309**
Autographs | Christmas | Commemorative | Commemorative - Royalty | Musical Groups | Souvenir Ware - Australian | Souvenir Ware - New Zealand | Sporting - AFL/VFL | Sporting - Cricket | Sporting - Golf | Sporting - Olympics | Sporting - Other | Transport - Aeronautical | Transport - Motoring | Transport - Nautical | Transport - Railways | Transport - Other | Other Memorabilia

Militaria   **310 – 312**

Numismatics & Scrip   **313**

Oriental   **314 – 319**
Ceramics | Other

Precious Objects   **320 – 321**
Money Boxes | Other

Printed Material   **322 – 346**
Books | Books - Australian | Comics - Australian | Comics - Spiderman | Comics - Phantom | Comics - Other | Magazines | Movie Posters | Other

Recreations & Pursuits   **347 – 357**
Alcohol Related | Photographic - Cameras | Photographic - Other | Sewing | Games & Puzzles | Smoking Related | Sporting Equipment | Writing

Silver   3

Silver Plate   3

Toys   **360 – 3**
Boats | Cars | Dinky | Games & Puzzles | Trains | Trucks & Busses | Movie & Television - Disney | Movie & Television - Star Wars | Movie & Televisio Other | Tinplate | Other

Contributing Dealer's Index   **388 – 4**

Index   **403 – 4**

ADVERTISER'S INDEX

Antiques & Art Australia

Australian Art Sales Digest

Books On Antiques

Burtons Colossal Fairs

CARTER'S Collecting Australiana

CARTER'S Mid 20thC Design

CARTER'S Price Guide to Antiques

Chapel Street Bazaar

Circa Vintage Clothing   1

Collectables Trader

Collectible Momentos   10 & 2

Goodwood House Antiques

Three Quarters 20th Century Furnishings

Lawson ~ Menzies

Maxine's Collectibles

Phillicia Antiques

The Botanic Ark

ACKNOWLEDGEMENTS

e publishers would like to thank our staff, photographers contributing dealers, designers
d printers whose contributions made this book a reality.

int Editors:

John Furphy
Trent McVey

blisher:

John Furphy Pty Ltd trading as
CARTER'S ANTIQUES & COLLECTABLES PRICE GUIDE
ABN 37 005 508 789

oduction Team,
pesetters:

Sue Stafford-Hickson, Dylan Davies, Dane Gardiner,
Linda Furphy, Nicola Ellis, Rosalind Toombs, Sam Furphy,
Jill Vincent, Peter Ellis, Emma Storey

dditional research
aterial provided by:

Dean Angelucci, David Atkinson, Elaine Atkinson, Kathy
Blackmore-Palmer, Mike Dawborn, Tiffany Dodd, Richard
Dowe, David Ferguson, Peter Ford, Brett Forde, David
Gonzales, Nola Hargreaves, John Hungerford, Alistair
Knight, Natalie McLaughlin, Robert Neilson, Kim
Wallace-Wells

hotographers:

Chris Elfes (NSW, WA, NZ), John Mildwaters (QLD), Tira
Lewis (VIC), Rick Merrie (VIC), Len Weigh (VIC), Chris Maait
(NSW), Simon Grimmett (NSW), Jake Jacobson (TAS),
Robin Cornwell (SA), Matthew Abbott (NSW)

ecial Thanks To:

William and Dorothy Hall

ge Design and
e Press:

Campbell Murray Creating, Sydney

ver Design:

Andrew Hogg Design, Melbourne

inters:

SNP SPrint Pte Ltd, Singapore

INTRODUCTION

There has long been a need for a Price Guide to complement CARTER'S Price Guide to Antiques in Australasia®, to cover items that people collect, but are not antique. This raises the problem of what is an 'antique'. For Australian Customs purposes, an antique is defined as an item that was manufactured over 100 years ago, but in popular usage, an 'antique' is an item that was manufactured in the unspecified past decades, but less than 100 years.

Over the last decade, the cut-off date that must be met for an item to be classed as an antique has become increasingly elastic. The two premier London antique fairs, the *Grosvenor House Antiques Fair and the Spring Olympia Fair* over the last 10 years have changed their exhibition criteria and dropped any specification as to the age of the items that dealers may exhibit. In Australia the Australian Antique Dealers Association set a dateline of pre-1950 as the age of items that may be exhibited at their annual fair.

For the purpose of this book, we have used post-1950 manufacture as an indicative guide to items that are eligible for inclusion. However, we also include some pre-1950 items, as in many areas covered in this book, 1950 did not represent a turning point in design, materials or manufacturing methods and production of some of the items continued from pre-1950, through the 1950s and later.

The next problem we had was that there was no generally accepted term to refer to items manufactured after 1950, which are sought or collected. The term 'collectable' refers to a large body of these items, but buyers of a Tessa lounge suite, a Norma Tullo dress or Georg Jensen jewellery would not consider they were purchasing a collectable.

To indicate the book covered more than just collectables, we chose the title 'Everything Vintage', with one dictionary definition of vintage being, *Classic. Of old, recognized, and enduring interest, importance, or quality.*

We hope you find our new publication informative and rewarding.

John Furphy,
John Furphy,
Publisher

FOREWORD

ENJOYING COLLECTABLES
By William and Dorothy Hall

"Everyone collects something." Whenever we say this to groups of people there are always those who question the statement, but it doesn't take us long to discover what they collect. It might be holiday match booklets, old tools stored in the shed, recipes carefully kept in folders, or vintage clothing that is bought to wear. When we've discovered their collecting passion, people usually retort with, "I'd never thought of that as a collection."

Some of us might not think of ourselves as collectors, but we are, even if we don't use that description of ourselves, such as those of us who search out and buy mid 20th century furniture for our homes. We do this because we regard such furniture as representing excellent design. So in this case our interest is mainly décor rather than to build up a collection. (We should mention that we are also keen collectors of mid 20th century glass.)

Once we've shown that everyone is a collector, we delight in pointing out Australia's most popular collectable. The answer might surprise you: it's sea shells. About one-half of the population collects them, but only two percent of the population are conchologists, that is serious shell collectors. One friend said he'd never thought of himself as a shell collector, but on considering it realised he had shells all over the place.

WHAT IS A COLLECTABLE?

Already in this short article we've used 'collect' as a word, or part word, many times without defining what we mean by 'collectable'. "But doesn't everyone know the definition of collectable?" you ask.

Well, no they don't, and debate about the definition has continued for many years, especially the argument about the link between 'antique' and 'collectable'.

Antiques may be collectable, and collectables may be antiques. And what is an 'antique'? There can be no firm dividing line, a fact long recognised by dealers throughout the world. Fortunately, and sensibly, this price guide has defined a collectable as anything produced after 1950. Unsurprisingly, some 'collectable' items were also made before 1950, so there can be no rigidity to the definition, it is just a guide.

CARTER'S publications define an antique as anything made over 50 years ago, which is a definition being increasingly adopted internationally, even though it is not the customs definition – their definition is 100 years.

WHAT THINGS ARE COLLECTABLE?

The answer is – everything. Not only does everyone collect something, everything is collectable. The strangest collectables we've come across are air sickness bags, sliced bread wrapper date tags and toilet rolls (the army camouflage rolls being the most sought after). The most popular collectables include pottery, glass, toys, postage stamps, printed ephemera, wine, and many more – which is why we need this price guide, to learn about the huge range of collectables available in Australia and New Zealand, and how much they cost.

We know a collector with over one million picture postcards, another whose house boasts huge illuminated display cabinets holding his pressed glass collection, another with hundreds of cookery books and another who has built a huge shed to house his furniture collection. In every case, they have found it essential to classify their collections.

A vast range of collectables is displayed in this publication. Not only will it serve as a price guide, it will also give readers important information on collectables presently available on today's market and give lots of ideas about classifying their collections. It will also be helpful to those of us who are décor conscious.

WHAT WILL BECOME COLLECTABLE?

The honest answer is that nobody knows. And yet a common mistake made by some people is to try to make predictions about collectability and to buy accordingly. So let's emphasise something we've said many times: don't collect with investment as the primary motive.

A person we know tried to do this with 1950s black lady table lamps. He saw that they had doubled in value in a few months, and so bought every lamp he could find. Now his shed is full of them and he cannot even give them away. This shows that some collectables can be fickle, popular one week and of little interest the next. (But, then, we must admit that in ten years time, they may regain popularity. So perhaps the black lady lamp will eventually prove to be a good investment, after all.)

WHY DO PEOPLE COLLECT?

If investment is not a recommended motive, what should the motive be? Quite simply, we should collect because we enjoy doing it. Full enjoyment can come through knowing about our collectables (history, maker, conservation, and so on) and by displaying, using, or wearing the collection to good effect.

This price guide is indispensable to gain much essential knowledge; so are good reference books. As well, you should consider joining a collectors' club. There are many specialist groups, such as those for glass and bottle collectors and good general clubs like the Australiana Society. We belong to the Adelaide Society of Collectors that meets every month.

Then there is the internet. A few well selected words (note 'well selected') will enable the search engine to reveal numerous references. As well, talking to knowledgeable dealers can be helpful, and in turn they get to know what interests you.

HOW MAY WE BUY AND SELL COLLECTABLES?

A good place to start is by examining the names and addresses of dealers in this price guide. Also, the Yellow Pages can be helpful; and dealers will often tell you about other retailers who sell the collectables that interest you. You'll discover that bric-a-brac shops and antiques markets stock many collectables, but even traditional antiques shops may be worth exploring, especially if you tell the proprietor what you're looking for. In New Zealand an antiques dealer who had no interest in old books pointed us to an antique dresser that contained a few hidden books, including Dr Johnson's leather bound pocket dictionary. We bought it for $10.

Auction houses have become collector friendly and so you should feel free to attend inspections, and to bid for items that interest you. But remember the buyer's premium. Auction houses are also good places to make a quick sale if you want to turn a collectable into cash.

Many of our cities and towns hold regular antiques, collectables and bric-a-brac fairs. They can be good places to see a wide range of collectables shown by dealers from around the country. It is often possible to compare prices.

Garage sales, car boot sales, church and school fetes and 'op' shops – such as those operated by the Salvation Army – are often worth exploring for the occasional bargain, especially vintage clothing. Our experience is that lots of time may be spent before something worthwhile turns up – but many collectors enjoy the fun of the chase, which is an important part of the collecting process to them.

Collecting is a fascinating, stimulating hobby and you will meet many interesting people. We collectors have needed an Australian collectables price guide for many years. Now we have one. The guide itself should become a collectable, and what better place to start your collection than with 'number one'.

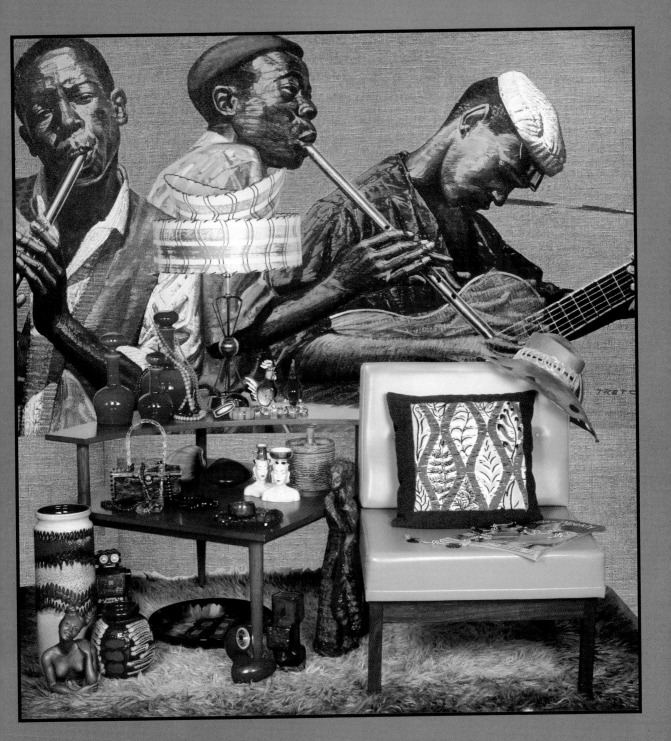

CHAPEL STREET BAZAAR

80 Independent dealers • Open 7 days 10am – 6pm

Chapel Street Bazaar • 217–223 Chapel Street • Prahran VIC 3181
Tel: 03 9529 1727 • Fax: 03 9521 3174

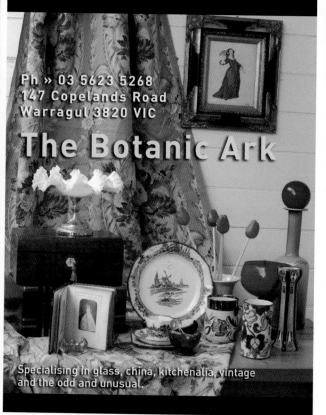

LAWSONS

entries invited

RETRO COLLECTABLES

20TH CENTURY FURNITURE, ART GLASS + CERAMICS, TOYS + COLLECTABLES
COMICS + BOOKS, RETRO FASHION, JEWELLERY + RETRO ART

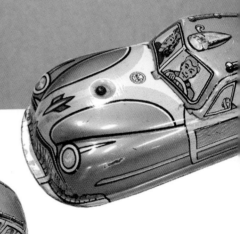

LAWSONS

1A The Crescent Annandale 2038
tel 02 9566 2377 **fax** 02 9566 2388
www.lawsons.com.au

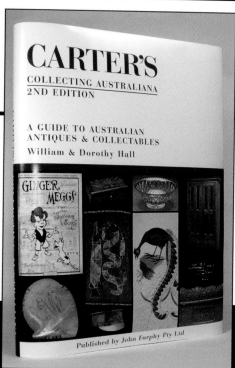
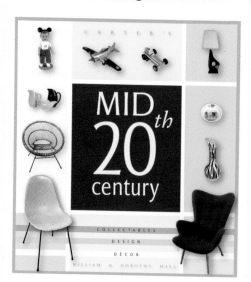

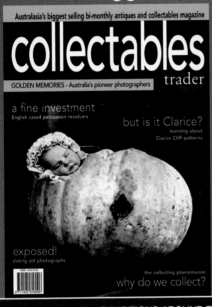
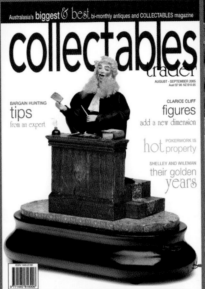

2006 CARTER'S
PRICE GUIDE TO
ANTIQUES IN AUSTRALASIA®

Published by John Furphy Pty Ltd

 1985
 1986
 1987
 1988
 1989
 1990
 1991
 1992
 1993

 1994
 1995
 1996
 1997
 1998
 1999

 2000
 2001
 2002
 2003
 2004
 2005

The 2006 edition, is available now and has:
- Improved, easier to follow and neater layouts
- Easier to follow and more detailed categorisation
- Wider category coverage
- More contributing dealers
- More comprehensive indexing

22nd EDITION
ORDER NOW FOR IMMEDIATE DELIVERY

$125

With 22 years of annual editions since 1985, CARTER'S Price Guide to Antiques in Australasia® is the longest running continuous series of books on antiques and collectables in Australia and New Zealand.
And with nearly 200,000 items covered in the series, from 1985 to 2006, there's little wonder why a full set of CARTER'S Price Guides has become such a sought after commodity.

Order directly through our office by calling toll free 1800 670 630 or from your local book or antique store.

Please note that CARTER'S Price Guide to Antiques in Australasia® is a registered trademark. If it doesn't carry this title it is not a genuine CARTER'S Price Guide and cannot possibly be a continuation of your collection.
John Furphy Pty Ltd ABN 37 005 508 789.
Trading as CARTER'S Antiques & Collectables Price Guide

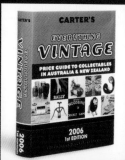

You've read the book now visit the dealers

To view antiques and collectables for sale,
locate dealers for any area, or get fair
details visit the Antiques & Art Australia site:

www.antique-art.com.au

The site contains thousands of items for sale from dealers located in Australia and New Zealand and are categorised, by dealer and item category.

Many of the dealers included in CARTER'S PRICE GUIDE showcase their items on this site.

If you find something you like, you correspond direct with dealer. There are no middlemen involved.

The Antiques & Art Australia domain is the largest, longest established and most comprehensive antiques and collectables site in Australasia.

DEALERS: The Antiques & Art Australia site is sponsored by CARTER'S PRICE GUIDE enabling you to list your items free of charge.

To register, go to the site and click on the 'How to List' link on the front page.

'Grants' Scotch Whisky tray with glamour gir, c1960, 34cm wide, 34cm high.

$65 - $85   **Born Frugal, VIC**

Whisky tin advertising tray, c1950, 35cm wide.

$45 - $65   **Towers Antiques & Collectables, NSW**

A large rectangular electric Johnny Walker clock, with inbuilt lights, c1950, 80cm wide, 115cm high.

$2400 - $2600   **Granny's Market Pty Ltd, VIC**

Tooth KB lager beer can cooler, gold with red KB, made by Willow Australia, c1980, 12cm long, 16cm diameter.

$15 - $25   **Alan's Collectables, NSW**

Original 'Ballarat Bitter' beer bag, c1950, 34cm wide, 74cm high.

$80 - $100   **Antiques, Goods & Chattels, VIC**

'Mudgee Ale' bottle, Federal Brewery, sealed and full, c1948, 28cm high.

$140 - $160   **Settlers Store, NSW**

Droving VB can, unopened from Newcastle water, N.T to Longreach, Qld May-September 1988, from CUB Breweries, c1988.

$10 - $20   **Alan's Collectables, NSW**

Advertising playing card for 'Smith's Yalumba Ports' situated in S.A.'s Barossa Valley, c1950, 9cm wide, 5.5cm high.

$5 - $10   **Philicia Antiques & Collectables, SA**

Advertising playing card for 'Kaiser-Pearl' sparking white wine, from a Barossa Valley winery in S.A., c1960, 5.5cm wide, 9cm high.

$5 - $10   **Philicia Antiques & Collectables, SA**

'The Swagman', a Jim Beam Australian decanter by Regal China, c1979, 36cm high.

$330 - $370   **Alan's Collectables, NSW**

'Clan Wallace Special Blend' empty Scotch whisky decanter, depicting a Scotsman in tartan kilt, c1960, 12.5cm wide, 46cm high.

$90 - $110   **Abra Card Abra Roycroft, VIC**

'Kangaroo' Jim Beam Australian decanter by Regal China, c1977, 30cm high.

$115 - $135　　**Alan's Collectables, NSW**

'Koala's' Jim Beam Australian decanter by Regal China, c1973, 25cm high.

$205 - $245　　**Alan's Collectables, NSW**

Australian 'Vickers Gin' advertising rooster figure, by Diana Pottery, c1950, 20cm high.

$110 - $130　　**Brae-mar Antiques, NSW**

Painted plaster bust on a base for 'Beenleigh Rum', 19cm deep, 22cm wide, 48cm high.

$940 - $1040　　**Alan Syber's Antiques Antiquarian, VIC**

'Black and White Scotch Whisky' plaster bar figure of two Scottish Terriers, c1950, 32cm long, 24cm deep.

$225 - $265　　**Ardeco Antiques & Collectables, WA**

Early hard rubber Dewar's scotch whisky advertising statue, 23cm wide.

$190 - $210　　**Tyabb Hay Shed, VIC**

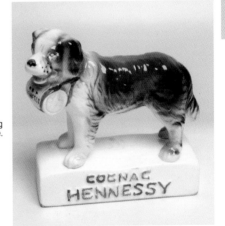

Small ceramic figure advertising 'Hennesy Brandy', c1950.

$140 - $160　　**Ardeco Antiques & Collectables, WA**

Jim Beam thermometer, fahrenheit and celsius, made of painted tin, c1960, 24cm wide, 64cm high.

$185 - $205　　**Chapel Street Bazaar, VIC**

'Beefeater Gin' advertising statue with old bottle, 43cm high.

$85 - $105　　**Bob Butler's Sentimental Journey, QLD**

Advertising figure of a woodpecker for 'Bulmers Cider', painted plastic, c1950, 6cm wide, 16cm high.

$55 - $75　　**Chapel Street Bazaar, VIC**

Jim Beam 'Australian' Fox commemorative statuette, Gawler River Beamers 5th birthday 11th July 1987, 14cm high.

$65 - $85　　**Alan's Collectables, NSW**

'Old Parr Whisky' jug, the base stamped 'Wade PDM England', 13cm high.

$110 - $130   **Granny's Market Pty Ltd, VIC**

Lilac coloured 'Johnnie Walker' jug and ashtray by Moulin Des Loups.

$770 - $870   **Kings Park Antiques & Collectables, SA**

Cylindrical, deep green water jug with advertising for 'Cutty Sark Scotch Whiskey', c1990, 19cm high.

$85 - $105   **Kenny's Antiques, VIC**

Square section, green water jug with recessed handle and advertising to three sides for 'Passport Scotch Whisky', manufactured by Wade, England, c1990, 20cm high.

$70 - $90   **Kenny's Antiques, VIC**

Square section, white water jug with vertical transfer print advertising 'Haig Scotch Whisky', recessed handle, unmarked, c1990, 20cm high.

$65 - $85   **Kenny's Antiques, VIC**

'Beefeater Gin' ice bucket, c1960, 20cm long, 15cm deep, 27cm high.

$150 - $180   **Newport Temple Antiques, VIC**

Cream coloured water jug with transfer printed advertising to two sides for 'Beefeater Gin', manufactured by Wade, England, c1990, 14cm high.

$85 - $105   **Kenny's Antiques, VIC**

Novelty radio advertising 'Swan Lager', c1970, 12cm high.

$20 - $30   **Secondhand Furniture Mart, TAS**

'Usher Whisky' advertising bottle display stand with Ushers Whisky bottle (full), not original, statue made of plaster for the USA market, c1935.

$1100 - $1300   **Mac's Collectables**

Royal Doulton 'King George IV, Top-Notch Whisky' matchbox holder and ashtray.

$400 - $450   **Old Bank Antiques, NSW**

'Teacher's Whisky' lidded box inscribed 'The Right Spirit Teacher's Whisky' inside the lid and, 'The Whisky of the Good Old Days Teacher - Estab. 1830' inside the box, c1930, 27cm deep, 42cm wide, 12cm high.

$155 - $175   **Timeless Treasures, WA**

Penfolds Royal Reserve Port advertising pub mirror, back painted with elaborate gilding featuring grape leaves, later fitted with frame, c1950, 51cm wide, 66cm high.

$825 - $925

Shenton Park Antiques, WA

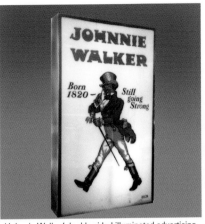

'Johnnie Walker' double sided illuminated advertising sign, manufactured by Delta, c1960, 20cm deep, 920cm wide, 1770cm high.

$1550 - $1750

Kings Park Antiques & Collectables, SA

Illuminated bar sign for 'Guinness Stout' with a 12 volt light and 240 volt to 12 volt transformer, c1998, 18cm deep, 20cm wide, 30cm high.

$330 - $370

The Evandale Tinker, TAS

'Kilkenny Irish Beer' illuminated sign, with 12 volt globe and 240 volt to 12 volt transformer, c1996, 15cm wide, 8cm high.

$330 - $370

The Evandale Tinker, TAS

McWilliams Wines tin advertising sign, c1950, 70cm long, 40cm high.

$65 - $85

Towers Antiques & Collectables, NSW

American 'Budweiser' 150 volt, red and white neon sign with transformer, 72.5cm long, 20cm deep, 60cm high.

$725 - $825

Tyabb Hay Shed, VIC

'Ad Ball' revolving advertising sign for 'Carlton Cold' beer, c2000, 39cm high, 32cm diameter.

$430 - $470

Old World Antiques, NSW

Illuminated 'Cascade Premium Light Beer' sign, 240 volts, c1998, 50cm deep, 33cm wide, 30cm high.

$265 - $305

The Evandale Tinker, TAS

'Johnny Walker' Scotch Whisky 'Wade' London, England, 9cm wide, 15cm high.

$55 - $75

Seguin's Antiques & Café, NSW

Advertising playing card for 'Melbourne Bitter Ale', c1950, 5.5cm wide, 9cm high.

$5 - $10

Philicia Antiques & Collectables, SA

'Johnnie Walker' Scotch Whisky advertising figure of a striding man, 27cm high.

$370 - $410

Kings Park Antiques & Collectables, SA

COCA-COLA

Boxed Coca-Cola phone in the shape of a bottle, Model 500, full featured electronic, c1985, 5cm long, 5cm wide, 25cm high.

$120 - $140 — **Alan's Collectables, NSW**

Coca-Cola clip on radio and compass, boxed, c2002.

$10 - $20 — **Alan's Collectables, NSW**

Coca-Cola advertising thermometer, c1955, 24cm long, 8cm high.

$135 - $155 — **Kings Park Antiques & Collectables, SA**

'Drink Coca-Cola' radio depicting a vending machine, c1965, 4cm deep, 9cm wide, 20cm high.

$360 - $400 — **Treats & Treasures, NSW**

Sydney Olympic 2000 'Months to Go' Coca-Cola bottles, set of five with tags, badges and pin trading kiosk.

$1400 - $1600 — **The Glass Stopper, NSW**

Miniature wooden box of twenty four Coke bottles and caps, c1950.

$380 - $420 — **The Glass Stopper, NSW**

Souvenir Coca-Cola bottle, gold print of the first 100 bottles, sealed, c1975.

$165 - $185 — **The Glass Stopper, NSW**

Coca-Cola Bon Jovi promotion can sealed and empty, fully autographed by the band with a certificate of authenticity, c1993.

$500 - $600 — **Chapel Street Bazaar, VIC**

Crystal commemorative Coca-Cola bottle, 'Opening Ceremony, Sydney Olympics 2000', boxed and numbered, c2000.

$325 - $365 — **The Glass Stopper, NSW**

Coca-Cola Ghostbusters can, never opened, c1989.

$10 - $15 — **The Glass Stopper, NSW**

Penfolds Royal Reserve Port advertising pub mirror, back painted with elaborate gilding featuring grape leaves, later fitted with frame, c1950, 51cm wide, 66cm high.

$825 - $925   **Shenton Park Antiques, WA**

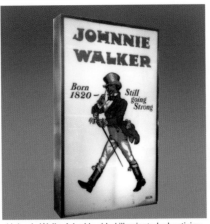

'Johnnie Walker' double sided illuminated advertising sign, manufactured by Delta, c1960, 20cm deep, 920cm wide, 1770cm high.

$1550 - $1750   **Kings Park Antiques & Collectables, SA**

Illuminated bar sign for 'Guinness Stout' with a 12 volt light and 240 volt to 12 volt transformer, c1998, 18cm deep, 20cm wide, 30cm high.

$330 - $370   **The Evandale Tinker, TAS**

'Kilkenny Irish Beer' illuminated sign, with 12 volt globe and 240 volt to 12 volt transformer, c1996, 15cm wide, 8cm high.

$330 - $370   **The Evandale Tinker, TAS**

McWilliams Wines tin advertising sign, c1950, 70cm long, 40cm high.

$65 - $85   **Towers Antiques & Collectables, NSW**

American 'Budweiser' 150 volt, red and white neon sign with transformer, 72.5cm long, 20cm deep, 60cm high.

$725 - $825   **Tyabb Hay Shed, VIC**

'Ad Ball' revolving advertising sign for 'Carlton Cold' beer, c2000, 39cm high, 32cm diameter.

$430 - $470   **Old World Antiques, NSW**

Illuminated 'Cascade Premium Light Beer' sign, 240 volts, c1998, 50cm deep, 33cm wide, 30cm high.

$265 - $305   **The Evandale Tinker, TAS**

'Johnny Walker' Scotch Whisky 'Wade' London, England, 9cm wide, 15cm high.

$55 - $75   **Seguin's Antiques & Café, NSW**

Advertising playing card for 'Melbourne Bitter Ale', c1950, 5.5cm wide, 9cm high.

$5 - $10   **Philicia Antiques & Collectables, SA**

'Johnnie Walker' Scotch Whisky advertising figure of a striding man, 27cm high.

$370 - $410   **Kings Park Antiques & Collectables, SA**

Boxed Coca-Cola phone in the shape of a bottle, Model 500, full featured electronic, c1985, 5cm long, 5cm wide, 25cm high.

$120 - $140   **Alan's Collectables, NSW**

Coca-Cola clip on radio and compass, boxed, c2002.

$10 - $20   **Alan's Collectables, NSW**

Coca-Cola advertising thermometer, c1955, 24cm long, 8cm high.

$135 - $155   **Kings Park Antiques & Collectables, SA**

'Drink Coca-Cola' radio depicting a vending machine, c1965, 4cm deep, 9cm wide, 20cm high.

$360 - $400   **Treats & Treasures, NSW**

Sydney Olympic 2000 'Months to Go' Coca-Cola bottles, set of five with tags, badges and pin trading kiosk.

$1400 - $1600   **The Glass Stopper, NSW**

Miniature wooden box of twenty four Coke bottles and caps, c1950.

$380 - $420   **The Glass Stopper, NSW**

Souvenir Coca-Cola bottle, gold print of the first 100 bottles, sealed, c1975.

$165 - $185   **The Glass Stopper, NSW**

Coca-Cola Bon Jovi promotion can sealed and empty, fully autographed by the band with a certificate of authenticity, c1993.

$500 - $600   **Chapel Street Bazaar, VIC**

Crystal commemorative Coca-Cola bottle, 'Opening Ceremony, Sydney Olympics 2000', boxed and numbered, c2000.

$325 - $365   **The Glass Stopper, NSW**

Coca-Cola Ghostbusters can, never opened, c1989.

$10 - $15   **The Glass Stopper, NSW**

Coca-Cola green 'Super' yo-yo, c1980, 5.5cm diameter.

$35 - $45 — **Treats & Treasures, NSW**

Coca-Cola 'Sprite', paper labeled yo-yo, c1975, 6cm diameter.

$330 - $370 — **Old World Antiques (NSW), NSW**

Coca-Cola yo-yo, c1966.

$80 - $100 — **Gardenvale Collectables, VIC**

Red and white 'Russell' Coca-Cola advertising yo-yo, c1970, 6cm diameter.

$25 - $35 — **Grant & Wendy Brookes, VIC**

Coca-Cola tin yo-yo, made in Hong Kong, c1960.

$380 - $420 — **The Glass Stopper, NSW**

Coca-Cola yo-yo Special Executive version, c1970.

$500 - $600 — **The Glass Stopper, NSW**

Green Coca-Cola 'Pause' yo-yo, c1960.

$255 - $295 — **The Glass Stopper, NSW**

Original box of Fanta yo-yos, twelve in box, c1966.

$500 - $600 — **The Glass Stopper, NSW**

Red Coca-Cola championship yoyo, logo on one side, slogan 'Things Go Better With Coke' on other side, c1960, 6cm diameter.

$40 - $50 — **Northside Secondhand Furniture, QLD**

Coca-Cola black 'Master' yo-yo, c1980, 5.5cm diameter.

$50 - $70 — **Treats & Treasures, NSW**

Coca-Cola badge, for the Royal Melbourne Golf Club 1990 Pro-AM Guest International Coca-Cola golf classic, c1990, 3cm long, 3cm wide.

$3 - $13 — **Alan's Collectables, NSW**

Red and white double frisby advertising Coca-Cola, c1989, 31cm long, 20cm wide.

$10 - $20 — **Alan's Collectables, NSW**

Advertising display for Coca-Cola, 'Win A Prize', c1980, 47cm long, 17cm deep, 44cm high.

$70 - $90 — **Burly Babs Collectables/Retro Relics, VIC**

Coca-Cola thongs on a board with Coke key ring still in bag, c2002, 24cm wide, 35cm high.

$20 - $30 — **Alan's Collectables, NSW**

Cast metal plaque by Geo J Meyer Manufacturing Co. model 324-PT, no. BH3354, built specially for Coca-Cola Bottling Company, c1963, 69cm long, 28cm high.

$1150 - $1350

Kings Park Antiques & Collectables, SA

Assortment of five Australian Coca-Cola metal advertising signs, c1955, 45cm wide, 137cm high.

$825 - $925

Kings Park Antiques & Collectables, SA

Coca-Cola tin sign, c1965, 45cm wide, 137cm high.

$430 - $470

The Restorers Barn, VIC

Pictorial enamel Coca-Cola sign, c1960, 152cm long, 91cm high.

$1900 - $2100

Salt's Antiques, QLD

Coca-Cola magazine advertisement, 'Be really refreshed - pause for Coke!', c1961, 29cm wide, 38cm high.

$20 - $30

The Restorers Barn, VIC

Coca-Cola, Santa 'Merry Christmas' enamel sign, 400cm long, 280cm high.

$280 - $320

The Glass Stopper, NSW

Coca-Cola calendar, printed by S.T. Leigh & Co. Pty Ltd, c1952.

$140 - $160

Old World Antiques (NSW), NSW

Coca-Cola magazine advertisement, c1958, 12cm wide, 18cm high.

$9 - $15

The Restorers Barn, VIC

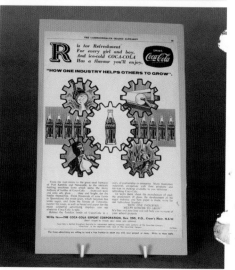

Coca-Cola magazine advertisement, c1950, 17cm wide, 25cm high.

$4 - $9

The Restorers Barn, VIC

Coca-Cola collectable pins, an official Coca-Cola licensed product, c1998.

$25 - $35

Alan's Collectables, NSW

Coca-Cola plastic ice bucket, c1960, 21cm high, 23cm diameter.

$85 - $105

Town & Country Antiques, NSW

Waxed Coke, Schweppes and Dickson advertising drink cups, c1960, 10cm high, 7.3cm diameter.

$10 - $20

Wooden Pew Antiques, VIC

Coca-Cola collectable toy, c1983.

$10 - $20

Coming of Age Antiques, QLD

FIFA soccer ball advertsising Coca-Cola with the slogan 'Coke Adds Life', c1960.

$165 - $185

The Glass Stopper, NSW

Advertisement for Coca-Cola from the 'Reader's Digest', September 1953, 14cm wide, 19cm high.

$20 - $30

Philicia Antiques & Collectables, SA

Wind up Coca-Cola train with carriage, c1960, 10cm long.

$30 - $40

Marge's Antiques & Collectables, NSW

Coca-Cola branded salt and pepper shakers in original box, c2002, 10cm deep, 5cm diameter.

$10 - $20

Kenny's Antiques, VIC

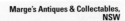

Coca-Cola bottle tops produced three sets of football faces and a 'How to Play Football' series from 1963 to 1968, 2.7cm diameter.

$5 - $10

At The Toss of A Coin, SA

Wax paper Coca-Cola cup for the America's Cup 1987, as official soft drink and major sponsor, c1987, 11cm high, 14cm diameter.

$2 - $7

Alan's Collectables, NSW

Plastic 'Boomer' bubblegum dispenser, c1990, 30cm high.

$50 - $70 — **Kingston Antiques, VIC**

Qantas plastic model of a '747-Classic' aeroplane, made in Taiwan, c1990, 27cm long.

$55 - $75 — **The Bottom Drawer Antique Centre, VIC**

'Alien Popps' lollypop dispenser with alien head, c1990, 22cm wide, 32cm high.

$45 - $65 — **Wooden Pew Antiques, VIC**

English 'Homepride' (Bread) salt and pepper shakers, modelled on the 'Fred' theme, c2004, 14cm long, 12cm high.

NZ$75 - $95 — **South Auckland Antiques & Collectables, New Zealand**

'Fred' of Homepride

In 1965, 'Fred' the flour grader, the little man in the bowler hat, first appeared on the packaging for 'Homepride' flour. He was so successful that Homepride moved him to television advertisements from the late Sixties onwards, along with his friends, promoting 'Homepride' flour, home baking products and cooking sauces.

The actor John Le Mesurier (1912 - 1983), was the original voice of 'Fred' in the TV commercials from the mid-1960s until his death, however the character lives on, voiced by other actors.

Following the success of the TV commercials, a series of kitchen accessories were created based on 'Fred', including flour sifters, mugs, vases, pie funnels, and fridge magnets.

Fred is still the mascot for Homepride and new accessories are being introduced on a regular basis.

Royal Doulton 'Fred' Homepride 40 year anniversary plate, c2004, 26cm diameter.

NZ$40 - $50 — **South Auckland Antiques & Collectables, New Zealand**

Moulded plastic 'Big Boy' figure, the mascot for US restaurant chain of the same name, c1980, 22cm high.

$55 - $75 — **Chapel Street Bazaar, VIC**

Dough boy figure, mascot for 'Pillsbury' packet cake mixes, first registered in 1971, c1985, 9cm wide, 19cm high.

$20 - $30 — **Chapel Street Bazaar, VIC**

Plush toy 'M & M Fun Friend' produced by Mars Confectionary Company, c1998, 30cm wide, 29cm high.

$13 - $23 — **Chapel Street Bazaar, VIC**

Plastic 'Smiths Crisps' container, c1960, 23cm wide, 33cm high.

$115 - $135 — **Chapel Street Bazaar, VIC**

Butcher's window display of an automated pig and piglets, tails wiggle and large pig's ear and eye move, 74cm long, 64cm deep, 33cm high.

NZ$2400 - $2600 — **Bulls Antiques & Collectables, New Zealand**

Timber sign, 'Kookaburra Underwear 51% Wool, 49% Cotton', 32cm long, 40cm high.

$430 - $470 — **Shop L21, Mittagong Antiques Centre, NSW**

Magazine 'Sunbeam Mixmaster' advertisement, c1954, 26cm wide, 34cm high.

$9 - $15

The Restorers Barn, VIC

'Fire Prevention Week' magazine advertisement, c1950, 27cm wide, 34cm high.

$9 - $15

The Restorers Barn, VIC

Bell Telephone system magazine advertisement, c1950, 16cm wide, 23.5cm high.

$5 - $10

The Restorers Barn, VIC

Magazine 'Band-Aid' advertisement, c1950, 21.5cm wide, 29cm high.

$4 - $10

The Restorers Barn, VIC

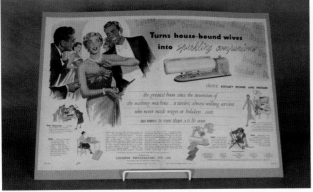

Magazine 'Coldspot Refrigerators Pty Ltd. Electric Rotary Ironer and Presser' advertisement, c1951, 57cm wide, 38cm high.

$9 - $15

The Restorers Barn, VIC

'Saxone' shoes magazine advertisement, c1963, 19cm wide, 13.5cm high.

$5 - $10

The Restorers Barn, VIC

An advertising playing card for 'AMSCOL' butter of Adelaide, S.A., c1950, 8.5cm wide, 5.5cm high.

$5 - $10

Philicia Antiques & Collectables, SA

Magazine 'Nescafe' advertisement, c1961, 28cm wide, 37cm high.

$15 - $20

The Restorers Barn, VIC

Magazine 'Lifesavers' advertisement, c1950, 12cm wide, 21cm high.

$9 - $15

The Restorers Barn, VIC

Cadbury's Nut Milk Chocolate wrapper, c1960.

$170 - $190

Gardenvale Collectables, VIC

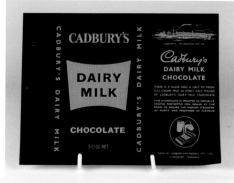

Cadbury's Dairy Milk Chocolate wrapper, c1960.

$170 - $190   **Gardenvale Collectables, VIC**

Cadbury's Fruit & Nut Chocolate wrapper, c1960.

$170 - $190   **Gardenvale Collectables, VIC**

An English advertising playing card for 'Army Club' cigarettes, c1948, 5.5cm wide, 9cm high.

$2 - $6   **Philicia Antiques & Collectables, SA**

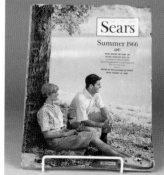

Sears catalogue, excellent reference source for American fashion, furnishings, sporting gear and camping trends of the mid 1960s, c1966.

$20 - $30   **Chapel Street Bazaar, VIC**

'Holden' motor vehicles, advertising playing card, c1950, 5.5cm wide, 9cm high.

$5 - $10   **Philicia Antiques & Collectables, SA**

Carr Fastener Co. advertising playing card, c1950, 5cm long, 9cm high.

$5 - $10   **Philicia Antiques & Collectables, SA**

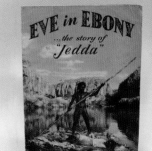
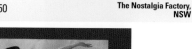

Movie booklet, 'Eve in Ebony. The Story of Jedda', c1956.

$40 - $50   **The Nostalgia Factory, NSW**

Magazine 'Buy Australian Made' advertisement, c1961, 29cm wide, 37cm high.

$11 - $20   **The Restorers Barn, VIC**

Mail-order catalogue for Peoplestores Ltd. Adelaide showing mostly fashion items available, 30 pages, c1950, 19cm wide, 25cm high.

$20 - $30   **Philicia Antiques & Collectables, SA**

An advertising playing card for Australia's Holden car, c1950, 5.5cm wide, 9cm high.

$5 - $10   **Philicia Antiques & Collectables, SA**

Advertising lima beans label for 'Fern Park', Chicago, Illinois, c1930, 28cm wide, 10.5cm high.

$17 - $22

Philicia Antiques & Collectables, SA

American advertising label for 'Blushing Melons', Yuma, Arizona, c1940, 25cm wide, 10cm high.

$30 - $40

Philicia Antiques & Collectables, SA

American advertising label for 'Foot High Melons', Yuma, Arizona, c1940, 24cm wide, 11cm high.

$30 - $40

Philicia Antiques & Collectables, SA

'Red Mule' advertising label from Eseter, California, c1950, 28cm wide, 10cm high.

$15 - $20

Philicia Antiques & Collectables, SA

American 'Defender' brand tomatoes label from Maine, c1930, 23cm wide, 10cm high.

$40 - $50

Philicia Antiques & Collectables, SA

Advertising label for 'Rosella' jams in Adelaide, S.A., c1950, 10cm wide, 21cm high.

$17 - $22

Philicia Antiques & Collectables, SA

American advertising produce label for 'Sunflower', Selma, California, c1950, 28cm wide, 10cm high.

$13 - $18

Philicia Antiques & Collectables, SA

American advertising label for 'Buxom Melons', Yuma, Arizona, c1940, 25cm wide, 10cm high.

$30 - $40

Philicia Antiques & Collectables, SA

Qantas Airlines baggage, adhesive silver label, c1950, 13cm long, 9cm high.

$30 - $40

Philicia Antiques & Collectables, SA

Advertising label for 'Smooth Apricot Jam' made by The N.S.W. Co-op Wholesale Society Ltd, Sydney, c1950, 28.5cm wide, 10cm high.

$13 - $18

Philicia Antiques & Collectables, SA

Advertising apple fruit jelly label, for 'Sundowner' Jams of Melbourne, c1950, 28cm wide, 10cm high.

$20 - $30

Philicia Antiques & Collectables, SA

Enamel sign for 'Shell Depot', c1950, 180cm long, 92cm high.

$430 - $470

Salt's Antiques,
QLD

Michelin sign, c1965, 40cm long, 20cm high.

$90 - $110

Unique & Antique,
VIC

'Stephens' Inks' enamel sign by Patent Enamel Co., London, c1910, 170cm long, 72cm high.

$430 - $470

Salt's Antiques,
QLD

Reproduction 'Castrol' enamel sign, 35cm long, 30cm high.

$135 - $155

Unique & Antique,
VIC

Pictorial 'Michelin' enamel sign, c1970, 65cm wide, 65cm high.

$500 - $600

Salt's Antiques,
QLD

'Harrisons Motor's Used Car Specialists' wooden entrance sign, timber, hand shaped, 100cm wide, 42cm high.

$190 - $210

The Mill Markets,
VIC

Painted metal Motor Traders Association of NSW, members sign, c1950, 29cm diameter.

$145 - $165

Old World Antiques (NSW),
NSW

Victorian Railways Advertising Division enamel sign, c1950, 244cm long, 30cm high.

$650 - $750

Victorian Railway Workshops Art & Antiques,
VIC

Four 'N Twenty pie enamel sign, c1960, 180cm long, 60cm high.

$225 - $265

Unique & Antique,
VIC

Enamel 'Spratts Ovals' dog biscuit sign, c1950, 76cm long, 30cm high.

$230 - $270

Salt's Antiques,
QLD

'Arnott's' biscuit, original shop display tin sign, c1950, 30cm deep, 50cm wide.

$185 - $205

The Wool Exchange Geelong,
VIC

Reproduced 'Peter's' ice cream cone light, 80cm long.

$550 - $650   **The Bottom Drawer Antique Centre, VIC.**

Tin advertising sign for 'Granny Davis Bread', c1970, 75cm long, 48cm wide, 75cm high.

$250 - $350   **Dr Russell's Emporium, WA**

'Lifebuoy' circular advertising mirror, c1950, 450mm diameter.

$475 - $515   **The Glass Stopper, NSW**

'Wundawax', screen printed metal, grocers counter sign, 25cm long, 40cm high.

$155 - $175   **Unique & Antique, VIC**

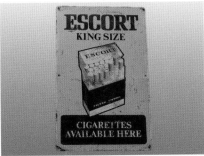

'Escort King Size' screen printed sign, c1970, 30cm long, 60cm high.

$165 - $185   **Unique & Antique, VIC**

'Cadbury's Bournvita' screen printed sign, c1955, 25cm long, 37cm high.

$90 - $110   **Unique & Antique, VIC**

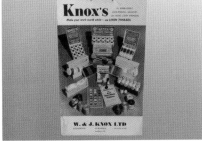

Advertising card for 'Knox's linen threads for embroidery, lace-making, crochet and hand loom weaving', c1950, 28cm wide, 44cm high.

NZ$110 - $130   **Antiques of Epsom, New Zealand**

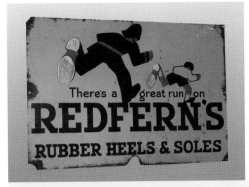

'Redfern's Rubber Heels & Soles', pictorial enamel sign, c1950, 77cm long, 51cm high.

$430 - $470   **Salt's Antiques, QLD**

Reproduction 'Hudsons Soap' enamel sign, 45cm long, 35cm high.

$165 - $185   **Unique & Antique, VIC**

'Players Please' cigarette advertising enamel sign, double sided, c1930, 43cm long, 40cm wide.

$300 - $340   **Wooden Pew Antiques, VIC**

'Four Square Cigarettes' tin advertising sign, c1955.

$190 - $210   **Glenn Stevens Antiques, VIC**

Advertising mirror for Laroche perfume, in wooden frame, c1970, 48cm wide, 59cm high.

$185 - $205   **Helen's On The Bay, QLD**

A northern England pub sign for 'Greenalls Beer', suspended on an iron frame, c1950, 65cm wide, 45cm high.

$745 - $845

Granny's Market Pty Ltd, VIC

Metal letter 'U', from old signage, c1980, 70cm high.

$140 - $160

Tarlo & Graham, VIC.

Original 'Solpah' paint advertising display showcard, c1950, 43cm high.

$85 - $105

The Wool Exchange Geelong, VIC

Royal Albert advertising plaque for shop display, c1955, 2.5cm deep, 11cm wide, 7cm high.

$85 - $105

Kookaburra Antiques, TAS

French hanging double sided enamel sign 'Agence Postale', c1910, 70cm wide, 36cm high.

$360 - $400

Seguin's Antiques & Café, NSW

Electrical advertising sign for 'Philips Lamps', constructed from masonite and timber, c1955, 66cm wide, 80cm high.

$475 - $515

Kenny's Antiques, VIC

Royal Insurance Company Limited, diamond shaped enamel sign, 45cm wide, 53cm high.

$480 - $520

The Mill Markets, VIC

Framed advertisement for 'Wards English Hats', 32cm wide, 37cm high.

$190 - $210

The Mill Markets, VIC

Firezone rectangular sign 'Saves Engine Ware', c1960, 90cm long, 15cm wide.

$280 - $320

The Mill Markets, VIC

White acrylic letters from old signage, c1980, 31cm high.

$50 - $70

Tarlo & Graham, VIC

Free-standing, fold out advertising show card for 'AWA Radiola Portable Stereophonic Gram' model 1045, c1950, 20cm long, 16cm high.

$135 - $155

Philicia Antiques & Collectables, SA

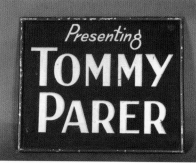

'Presenting Tommy Parer' sign, 44cm wide, 35cm high.

$190 - $210

The Mill Markets, VIC

Biscuit tin, 'Swallow's Centenary Gift Box' celebrating the company's centenary year, c1954, 24cm long, 14cm deep.

$25 - $35   **Shirley & Noel Daly Antiques, VIC**

Phoenix biscuit tin, made by Willow, picturing Spring St. Melbourne, with FB and FC Holdens, c1960.

$30 - $40   **Chris' Antiques & Collectables, VIC**

Golliwog tin, embossed triangle shape in green, red, black and white, c1955, 15cm long, 15cm wide.

$115 - $135   **Retro Relics, VIC**

'Golden Fleece' auto transmission fluid tin, one imperial quart with original contents, c1950, 30cm high.

$55 - $75   **Western District Antique Centre, VIC**

Shell Motor Oil tin, one gallon, c1950, 17cm long, 12cm deep, 17cm high.

$45 - $65   **Towers Antiques & Collectables, NSW**

'Golden Fleece' one gallon flushing oil tin, c1950, 13cm deep, 17cm wide, 24cm high.

$40 - $50   **Town & Country Antiques, NSW**

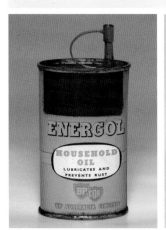

'Energol' oval household oil tin, featuring advertising for 'BP' and 'COR', paper sticker for sewing centre, c1960, 9cm high.

$40 - $50   **The Bottom Drawer Antique Centre, VIC**

'Inglis Goldenia Coffee' eight lb tin with paper-label, c1950, 26cm deep, 20cm high.

$70 - $90   **Treats & Treasures, NSW**

Edmonds 4lb custard powder tin made by T. J. Edmonds, Christchurch, N.Z., c1950, 18cm high, 15cm diameter.

NZ$30 - $45   **Memory Lane, New Zealand**

'Glaxo' milk food tin by Glaxo Laboratories New Zealand Ltd, c1955, 16.5cm high, 15cm diameter.

NZ$20 - $30   **Memory Lane, New Zealand**

Pascall's 'Robin Hood' toffee tin, c1950, 18cm deep, 22cm wide, 13cm high.

$165 - $185

Glenn Stevens Antiques, VIC

'Griffiths Sweets' tin from Ansett-ANA, c1960, 24cm long, 10cm deep, 3cm high.

$140 - $160

Southside Antiques Centre, QLD

'Chupa Chups' tin, French, c1975, 15cm wide, 24cm high.

NZ$25 - $35

Oxford Court Antiques Centre, New Zealand

Cadbury Roses chocolate 5lb tin, c1950, 21cm high, 19cm diameter.

$30 - $40

Chapel Street Bazaar, VIC

'Pascall Fruit Bon Bon' tin, made in Claremont, Tasmania, 15cm wide, 22cm high.

$185 - $205

The Rustic Rose, VIC

Early Bushells tea tin 'Tea of Flavor', 'First Grade 1lb net' on base, c1950, 12cm wide, 16cm high.

$55 - $75

Maryborough Station Antique Emporium, VIC

'ETA' brand sugar coated peanuts bulk tin with paper label, c1950, 10cm long, 20cm deep.

$60 - $80

Treats & Treasures, NSW

'Anchor Milk Powder', 2 1/2lb tin, by New Zealand Dairy Co. Ltd., c1955, 18cm high, 14cm diameter.

NZ$30 - $40

Memory Lane, New Zealand

Berry's 'Glen Valley Tea' tin, 24cm high, 21cm diameter.

$80 - $100

Kingston Antiques, VIC

'ETA' brand nuts tin made by Willow Australia, c1950, 15cm wide, 11cm high.

$20 - $30

The Rustic Rose, VIC

'ETA' brand salted peanuts bulk tin with paper label, c1950, 20cm wide, 10cm high.

$80 - $100

Treats & Treasures, NSW

Financial year 1981-82 Big M Girl calendar, photographed by thirteen leading Australian photographers, sexist pin-up style advertising promoting flavoured milk, c1981, 48cm long, 35cm wide.

$40 - $50   **Image Objex, VIC**

A cheesecake glamour advertising calendar for 'Hamilton Ewell' wines and spirits, c1960, 28cm wide, 56cm high.

$115 - $135   **Philicia Antiques & Collectables, SA**

'Golden Fleece' calendar, c1961, 24cm wide, 29cm high.

$75 - $95   **Chapel Street Bazaar, VIC**

Arnott's '130 years of Arnotts' porcelain collector's plate, including certificate of authenticity, 24cm diam.

$145 - $165   **Treats & Treasures, NSW**

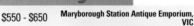

Mannequin, dressed in turn of the century nurse's uniform, c1960, 177cm high.

$550 - $650   **Maryborough Station Antique Emporium, VIC**

Square sided water jug with transfer print advertising 'Dunhill' brand cigarettes, made by Wade, England, c1990.

$85 - $105   **Kenny's Antiques, VIC**

Labelled bottle of 'New Era Furniture Reviver', label to rear of bottle, city distributor, Boans of Perth, c1950, 15cm high.

$35 - $45   **Ardeco Antiques & Collectables, WA**

'Tarax' and 'Cottee's' soft drink bottles.

$40 - $50   **Gardenvale Collectables, VIC**

Complete unopened box of Federal matches containing 12 individual boxes.

$35 - $45   **Home Again, NSW**

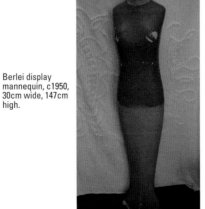

Berlei display mannequin, c1950, 30cm wide, 147cm high.

$305 - $345   **Town & Country Antiques, NSW**

Fold out brochure for Southern Cross Seneschal Windmills, c1940, 20cm long, 27cm high.

$30 - $40   **Philicia Antiques & Collectables, SA**

Lucky charm pin back, c1950, 3cm diameter.

$9 - $19

Southside Antiques Centre,
QLD

A large plastic working advertising 'Swatch' watch, c1970, 65cm high.

NZ$245 - $285

Banks Peninsula Antiques,
New Zealand

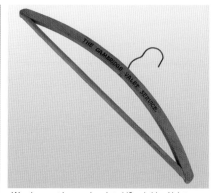

Wooden coat hanger imprinted 'Cambridge Valet Service'.

$40 - $50

Tyabb Hay Shed,
VIC

'McAlpines Self Raising Flour', two cup, tin sieve, made by Wilson Bros Pty. Ltd, c1930, 12cm long, 7cm high, 8cm diameter.

$48 - $68

Mt Dandenong Antique Centre,
VIC

Black glass 'Brylcreem' hair gel dispenser, as used in a barber's shop, c1950, 25cm high.

NZ$275 - $315

Banks Peninsula Antiques,
New Zealand

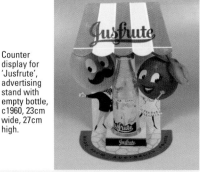

'Life Savers' show bag.

$380 - $420

Gardenvale Collectables,
VIC

Thermometer with advertising for 'Zig-Zag' rice cigarette papers, c1950, 25cm long, 11cm wide.

$115 - $135

Wooden Pew Antiques,
VIC

Miniature working model of a Hills Hoist, c1950, 62cm high, 84cm diameter.

$455 - $495

Burly Babs Collectables/Retro Relics,
VIC

Counter display for 'Jusfrute', advertising stand with empty bottle, c1960, 23cm wide, 27cm high.

$80 - $100

Chapel Street Bazaar,
VIC

Counter display for 'Dr. MacKenzies Menthoids', painted wood, c1950, 18cm wide, 20cm high.

$85 - $105

Chapel Street Bazaar,
VIC

'Arnotts' Sao' advertising tray, 49.5cm long, 34cm wide.

$66 - $86

Treats & Treasures,
NSW

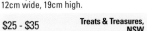

Jaffas jar, ex-Bushells Coffee, c1950, 12cm wide, 19cm high.

$25 - $35   **Treats & Treasures, NSW**

'Smalls' show bag.

$170 - $190   **Gardenvale Collectables, VIC**

'Hoadleys' show bag.

NZ$170 - $190   **Gardenvale Collectables, VIC**

Giant pencil, advertising Staedtler, c1950, 74cm long.

$175 - $195   **All In Good Time Antiques, SA**

Set of four, promotional sample, multi coloured Bakelite cups with 'Kraft Foods' embossed to the base of each cup, c1950, 7cm high, 5cm diameter.

$45 - $65   **Mt Dandenong Antique Centre, VIC**

Ampol, orange coloured four person picnic set of four cups, four plates, four bowls, a serving plate, two salad bowls and two salt and pepper shakers, from an Ampol sales promotion, c1970, 23cm deep, 23cm wide, 20cm high.

$30 - $40   **Bowhows, NSW**

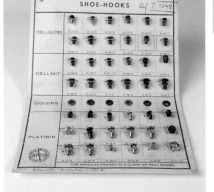

Shoe hook sample card, c1950.

$20 - $30   **Victory Theatre Antiques, NSW**

Presidential pin, painted metal, c1956, 0.5cm wide, 2cm diameter.

$45 - $65   **Bowhows, NSW**

'Golden Fleece' drum caps, c1970, 3.5cm diameter.

$30 - $40   **Wooden Pew Antiques, VIC**

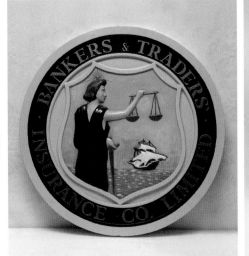

'Bankers & Traders Insurance Company' wood, plaster and fibreglass circular sign, c1970, 63cm diameter.

$405 - $445   **Wooden Pew Antiques, VIC**

Sewing cotton sample card, c1950.

$20 - $30   **Victory Theatre Antiques, NSW**

ARTEFACTS – AUSTRALIAN ABORIGINAL

Ceremonial Aboriginal headdress from Mornington Island, made from paper bark, supporting spun human hair string, topped with emu feathers and ochre pigments, c1970, 36cm high.

$475 - $515

Rose Cottage Antiques, ACT

Aboriginal bark, string woven dilly bag with pigment decoration., c1960, 25cm high.

$155 - $175

Rose Cottage Antiques, ACT

An Ilford 35mm colour slide of famed artist Albert Namatjira and his wife Rubina, at Hermannsberg Mission in Central Australia, c1952, 5cm wide, 5cm high.

$115 - $135

Philicia Antiques & Collectables, SA

Pukamani post, carved in iron wood and decorated with ochre, from the Melville and Bathurst Islands, Northern Territory. c1950, 62cm high.

$2300 - $2500

Rose Cottage Antiques, ACT

Collecting Aboriginal Artifacts.

Aboriginal art and artifact collecting goes back to early first contact times. In fact local Aboriginals around Sydney use to trade artifacts with visiting ships from the earliest days. Curio collecting has always been part of early exploration of the new world.

Ceremonial adornment items that were made of perishable material were not preserved for future use and so early examples are very collectable. Early shields, clubs and boomerangs that were cherished as favorites and had developed a deep colour and patina are preferred. Historical items that were collected by early notable pioneers, explorers or anthropologists are of high interest to collectors. Some areas are collected because the artistic expression makes them more appealing when displayed.

Production of artifacts has never ceased and are still made today for sale.

Bark painting production started in mass in the 1950's and were sold via missionary shops. The earlier barks are more sought after. Now with many of the early artists and their roll in the maintenance of culture recognized, these barks are seen as important expressions of a past lifestyle.

Aboriginal ironwood bird figure, from Bathurst and Melville Islands in Northern Territory, c1980, 63cm high.

$475 - $515

Rose Cottage Antiques, ACT

Aboriginal dance ceremonial object, of emu feather and ochre on wood, from Arnhem Land Northern Territory, c1960, 32cm high.

$900 - $1000

Rose Cottage Antiques, ACT

Aboriginal mimi carving by Lena Gwinyin, carved wood and decorated with ochre, c1990, 123cm high.

$745 - $845

Rose Cottage Antiques, ACT

Australian Aboriginal hand spun bush string dilly bag, c1950, 22cm wide, 45cm high.

$150 - $170

The Junk Company, VIC

West Australian didgeridoo, c1950, 127cm long, 22cm diameter.

$185 - $205

Antiques, Goods & Chattels, VIC

Australian tourist boomerang depicting the Flinders Ranges, South Australia, signed Ray Hurst, an Aboriginal artist, Taree NSW, 55cm long, 8cm wide.

$70 - $90

Antiques, Goods & Chattels, VIC

A 'Gope' ancestral spirit board from the Gulf of Papua, hand carved from very old canoe plank as wood was scarce, lime charcoal and ochre natural pigments. Kept in men's house, wide boards like this are good compared to most narrow pieces, c1970, 33cm wide, 125cm high.

$420 - $460   **The New Farm Antique Centre, QLD**

Quality old Upper Sepik River carved cult mask, strong with good colour and great patination, c1960, 16cm wide, 100cm high.

$730 - $830   **The New Farm Antique Centre, QLD**

Sepik River Kundu drum with intact lizard skin, handle has abstract bird head carvings, c1960, 62.5cm high.

$375 - $415   **Rose Cottage Antiques, ACT**

Figure from the Papuan Gulf, carved wood and ochre on stand, c1960, 76cm high.

$800 - $900   **Rose Cottage Antiques, ACT**

Helmet mask, from Vitu Island near New Britain, PNG, carved wood and post WWII house paints, on stand.

$1750 - $1950   **Rose Cottage Antiques, ACT**

Collecting Oceanic Artifacts

Expressions of sublime beauty with a sense of purified expression. Pre-contact pieces all shaped by stone and shell, gives them a softer look because early tools required more time to a more exact form. Once a great item is created it is always kept in a safe place, often in a special hut or abode that was specially built and also being off limits to women and children.

There are many different language groups to Papua New Guinea, each having a slightly different culture with differences in their cultural objects. The Sepik River holds many of these tribal cultures and has a huge production of ephemeral, adornment and cultural objects. Pre European contact pieces are the most sought after because they reflect a culture that goes back tens of thousands of years and the expressions probably haven't changed much over that time, c1960, 46cm high.

PNG figure from the Sepik River district, c1960, 63cm high.

$180 - $200   **Paddington Antique Centre Pty Ltd, QLD**

Authentic coastal Ranui dance mask with slanting shell eyes, red, black and white trade paint and carved wooden tusks, c1950, 51.5cm high.

$1800 - $2000   **B.C. Galleries, VIC**

Beautiful New Guinean doll, dressed in its original hand made costume consisting of beads and woven materials, c1955, 6cm deep, 13cm wide, 25cm high.

$90 - $110   **Mac's Collectables**

New Britain PNG war shield, carved wood and enamel house paint, c1960, 29cm wide, 137cm high.

$645 - $745   **Rose Cottage Antiques, ACT**

Asmat, Irian Jaya shield, carved wood and ochre, c1960, 38cm wide, 1170cm high.

$375 - $415   **Rose Cottage Antiques, ACT**

Original vintage poster, for the 'Pacific Rotary Conference', by the artist Trompf, c1930, 51cm wide, 62cm high.

$1400 - $1600

Galerie Montmartre, VIC

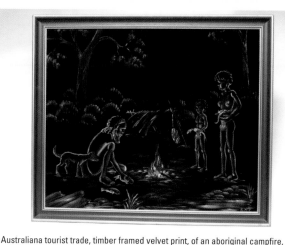

Australiana tourist trade, timber framed velvet print, of an aboriginal campfire, c1970, 67cm wide, 57cm high.

$110 - $130

The Bottom Drawer Antique Centre, VIC

Original vintage poster, 'Orient-Royal Mail to Australia', artist John Hassal, c1920, 64cm wide, 94cm high.

$1400 - $1600

Galerie Montmartre, VIC

Framed reproduction print of a 'Billy Tea' advertising poster, 49cm wide, 61cm high.

$60 - $80

Treats & Treasures, NSW

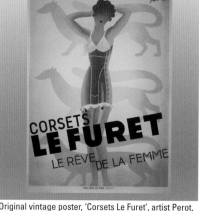

Original vintage poster, 'Corsets Le Furet', artist Perot, c1933, 100cm wide, 140cm high.

$2100 - $2300

Galerie Montmartre, VIC

Victorian Railways travel poster by 'Trompf' depicting Lake Wendouree and Sturt St., Ballarat, c1950.

$330 - $370

Glenn Stevens Antiques, VIC

Original vintage poster, 'Priceless Oil', artist Laurencin, c1920, 120cm wide, 160cm high.

$1100 - $1300

Galerie Montmartre, VIC

Orangina B. Vellemot original lithographic poster, linen backed, condition A, c1982, 240cm wide, 160cm high.

$4300 - $4500

Vintage Posters Only, VIC

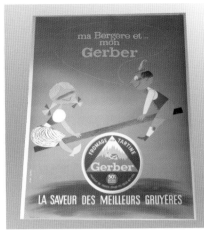

Gerber, Jean Ferry original lithographic poster, linen backed c1954, 120cm wide, 160cm high.

$1400 - $1600   **Vintage Posters Only, VIC**

Pasta Agnesi 1961, Raymond Savignac original lithographic poster, linen backed, c1961, 130cm wide, 200cm high.

$4300 - $4500   **Vintage Posters Only, VIC**

'Bally Lotus', Bernard Vellemot original linen backed lithographic poster, c1973, 120cm wide, 120cm high.

$1900 - $2100   **Vintage Posters Only, VIC**

'Apple' label, c1950, 11cm wide, 10cm high.

$15 - $25   **Chapel Street Bazaar, VIC**

Original vintage poster, 'Kinalillet', artist Robys, c1937, 130cm wide, 200cm high.

$2100 - $2300   **Galerie Montmartre, VIC**

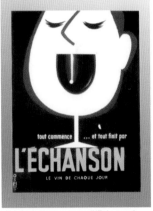

Original vintage poster, 'L'Echanson', artist Seguin, c1950, 120cm wide, 160cm high.

$2500 - $2700   **Galerie Montmartre, VIC**

Original vintage poster, 'Favor girl', artist Bellenger, c1950, 115cm wide, 155cm high.

$1300 - $1500   **Galerie Montmartre, VIC**

L'equipment de Bureau, original lithographic poster, linen backed, c1959, 120cm wide, 160cm high.

$1400 - $1600   **Vintage Posters Only, VIC**

Contrex B. Vellemot, 1977 original lithographic poster, linen backed, 120cm wide, 160cm high.

$1100 - $1300   **Vintage Posters Only, VIC**

Australian National Travel Association poster, c1960, 48cm wide, 76cm high.

$80 - $100   **Chapel Street Bazaar, VIC**

Original vintage poster 'Bally Kick', artist Bernard Villemot, c1989, 116cm wide, 162cm high.

$1400 - $1600 **Galerie Montmartre, VIC**

Pan American Airways travel poster, c1950, 60cm wide, 90cm high.

$200 - $240 **Chapel Street Bazaar, VIC**

Poster for a Robert Indianna exhibition, c1966, 28cm wide, 39.5cm high.

$70 - $90 **506070, NSW**

Original vintage poster 'Nice Travail and Joie', artist Matisse, c1947, 65cm wide, 98cm high.

$1200 - $1400 **Galerie Montmartre, VIC**

Original vintage poster 'Relax', artist Rene Gruau, c1960, 63cm wide, 97cm high.

$1000 - $1200 **Galerie Montmartre, VIC**

Original Vintage Poster 'Cinzano', artist Fatio, c1948, 90cm wide, 128cm high.

$1650 - $1850 **Galerie Montmartre, VIC**

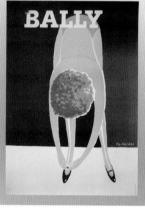

Original vintage poster 'Bally Dancer', artist Fix-Masseau, c1985, 116cm wide, 165cm high.

$950 - $1050 **Galerie Montmartre, VIC**

Original vintage poster 'Bally Legs Noir', artist Bernard Villemot, c1979, 116cm wide, 172cm high.

$950 - $1050 **Galerie Montmartre, VIC**

Original vintage poster, 'Cigarettes Saphir', artist Stephano, c1920, 80cm wide, 120cm high.

$1500 - $1700 **Galerie Montmartre, VIC**

Original vintage poster 'Brummel', artist Rene Gruau, c1950, 120cm wide, 160cm high.

$1500 - $1700 **Galerie Montmartre, VIC**

Original vintage poster 'Olio Radino', artist Boccasile, c1950, 140cm long, 100cm high.

$1900 - $2100 **Galerie Montmartre, VIC**

Original vintage poster, 'Biscotti Lazzaronia', artist Muggiani, c1930, 140cm wide, 198cm high.

$2200 - $2400   **Galerie Montmartre, VIC**

Original vintage poster 'Kangourou', artist Seguin, c1950, 114cm wide, 156cm high.

$1900 - $2100   **Galerie Montmartre, VIC**

Original vintage poster 'Vivor', artist Gabriel, c1950, 115cm wide, 160cm high.

$1000 - $1200   **Galerie Montmartre, VIC**

Original vintage poster, 'Cycles Louvet', Artist Mich, c1930, 80cm wide, 112cm high.

$1900 - $2100   **Galerie Montmartre, VIC**

Original vintage poster, 'Escargot Menetrel', artist Rudd, c1920, 115cm wide, 147cm high.

$1300 - $1500   **Galerie Montmartre, VIC**

Original vintage poster, 'Grand Pasteur', artist Villot, c1930, 120cm wide, 160cm high.

$1300 - $1500   **Galerie Montmartre, VIC**

Original vintage poster, 'Agua de Vilajuiga', artist Leonetto Cappiello, c1910, 96cm wide, 135cm high.

$1500 - $1700   **Galerie Montmartre, VIC**

Original vintage poster, 'Sardegna Cycles', artist Maga, c1930, 100cm wide, 140cm high.

$3400 - $3600   **Galerie Montmartre, VIC**

Original vintage poster, 'Australia', signed Annand, c1937, 30cm wide, 50cm high.

$850 - $950   **Galerie Montmartre, VIC**

Original vintage poster 'Tat Newspaper', artist Herbert Leupin, c1959, 90cm wide, 128cm high.

$1100 - $1300   **Galerie Montmartre, VIC**

Original vintage poster 'Thermogene', artist Leonetto Cappiello, c1949, 80cm wide, 120cm high.

$850 - $950   **Galerie Montmartre, VIC**

PRINTS & PAINTINGS

Oil on paper, 'Hughie Grigg' by Jason Monet, c1976, 71cm wide, 103cm high.

$1850 - $2050

Chapel Street Bazaar, VIC

Abstract oil painting on canvas with brown tonings, 102cm long, 51cm high.

$120 - $150

The Junk Company, VIC

Retro kitsch Tretchikoff print of the Chinese girl, re-framed with glass, c1950, 57.5cm wide, 67.5cm high.

$330 - $370

River Emporium, NSW

Martin Sharp screen-print, 'Bloom', on celluloid, framed between two pieces of perspex in limited edition 5th of 10. c1960, 86.5cm wide, 113.5cm high.

$2900 - $3100

506070, NSW

Martin Sharp

Martin Sharp is a Sydney artist well known for his support and promotion through graphic posters, of amongst others, Tiny Tim, Luna Park and Arthur Stace, the 'Eternity Man'.

In the early 1960s along with Richard Walsh and Richard Neville he started the controversial underground satirical magazine 'Oz' and provided many of the graphic illustrations. In the late 1960s he designed iconic psychedelic album covers for Donovan's 'Sunshine Superman' and Cream's 'Disraeli Gears' as well as psychedelic posters for Bob Dylan and Jimi Hendrix.

In 1970 on his return to Sydney he set up the 'Yellow House' exhibition space at 59 Macleay Street, Potts Point which was based on the idea of a community of artists in the way of Van Gogh's Yellow House at Arles. Artists involved included George Gittoes, Peter Powditch, Peter Kingston and Brett Whitely.

'Bloom', as shown, was a continuation of similar works on celluloid sold through Oz Magazine and advertised for sale by mail order on the back cover of Oz Magazine. This particular work was produced in a very small edition for the first exhibition of the Yellow House.

'Europa and the Bull' by Hans Erni, signed print, limited edition, 92/150, 65cm wide, 83cm high.

$480 - $520

Vintage Living, ACT

Limited edition signed print, no. 148 of 175 framed behind glass, artist Menwuy, c1965, 89cm long, 67cm wide.

$175 - $195

The Bottom Drawer Antique Centre, VIC

Beautifully framed retro kitch print by Leo Jansen, c1965, 61.25cm wide, 70.25cm high.

$330 - $370

River Emporium, NSW

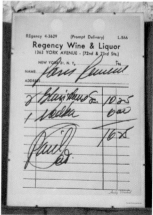

'Banksia Ornata', limited edition print 8/100 by Celia Rosser from 'The Banksias of Victoria', c1980, 350cm wide, 500cm high.

$230 - $270

Antique Prints and Maps at Full Circle, VIC

Andy Warhol poster depicting a bill from a New York restaurant, c1970, 28cm wide, 39.5cm high.

$70 - $90

506070, NSW

Pair of 'Solo Dancer' prints by Bjorn Wiinblad, c1970.

$430 - $470

Toowoomba Antiques Gallery, QLD

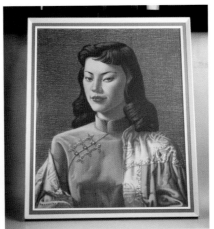

Framed Vladimir Tretchikoff print of 'Miss Wong', c1950, 58cm wide, 66cm high.

$310 - $350

Chapel Street Bazaar, VIC

'Solo Dancer' print by Bjorn Wiinblad, c1970.

$430 - $470

Toowoomba Antiques Gallery, QLD

Print by Tretchikoff, 'Lady of the Orient' in original frame, c1955, 76cm long, 2cm deep, 76cm wide, 66cm high.

$310 - $350

Dr Russell's Emporium, WA

Picasso's 'Portrait of Madame Z' in original 1950's blonde wood frame, c1950.

$100 - $120

Retro Active, VIC

Framed print by Brownie Downing, c1950, 20cm wide, 22cm high.

$65 - $85

Alan's Collectables, NSW

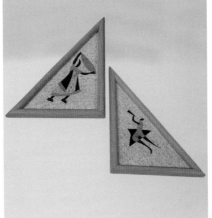

Contemporary linocut wall plaques, manufactured by Universal Wood Art, Sydney, c1950, 27cm high.

$65 - $85

Rosebud Antiques, NSW

Van Cleef girlie print, artist framed, no glass, c1960, 60cm wide, 70cm high.

$45 - $65

Fat Helen's, VIC

SCULPTURE

Stylised red cat ornament, red over glaze/paint with plastic diamantes, c1960, 28.5cm high.

$30 - $40

Fat Helen's, VIC

Plaster fairground figure of two black and white puppies, 20cm wide, 19cm high.

$40 - $50

The Restorers Barn, VIC

Bronze statue of a 'Mama and baby Grizzly' by Hyatt.

$480 - $520

Chilton's Antiques & Jewellery, NSW

Giraffe figurine with a hi-gloss finish, c1965, 9cm wide, 15cm high.

$115 - $135

Helen's On The Bay, QLD

Plaster bust of Sir Robert Menzies, Australia's longest serving Prime Minister, c1970.

$380 - $420

Timeless Treasures, WA

Pair of alabaster busts with original marble stands, 14cm wide, 18cm high.

$480 - $520

Sherwood Bazaar, QLD

David Phillips Koru head, c1968, 13cm wide, 31cm high.

NZ$330 - $370

Oxford Court Antiques Centre, New Zealand

Ceramic umbrella stand in the form of a an owl, c1970, 30cm deep, 28cm wide, 40cm high.

$265 - $305

The Junk Company, VIC

Large plaster figure of a spaniel, used as a top shelf side show prize in the 50's and 60's, part of the collection of side show items used by a one man outfit in South East Queensland and Northern NSW, c1955, 40cm long, 37.5cm high.

$100 - $120

River Emporium, NSW

Wooden and bronze bookends, decorated with dolphins cast in bronze. These bookends were made at Devon Port Naval Dockyard, New Zealand, 15cm long, 13cm wide, 20cm high.

NZ$70 - $90

Casa Manana Antiques & Collectables, New Zealand

Set of four terracotta hand built and painted figures, flute player, vocalist, sitar and drum player, all by Bjorn Wiinblad from his own studio in Copenhagen, Denmark, c1962.

$2980 - $3180

Toowoomba Antiques Gallery, QLD

Hand carved Italian palm wood Cubirt figure of Pan, c1950, 12.5cm wide, 25cm high.

$480 - $520   **Barry McKay, NSW**

Bronze statue by Lucy Boyd, c1960, 17.5cm high.

$750 - $850   **Alan Syber's Antiques Antiquarian, VIC**

Spelter figurine of a shepherd girl by 'L.F. Moreau' with a foundry stamp, c1980, 17cm wide, 56cm high.

$1080 - $1280   **Mentone Beach Antiques Centre, VIC**

Earthenware sculpture by Melbourne artist Trudi Fry, titled 'Earth Women', c1974, 54cm high.

$380 - $420   **Chapel Street Bazaar, VIC**

Wooden mounted, embossed leather head of an old Maori lady, modelled on a C. F. Goldie painting, c1950, 4cm deep, 27cm diameter.

NZ$55 - $75   **Memory Lane, New Zealand**

Pitcairn Island flying fish made by Calvert Warren, c1950, 32cm wide, 17cm high.

NZ$350 - $390   **Antiques of Epsom, New Zealand**

Three dimensional sculptured glass by Vicki Lindstrand from his glazier series featuring a hand etched eskimo canoeing, signed, c1960, 16cm wide, 13cm high.

$330 - $370   **Virtanen Antiques, VIC**

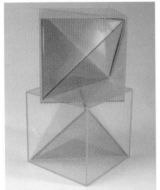

Clement Meadmore Rainbow educational boxes of perspex, clear cube with coloured planes of perspex inside that when held at different angles illustrate the mixing of colours, c1960, 10cm long, 10cm deep, 10cm high.

$110 - $130   **506070, NSW**

Bossons 'Sherpa', wall mounted figurine, c1960, 17cm wide, 38cm high.

$380 - $420   **Philicia Antiques & Collectables, SA**

Plaster fairground figure of a cheeky girl, 'My First Cam', 56cm high.

$480 - $520   **Antiques On Macquarie, TAS**

Papier mache policeman, 'Bobby Sheen', c1930.

$185 - $205   **Victory Theatre Antiques, NSW**

Royal Winton 'Wellbeck' lidded sugar bowl, 8cm deep, 7cm high.

$275 - $315

Antiques On Macquarie, TAS

Royal Winton breakfast set in the 'Marion' pattern, c1950.

$1550 - $1750

Alan Syber's Antiques Antiquarian, VIC

Royal Winton 'Old Cottage Chintz' vase, pattern no. 9632, in production 1930-60, 16cm high.

$255 - $295

Armadale Antique Centre, VIC

Lord Nelson 'Country Lane', three piece cruet set, c1940, 16cm long, 6cm deep, 8cm high.

$205 - $245

White Park Antiques, SA

Royal Winton 'Evesham' two slice toast rack, Pattern No. 404, c1950, 11.5cm long.

$475 - $515

Armadale Antique Centre, VIC

James Kent 'Du Barry' pattern trio, c1950.

$155 - $175

Antipodes Antiques, QLD

'Evesham' pattern trio by Royal Winton, c1951.

$255 - $295

Margaret Sutherland Antiques, VIC

Royal Winton all over floral chintz 'Dorset' demitasse, c1950.

$415 - $455

Sturt Street Antiques & Art, VIC

Shelley 'Rock Garden' trio, 7.5cm high, 16cm diameter.

$245 - $285

White Park Antiques, SA

Royal Winton 'Old Cottage Chintz' stacking teapot, pattern number 9632 and in production from 1930 to 1960, 14cm high.

$1295 - $1495   **Armadale Antique Centre, VIC**

Royal Winton 'Old Cottage Chintz' six cup 'Albans' teapot, Pattern No. 9632 in production 1930-60's, 16cm high.

$845 - $945   **Armadale Antique Centre, VIC**

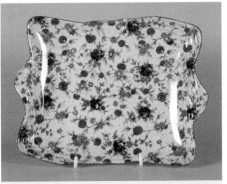

Royal Winton 'Old Cottage chintz' rectangular plate, c1945, 23cm wide.

$110 - $130   **Street Antiques & Art, VIC**

Maling Chintz all over floral comport with lustre finish, c1949, 27cm deep.

$260 - $300   **Yesterday's Gems, NSW**

Royal Winton all over floral comport in the 'Crocus' pattern, c1950, 16cm wide, 7cm high.

$205 - $245   **Gumnut Antiques & Old Wares, NSW**

Royal Winton 'Sunshine' comport, c1950, 17.5cm wide, 6.5cm high.

$415 - $455   **Sturt Street Antiques & Art, VIC**

Royal Winton 'Summertime' pattern tri-section chintz dish, c1950, 25cm diameter.

$310 - $350   **Alan Syber's Antiques Antiquarian, VIC**

Royal Winton 'Evesham' three tier cake stand, c1950, 35cm high.

$545 - $645   **Armadale Antique Centre, VIC**

Royal Winton all over floral honey pot, with under dish, in the 'Julia' pattern, c1950, 10cm high.

$325 - $365   **Western District Antique Centre, VIC**

Royal Winton 'Beeton' jam jar on tray pattern No. 2203, 11cm wide, 9cm high.

$305 - $345   **Nostalgia Antiques Pty Ltd, VIC**

Royal Winton 'Joyce-Lynn' jam pot and liner, Pattern No. 275, c1950, 10.5cm high.

$405 - $445   **Armadale Antique Centre, VIC**

Small boxed lidded pot with decorative lid, 'Les Blakebrough' signed to lid. Les Blakebrough is a distinguished Australian potter represented in all state Public Art Collections and National Gallery of Canberra, and has worked extensively in Australia and Japan, c1970, 6cm long, 6cm deep, 6cm wide, 6cm high.

$255 - $295   **Malvern Antique Market, VIC**

Large casserole pot with handle and subtle abstract design in soft pastel glazes, signed Tom Sanders and dated 1963. Tom Sanders worked with Guy Boyd in late 1940s, John Perceval in 1953 and had association with artist Fred Williams, travelled and worked in London and Paris in late 1950s, early 1960s, c1963, 23cm wide, 22cm high.

$650 - $750   **Malvern Antique Market, VIC**

Startling 'Olive Tree' ginger jar of elongated globe form with accentuated neck, boldly painted on a copper red background are startling images of fruit laden olive trees wandering all over the exterior surface with spasmodic veined leaves, majolica gloss glazes, charcoal, yellow, blues, ochre, chocolate. Signed 'A. Copeland 3.7.2002' impressed mark, 22cm high, 19cm diameter.

$380 - $420   **Hurnall's Antiques & Decorative Arts, VIC**

David and Hermia Boyd oil/vinegar jug, c1960, 15cm wide, 20cm high.

$1050 - $1250   **The Wool Exchange Geelong, VIC**

'The Owl and the Pussycat' large jug of spectacular tall conical form with prominent handle to one side, complementary pouring throat, realistically decorated with a large endearing owl and pussycat, both very animated with particular emphasis to their faces, eyes, the cat's long whiskers and pronounced tail, both surrounded by a variety of grasses, flowers and plant life. Bright, cheerful, majolica gloss glazes teal, turquoise, royal blue, ochre, chocolate, coffee and tan. Boldly signed 'Alexandra Copeland', impressed mark. c1999, 31.5cm high, 28cm diameter.

$4850 - $5050   **Hurnall's Antiques & Decorative Arts, VIC**

Alexandra Copeland

Alexandra Copeland is a Melbourne born artist who has had solo exhibitions since 1983.

The National Gallery of Australia, Canberra, National Gallery of Victoria, Melbourne, Queensland Art Gallery, Brisbane and Tasmanian Museum & Art Gallery, Hobart are amongst the public galleries in which she is represented.

Alexandra has been guest artist-in-residence for six years running at Dartington Pottery in Devon, UK, a studio founded by Bernard Leach in 1930 with a unique approach to stoneware production.

Large hand constructed ceramic candelabra, signed Arthur Halpern to base. Arthur Halpern is an important Victorian potter, who in 1958 was a founding member of Potters Cottage in Warrandyte. Other founding members were Reg Preston, Charles Wilton and Gus McLaren, c1960, 8cm deep, 29cm wide, 33cm high.

$470 - $510   **Malvern Antique Market, VIC**

Large lidded terracotta pot with earthy decorative abstract design, signed 'John Moore' on base, c1970, 33cm high, 23cm diam.

$360 - $400   **Malvern Antique Market, VIC**

Small highly decorated bowl with abstract pattern, signed to base 'Lucy Hatton Beck', c1960, 5cm high, 11cm diameter.

$75 - $95   **Malvern Antique Market, VIC**

Large ceramic bowl with decorative abstract design, signed 'Charles Wilton' to base. Charles Wilton is a Victorian potter and co-founder of Potters Cottage, Warrandyte in 1958. Other members included Reg Preston, Gus McLaren and Artur Halpern, c1960, 13cm high, 24cm diam.

$175 - $195   **Malvern Antique Market, VIC**

Large Ric Pearce stoneware candlestick, signed to base 'Ric'. Ric Pearc was a well known potter and ceramics lecturer in Melbourne in 1970s and 1980s, c1970, 34cm high, 10cm diameter.

$260 - $300   **Malvern Antique Market, VIC**

Large earthy stoneware bowl with floral motif by Victor Greenaway and artist's mark to base. Important and distinguished Victorian, Vic Greenaway is represented in most state Public Art Collections and the National Gallery of Canberra and had many exhibitions in Australia and overseas, c1975, 16cm high, 34cm diameter.

$520 - $620 **Malvern Antique Market, VIC**

Large stoneware platter with abstract design and luscious glazes by Reg Preston, signed to base. Reg Preston is an important and noted Victorian potter, co-founder of Potters Cottage, Warrandyte in 1958, and is represented in The National Gallery of Victoria and National Gallery of Canberra and many exhibitions in Australia, c1960, 32cm diameter.

$480 - $520 **Malvern Antique Market, VIC**

Large ceramic stoneware platter with an eagle perched on rocky outcrop and artist's initials 'R.U.' incised to base, c1960, 36cm diameter.

$380 - $420 **Malvern Antique Market, VIC**

Australian Pottery lizard on a tree trunk, sculpture moulded initials MM, 14cm wide.

$1350 - $1550 **Deco Down Under, WA**

Large ceramic bowl with rich earthy glazes and abstract design with 'Cynthia Mitchell's' mark to base. Cynthia Mitchell is an important and noted Tasmanian Potter who began potting with Maud Poynter in her early development and is represented in many public and private collections, c1960, 10cm high, 29cm diam.

$340 - $380 **Malvern Antique Market, VIC**

Small highly glazed jug, strong abstract incised design with aboriginal influence, signed 'Rosa Whitlam' to base and dated 1955, c1955, 13cm long, 11cm high.

$245 - $285 **Malvern Antique Market, VIC**

Large Bill Byrnes ceramic vase with abstract design, signed to base, c1960, 43cm high, 15cm diameter.

$330 - $370 **Malvern Antique Market, VIC**

Large stoneware exhibition platter with abstract landscape theme, signed 'Bryan Truman' to base and dated 1979. Bryan Truman is an important potter from England who worked in Australia in the 1970s and early 1980s, and is represented in The National Gallery of Victoria's ceramic collection, c1979, 35cm diameter.

$380 - $420 **Malvern Antique Market, VIC**

Large exhibition stoneware platter with luscious glazes, abstract design and signed to base 'Robert Barrow'. Robert Barrow is a master potter, and represented in numerous public and private collections. He has exhibited in many solo and group exhibitions in Australia and overseas, c1980, 43cm diameter.

$600 - $700 **Malvern Antique Market, VIC**

Large highly textured vase with heavily incised abstract design, signed 'Margot Manchester' to base. Margot Manchester is a master Tasmanian potter who experiments with a variety of clays and highly textured surfaces. Represented in Public Art Gallery of Tasmania and many private collections, c1970, 29cm high, 25cm diameter.

$480 - $520 **Malvern Antique Market, VIC**

CERAMICS

Ceramic vase with highly textured abstract design, signed 'Rynne Tanton' to base. Rynne Tanton is a master Tasmanian potter and ceramics lecturer in Tasmania, and is represented in state Public Art Collections in Tasmania and Victoria, c1970, 18cm high, 15cm diameter.

$260 - $300   **Malvern Antique Market, VIC**

Wheel and hand constructed ceramic vase with floral motif, dated 1984 to base with artist's initials 'L.B.' Les Blakebrough is one of Australia's most distinguished living Potters. Represented in most state Public Art Collections and The National Gallery of Canberra, he has been a Senior Lecturer in ceramics and travelled and worked extensively in Japan, c1984, 13cm high, 11cm diameter.

$260 - $300   **Malvern Antique Market, VIC**

Sculptural ceramic stoneware vessel featuring groups of horse riders on a worn landscape, 21cm high, 22cm diameter.

$330 - $370   **Malvern Antique Market, VIC**

Pair of salt glaze ceramic goblets, Janet Mansfield's initials incised. Janet Mansfield is a distinguished Australian potter and author of many books and journals on ceramics, and is represented in most state Public Art Collections and The National Gallery of Canberra. Best known for her salt glaze finishes, c1970, 13cm high, 8cm diameter.

$80 - $100   **Malvern Antique Market, VIC**

Large decorative hand constructed stoneware vase, Col Levy's impressed initials to base. Col Levy is a distinguished living Australian Potter from NSW, who started working with Ivan McMerkin at Sturt Pottery, Mittagong NSW in 1958. He has held numerous exhibitions in Australia and Japan and is represented in most state Public Art Collections and The National Gallery of Canberra, c1970, 30cm high, 10cm diam.

$900 - $1000   **Malvern Antique Market, VIC**

Small work by David and Hermina Boyd with classical theme, signed 'Boyd, England 1955', c1955, 5cm high, 11cm diameter.

$450 - $490   **Malvern Antique Market, VIC**

Hand painted deco platter, signed by Melbourne artist, Nina Gregory', a one off design, c2003, 40cm diameter.

$330 - $370   **Chapel Street Bazaar, VIC**

Raku fired ceramic vase with decorative abstract design, signed 'J. Blight' to base and dated 1986, 18cm high, 15cm diameter.

$245 - $285   **Malvern Antique Market, VIC**

Indigenous hand painted art vase with integral flower frog, produced by The Little Sydney Pottery Co, c1950, 20cm wide, 25cm diameter.

$230 - $270   **Fyshwick Antique Centre, ACT**

Very large ceramic sculptural work with highly textured finish, c1970, 70cm high, 40cm diameter.

$1700 - $1900   **Malvern Antique Market, VIC**

Joliffe blue glazed jug, incised 'Hand built by Joliffe 1945', c1945, 12.5cm high.

$1000 - $1200 **Armadale Antique Centre, VIC**

Australian pottery vase by Adelaide potters John and Dulcie Dodd, c1950.

$230 - $270 **The Exchange Galleries, NSW**

Handbuilt Australian ceramic vase with three spouts, signed 'Val Lindar' and dated 1976, 10cm deep, 15cm wide, 42cm high.

$225 - $265 **The Junk Company, VIC**

Jeff Mincham, raku fired lidded pot, dated 1989, represented in over fifty public and private collections in Australia and overseas and the winner of the prestigious Fletcher Challenge award in 1985 and 1989, 25cm deep, 22cm high.

$1700 - $1900 **Malvern Antique Market, VIC**

Studio pottery decanter with stopper and six beakers by Alan Lowe, with inscribed signature to base and hand decorated in a high gloss glaze, c1950.

$230 - $270 **Born Frugal, VIC**

Australian pottery wall plaque by Trudi Fry, c1965.

$750 - $850 **Design Dilemas, VIC**

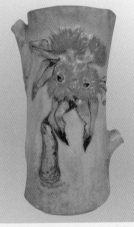

Studio pottery vase, heavily decorated with gumnuts, blossoms and gumleaves, attributed to Daisy Merton, 12cm wide, 19cm high.

$1800 - $2000 **Collector's Cottage Antiques, NSW**

Funky teapot and cup, designed by Michele Finch, well known Australian potter, 16cm high.

$230 - $270 **R. Johansson, NSW**

Ceramic twenty three piece, one off design tea set, hand painted by Melbourne artist Nina Gregory, c1998.

$2400 - $2600 **Chapel Street Bazaar, VIC**

Semi-circular vase featuring gum nuts and gum leaves, attributed to Delamere Studio, c1950, 30cm wide, 8cm high.

$175 - $195 **Collector's Cottage Antiques, NSW**

BESWICK

Beswick ceramic bird figurine 'Gold Crest' no. 2415, 6.5cm wide, 6.5cm high.

$80 - $100   **The Exchange Galleries, NSW**

Beswick model of a song thrush with brown - speckled breast, designer Albert Hallan, model no. 2308, in production 1970-1989, 14.6cm high.

NZ$310 - $350 **Country Charm Antiques, New Zealand**

Beswick model of a Gouldian finch with wings, designer Arthur Gredington, model no. 1179, purple, green and yellow gloss, in production 1949-1959, 12cm high.

NZ$650 - $750 **Country Charm Antiques, New Zealand**

Beswick model of a seagull, number 922/3, issued between 1941and 1971, 17cm long, 3.5cm deep, 21.5cm high.

$185 - $205   **White Park Antiques, SA**

Beswick model of a Kingfisher, model 237, 13cm high.

NZ$190 - $210   **Antiques On Victoria, New Zealand**

Beswick model of a Mallard settling, model no. 750, browns, teal green and white gloss, designed by Arthur Gredington, in production 1939-1965, 16.5cm high.

NZ$500 - $600   **Country Charm Antiques, New Zealand**

Beswick model of a Mallard duck, model number 596/1, 26cm long, 6cm deep, 24cm high.

$205 - $245   **White Park Antiques, SA**

Set of four Beswick ducks, model numbers 5961-2-3-4.

$950 - $1050   **The Silky Oak Shop, QLD**

Three Beswick 'Swallows' model numbers 757-1/2/3, c1950.

$600 - $700   **Upwell Antiques, ACT**

Beswick flight of pheasants, in production 1938-71.

$550 - $650   **Shenton Park Antiques, WA**

Beswick figure of a kookaburra, c1960, 14cm high.

$275 - $315 **Paddington Antique Centre Pty Ltd, QLD**

Set of three Beswick figures of seagulls with wings up, No. 922, designer Arthur Gredington, in production 1941 - 1971.

$700 - $800 **Glenelg Antique Centre, SA**

Beswick model of a lioness, c1960, 12cm high.

$250 - $300 **Goodwood House Antiques, WA**

Beswick 'Penguin Family' of four, produced from 1940-1973, c1940.

$275 - $315 **Brae-mar Antiques, NSW**

Beswick mallard wall pocket, model number 396/3, 18cm long, 4.5cm deep, 18cm high.

$185 - $205 **White Park Antiques, SA**

Beswick model of a Nut Hatch Finch, No. 2413, 9cm wide, 8cm high.

$115 - $135 **Copperfield Antiques - NSW, NSW**

Beswick 'Pink Legend' partridge wall plaque #1188/1 large, in production 1950-67, 26cm wide.

$275 - $315 **Sherwood Bazaar, QLD**

Beswick black puma, c1960, 15cm high.

$310 - $350 **David Barsby Antiques, NSW**

Beswick figure of a smokey black cat, model no. 1030, designer Arthur Gredington, 1945-1970, 12cm wide, 16cm high.

$255 - $295 **Glenelg Antique Centre, SA**

Beswick figure of a Siamese cat model no. 1887, designer Albert Hallam, in production 1971-1989, 8cm wide, 11cm high.

$135 - $155 **Glenelg Antique Centre, SA**

Beswick 'Puma on Rock', No. 1702 in tawny matt glaze, produced from 1970-1973, c1970, 28cm long, 20cm high.

$380 - $420 **Brae-mar Antiques, NSW**

BESWICK

Beswick figure of a Tigeress, issued from 1957-1975, 20cm long.

$460 - $500

Western District Antique Centre, VIC

Beswick model of a lion cub, c1970, 10cm high.

$200 - $230

Goodwood House Antiques, WA

Beswick model of Siamese kittens with copper lustre, No. 1296, c1971.

NZ$200 - $235

Country Charm Antiques, New Zealand

Early Beswick figure of Siamese kittens, No.1296 designed by Miss Granoska, c1953, 10cm long.

$65 - $85

Paddington Antique Centre Pty Ltd, QLD

Beswick grey Persian cat, standing, with original sticker, 6cm deep, 14cm wide, 13cm high.

$120 - $140

Shop 15, Antiques & Collectables - Hamilton, NSW

Pair of Beswick models of grey striped seated kittens, No. 1316, designed by Miss Granoska, in production 1962-1973, 8.9cm high.

$270 - $300

Jennifer Elizabeth Antiques, VIC

Seated cat looking forward, No. 1031, designed by Arthur Gredington, produced between 1945-1970, 11.9cm high.

$190 - $230

Jennifer Elizabeth Antiques, VIC

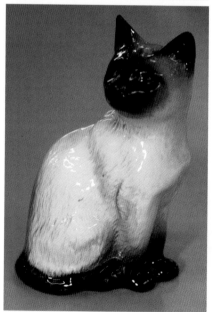

Beswick Siamese cat, model no.1887 designed by A. Hallam, seal point gloss, made from 1963-1989, green and gold label to underside 'Beswick England', also stamps embossed 1837 and makers stamp, 10cm high.

$260 - $300

Seguin's Antiques & Café, NSW

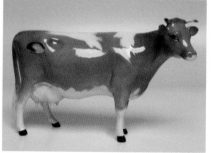

Bewsick model of a Guernsey cow, c1960, 18cm long, 10cm high.

NZ$620 - $720

Antiques On Victoria, New Zealand

Collecting Beswick Figures

From the establishment of the Beswick factory in Longton, Stoke on Trent in 1894, animal figures of a very high quality and at an affordable price to the collector with a modest budget, have been represented in Beswick sales catalogues and advertising material.

The production of Beswick figures can be divided into two periods. From the 1890's to the mid 1930's the Beswick factory produced, in the Staffordshire traditional form, a combination of table ware, decorative porcelain, majolica and a range of figures and animals such as generals, milkmaids, mantle dogs, cattle and horses. Critics of the time described their models to be of a higher quality than those of their precursors. Unfortunately for collectors, Beswick followed the early Staffordshire tradition of not marking their figures and as a consequence, it is very difficult to identify the names of the modellers, designers and artists from that period until the 1930's.

In 1934 after the death of his father, John (Ewart) took over as managing director and moved the company away from the production of tableware to placing a greater emphasis on figurines. And most importantly for collectors, introduced a 'shape book' and a systematic numbering catalogue recording the impressed mark and backstamp on the full range of Beswick products.

They also appointed Arthur Gredington as the company's first full time modeller in 1939. The combination of these two events created the golden age of Beswick which continued until the factory closed in 2002.

Beswick figure of a dairy short horn bull champion 'Gwerslyt Lord Oxford' 74th, 1957-1973 12.7cm high.

NZ$1490 - $1690   **Country Charm Antiques, New Zealand**

Beswick model of a Hereford calf, model no. 854, second version, designer Arthur Gredington, c1957, 9.5cm high.

NZ$1180-$1380   **Country Charm Antiques, New Zealand**

Beswick model, 'Champion of Champions' Hereford bull, c1950, 20cm long, 12cm high.

NZ$600 - $700   **Antiques On Victoria, New Zealand**

Beswick model of a 'Red Poll Cow', rare breeds, red gloss, designer Robert Donaldson, 2001-2002, 16cm high.

NZ$720 - $820   **Country Charm Antiques, New Zealand**

Beswick model of a Highland bull, model no. 2008, designer Arthur Gredington, in production 1965-1990, 12.7cm high.

NZ$1170 - $1370   **Country Charm Antiques, New Zealand**

Beswick model of a Jersey cow 'Newton Tinkle', designer Arthur Gredington, model no. 1345, in production 1954-1997,10.8cm high.

NZ$480 - $520   **Country Charm Antiques, New Zealand**

Beswick model of a Charolais bull, model no. 2463, designer Alan Maslankowski, in production 1978-1993, 12.7cm high.

NZ$650 - $750   **Country Charm Antiques, New Zealand**

Beswick model of a Jersey bull 'Dunsley Toy Boy' model no. 1422, designer Arthur Gredington, in production 1956-1997, 12cm high.

NZ$650 - $750   **Country Charm Antiques, New Zealand**

Beswick Ayrshire bull 'White Hill Mandate' gloss no. 1454 B, c1950, 13.5cm high.

$740 - $840

Turn O' The Century, **QLD**

Beswick model of a Charolais bull, c1950, 23cm long, 13cm high.

NZ$650 - $750

Antiques On Victoria, **New Zealand**

Large Beswick figure of a bull, light brown colourway with yellow horns, c1950, 24cm long, 15cm high.

$650 - $750

Richmond Antiques, **TAS**

Beswick model of a goat, model no. 1035, designer Arthur Gredington, in production 1945-1971, 14cm high.

NZ$410 - $450

Country Charm Antiques, **New Zealand**

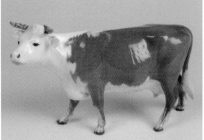

Beswick Hereford cow, model No. 948, 2nd version designer, Arthur Gredington., c1941.

NZ$1100 - $1300

Country Charm Antiques, **New Zealand**

Beswick model of a highland cow, model no. 1740, designer Arthur Gredington, in production 1966-1990, 3.3cm high.

NZ$900 - $1000

Country Charm Antiques, **New Zealand**

Beswick figure of 'Pig & Piglet Piggy Bank', model No.2746, designer Graham Tongue, in production 1983-1994 and piglet model No.2746, in production 1940-1971, 16.5cm wide.

$200 - $240

Newlyn Antiques, **VIC**

Beswick model of a Pekinese dog, 10cm long, 12cm high.

$170 - $190

Camberwell Antique Centre, **VIC**

Beswick model of a sheep dog, pattern D1792, 27cm long, 16cm high.

$180 - $200

Camberwell Antique Centre, **VIC**

Beswick model of a pug dog, 12cm long, 12cm high.

$180 - $200

Camberwell Antique Centre, **VIC**

Beswick model No.1791, large Collie 'Lochinvar of Ladypark', designer Arthur Gredington, in production 1961-94, 14.6cm high.

$225 - $265

Newlyn Antiques, **VIC**

Beswick model of a seated dog with a white and tan gloss finish. No. 286, designed by Mr. Watkin, in production 1934-1954, 15.9cm high.

$250 - $300   **Jennifer Elizabeth Antiques, VIC**

Beswick model of a seated terrier dog, model No. 286, in production between 1934-1954, 20cm long, 16cm high.

$190 - $230   **Camberwell Antique Centre, VIC**

Beswick bull terrier figurine, HN1132 in production from 1937 to 1960, 20cm long, 6.5cm deep, 16cm high.

$1900 - $2100   **Southside Antiques Centre, QLD**

Beswick model of a greyhound, model number 972, 'Jovial Roger', in production 1942-1990, 18cm long, 14cm high.

$360 - $390   **Southside Antiques Centre, QLD**

Beswick Yorkshire Terrier, model 2102, in production between 1967-1972, 8cm high.

$110 - $130   **Camberwell Antique Centre, VIC**

Beswick cast iron monarch Airedale terrier MN962, 6cm deep, 17cm wide, 14cm high.

$360 - $400   **Southside Antiques Centre, QLD**

Beswick model No.361, dachshund standing, designer: Mr. Watkin, in production 1936-83, 14cm high.

$165 - $185   **Newlyn Antiques, VIC**

Beswick figure of a boxer, model 3081, c1999, 16cm long, 14cm high.

$160 - $180   **Camberwell Antique Centre, VIC**

White Beswick model of a bull terrier, stand added, 17cm high.

$205 - $245   **Shop 7, Centenary Antique Centre, NSW**

Beswick ceramic figure of a daschhund, 10cm long, 7cm high.

$75 - $95   **The Exchange Galleries, NSW**

Beswick model of a basset hound, model 2045A, in production between 1965-1994, 19.5cm long, 13cm high.

$210 - $250   **Camberwell Antique Centre, VIC**

Beswick figurine of an English Setter, Baycoone Baronet, MN973. 1942-1989, 4.5cm deep, 23cm wide, 14cm high.

$330 - $370   **Southside Antiques Centre, QLD**

Beswick figure of a labrador, 8cm high.

$90 - $110 **Shirley & Noel Daly Antiques, VIC**

Beswick sheepdog figurine in production from 1961 to 1997, 16cm long, 13cm high.

$130 - $170 **Southside Antiques Centre, QLD**

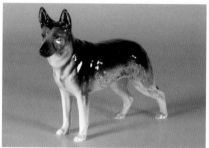

Beswick dog model No.969, a large Alsation 'Ulrica of Brittas', designer, Arthur Gredington, in production 1942-94, 14.6cm high.

$200 - $240 **Newlyn Antiques, VIC**

Poodle on a cushion, matt finish, No. 2985, designed by Alan Maslamkowski from the good companions series, only in production for two years, c1988, 14cm high.

$390 - $450 **Jennifer Elizabeth Antiques, VIC**

Beswick figure of border collie dog, c1980, 7.5cm high.

$90 - $110 **Shirley & Noel Daly Antiques, VIC**

Beswick model of a hare, model no. 1024, tan and gloss, designer Arthur Gredington, in production1945-1963, 12.7cm high.

NZ$1100 - $1300 **Country Charm Antiques, New Zealand**

Beswick curled fox, model no. 1017, 10cm long, 3.2cm high.

NZ$275 - $315 **South Auckland Antiques & Collectables, New Zealand**

Beswick standing fox, model no. 1016A, 21cm long, 14cm high.

NZ$275 - $315 **South Auckland Antiques & Collectables, New Zealand**

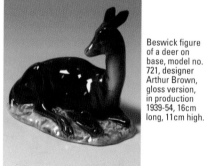

Beswick figure of a deer on base, model no. 721, designer Arthur Brown, gloss version, in production 1939-54, 16cm long, 11cm high.

$205 - $245 **Glenelg Antique Centre, SA**

Beswick stag and deer with green stickers, c1970, 19cm long, 20cm high.

NZ$530 - $630 **South Auckland Antiques & Collectables, New Zealand**

Beswick figure of a wild animal model No. 954, Stag - Lying, designer Arthur Gredington, in production 1945-75, 14cm high.

$170 - $190 **Newlyn Antiques, VIC**

Beswick model of a stag, standing model no. 981, designer Arthur Gredington, light brown gloss, in production 1942-1997, 20.3cm high.

NZ$480 - $520 **Country Charm Antiques, New Zealand**

Beswick model of a shire mare, model no. 818, designer Arthur Gredington, rockinghorse grey, in production 1940-1962, 21.6cm high.

NZ$1350 - $1550   **Country Charm Antiques, New Zealand**

Beswick figure of a foal, c1950, 13cm long, 6cm wide, 12.5cm high.

$110 - $130   **Kookaburra Antiques, TAS**

Beswick brown matt glaze horse figurine, c1970, 20cm high.

$135 - $155   **Brae-mar Antiques, NSW**

Beswick model of a highland pony, 'Mackionneach' mountain and Moorland ponies, designer Arthur Gredington, in production 1961-1989, 18.4cm high.

NZ$480 - $520   **Country Charm Antiques, New Zealand**

Beswick model of a thoroughbred stallion, designer Arthur Gredington, second version, model no. 1772, in production1961-1989, 20.3cm high.

NZ$690 - $790   **Country Charm Antiques, New Zealand**

Beswick figure of an Arab pony, designed by Arthur Gredington, model No. 1407, grey gloss, in production 1961-1989, 12cm high.

NZ$380 - $420   **Country Charm Antiques, New Zealand**

Beswick figure of a wooly Shetland pony, manufactured 1945-1989, c1970, 20cm long, 14cm high.

NZ$480 - $520   **Colonial Heritage Antiques Ltd, New Zealand**

Beswick figure of a Welsh mountain pony, 'Coed Coch Madog', series of Mountain and Moorland ponies, in production 1961 to the present, 16cm high.

NZ$650 - $750   **Country Charm Antiques, New Zealand**

Beswick figure of a shire foal, model #951 designed by Arthur Gredington, manufactured 1941-1971, 16cm high.

NZ$275 - $315   **Colonial Heritage Antiques Ltd, New Zealand**

Beswick figure of a Shetland foal designed by Arthur Greddington, manufactured 1945-1989, c1970, 10cm long, 8cm high.

NZ$275 - $315   **Colonial Heritage Antiques Ltd, New Zealand**

Beswick figure of an Appaloosa horse, second issue discontinued 1989, 23cm long, 20cm high.

NZ$750 - $850   **Colonial Heritage Antiques Ltd, New Zealand**

Beswick model of a huntsman on rearing horse, model no. 868, second version, designed by Arthur Gredington, in production 1952-1995, 25.4cm high.

NZ$940 - $1040   **Country Charm Antiques, New Zealand**

Arthur Gredington

Beswick was a tight knit family firm which was renowned for its ability to produce high quality traditional Staffordshire figures and table ware from its formation in 1894. By the time John (Ewart) Beswick took over as Managing Director in 1934 the firm had prospered under three generations of Beswick management. John, along with his Uncle Gilbert who worked alongside with him as Sales Director, worked to change the direction of the company from producing tableware to the production of figurines. This required the recruitment of a modelling team. In 1939 Arthur Gredington was appointed as the company's first full time modeller.

Beswick horse and jockey standing still, model No. 1862. Designed by Arthur Gredington, in production 1963-1984. 20.3cm high.

NZ$1480 - $1680

Country Charm Antiques, New Zealand

Beswick figure of a horse and rider, 27cm long, 25cm high.

$1600 - $1800

Chelsea Antiques & Decorative Art Centre P/L, QLD

This was an inspired choice as the team of Ewart, Gilbert and Arthur Gredington created the Beswick golden age, which lasted to the 1990's, long after all three had left the Company.

Arthur Gredington's influence at Beswick was enormous. He had a great talent for modelling with his accurate and realistic creation of animals of all kinds such as horses, dogs, cats, birds, wild animals, farm animals, fish and more all of the highest quality. He also displayed versatility and humour with his design of the wide range of Beswick story book figurines where he gave human characteristics to the story book animals. Gredington designed and modelled the first Beatrix Potter figurines in 1947 and from this base, Beswick produced a vast array of cartoon figures, character animals, Brambly Hedge and other story book figures.

Arthur Gredington retired in 1968. Ewart and Gilbert Beswick, with no successors to take over the business, sold to Royal Doulton in 1969. However, such was his skill and talent, that many of Gredington's models remained in production to ensure that the Beswick factory continued to produce the highest quality figurines until the factory closed in 2002.

Beswick figure of a horse model No.1037, 'jockey walking racehorse', colourway number 2 (number on saddle cloth), horse in brown gloss. Designer: Arthur Gredington, in production 1945-76, 21.6cm high.

$1500 - $1700

Newlyn Antiques, VIC

Beswick model of a Barracuda, model 1236, designer Arthur Gredington blue and silver, in production 1952-1968, 12cm long.

NZ$1200 - $1400

Country Charm Antiques, New Zealand

Beswick sea lion shape No.383 in matt white finish, c1940, 18cm wide, 26cm high.

$545 - $645

Philip Cross Antiques, NSW

Beswick figure of a trout, model no. 1032, designer Arthur Gredington, in production 1945-75, 15.9cm high.

$470 - $510

Newlyn Antiques, VIC

Beswick Decanic Bonito fish, designed by Arthur Gredington, in blue, silver and green gloss, model No. 1232, in production 1952-1968, 18.4cm long.

NZ$1000 - $1200

Country Charm Antiques, New Zealand

Beswick model of an Atlantic salmon, designed by Arthur Gredington, in blue, silver and green gloss, model no. 1233, in production 1952-1970, 16.5cm high.

NZ$1100 - $1300

Country Charm Antiques, New Zealand

Beswick figurine of a man pushing donkey, 17cm wide, 9cm high.

NZ$115 - $135   **Country Charm Antiques, New Zealand**

Beswick figure of a monkey smoking pipe, introduced 1946, withdrawn 1969, 11cm high.

$220 - $260   **Western District Antique Centre, VIC**

Beswick wild animal model No.853, giraffe small, designer: Arthur Gredington, in production 1940-75, 18.4cm high.

$230 - $270   **Newlyn Antiques, VIC**

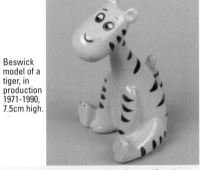

Beswick model of a tiger, in production 1971-1990, 7.5cm high.

$300 - $340   **Antique Centre of Stonnington, VIC**

Beswick 'Mock Turtle' from Alice in Wonderland, 1st series, in production 1973-83, 10cm high.

$230 - $270   **East West Collectables, NSW**

Beswick 'Bill Badger' from the Rupert the Bear series, c1981, 7cm high.

$480 - $520   **Brae-mar Antiques, NSW**

Highly collectable 'Rupert the Bear Snowballer', Beswick, and boxed, c1990, 3.5cm wide, 11.25cm high.

$1400 - $1600   **Barry McKay, NSW**

Beswick figure 'Lady Mouse', in production 1950-1988, 7cm wide, 10cm high.

$90 - $110   **Antique General Store, NSW**

Beswick figure 'Ribby', c1973, 7cm wide, 9cm high.

$150 - $170   **Antique General Store, NSW**

Beswick three piece vase setting designed by Kathy Urbach, the doves 29cm long, the vase 19cm high, c1960.

NZ$850 - $950   **Banks Peninsula Antiques, New Zealand**

Beswick 'Rabbit' from the Winnie the Pooh series, in production 1965-90.

$170 - $220   **East West Collectables, NSW**

Classic Beswick vase, c1950.

NZ$110 - $130

**Maxine's Collectibles,
New Zealand**

Beswick lavender palm tree jug no. 1074, in production 1947-63, 14cm wide, 18cm high.

NZ$350 - $390

**Country Charm Antiques,
New Zealand**

Large retro vase, maker Beswick English Pottery, designer Albert Hallam, c1960, 24cm high.

$165 - $185

**Urbanized,
VIC**

Beswick 'Tony Weller' jam pot, model 1207, c1950, 8.5cm high, 7cm diameter.

$165 - $185

**Arleston Antiques,
VIC**

English Beswick glazed urn, model 1190, c1950, 26cm high, 23cm diam.

$165 - $185

**Heartland Antiques & Art,
NSW**

Beswick footed trough vase with bright copper glaze, c1950, 14cm deep, 32cm wide, 14cm high.

$45 - $65

**Antiques & Collectables Centre - Ballarat,
VIC**

Beswick vase, red interior and zebrette style exterior, in clam style, c1950, 14cm deep, 20cm wide, 15cm high.

$185 - $205

**Chapel Street Bazaar,
VIC**

Beautifully glazed Beswick vase, c1950, 10cm long, 15cm high.

$50 - $70

**Fyshwick Antique Centre,
ACT**

Beswick vase in Art Deco shape, No. 190, c1950, 19cm high, 13cm diameter.

$115 - $135

**Dr Russell's Emporium,
WA**

Retro vase, maker Beswick, designer Albert Hallam, c1960, 16cm high.

$105 - $125

**Urbanized,
VIC**

Beatrix Potter's 'The Old Woman Who Lived In A Shoe' figurine, c1959, 7cm high.

$85 - $105   **Sherwood Bazaar, QLD**

Beswick Beatrix Potter 'Appley Dapply' 1st version BP30, 1973-74, 8cm high.

$245 - $285   **Yanda Aboriginal Art Melbourne, VIC**

Beatrix Potter 'Little Pig Robinson' with a gold stamp, in production 1948-1974, 9.5cm high.

NZ$620 - $670   **Country Charm Antiques, New Zealand**

Beswick figure 'Foxy Whiskered Gentleman', c1980, 13cm high.

$110 - $130   **Antique General Store, NSW**

Beswick Beatrix Potter 'Squirrel Nutkin' 1st version BP3A, 1974-75, 9.5cm high.

$155 - $175   **Yanda Aboriginal Art Melbourne, VIC**

Beswick Beatrix Potter 'Tommy Brock' figurine, BP3b second version, 7.5cm high.

$100 - $135   **East West Collectables, NSW**

Beswick Beatrix Potter 'Lady Mouse' with a gold back stamp, 10cm high.

$270 - $320   **East West Collectables, NSW**

'The Old Woman Who Lived in the Shoe, Knitting' from the Beatrix Potter series, c1983, 7cm high.

$280 - $320   **Brae-mar Antiques, NSW**

Beatrix Potter model of 'Yock Yock In The Tub', c1999, 8cm high, 7cm diameter.

$115 - $135   **Glenelg Antique Centre, SA**

Beswick Wren, No. 993, c1940.

NZ$105 - $125   **Antiques On Victoria, New Zealand**

Small decorative gilded plate from the 'Magic Flute' series by Bjorn Wiinblad, Rosenthal Germany, c1980, 10cm diam.

$185 - $205   **Toowoomba Antiques Gallery, QLD**

Bjorn Wiinblad

Born in Copenhagen, Denmark in 1919, Bjorn Wiinblad is regarded as one of the most imaginative artists of our time. Currently residing in Copenhagen, and at the age of 86, he still works from his own studio and shows no sign of retiring. Working in as many mediums as possible, Wiinblad has created pieces in porcelain, terracotta, glass and silver, as well as numerous designs on paper, and all manner of textiles.

With his world of fairy tales and myths, and use of the nymph figure, Wiinblad's designs appeal to all age groups, from the very young, to the mature collector and decorator.

Mostly these characters are rotund, often sad but always with overtones of amusement and mischievousness. These simple elements of design have propelled Wiinblad to the forefront of the modern day collectables market. Chief designer with Rosenthal Germany for 35 years, he is represented in major collections, galleries and museums throughout the world.

'Year of the Rooster' plate designed by Bjorn Wiinblad with stylized central rooster figure and matching border, made by Rosenthal Germany, c1974, 28.5cm diam.

$480 - $580   **Toowoomba Antiques Gallery, QLD**

Very large and impressive pair of Bjorn Wiinblad vases from the Quatre Couleurs 'Head Dress' series, 'Quatre Couleurs' indicates four different carats of gold used in the gilding, c1970, 10cm deep, 27cm wide, 32cm high.

$5300 - $5700   **Toowoomba Antiques Gallery, QLD**

The 'Four Seasons' figures by Bjorn Wiinblad, Summer, Spring, Winter and Fall, all hand built of terracotta and decorated in blue and white with applied decorative relief c1977, 33cm high.

$7750 - $8150   **Toowoomba Antiques Gallery, QLD**

Bjorn Wiinblad musician plate in theatrical dress, cobalt blue background with gold and platinum highlights, c1970, 31cm long, 31cm high.

$650 - $750   **Toowoomba Antiques Gallery, QLD**

Pair of Mermaid candleholders in stark white with hand gilded highlights, designed by Bjorn Wiinblad, and produced in limited quantities by Rosenthal Germany, c1980, 34cm high.

$3400 - $3600   **Toowoomba Antiques Gallery, QLD**

Bjorn Wiinblad figural candlestick, Wiinblad Studio Copenhagen Denmark, hand sculpted and painted., c1988, 64cm high.

$4850 - $5050   **Toowoomba Antiques Gallery, QLD**

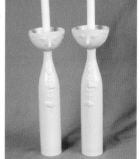

Pair of 'Romanze' figural candle holders, each detailed with applied relief on stark white. Designed by Bjorn Wiinblad and produced by Rosenthal of Germany, c1980, 35cm high.

$2640 - $2840   **Toowoomba Antiques Gallery, QLD**

Bjorn Winblad cylinder vase, white with black transfer of naked maidens, c1960, 28cm high, 9.5cm diam.

$165 - $185   **Cool & Collected, SA**

Pair of large vases decorated with horse and rider, vibrant colours over a cobalt blue background, designed by Bjorn Wiinblad, produced at Rosenthal Germany, c1970, 30cm long, 13cm wide, 33cm high.

$6300 - $6700   **Toowoomba Antiques Gallery, QLD**

Pair of Bjorn Wiinblad designed vases featuring a lady with bunches of flowers with Pagoda style hat, all hand gilded with four different carats of gold, by Rosenthal Germany, c1980, 31cm high.

$1890 - $2090   **Toowoomba Antiques Gallery, QLD**

Painted plate with landscape, incised 'Guy Boyd Australia', signed J. F., c1950, 16cm diameter.

$155 - $175

Ainsley Antiques, VIC

Endearing bottlebrush biscuit barrel with prominent finial, in the traditional form, both face and back painted with clusters of flowering bottlebrushes and leaves, the lid also painted with leaves, gloss glazes of red, pink, greens, ochre, chocolate , incised 'Guy Boyd' painted signature 'H. Illich', c1955, 17cm high, 14cm diameter.

$480 - $520

Hurnall's Antiques & Decorative Arts, VIC

Guy Boyd fifteen piece coffee set, speckled pink body with beige accents, signed Guy Boyd on bases, c1950, 1.25cm wide, 2.3cm high, 1.15cm diameter.

$230 - $270

Hamilton Street Antiques, VIC

'Dreamtime' cave paintings platter, the surface deeply incised with a large mythical kangaroo holding a spear, defending itself against an armed Aboriginal hunter, deep yellow, charcoal, chocolate, tan gloss glazes, incised 'Guy Boyd', c1955, 23cm diameter.

$4350 - $4550

Hurnall's Antiques & Decorative Arts, VIC

Martin Boyd handpainted mug, numbered and signed, c1950, 12cm high, 8cm diam.

$135 - $155

Kollectik Pty Ltd, NSW

Martin Boyd 'Mr Winkle' mug, c1950, 8cm high.

$85 - $105

Antiques Down Under, NSW

Australian pottery salt and pepper, 4.5cm high, 3.5cm diameter.

NZ$60 - $80

Country Charm Antiques, New Zealand

Australian ceramic dish, signed Martin Boyd, 3cm high, 11cm diameter.

NZ$155 - $175

Country Charm Antiques, New Zealand

One of a set of six soup coupe's, hand painted, each piece with different decoration, c1960.

$330 - $370

Shop 18, Centenary Antique Centre, NSW

Two Martin Boyd hand painted pots with wattle, yellow and green decoration with pink and grey bird, c1950, 9cm diameter.

NZ$90 - $110

Strangely Familiar, New Zealand

Sculpted Merric Boyd jug, decorated on reverse with leaves and to the front with quinces and leaves, incised 'Merric Boyd 1947', 19cm high.

$3850 - $4050

Armadale Antique Centre, VIC

Large Brownie Downing plate, registered design No. 35059, 21cm diameter.

$80 - $100

The Mill Markets, VIC

Australian aboriginal figure riding a turtle, by Brownie Downing, c1950, 9cm deep, 6cm wide, 7cm high.

$100 - $120

The Junk Company, VIC

Brownie Downie 'Mexican Boy' plate, c1950.

$30 - $60

Rose Cottage Antiques, ACT

Brownie Downing tea pot, c1960, 10cm high.

$410 - $450

Debbie Pech, VIC

Brownie Downing salt and pepper shakers featuring piccaninnies with a kookaburra and flowers, signed to the front and stamped to the base, c1950, 8cm high, 4cm diameter.

$115 - $135

Mt Dandenong Antique Centre, VIC

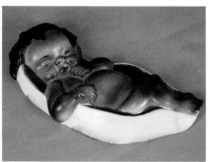

Brownie Downing figure, 'Sleeping Piccaninny' No. 35057, 16cm long.

$180 - $200

Paddington Antique Centre Pty Ltd, QLD

Brownie Downing figurine of an aboriginal girl with two birds, including a kookaburra, c1950, 7cm high.

$115 - $135

Camberwell Antique Centre, VIC

Large Brownie Downing plate, c1950, 20cm diameter.

$155 - $175

Antipodes Antiques, QLD

'Widpy-Woo', unmarked koala wall plaque by Brownie Downing, 14cm high.

$255 - $295

Mooney Collectables, NSW

Two part dish of unusual shape with handle, by Brownie Downing, c1950, 20cm long, 12cm wide.

$100 - $120

Collector's Cottage Antiques, NSW

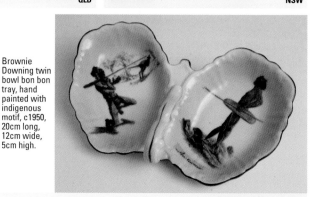

Brownie Downing twin bowl bon bon tray, hand painted with indigenous motif, c1950, 20cm long, 12cm wide, 5cm high.

$120 - $140

Fyshwick Antique Centre, ACT

Carlton Ware Rouge Royale with stork pattern, c1950, 17cm high.

$480 - $520
Western District Antique Centre, VIC

Carlton Ware 'Briar Rose' jug, 18cm long, 8cm deep, 13cm high.

$140 - $170
Sherwood Bazaar, QLD

Large Carlton Ware jug with grape decoration, c1950, 19cm wide, 20cm high.

NZ$215 - $255
Country Charm Antiques, New Zealand

Carlton Ware jug, c1950, 11cm deep, 18cm wide, 17cm high.

$135 - $155
Kookaburra Antiques, TAS

Carlton Ware 'Gumnut' jug, 12cm wide, 4cm high.

NZ$90 - $110
Country Charm Antiques, New Zealand

Carlton Ware 'Blue Royale' jug, c1950, 17cm high.

$135 - $155
Yanda Aboriginal Art Melbourne, VIC

Carlton Ware pink buttercup jug, c1950, 14cm wide, 10cm high.

$225 - $265
Camberwell Antique Centre, VIC

Carlton Ware langouste salad sauce jug, dish and spoon with hand painted lobster, c1958, 13cm long, 5cm high.

NZ$140 - $180
Country Charm Antiques, New Zealand

Carlton Ware yellow 'Apple Blossom' teapot, c1940, 23cm wide, 10cm high.

$350 - $390
Camberwell Antique Centre, VIC

Carlton Ware leaf patterned plate, c1930, 20cm long, 20cm wide, 4cm high.

$30 - $40
Kenny's Antiques, VIC

Carlton Ware 'Rouge Royale' sugar bowl and creamer, c1950.

$360 - $410
H.O.W Gifts & Collectables, QLD

CARLTON WARE

Carlton Ware leaf plate, 22cm long, 19cm wide.

$40 - $50

**Laidley Old Wares,
QLD**

Large Carlton Ware platter with five segments and embossed grape design, c1950, 7cm high, 34cm diam.

$185 - $205

**White Park Antiques,
SA**

Carlton Ware Australian design lobster egg server platter, c1950, 30cm diameter.

NZ$75 - $95

**Peachgrove Antiques,
New Zealand**

Carlton Ware plate, 32cm diameter.

$250 - $300

**Pedlars Antique Market,
SA**

Carlton Ware lustre glaze 'Bunnies' design vase, 11.5cm high, 11cm diameter.

$700 - $800

**Rose Cottage Antiques,
ACT**

Carlton Ware 'Hydrangea' wall pocket, c1950, 12cm wide, 17cm high.

$205 - $245

**Camberwell Antique Centre,
VIC**

Carlton Ware vase in the 'New Stork' pattern, No. 1640, c1950, 13cm wide, 13cm high.

$330 - $370

**Mentone Beach Antiques Centre,
VIC**

Carlton Ware studio ribbed vase, c1950, 16cm high, 15cm diameter.

$185 - $205

**Antiques & Collectables Centre - Ballarat,
VIC**

Carlton Ware vase, c1950, 10cm deep, 13.5cm high.

$55 - $75

**Antiques Down Under,
NSW**

Carlton Ware 'Blackberry' bowl, c1940, 27cm long.

$125 - $145

**Camberwell Antique Centre,
VIC**

Carlton Ware 'Wild Rose' salad bowl and servers, c1940, 29cm long, 21cm wide.

$310 - $350

**Camberwell Antique Centre,
VIC**

Carlton Ware sauce boat in the 'Gumnut' pattern, 14cm wide, 5cm high.

NZ$100 - $120

Country Charm Antiques, New Zealand

Carlton Ware 'Spring Flowers', large dish moulded in relief, Australian design, 30cm long, 18cm deep, 3cm high.

$175 - $195

Laidley Old Wares, QLD

Carlton Ware dish, c1950, 25cm deep, 26cm wide.

NZ$255 - $295

Country Charm Antiques, New Zealand

Carlton Ware 'Blue Royal New Stork' pattern bowl, c1950, 16cm deep, 27cm wide.

NZ$360 - $400

Country Charm Antiques, New Zealand

Carlton Ware 'Vert Royale New Stork' pattern dish, c1950, 17cm deep, 25cm wide.

$275 - $315

Glenelg Antique Centre, SA

Carlton Ware bowl in black and gold, c1955, 25cm diam.

$330 - $370

Cedar Lodge Antiques, VIC

Unusual Carlton Ware bowl, c1950, 13cm high.

$185 - $205

Western District Antique Centre, VIC

Carlton Ware grape entrée handle dish with two bowls, c1950, 25cm deep, 26cm wide.

NZ$255 - $295

Country Charm Antiques, New Zealand

'Grape' pattern coffee cup and saucer with gilded interior and handle, c1950, 7cm high.

$85 - $105

Sherwood Bazaar, QLD

Rouge Royale sugar and creamer, #3965, gold trim.

$380 - $420

H.O.W Gifts & Collectables, QLD

Carlton Ware cigarette box, c1950, 13cm long, 10cm deep, 4cm high.

$125 - $145

Days of Olde Antiques & Collectables, VIC

Fifteen piece Carlton Ware, polka dot 'Rouge Royale' coffee set, c1950.

$1480 - $1680

Cedar Lodge Antiques, VIC

Novelty Carlton Ware teapot in the shape of a camel, c1976, 20cm wide, 19cm high.

$110 - $130

The Botanic Ark, VIC

Carlton Ware bowl on tray, 9cm high.

$40 - $50

Paddington Antique Centre Pty Ltd, QLD

Large Carlton Ware foxglove bowl with original servers, c1940, 27cm long, 22cm deep, 10cm high.

$320 - $350

Sturt Street Antiques & Art, VIC

Carlton Ware dark blue hand enamelled and gilded lustre bowl in the 'New Stork' pattern, c1950, 18cm long, 6cm high.

$340 - $370

Sturt Street Antiques & Art, VIC

'Poppies & Daises' Carlton Ware milk jug and sugar bowl, c1950.

$175 - $195

Debbie Pech, VIC

Carlton Ware embossed pink hydrangea serving dish on green background, c1950, 30cm long, 15cm deep.

Carlton Ware embossed hydrangea serving dish on pale blue background, c1950, 27cm long, 14cm deep.

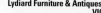

$165 - $185

Lydiard Furniture & Antiques, VIC

$165 - $185

Lydiard Furniture & Antiques, VIC

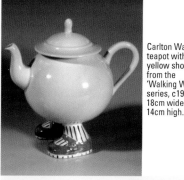

Carlton Ware teapot with yellow shoes from the 'Walking Ware' series, c1970, 18cm wide, 14cm high.

$185 - $205

White Park Antiques, SA

White and gold Carlton Ware wine decanter and six goblets, c1970, 36cm high.

NZ$230 - $270

Maxine's Collectibles, New Zealand

Set of six white Carlton Ware mugs with ribbed sides, pink and red flower decoration, 14cm high.

NZ$280 - $320

Maxine's Collectibles, New Zealand

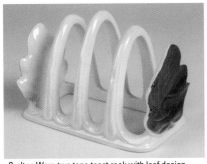

Carlton Ware two tone toast rack with leaf design, c1950, 12cm long, 7cm wide, 8cm high.

NZ$65 - $85

Strangely Familiar, New Zealand

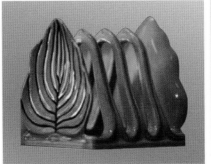

Carlton Ware pinstripe and cream toast rack.

$115 - $125

Bower Bird Art & Antiques, QLD

Carlton Ware green 'Rosebud' toast rack, c1950, 9cm high.

$175 - $195

Western District Antique Centre, VIC

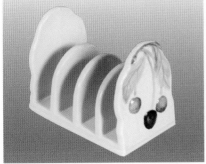

Carlton Ware toast rack.

$100 - $130

20th Century Antiques & Collectables Market, QLD

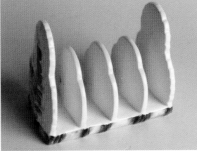

Carlton Ware 'Foxgloves' toast rack, 10cm long, 8cm high.

$120 - $140

Treats & Treasures, NSW

Carlton Ware yellow apple blossom serviette ring, c1940, 6cm diameter.

$125 - $145

Camberwell Antique Centre, VIC

Carlton Ware mushroom shaped, four piece cruet set, c1950, 15cm diameter.

$155 - $175

Gumnut Antiques & Old Wares, NSW

Carlton Ware salt and pepper shakers in the form of owls, c1950, 5cm wide, 17cm high.

NZ$20 - $30

Casa Manana Antiques & Collectables, New Zealand

Carlton Ware hand painted sugar shaker in the shape of a house, c1950, 8cm wide, 14cm high, 7cm diameter.

Ceramic pink pig bookends by Carlton Ware, c1950, 15cm high.

$175 - $195

The Bottom Drawer Antique Centre, VIC

Carlton Ware musical decanter, Swiss made with original sticker, c1950, 14cm wide, 24cm high, 14cm diam.

$370 - $410

Urbanized, VIC

$430 - $470

Camberwell Antique Centre, VIC

Clarice Cliff Bizarre cup and saucer, decorated in the 'Applique Auignon' pattern.

$850 - $950   **Deco Down Under, WA**

Clarice Cliff 'Drummer' double sided figurine, 30cm high.

NZ$120 - $140   **Memory Lane, New Zealand**

Clarice Cliff 'Blue Dancer' double sided figurine, 20cm high.

NZ$245 - $285   **Memory Lane, New Zealand**

Clarice Cliff Fantasque octagonal sandwich plate, decorated in the 'Gibraltar' pattern, 14cm diameter.

$1850 - $2050   **Deco Down Under, WA**

Clarice Cliff sandwich plate in 'Crocus' pattern, Clarice Cliff mark, c1940, 30cm wide, 10cm high.

$700 - $800   **Moor-Cliff, NSW**

Clarice Cliff square hand painted bowl decorated with an orchid, c1950.

$480 - $520   **Chilton's Antiques & Jewellery, NSW**

Clarice Cliff 'Dance Pair' double sided figurine, 50cm high.

NZ$380 - $420   **Memory Lane, New Zealand**

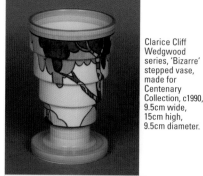

Clarice Cliff 'Swan' vase, 14cm high.

NZ$380 - $420   **Colonial Antiques, New Zealand**

Clarice Cliff Wedgwood series Bizarre ware 'Lido Lady', made for The Centenary Collection, c1990, 11cm wide, 16cm high, 15cm diam.

$360 - $400   **Hermitage Antiques - Geelong Wintergarden, VIC**

Clarice Cliff Wedgwood series, 'Bizarre' stepped vase, made for Centenary Collection, c1990, 9.5cm wide, 15cm high, 9.5cm diameter.

$480 - $520   **Hermitage Antiques - Geelong Wintergarden, VIC**

Clarice Cliff 'Harvest' teapot, c1950, 17cm high.

$550 - $650   **Yanda Aboriginal Art Melbourne, VIC**

Crown Devon bowl, 33cm long, 9cm high.

$850 - $880

Bayside Antiques Centre, VIC

Part of a Crown Devon Fieldings tea set in the Stockholm pattern, comprising of eight trios, tea pot, milk jug and sugar bowl, c1950.

$390 - $430

frhapsody, WA

Crown Devon twin handled vase, 30cm long, 12cm high.

$650 - $68

Bayside Antiques Centre, VIC

Crown Devon cup and saucer featuring a striking black and yellow design, c1950, 28cm long, 16cm wide.

$60 - $80

Sturt Street Antiques & Art, VIC

Crown Devon Fairy Castle Rouge vase, 21cm high.

$2200 - $2400 **Bayside Antiques Centre, VIC**

Crown Devon fairy vase, 31cm high.

$2100 - $2300 **Bayside Antiques Centre, VIC**

Crown Devon spider web vase with matt finish, 19cm high.

$1000 - $1200 **Bayside Antiques Centre, VIC**

Crown Devon lustre vase, 15cm high.

$900 - $950 **Bayside Antiques Centre, VIC**

Crown Devon parrot and cloud, matt green jug, 23cm high.

$2700 - $2900 **Bayside Antiques Centre, VIC**

Crown Devon handpainted spiral castor, 14cm high.

$75 - $95 **Paddington Antique Centre Pty Ltd, QLD**

Crown Devon Fieldings 'Oceania' plate, hand painted with scene of crayfish, sea horse, two fish and shell, 25cm diameter.

$70 - $90 **Bower Bird Art & Antiques, QLD**

Crown Lynn

The Crown Lynn story is part of the New Zealand's heritage. Operating during the period 1948 - 1989, the factory produced domestic ware commonly used in most New Zealand homes c1950. The story began in the 1860s, at Hobsonville where a farmer, R. O. Clark, encountering drainage problems, made his own clay drainage pipes. Demand was such that he went into business as a manufacturer of bricks and tiles and began a family business which was to have a lasting impact on New Zealand households.

In 1931 Thomas Clark, the great grandson of the original owner joined the firm. He realised the oportunities and expanded into domestic ware, opening a porcelain Specials Department in 1937. During WW2 the Specials Department was declared an essential industry and moved into making vitrified mugs and cereal bowls for the American Forces in the Pacific. Until 1947 half the production from the specials department was exported to Australia. The Specials Department became a separate company in 1948, and was called Crown Lynn. Important designers include Dave Jenkin, Mirek Smizek, Frank Carpay, Daniel Steenstra, Ernest Shufflebottom, Dorothy Thorpe.

By 1959 Crown Lynn Potteries had produced its 100 millionth article, and at their peak in the 1960's Crown Lynn employed 650 people in their Auckland potteries, manufactured around 17 million pieces of dinnerware annually in over 82 patterns and exported half of their production.

Crown Lynn became Ceramco in 1974 and diversified into a series of new interests, including electronics, appliance wholesaling and making acquisitions including Bendon lingerie. The Crown Lynn pottery factory closed in 1989, unable to compete with foreign competitors.

Sir Thomas Clark died in 2005.

Crown Lynn coffee pot in the 'Palm Springs' pattern, designed by Dorothy Thorpe, c1968, 30cm high.

NZ$850 - $950   **Banks Peninsula Antiques, New Zealand**

Set of three graduated Crown Lynn handpotted vases, the tallest 23 cm high.

NZ$1400 - $1600

Banks Peninsula Antiques, New Zealand

Vase with hand incised marks to base 'Crown Lynn, H. Made', with a rough royale type glaze, c1950, 9cm wide, 17cm high.

NZ$270 - $310   **Antiques of Epsom, New Zealand**

Crown Lynn ball handled coffee cup and saucer in the 'Monterrey' pattern, designed by Dorothy Thorpe, c1968.

NZ$280 - $320   **Banks Peninsula Antiques, New Zealand**

Crown Lynn ball handled milk jug and sugar bowl in 'Monterey' pattern, designed by Dorothy Thorpe, c1968, 11cm high.

NZ$280 - $320   **Banks Peninsula Antiques, New Zealand**

Crown Lynn vase decorated with an abstract floral pattern, c1960, 25cm long, 8cm high.

NZ$65 - $85   **Maxine's Collectibles, New Zealand**

'Ascot' dish by Crown Lynn, c1960, 18cm diameter.

NZ$20 - $30   **Woodville Mart, New Zealand**

Crown Lynn hand painted powder blue glazed vase by Ernest Shufflebottom, c1950, 10cm wide, 19cm high.

NZ$370 - $410   **Antiques of Epsom, New Zealand**

Pair of Crown Lynn slip cast wall vases, number 544 in the 'Tree Trunk' pattern, c1960, 8cm deep, 20cm wide, 20cm high.

NZ$140 - $160   **Memory Lane, New Zealand**

NZ Army milk jug by 'Crown Lynn', c1960, 13cm high.

NZ$13 - $23   **Woodville Mart, New Zealand**

Crown Lynn lamp base, the 'Three Faces of Eve', signed by the modeller, c1950, 32cm high, 16cm diameter.

NZ$490 - $590   **Antiques & Curiosities, New Zealand**

Pair of Crown Lynn entrée plates, 'Last Wave', c1960, 23.5cm long, 15.5cm wide.

NZ$40 - $60

Country Charm Antiques, New Zealand

NZ Army salt and pepper set by 'Crown Lynn', c1960, 6cm high.

NZ$10 - $20

Woodville Mart, New Zealand

Crown Lynn 'Little Bo-Peep' childs plate, c1947, 4cm high, 19.5cm diameter.

NZ$40 - $60

Country Charm Antiques, New Zealand

Crown Lynn baby plate, 'Bunny by Crown Lynn', with backstamp, c1950, 4.5cm high, 15.5cm diameter.

NZ$40 - $60

Country Charm Antiques, New Zealand

Transfer printed Crown Lynn cabinet plate, c1960, 3cm high, 23cm diameter.

NZ$30 - $40

Memory Lane, New Zealand

Pair of 'Crown Lynn' porcelain door handles, c1970, 5cm diameter.

NZ$20 - $30

Woodville Mart, New Zealand

Pair of polar bear bookends by Crown Lynn Potteries, 12cm long, 10cm high.

NZ$410 - $450

Bulls Antiques & Collectables, New Zealand

Crown Lynn hand potted and decorated vase, c1960, 14cm high.

NZ$460 - $500 **Banks Peninsula Antiques, New Zealand**

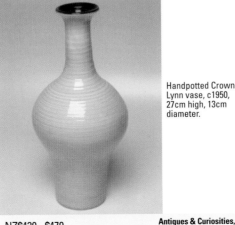

Handpotted Crown Lynn vase, c1950, 27cm high, 13cm diameter.

NZ$430 - $470

Antiques & Curiosities, New Zealand

Crown Lynn dog, number 178, c1950, 17cm high.

NZ$225 - $265

Antiques of Epsom, New Zealand

Crown Lynn hand crafted vase, shape #58 features a multi-ribbed body, 14cm wide, 18cm high.

NZ$510 - $610 **Antiques of Epsom, New Zealand**

Crown Lynn handpotted vase, in cream colours with three rings around the top, c1950, 18.5cm high, 12cm diameter.

NZ$430 - $470 **Maxine's Collectibles, New Zealand**

Crown Lynn boxed set of vases, c1965, 5cm wide, 7.5cm high.

NZ$75 - $95 **Oxford Court Antiques Centre, New Zealand**

NZ Army egg cup by 'Crown Lynn', c1960, 4.5cm high.

NZ$3 - $13 **Woodville Mart, New Zealand**

Set of six Crown Lynn coffee cans and saucers by Gail Henry, c1960, 14.5cm long, 7.5cm high.

NZ$110 - $130 **Maxine's Collectibles, New Zealand**

Crown Lynn trickle glaze character jug in dark brown, showing a gentleman in three cornered hat, c1950, 15cm long, 13cm wide, 13cm high.

NZ$40 - $50 **Casa Manana Antiques & Collectables, New Zealand**

Crown Lynn large swan vase, c1955, 19cm wide, 21.5cm high.

NZ$50 - $70 **Country Charm Antiques, New Zealand**

Crown Lynn hound dog, c1960, 12cm long, 10cm high.

NZ$280 - $320 **Banks Peninsula Antiques, New Zealand**

Crown Lynn Santa Barbara cup and saucer design by Dorothy Thorpe, c1960.

NZ$300 - $340 **Antiques of Epsom, New Zealand**

Crown Lynn server, c1970, 26cm wide, 26cm high.

NZ$100 - $120 **Oxford Court Antiques Centre, New Zealand**

Very large jug with embossed design in olive and ochre coloured glaze, West Germany, c1960, 40cm high.

$85 - $105   **Vintage Living, ACT**

West German ceramic vase, bold orange spot design on classic 70's brown, c1975, 20cm wide, 55cm high.

$120 - $140   **Chapel Street Bazaar, VIC**

Cylindrical large West German vase, classic orange, beige and brown tones, c1974, 16cm wide, 42cm high.

$85 - $105   **Chapel Street Bazaar, VIC**

German Scheurich urn shaped vase with handle, moulded marks to base, c1970, 32cm high.

NZ$60 - $80   **Collector's Choice, New Zealand**

Tall cylindrical German Scheurich vase, moulded 'W. Germany' on base, c1970, 41cm high.

NZ$175 - $195   **Collector's Choice, New Zealand**

German Keriska pottery vase with stylised glazed circle decorations and all over matt glazed finish, signature and inscription to base, c1950, 24cm high, 9cm diameter.

$200 - $240   **Garden Street Bazaar, NSW**

Retro urn vase, made in West Germany, impressed on base, rich high gloss 'lava' glaze over upper body of vessel and handle, c1960, 30cm high, 18cm diameter.

$85 - $105   **Born Frugal, VIC**

Vase, marked 'W. German', c1970, 27cm high, 10cm diameter.

$85 - $105   **Antique Centre of Stonnington, VIC**

Large piece of West German pottery with lustre glaze in brown and orange banding, 23cm long, 50cm high.

$90 - $110   **The Mill Markets, VIC**

West German pottery vase in rich orange and green glaze, c1960, 17cm long, 17cm deep, 17cm wide, 36cm high, 17cm diam.

$70 - $90   **Dr Russell's Emporium, WA**

Colourful retro German vase, c1970, 17cm long, 42cm high, 17cm diameter.

$55 - $75   **Towers Antiques & Collectables, NSW**

GOEBEL

Goebel ceramic elephant, produced for Q.V.C. America, c1956, 16cm high.

$205 - $245   **Sturt Street Antiques & Art, VIC**

Limited edition of an English robin, by Goebel Germany, c1965, 12cm high.

NZ$155 - $175   **Peachgrove Antiques, New Zealand**

Pair of Goebel figurines of praying children.

$150 - $200   **Lilydale Antique Centre, VIC**

A Goebel figure of a cat 'Julia' from the series by Rosina Wachtmeister, c2000, 9cm high.

$80 - $100   **Grant & Wendy Brookes, VIC**

A Goebel figure of a titmouse, reg number 88016-10, 10cm high.

$75 - $95   **Shirley & Noel Daly Antiques, VIC**

Goebel figure of a chicken, dated to underside, c1987, 10cm high.

$50 - $70   **Shirley & Noel Daly Antiques, VIC**

A Goebel figure of a robin, c1978, 9cm high.

$75 - $95   **Shirley & Noel Daly Antiques, VIC**

Goebel novelty clown sugar pot and creamer set on tray, c1940, 12cm high.

$350 - $400   **Steven Sher Antiques, WA**

Friar jug by Goebel, 14.5cm high.

$185 - $205   **Den of Antiquities, VIC**

Goebel salt and pepper shakers modelled as poodles, c1955, 9cm high.

$110 - $130   **Shenton Park Antiques, WA**

A Goebel figurine of two cats 'Angelo and Angelina', from the series R. Wachtimeister, c2000, 7cm high.

$85 - $105   **Grant & Wendy Brookes, VIC**

Hummel figure 'The Little Gardener',
No. 74, c1963, 11cm high.

$115 - $135   **Shirley & Noel Daly Antiques, VIC**

Hummel 'Doctor' figure, c1966, 12cm
high, 6cm diameter.

$165 - $185   **Southside Antiques Centre, QLD**

M. I. Hummel by Goebel figure
HUM#15/0, 'Hear Ye, Hear Ye' TMK3, in
production 1958-1972, 12.5cm high.

$360 - $400   **Roundabout Antiques, QLD**

M. I. Hummel by Goebel figure
HUM#130, 'Duet' TMK2, in production
1940-1959, 13.5cm high.

$550 - $650   **Roundabout Antiques, QLD**

Hummel figure, c1970, 15cm high,
6cm diameter.

$275 - $315   **Glenelg Antique Centre, SA**

Hummel 'Globetrotter' pattern figure,
c1966, 9cm deep, 5cm wide, 13cm high.

$320 - $360   **Southside Antiques Centre, QLD**

M. I. Hummel by Goebel figure
HUM#394, 'Timid Little Sister' TMK6, in
production 1979-1991, 18cm high.

$550 - $650   **Roundabout Antiques, QLD**

Hummel figure 'Retreat to Safety', c1979.

$130 - $150   **Shirley & Noel Daly Antiques, VIC**

M. I. Hummel by Goebel figure
HUM#6/I, 'Sensitive Hunter' TMK3, in
production 1958-1972, 14.5cm high.

$410 - $450   **Roundabout Antiques, QLD**

M. I. Hummel by Goebel figure HUM#71,
'Stormy Weather' TMK4, in production
1964-1972 16cm high.

$650 - $750   **Roundabout Antiques, QLD**

M. I. Hummel Figures

With cherubic grins and blushed cheeks you would just love to
pinch, how could anyone not fall in love with the adorable little
figures of boys in lederhosen and girls with pigtails that are known
as 'Hummels'?

MI Hummel figures are produced by renowned German porcelain
manufacturer W Goebel Porzellainfabrik ('Goebel'). In the last few
years these figures have gained a large collecting base in Australia
and New Zealand.

The figures are based on the caricatures of Maria Innocentia
('Berta') Hummel – an extremely talented German art student who
went on to became a nun. Hummel figures have been produced
by Geobel since 1935 and production continues today. All figures
are readily identified by the engraved script MI Hummel trademark
somewhere on the figure, usually on the base rim.

Interestingly, the ownership of the designs and approval of
production of all figures, still rests with Maria Innocentia Hummel
(now deceased) and the Convent of Siessen, even through to
current releases.

M. I. Hummel by Goebel figure HUM#67,
'Doll Mother' TMK3, in production 1957-
1972, 11.5cm high.

$380 - $420   **Roundabout Antiques, QLD**

GOEBEL - HUMMEL

Hummel figure of the 'Happy Traveller' manufactured by Goebel, West Germany, c1980, 13cm high.

$135 - $155

Shirley & Noel Daly Antiques, VIC

Hummel Apple Tree Girl #143, Apple Tree Boy #142, c1970, 15cm high.

$470 - $510

Shop 21, Southern Antique Centre, NSW

Hummel figure of a boy with accordion, 7.5cm high.

$85 - $105

Shirley & Noel Daly Antiques, VIC

M. I. Hummel by Goebel figure HUM#132, 'Star Gazer' TMK3, in production 1958-1972, 12cm high.

$430 - $470

Roundabout Antiques, QLD

M. I. Hummel by Goebel figure HUM#141/I, 'Apple Tree Girl' TMK5, in production 1972-1979, 16cm high.

$360 - $400

Roundabout Antiques, QLD

Hansel and Gretel, M. I. Hummel backstamp 'TMK 2B, Germany', c1952.

NZ$480 - $520

Collector's Choice, New Zealand

Girls Dancing, M. I. Hummel backstamp 'TMK 4A Springdance', c1968, 11cm wide, 18cm high.

NZ$730 - $830

Collector's Choice, New Zealand

M. I. Hummel by Goebel figure HUM#86, 'Happiness' TMK3, in production 1958-1972, 12cm high.

$280 - $320

Roundabout Antiques, QLD

M. I. Hummel by Goebel figure HUM#314, 'Confidentially' TMK6, in production 1979-1991, 14cm high.

$370 - $410

Roundabout Antiques, QLD

M. I. Hummel by Goebel figure HUM#396, 'Ride into Christmas' TMK5, 14.5cm high.

$580 - $680

Roundabout Antiques, QLD

M. I. Hummel by Goebel figure HUM#127, 'Doctor' TMK3, in production 1958-1972, 12cm high.

$275 - $315

Roundabout Antiques, QLD

Hummel figure group of 'Happy Days', c1980, 7cm wide, 12cm high.

$275 - $315 **Glenelg Antique Centre, SA**

M. I. Hummel by Goebel figure HUM#136/I, 'Friends' TMK4, in production 1964-1972, 14cm high.

$310 - $350 **Roundabout Antiques, QLD**

Figurine of girl and boy going to market, backstamp 'M. I Hummel 49/0 U.S Zone Germany', c1952, 14cm long.

NZ$460 - $500 **Collector's Choice, New Zealand**

Hummel figure group, 'The Photographer', c1980, 10cm wide, 13cm high.

$410 - $450 **Glenelg Antique Centre, SA**

M. I. Hummel by Goebel figure HUM#182, 'Good Friends' TMK3, in production 1958-1972, 10cm high.

$320 - $360 **Roundabout Antiques, QLD**

Hummel figure group of 'Little Goat Herder', c1960, 14cm high, 9cm diameter.

$380 - $420 **Glenelg Antique Centre, SA**

M. I. Hummel by Goebel figure HM#128, 'Baker' TMK3, in production 1958-1972, 12cm high.

$310 - $350 **Roundabout Antiques, QLD**

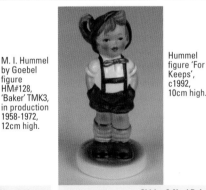

Hummel figure 'For Keeps', c1992, 10cm high.

$85 - $105 **Shirley & Noel Daly Antiques, VIC**

M. I. Hummel by Goebel figure HUM#59, 'Skier' TMK6. Earlier versions have wooden poles, later versions have metal poles, in production 1979-1991, 13cm high.

$280 - $320 **Roundabout Antiques, QLD**

M. I. Hummel by Goebel figure HUM#III/I, 'Wayside Harmony' TMK4, in production 1964-1972, 12.5cm high.

$370 - $410 **Roundabout Antiques, QLD**

M. I. Hummel by Goebel figure HUM#13/0 'Meditation' TMK3, in production 1958-1972, 13.5cm high.

$370 - $410 **Roundabout Antiques, QLD**

M.I. Hummel by Goebel figure HUM#334, 'Homeward Bound' TMK5, in production 1972-1979, 12.5cm high.

$530 - $630 **Roundabout Antiques, QLD**

GOEBEL - HUMMEL

Hummel Goebel bell with 1983 on the back, c1983, 10cm wide, 16cm high.

$85 - $105   **Helen's On The Bay, QLD**

Hummel figure group 'Shepherds boy', c1980, 9cm wide, 15cm high.

$380 - $420   **Glenelg Antique Centre, SA**

M. I. Hummel quartet wall plaque with backstamp 'TMK 3 C West Germany', c1965, 3.5cm deep, 14cm wide, 16cm high.

NZ$460 - $500   **Collector's Choice, New Zealand**

Hummel annual plate 'Heavenly Angel' design, backstamp 'Hum 264, in commemoration of 100 year Goebel Hummel factory', c1971, 19cm diameter.

NZ$930 - $1030   **Collector's Choice, New Zealand**

M. I. Hummel by Goebel figure HUM#143/I, 'Boots' TMK5, in production 1972-1979, 17cm high.

$430 - $470   **Roundabout Antiques, QLD**

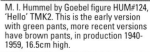

M. I. Hummel by Goebel figure HUM#124, 'Hello' TMK2. This is the early version with green pants, more recent versions have brown pants, in production 1940-1959, 16.5cm high.

$480 - $520   **Roundabout Antiques, QLD**

M. I. Hummel by Goebel HUM#360/A, 'Boy and Girl' wall vase TMK3. Some variations have the boy, some have the girl, few have both figures, in production 1958- 1972, 11.5cm wide, 15cm high.

$550 - $650   **Roundabout Antiques, QLD**

Pair of Hummel bookends, c1956, 12cm high.

$135 - $155   **Sturt Street Antiques & Art, VIC**

Hummel figure of the 'Apple Tree Boy', c1970, 10cm high, 5.5cm diameter.

$215 - $255   **Glenelg Antique Centre, SA**

M. I. Hummel by Goebel figure HUM#317, 'Not For You' TMK4, in production 1964-1972, 14cm high.

$380 - $420   **Roundabout Antiques, QLD**

Maling footed bowl with a pheasant pattern, c1950, 8cm high, 27cm diameter.

$185 - $205

White Park Antiques, SA

Set of four pink, blue, green and blue-grey Maling sweet dishes, 8.1cm high.

$170 - $190

Discovery Corner, QLD

Maling coffee pot, cobalt blue raised pattern, c1951, 18.5cm wide, 20.1cm high.

$700 - $800

Calmar Trading, VIC

Maling Ware green electric lamp base, embossed with 'Peony Rose' pattern, c1950, 35cm high, 15cm diameter.

$680 - $780

Mentone Beach Antiques Centre, VIC

Set of six Maling Ware dessert dishes, 'Tulip' pattern with blue lustre, c1950, 9cm high, 10cm diameter.

$200 - $240

Mentone Beach Antiques Centre, VIC

Maling vase 6567 with embossed blossom of blue flowers and ruby thumbprint, c1954, 7cm deep, 18cm high.

NZ$170 - $210

Country Charm Antiques, New Zealand

Stunningly bright Maling Clematis thumbprint and floral bowl, c1950, 6cm high, 23cm diameter.

$310 - $350

Bill & Janet White, WA

Maling basket with thumbprint decoration and lustre glaze, c1950, 12cm wide, 10cm high.

$225 - $265

Ainsley Antiques, VIC

Maling lustre elongated vase in a stunning light aqua colourway, set off by an edging of gold on the top rim, c1960, 27cm long, 9cm deep, 16.5cm high.

NZ$165 - $185

Classy Clutter And Collectables, New Zealand

Maling bowl in green thumbprint, 12cm high, 21cm diameter.

NZ$270 - $310

Memory Lane, New Zealand

Posy bowl, green lustre finish, flower and bird design, manufactured by Maling, Newcastle-on-Tyne, 11cm wide, 9cm high.

$70 - $90

Janet Smith, NSW

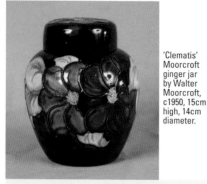

'Clematis' Moorcroft ginger jar by Walter Moorcroft, c1950, 15cm high, 14cm diameter.

$1850 - $2050   **Toowoomba Antiques Gallery, QLD**

Moorcroft flambe 'Leaf and Berries' charger plate, 30cm wide.

$2150 - $2350   **Chelsea Antiques & Decorative Art Centre P/L, QLD**

Moorcroft vase, trial colour variation of the Malahide pattern, an Australian bottlebrush, marked 'Trial 213.95' with usual Moorcroft marks. There was only one vase produced in this design, 11.9cm high.

$1300 - $1500   **Moor-Cliff, NSW**

Limited edition Moorcroft vase, Australian only range, 'Sturt Desert Pea' No. 143/500, shape 226/7, 19cm high, 10cm diameter.

$1200 - $1400   **Old Technology, NSW**

Moorcroft Australian Designs

By 1906 Moorcroft Pottery was available in Australia and in 1934/5 export markets for Moorcroft comprised Canada, Australia and New Zealand followed by the United States.

Australian inspired designs were introduced from about 1932 with William Moorcroft's 'Waratah' range. There was a gap until Marjorie Kubanda's 'Fruit and Vine' limited edition was released in 1986. Following are the Australian designs from 1986:

1986	'Fruit and Vine', 500 planters for Australian and Canadian markets
1987	'Banksia' Range, initially for the Australian market (withdrawn in 1990)
1988	'Wattle' Range, initially for the Australian market (withdrawn in 1990)
1988	'First Fleet' (H.M.S.Sirius) Large covered jar, Limit 25
1988	'First Fleet' (H.M.S.Sirius) 14 inch vase, 100 for Australia and 150 internationally.
1988	'First Fleet'(H.M.S.Sirius) Charger, 100 for Australia and 150 internationally.
1989	'Fruit and Vine', 75 x 8 inch plates, backstamped for Showplace Melbourne.
1989	'Fruit and Vine', 50 x 8 inch plates, without Showplace backstamp.
1991	'Magnolia' Range, new wine colourway Australia 1991 and worldwide in 1992.
1991	'Tasmanian Blue gum', 50 x 65/16 (Shape/Size in inches) vases.
1991	'Tasmanian Blue gum' 500 x 393/7 vases.
1996	'Sulphur Crested Cockatoo', 350 x 783/10 plates
1996	'Sulphur Crested Cockatoo', 60 x 4/10 vases.
2000	'Sturt Dessert Pea', 500 x 226/7 vases.
2000	'Sturt Dessert Pea', 100 x 62/11 vases.
2001	'Illyarie' Range, 7 shapes 2001 orders only
2002	'Rainbow Bee Eater', 2 x 398/14
2004	'Red Hairy Heath', 75 x 93/12 vases.
2004	'Red Hairy Heath', 150 x 93/8 vases.
200?	'Flannel Flowers', 200 x 128/8 vases., c2000

Moorcroft powder blue one person coffee pot, c1950, 14cm high, 8cm diameter.

$60 - $80   **The Botanic Ark, VIC**

Moorcroft vase in the 'Jumeirah' pattern by Beverly Wilks, c1999, 11cm high, 7cm diameter.

$700 - $800   **Mentone Beach Antiques Centre, VIC**

Moorcroft 'Coral Hibiscus' bowl, limited edition of 100, c1983, 27cm diameter.

NZ$1080 - $1280   **Kelmscott House Antiques, New Zealand**

Royal Doulton Moorcroft vase with Puffins, signed and stamped W.M, 19cm high.

NZ$1250 - $1450   **Antiques On Victoria, New Zealand**

'Illyarrie' vase by Moorcroft, shape 402/4, Australia Only Range 2001, designer Emma Bossons, c2001, 10cm high, 13.5cm diameter.

$700 - $800   **Old Technology, NSW**

'Honeycomb' pattern Moorcroft vase designed by Philip Richardson, issued 1987-89, c1987, 18cm high.

$1400 - $1600   **Armadale Antique Centre, VIC**

Moorcroft flambe orchid vase designed by William Moorcroft and executed by Walter Moorcroft, c1947, 24cm high.

$4400 - $4600   **Steven Sher Antiques, WA**

Walter Moorcroft vase, 'Hibiscus' design. 1953-78, 18cm high.

$1150 - $1350   **Elizabeth Antiques, NSW**

Moorcroft 'Bramble Berries' pattern small dish, c1994, 12cm diameter.

NZ$260 - $300   **Casa Manana Antiques & Collectables, NZ**

Vase, 'The Caravan' limited edition No. 98 of 100 vase by Moorcroft, shape 65/16, designer Rachel Bishop. c2003, 42cm high, 27cm diameter.

$9000 - $9400   **Old Technology, NSW**

Rachel Bishop

When Rachel Bishop joined Moorcroft in 1993, she was only the fourth Moorcroft designer in 100 years. She followed the founder of the the firm, William Moorcroft 1913-1945, his son William from 1945 to the 1980s, and Sally Tuffin to 1992.

In the 1970's the prosperity of the company continued to decline and the low point was reached in the mid 1980's at which time the company had only 16 employees remaining. The revival began when Moorcoft was purchased by Richard Dennis (the husband of Sally Tuffin) and Hugh Edwards. Richard Dennis and Sally Tuffin left the company in 1993, leaving the Edwards family in ownership.

The design vacuum was filled by Rachel Bishop, and although only 24 years old when she joined, she was soon to see sales of her William Morris inspired designs flourish and with it the company continued its revival, its' employees now numbering several hundred.

Her success was rewarded with the creation of the Moorcroft Design Studio in 1997, comprising eight designers with Rachel Bisop as the head designer.

Moorcroft 'Clematis', bulbous vase, c1948, 23cm high.

$2650 - $2850   **Timeless Treasures, WA**

Foxglove vase, c1989, 30cm high

$1800 - $2000   **Den of Antiquities, VIC**

Moorcroft silver fern vase, limited edition 48/150, c1995, 15cm high.

NZ$1350 - $1550   **Banks Peninsula Antiques, NZ**

'Dasara' limited edition Moorcroft Vase, No. 21 of 200, shape 111/14, designed by Kerry Goodwin, c2004, 37.5cm high, 18cm diameter.

$5200 - $5600   **Old Technology, NSW**

PATES POTTERY

Pates cornucopia, lustre glaze vase, c1950, 33cm long, 18cm deep, 18cm high.

$50 - $70

Galeria del Centro, NSW

Pates vase with original label, c1950, 20cm long, 12cm deep, 19cm high.

$40 - $60

Galeria del Centro, NSW

Pates pottery vase with pink and yellow glaze, c1950, 22cm wide, 30cm high.

$55 - $75

The Exchange Galleries, NSW

Pates float bowl, semi circular shape, c1950, 20cm long.

$30 - $40

Settlers Store, NSW

Australian pottery turtle by Pates Pottery, 15cm long, 9cm wide.

$70 - $90

Nana's Pearls, ACT

Tall, olive green drip glaze jug by Klytie Pate, c1960, 21cm high, 10cm diameter.

$480 - $580

Armadale Antique Centre, VIC

Australian Pates pottery planter or vase, 28cm long, 12cm high.

$75 - $95

Past Connections Antiques & Decorative Arts, NSW

Pates Australian Pottery swan vase, c1950, 26cm long, 17cm deep, 17cm high.

$55 - $75

Towers Antiques & Collectables, NSW

A large multicoloured display plate, incised 'Klytie Pate', c1955, 24cm wide.

$275 - $315

Sturt Street Antiques & Art, VIC

Majolica style glazed dish with dropped splash design, signed 'Klytie Pate' on reverse, c1950, 1.6cm high, 2.45cm diameter.

$275 - $315

Hamilton Street Antiques, VIC

Poole Pottery England 'Delphis' spear plate, signed and painted by Cynthia Bennett '71 - 77', c1970, 44cm long, 18cm wide.

$270 - $310   **Retro Active,**
                               VIC

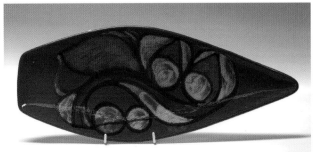

Poole Delphis retro design platter, c1960, 44cm long.

$150 - $170   **The Bottom Drawer Antique Centre,**
                               VIC

Poole plate, signed Margaret Anderson, decorated with blue flower, c1970, 20cm diameter.

NZ$205 - $245   **Moa Extinct Stuff,**
                               New Zealand

Hand painted Poole plate, c1970, 15cm long, 2.5cm deep, 10cm wide.

$15 - $25   **Bowhows,**
                               NSW

Large Poole charger, 'Delphis' pattern, c1965, 35cm diameter.

NZ$600 - $700   **Colonial Heritage Antiques Ltd,**
                               New Zealand

Poole Delphis vase, c1970, 23cm high.

NZ$245 - $285   **Right Up My Alley,**
                               New Zealand

Poole hand painted vase, shape 154, decoration HK, painted by Jean Cocktown (Wilson), c1948, 26cm high.

$750 - $850   **Ritzy Bits - ACT,**
                               ACT

Hand painted Poole Pottery lamp, marked 701A, c1950, 33cm high, 14cm diameter.

$650 - $750   **Shenton Park Antiques,**
                               WA

Poole 13 piece coffee set in grey and white, including creamer and sugar bowl, 15cm high.

$175 - $195   **Shaws Antiques,**
                               NSW

Poole Pottery England 'Agean' silhouette technique glaze bowl '4', c1960, 27cm diameter.

$175 - $195   **Retro Active,**
                               VIC

Blue glazed trout, Poole Pottery England, c1950, 80cm deep, 170cm wide, 125cm high.

$100 - $120   **Old World Antiques,**
                               SA

Royal Albert 'American Beauty' two section bowl, c1950, 19cm long, 17cm deep, 2.5cm high.

$90 - $110 **Southside Antiques Centre, QLD**

Royal Albert lidded tureen 'Lady Carlysle', c1970, 11cm high, 26cm diameter.

$175 - $195 **Northumberland Antiques & Restorations, NSW**

Royal Albert bone china eight cup tea pot in 'Old Country Roses' pattern, c1970, 20cm deep, 25cm high.

$140 - $160 **The New Farm Antique Centre, QLD**

Royal Albert 'Flower of the Month' three piece tea service, c1984, 15cm deep, 24cm wide, 19cm high.

$205 - $245 **Southside Antiques Centre, QLD**

Royal Albert 'Lady Carlisle' three piece tea service, c1970.

$275 - $315 **Northumberland Antiques & Restorations, NSW**

Royal Albert cup, saucer and plate, 'Lady Hamilton' pattern.

$40 - $50 **Antiques Down Under, NSW**

Royal Albert 'Memory Lane' oval tray, 13cm deep.

$20 - $30 **Things 4 U, NSW**

Royal Albert cup and saucer, 'Provincial Flowers', prairie lily, c1960.

$50 - $70 **Southside Antiques Centre, QLD**

One of a set of six 'Lady Carlisle' dinner plates, by Royal Albert, c1970, 26cm diameter.

$45 - $65 **Northumberland Antiques & Restorations, NSW**

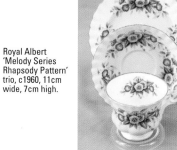

Royal Albert 'Melody Series Rhapsody Pattern' trio, c1960, 11cm wide, 7cm high.

$55 - $75 **Helen's On The Bay, QLD**

A Royal Albert figurine of 'Tom Kitten' from the Beatrix Potter series, c1989, 9cm high.

$35 - $45 **Grant & Wendy Brookes, VIC**

Royal Copenhagen vase, 30cm high.

$360 - $400 · **Paddington Antique Centre Pty Ltd, QLD**

Royal Copenhagen square vase, designed by 'Nils Thorsson' in the Baca series, 9.5cm long, 28.5cm high.

NZ$500 - $600 · **Heritage House Antiques, New Zealand**

Royal Copenhagen vase, c1960, 23cm high.

NZ$470 - $510 · **Tinakori Antiques, New Zealand**

Royal Copenhagen figure of 'The Little Mermaid', porcelain model No.4431, designed by Edvard Eriksen, c1990, 22cm high.

$850 - $950 · **Vintage Living, ACT**

Royal Copenhagen figure 'Girl on Rock', No. 4027, sculptor Adda Bonfils, c1987, 14.5cm high.

$390 - $410 · **Elizabeth Antiques, NSW**

Royal Copenhagen figurine 'The Fisher Boy' by Christian Thomsen, c1958, 17cm wide, 29cm high.

$1500 - $1700 · **Philicia Antiques & Collectables, SA**

Royal Copenhagen ceramic lamp, c1960, 10cm wide, 37cm high.

$360 - $400 · **Obsidian Antiques, NSW**

Royal Copenhagen Faience series teardrop vase signed CB, retro design, c1955, 40cm high.

$550 - $650 · **Woollahra Decorative Arts Gallery, NSW**

Royal Copenhagen coffee pot, c1950, 22cm diameter.

$155 - $175 · **Yanda Aboriginal Art Melbourne, VIC**

Royal Copenhagen 1977 Christmas plate, c1977.

$40 - $50 · **Victory Theatre Antiques, NSW**

Royal Copenhagen faience serving dish, c1970, 26cm long, 26cm wide.

NZ$225 - $265 · **Moa Extinct Stuff, New Zealand**

Royal Copenhagen faience hand painted slab form vase, c1960, 19cm long, 7cm deep, 15cm high.

$240 - $280 · **Cool & Collected, SA**

Royal Doulton Bunnykins figure DB103, 'Bedtime Bunnykins'. This figure was sold exclusively at the Special Events Tour functions in 1991, 8.5cm high.

$430 - $470   **Roundabout Antiques, QLD**

Royal Doulton Bunnykins DB34, 'Santa Bunnykins' music box, plays 'White Christmas', in production 1984-1991, 18.5cm high.

$330 - $370   **Roundabout Antiques, QLD**

Royal Doulton Bunnykins figure DB74A, 'Red Cross Nurse Bunnykins'. This figure was initially painted with a red cross on the forehead until it was changed to a green cross due to copyright infringements, in production 1989-1994, 11cm high.

$360 - $400   **Roundabout Antiques, QLD**

Royal Doulton 'Collector Bunnykins' DB54, exclusively for Royal Doulton Collectors Club, modelled by D. Lyttleton c. 1986, 10cm high.

$830 - $930   **H.O.W Gifts & Collectables, QLD**

Royal Doulton Bunnykins Figures

Very few 20th century collectables have seen a more stellar rise in price than Royal Doulton Bunnykins figures.

When Royal Doulton took over the Beswick factory in 1969, they acquired the modelling talents of Mr Albert Hallam who had previously worked on the similarly highly collectable Beswick Beatrix Potter figures. The first of the nine Royal Doulton Bunnykins figures were launched in 1972 with DB pattern numbers and they are approximately 4 inches in height. All were inspired by Royal Doulton Nurseryware patterns – this continued until 1974 when there were a total of 15 figures in the range.

The 1980's through to the present day has seen many general range, special colourway and Limited Edition Bunnykins figures released – with now well over 300 Royal Doulton Bunnykins figures for collectors to be enthused about.

Some of the Limited Edition figures have seen price rises of over 1000% in a very short time and with many of the figures in short supply and high demand, there is no reason for this collectables success not to continue unabated.

Royal Doulton Bunnykins figure DB134, 'John Bull Bunnykins', issued in 1993 in a limited edition of 1000 figures worldwide, 12cm high.

$600 - $700   **Roundabout Antiques, QLD**

Royal Doulton Federation Bunnykins D224 - Limited Edition of 2500 (No. 540) series 'Australian Heritage' with certificate and original box, designed by Brian Dalglish and Bill Bryant of Dalbry Antiques, Melbourne, c2000, 12.7cm high.

$360 - $400   **Elizabeth Antiques, NSW**

Royal Doulton Bunnykins figure DB136, 'Sergeant Mountie Bunnykins'. This figure was issued in 1993 in a special edition of 250 figures only and is widely regarded as the most desirable Bunnykins figure, 10cm high.

$1900 - $2100   **Roundabout Antiques, QLD**

Royal Doulton Digger Bunnykins - Limited edition of 2500 (No. 1182) series 'Australian Heritage' with certificate and original box, designed by Brian Dalglish and Bill Bryant of Dalbry Antiques, Melbourne, c2001, 14cm high.

$380 - $420   **Elizabeth Antiques, NSW**

Royal Doulton Bunnykins plate in the 'Family Cycling' pattern, 25cm wide, 22cm high.

$300 - $340 — Southside Antiques Centre, QLD

Royal Doulton Bunnykins 'Cycle Ride' porridge plate, signed Barbara Vernon, c1940, 19cm diameter.

NZ$165 - $185 — South Auckland Antiques & Collectables, New Zealand

Royal Doulton Bunnykins warming dish and lid with the 'Apple Picking' and 'Dressing Up' designs, 9cm high, 22cm diameter.

NZ$430 - $470 — South Auckland Antiques & Collectables, New Zealand

Royal Doulton Bunnykins mug 'Pressing Trousers' by Barbara Vernon, 7.5cm deep, 9cm high.

$155 - $175 — Southside Antiques Centre, QLD

Royal Doulton Bunnykins figure DB36, 'Happy Birthday Bunnykins' music box, plays 'Happy Birthday to You', in production 1984-1991, 18cm high.

$330 - $370 — Roundabout Antiques, QLD

Royal Doulton Bunnykins mug 'Family Going Out on Washing Day', signed Barbara Vernon, 7.5cm deep, 9cm wide, 9cm high.

$140 - $160 — Southside Antiques Centre, QLD

Royal Doulton Bunnykins bowl, signed Barbra Vernon, c1950, 15cm diameter.

$100 - $120 — Antiques, Goods & Chattels, VIC

Royal Doulton Bunnykins nursery lamp, never used, c1985, 33cm high.

$275 - $315 — Debbie Pech, VIC

Royal Doulton Bunnykins figure set DB23-27, 'Oompah Band', in production 1984-1990. This was a general issue set with pieces sold individually or otherwise.

$950 - $1050 — Roundabout Antiques, QLD

Set of six Ye Royal Doulton Bunnykins figures comprising 'The Jazz Band Collection'. Each figure is issued in a limited edition of 2500 figures, DP182 'Banjo Player', DB184 'Clarinet Player', DB185 'Double Bass Player', DB186 'Saxophone Player', DB210 'Trumpet Player' and DB250 'Drummer'. In production 1998-2001.

$205 - $245 — Roundabout Antiques, QLD

Royal Doulton Bunnykins figure DB14, 'Grandpa's Story Bunnykins', one of the original fifteen Bunnykins figures produced between 1972-1982, 10cm high.

$430 - $470   **Roundabout Antiques, QLD**

Royal Doulton Bunnykins figure DB54, 'Collector Bunnykins'. This figure was issued in 1987 and was only available to Royal Doulton International Collectors Club members. It is very difficult to obtain, 11cm high.

$800 - $900   **Roundabout Antiques, QLD**

Royal Doulton Bunnykins figure DB13, 'The Artist', one of the original fifteen Bunnykins figures produced between 1972-1982, 9.5cm high.

$500 - $600   **Roundabout Antiques, QLD**

Royal Doulton Bunnykins figure DB126, 'Magician Bunnykins', issued in 1992 in a limited edition of 1000 figures only, 12cm high.

$480 - $520   **Roundabout Antiques, QLD**

Royal Doulton Bunnykins figurine 'Jogging', c1982, 9cm long, 6.5cm high.

$110 - $130   **The Exchange Galleries, NSW**

Royal Doulton Bunnykins DB39, 'Mrs Bunnykins at the Easter Parade' music box, plays 'Easter Parade', in production 1987-1991, 18cm high.

$330 - $370   **Roundabout Antiques, QLD**

Royal Doulton Bunnykins DB33A, 'Tally Ho Bunnykins' music box, plays 'Rock a Bye Baby', in production 1984-1993, 18cm high.

$330 - $370   **Roundabout Antiques, QLD**

Royal Doulton Bunnykins figure DB165, 'Ringmaster Bunnykins', issued in a special edition in 1996 of 1500, 12cm high.

$380 - $420   **Roundabout Antiques, QLD**

Olympic Doulton Bunnykin figurine, Golden Jubilee, c1984, 9cm high.

$810 - $910   **Antique Centre of Stonnington, VIC**

Royal Doulton Bunnykins DB131, 'Master Potter' Bunnykins, issued in 1992-1993 as a special edition available to Royal Doulton International Collectors Club members, very difficult to obtain, 9.5cm high.

$360 - $400   **Roundabout Antiques, QLD**

Royal Doulton Bunnykins figure set DB96-100, 'Touchdown'. Each figure in this set was produced in a limited edition of 200 figures only and sold separately. Many less than 200 full sets of figures exist today. The rarest of all limited edition Bunnykins sets, c1990, 8.5cm high.

$3900 - $4100

Roundabout Antiques, QLD

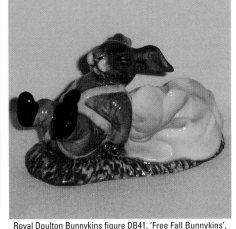

Royal Doulton Bunnykins figure DB41, 'Free Fall Bunnykins', in production 1986-1989, 6cm high.

$500 - $600

Roundabout Antiques, QLD

Royal Doulton Bunnykins DB163, 'Beefeater Bunnykins', issued in a limited edition of 1500 in 1996, 12cm high.

$480 - $520

Roundabout Antiques, QLD

Royal Doulton Bunnykins DB161, 'Jester Bunnykins', issued in 1995 in a limited edition of 1500, 12cm high.

$550 - $650

Roundabout Antiques, QLD

Royal Doulton Bunnykins figure DB58, 'Australian Bunnykins'. This figure was issued for the Australian Bicentenary in 1988 for sale on the Australian market. Highly sought after by collectors, they were never sold overseas, 10cm high.

$550 - $650

Roundabout Antiques, QLD

Royal Doulton Bunnykins figure DB3, 'Billie Bunnykins Cooling Off', one of the original fifteen Bunnykins figures produced between 1972-1982, 9.5cm high.

$280 - $320

Roundabout Antiques, QLD

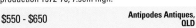

Royal Doulton Bunnykins DB7 'Spring Time' in production 1972-76, 7.5cm high.

$550 - $650

Antipodes Antiques, QLD

Royal Doulton Bunnykins figure DB174, 'Sweetheart Bunnykins' with heart inscribed 'I Love Bunnykins' issued in 1997 in a special edition of 2500 figures for UK Fairs Limited, 9.5cm high.

$310 - $350

Roundabout Antiques, QLD

Royal Doulton Bunnykins figure DB78, 'Tally Ho Bunnykins', issued as a special commission colourway in 1988 only, 10cm high.

$360 - $400

Roundabout Antiques, QLD

Royal Doulton large character jug 'St George' D6618, in production 1968-1971. This character jug is in English translucent chine (E.T.C.) and was made for only a few years, 19cm high.

$600 - $700

Roundabout Antiques, QLD

Royal Doulton large character jug 'King Henry VIII' D6888, issued in a limited edition of 1991 jugs, 18cm high.

$1150 - $1350

Roundabout Antiques, QLD

Royal Doulton large character jug 'Touchstone' D5613, in production 1936-1960, 18cm high.

$380 - $420

Roundabout Antiques, QLD

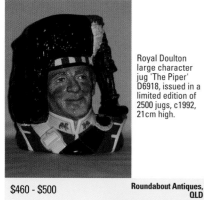

Royal Doulton large character jug 'The Piper' D6918, issued in a limited edition of 2500 jugs, c1992, 21cm high.

$460 - $500

Roundabout Antiques, QLD

Royal Doulton large character jug 'General Eisenhower' D6937, issued in a limited edition of 1000 jugs, c1993, 18cm high.

$480 - $520

Roundabout Antiques, QLD

Royal Doulton character jug of 'Long John Silver', early version, 23cm wide, 19cm high.

$255 - $295

The Exchange Galleries, NSW

Royal Doulton large character jug 'Mae West' D6688. American Express special edition, approx 500 jugs were created, c1983, 18cm high.

$480 - $520

Roundabout Antiques, QLD

Royal Doulton large character jug 'Punch and Judy Man' D6590, in production 1964-1969, 18cm high.

$1000 - $1200

Roundabout Antiques, QLD

Royal Doulton 'City Gent' character jug. D6815, c1988, 14cm wide, 16cm high.

$270 - $310

Mentone Beach Antiques Centre, VIC

Royal Doulton North American Indian large character jug, in production 1967-1991, 19cm high.

$235 - $275

Sturt Street Antiques & Art, VIC

Large Doulton 'Old Man' character jug, designed by Harry Tenton, c1948, 16cm high. PRICE:

$245 - $285

Sturt Street Antiques & Art, VIC

Royal Doulton miniature toby jug 'Mr Pickwick', in production 1947-1960, 3.5cm wide, 3.5cm high.

$275 - $315   **Turn O' The Century, QLD**

Royal Doulton character jug 'John Barleycorn', in production 1939-1960, 6cm wide, 6cm high.

$165 - $185   **Antique General Store, NSW**

Royal Doulton character jug 'Neptune', discontinued 1991, 10cm high.

$130 - $150   **Antique General Store, NSW**

Royal Doulton small character jug 'Gondolier' D6592, in production 1964-1969, 9.5cm high.

$115 - $135   **Yanda Aboriginal Art Melbourne, VIC**

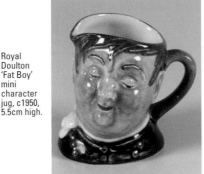

Royal Doulton 'Fat Boy' mini character jug, c1950, 5.5cm high.

$120 - $140   **Sturt Street Antiques & Art, VIC**

Royal Doulton small character jug 'Gulliver' D6563, in production 1962-1967, 10cm high.

$730 - $830   **Roundabout Antiques, QLD**

Royal Doulton large toby jug 'Cliff Cornell' version 3 with brown coat, issued in a limited edition of approx 500 as a special commission, c1956, 23cm high.

$600 - $700   **Roundabout Antiques, QLD**

Royal Doulton celebrity collection character jug, 'Groucho Marx' D6710, large size, signed by Michael Doulton 20/9/1984, c1984.

$610 - $710   **H.O.W. Gifts & Collectables, QLD**

Royal Doulton large character jug 'Johnny Appleseed' D6372, in production 1953-1969, 15cm high.

$650 - $750   **Roundabout Antiques, QLD**

Royal Doulton large three handled limited edition character jug, 'King Charles 1st' D6917, limited edition of 2500 with certificate. First character jug to be made with three handles, c1992. 18cm high.

$600 - $700   **Roundabout Antiques, QLD**

Royal Doulton large character jug 'William Shakespeare' D6933, issued in a limited edition of 2500 jugs in 1992, 18cm high.

$600 - $700   **Roundabout Antiques, QLD**

Royal Doulton 'Leopard on Rock' prestige figure, 41cm long, 23cm high.

$3400 - $3600   **Chelsea Antiques & Decorative Art Centre P/L, QLD**

Large Royal Doulton figure of a tiger, dated 1981 and designed by Charles Noke, 35cm long.

$1400 - $1600   **Antique Centre of Stonnington, VIC**

Royal Doulton flambe figure of an elephant 'Trunk in salute' HN941, c1950, 11.5cm high.

$500 - $600   **Roundabout Antiques, QLD**

Royal Doulton flambe figure 'Stalking Tiger' HN1082, signed 'Noke', c1950, 33.5cm long.

$1600 - $1800   **Roundabout Antiques, QLD**

Doulton bone china Mallard duck, HN807, c1950, 6cm high.

$175 - $195   **David Barsby Antiques, NSW**

Royal Doulton 'Cocker Spaniel' HN 1109, in production between 1937-1985, 18cm long, 14cm high.

$390 - $430   **Camberwell Antique Centre, VIC**

Royal Doulton Persian Cat HN2539, 1940-1969, 13cm high.

$700 - $800   **Shop 25, Southern Antique Centre, NSW**

Royal Doulton figure 'English Setter with Pheasant' HN 2529, 28cm long, 23cm high.

$1300 - $1500   **Camberwell Antique Centre, VIC**

Royal Doulton figure of a terrier sitting on its hind legs. 'Bone China' circle mark for Burslem small objects, in production 1902-1956, 3cm wide, 6.5cm high.

$185 - $205   **Turn O' The Century, QLD**

Royal Doulton pekinese figurine, issued between 1931 and 1955, 19cm long, 14.5cm high.

$1200 - $1400   **Antique Centre of Stonnington, VIC**

Royal Doulton character dog with bone HN1159, in production 1937-1985, 10cm high.

$205 - $245   **Shop 25, Southern Antique Centre, NSW**

Large Royal Doulton bulldog draped in Union Jack D5913, in production 1941-1961, 21cm long, 16cm high.

$1300 - $1500   **Camberwell Antique Centre, VIC**

Large Royal Doulton black cocker spaniel figurine No. HN1000, 15cm high.

$800 - $840   **East West Collectables, NSW**

Royal Doulton Dalmation HN 1113, in production between 1937-1985, 20cm long, 14cm high.

$340 - $380   **Camberwell Antique Centre, VIC**

Royal Doulton character figure 'Dog Yawning' HN 1099, in production between 1934-1985, 11cm high.

$230 - $270   **Camberwell Antique Centre, VIC**

Royal Doulton 'Wire Hair Fox Terrier' HN 1013, in production between 1931-1960, 20cm long, 14cm high.

$500 - $600   **Camberwell Antique Centre, VIC**

Royal Doulton bulldog HN 1047, in production between 1931-1985, 14cm long, 9cm high.

$330 - $370   **Camberwell Antique Centre, VIC**

Royal Doulton 'Dog with Slipper' HN 2654, in production between 1959-1985, 9cm long, 8.5cm high.

$170 - $190   **Camberwell Antique Centre, VIC**

Royal Doulton 'Scottish Terrier' model 1092, in production 1940-1977, 6.5cm long, 5.5cm high.

$150 - $170   **Camberwell Antique Centre, VIC**

Royal Doulton figure 'The Clown' HN2890, in production 1979-1988, designer W.K. Harper, 23cm high.

$600 - $700   **Roundabout Antiques, QLD**

Royal Doulton figurine 'A Jester' HN2106, in production 1949-1997, designer C. Noke, 25.5cm high.

$500 - $600   **Roundabout Antiques, QLD**

Royal Doulton 'Tiptoe' figurine, 23cm high.

$450 - $500   **Bayside Antiques Centre, VIC**

Royal Doulton figure 'Will he - Won't he?' HN3275, c1990, 24cm high, 12cm diameter.

$410 - $450   **Glenelg Antique Centre, SA**

Royal Doulton figurine HN 1843, 'Biddy Pennyfarthing', in production 1938-2000, designer L. Harradine, 23cm high.

$480 - $520   **Roundabout Antiques, QLD**

Royal Doulton "HN" numbering system

The Royal Doulton "HN" numbering system has proven to be a very orderly way of identifying each individual Royal Doulton figure.

The "HN" refers to Harry Nixon who was in charge of the new figure painting department in Doulton's very early years. The HN numbering system has endured the test of time to be still in effect today.

Over time, Royal Doulton has issued over 4000 individual HN numbers although they all are not new models – some are assigned to specific colourway variations and some cross over to be used to identify animal figures.

Royal Doulton 'Balloon Man' figurine HN 1954, designed by L. Harradine, c1940, 18cm high.

$580 - $680   **Armadale Antique Centre, VIC**

Royal Doulton figure of the 'Balloon Lady' HN2936, c1987, 13cm wide, 22cm high.

$500 - $600   **Glenelg Antique Centre, SA**

Royal Doulton figure 'Old Balloon Seller' HN 1315 by L. Harridine, issued 1929-1998.

$700 - $800   **Chilton's Antiques & Jewellery, NSW**

Royal Doulton figure 'Omar Kayam' HN 2247, designer M. Nicoll (1968-83), 16cm high.

$380 - $420   **Elizabeth Antiques, NSW**

Royal Doulton figurine 'Falstaff', c1949.

$310 - $350   **Copperfield Antiques - NSW, NSW**

Royal Doulton figurine 'Geisha' HN3229, flambe glaze, designer P. Parsons, issued only to members of the Royal Doulton International Collectors Club in 1989, 24cm high.

$700 - $800 **Roundabout Antiques, QLD**

Royal Doulton figurine 'Eastern Grace' HN3683, flambe glaze, limited edition of 2500, designer P. Parsons, c1995, 31.5cm high.

$800 - $900 **Roundabout Antiques, QLD**

Royal Doulton figurine 'Henry VIII' HN3458 limited edition of 9500, c1990, 23.5cm high.

$750 - $850 **Fyshwick Antique Centre, ACT**

Royal Doulton figurine 'The Chief' HN 2892, c1978, 18cm high.

$460 - $500 **Kings Park Antiques & Collectables, SA**

Royal Doulton figurine 'This Little Pig' HN1793, c1975, 10cm high.

$185 - $205 **Chapel Street Bazaar, VIC**

Royal Doulton figurine 'Good Friends' HN2783, designed by W. K. Harper, c1988, 14cm wide, 23cm high.

$370 - $410 **Mentone Beach Antiques Centre, VIC**

Royal Doulton figurine 'Coppelia' HN2115, in production 1953-1959, designer M. Davies, 18.5cm high.

$1100 - $1300 **Roundabout Antiques, QLD**

Royal Doulton figurine 'Blue Beard' HN2105, c1960, 26cm high.

$850 - $950 **Fyshwick Antique Centre, ACT**

Three of six Royal Doulton 'The Gentle Arts Collection' No.602, all figures on wooden stands, complete with certificates and boxes.

$7300 - $7700 **Chelsea Antiques & Decorative Art Centre P/L, QLD**

Royal Doulton figurine 'Afternoon Tea' HN1747, in production 1935-1982, designer P. Railston, 14.5cm high.

$900 - $1000 **Roundabout Antiques, QLD**

Royal Doulton Dickens series figurines, 10cm high.

$1070 - $1270

Sherwood Bazaar,
QLD

Royal Doulton 'The Wizard of Oz' Limited Edition Set, Dorothy, The Tin Man, Lion and Scarecrow, c1997, 15cm high.

$1550 - $1750

Armadale Antique Centre,
VIC

Royal Doulton figure of 'Alice' HN2158, c1959, 13cm high.

NZ$480 - $520

Colonial Heritage
Antiques Ltd, NZ

Royal Doulton 'The Detective' figurine designed by M. Nicole, c1980, 24cm high.

$500 - $600

Antique Centre of
Stonnington, VIC

Royal Doulton figurine 'Pied Piper' HN2102, in production 1953-1976, designer L. Harradine, 22cm high.

$550 - $650

Roundabout Antiques,
QLD

A Royal Doulton 'Fiddler' figure HN 2171, designer Nicoll, c1950, 14cm deep, 12cm wide, 22cm high.

$1200 - $1400

C. V. Jones Antiques &
Art Gallery, VIC

Royal Doulton 'The Orange Lady' HN 1759, in production 1936-1975, designed by L. Harradine, 22cm high.

$500 - $600

Armadale Antique Centre,
VIC

Royal Doulton figurine 'The Organ Grinder' HN 2173, in production 1956-65, designed by M. Nicholl, 22cm high.

$1800 - $2000

Armadale Antique
Centre, VIC

Royal Doulton figurine 'The Potter' HN1493, in production 1932-1992, designer C. J. Noke, 18cm high.

$700 - $800

Roundabout Antiques,
QLD

Royal Doulton 'The China Repairer' pattern No. 2943, designer R. Tabbenor, c1980, 17cm high.

$440 - $480

Armadale Antique Centre, VIC

Royal Doulton figurine 'Blue Bell Cottage Thank You' HN2732, c1982, 12cm wide, 21cm high.

$500 - $600

Glenelg Antique Centre, SA

Royal Doulton figurine 'The Cobbler' HN1706, in production 1935-1969, designer C.J. Noke, 21cm high.

$550 - $650

Roundabout Antiques, QLD

Royal Doulton figurine 'Royal Governors Cook' HN2233 from the series entitled 'Figures of Williamsburg', in production 1960-1983, designer M. Davies, 15cm high.

$800 - $900

Roundabout Antiques, QLD

Royal Doulton figurine 'The Rag Doll Seller' HN2944, c1983, 12cm wide, 29cm high.

$500 - $600

Glenelg Antique Centre, SA

Royal Doulton figurine 'Schoolmarm' HN2223, c1960, 7.5cm high.

$550 - $650

Fyshwick Antique Centre, ACT

Royal Doulton miniature 'Top Of The Hill' limited edition for Royal Doulton International Collectors Club, c1990, 10cm high, 7cm diameter.

$205 - $245

Glenelg Antique Centre, SA

Royal Doulton figurine, 'Lilac Time', c1953.

$480 - $520

Copperfield Antiques - NSW, NSW

Royal Doulton figure 'Sweet and Twenty' HN1298, in production 1928-1969, designer L. Harradine, 14.5cm high.

$700 - $800

Roundabout Antiques, QLD

Royal Doulton figurine HN1987, 'Paisley Shawl', in production 1946-1959, designer L. Harradine, 21cm high.

$650 - $750

Roundabout Antiques, QLD

Royal Doulton figurine 'Belle O the Ball' HN1997, in production 1947-1979, designer Rasplin, 15cm high.

$700 - $800

Roundabout Antiques, QLD

Royal Doulton figurine 'Penelope' HN1901, in production 1939-1975, designer L. Harradine, 18cm high.

$750 - $850

Roundabout Antiques, QLD

Royal Doulton figurine HN3834 'Mary Tudor', designer P. Parsons, limited edition of 5000 figures, produced in 1997 from the Tudor Roses series, 16cm high.

$850 - $950 — **Roundabout Antiques, QLD**

Royal Doulton figurine 'Reverie' HN2306, in production 1964-1981, 20cm wide, 18cm high.

$650 - $750 — **Glenelg Antique Centre, SA**

Royal Doulton 'Daydreams' HN1731, 14cm high.

NZ$330 - $370 — **Alexandra Antiques, New Zealand**

Royal Doulton figurine HN2028 'Kate Hardcastle', in production 1949-1952, designer L. Harradine. 19.5cm high.

$1000 - $1200 — **Roundabout Antiques, QLD**

Royal Doulton figurines

There have been over 4000 different models of Royal Doulton figurines for collectors to be captivated by.

Production of these figures has been from 1890s (Doulton Lambeth) through to the present day with rarity, age, theme, colour and variations of individual designer determining the value of each figure. The design of figures tends to reflect the taste of the times in which they are made.

There have been too many designers of figures to mention here, however the timeless 1920's and 1930's Leslie Harradine designs of bright young things in their negligees and lounging pyjamas will always tend to be the most desirable and widely collected of the entire range.

Many collectors collect to a particular theme, it may be strong male character figures of a nautical design or the ever popular 'Street Vendors' series from Edwardian England that represent something emotive to each individual collector.

Royal Doulton figurine 'Ninette', designer: M. Davies, part of the 'Pretty Ladies' series HN #2379, c1980, 16cm deep, 16cm wide, 22cm high.

$430 - $470 — **Rare Old Times Antiques & Collectables, SA**

Royal Doulton figurine, 'Sandra' HN2275, c1980, 13cm deep, 13cm wide, 19cm high.

$480 - $520 — **H.O.W Gifts & Collectables, QLD**

Royal Doulton figurine 'Laura' HN3136 Michael Doulton exclusive 1988, signed by Michael Doulton, 12cm deep, 12cm wide, 18cm high.

$550 - $650 — **H.O.W Gifts & Collectables, QLD**

Royal Doulton figurine 'Julia', c1975, 20cm high.

$255 - $295 — **Sturt Street Antiques & Art, VIC**

Royal Doulton figurine 'Fair Lady' HN2832, c1962, 18cm high.

NZ$300 - $340 — **Alexandra Antiques, New Zealand**

Royal Doulton figurine HN2471 'Victoria' in production 1973-2000, designer M. Davies, 16.5cm high.

$430 - $470   **Roundabout Antiques, QLD**

Royal Doulton figurine of 'Marie' HN1370, c1955, 13cm high.

NZ$310 - $350   **Colonial Heritage Antiques Ltd, New Zealand**

Royal Doulton figurine 'Isadora', c1985, 20cm high.

$530 - $630   **Gumnut Antiques & Old Wares, NSW**

Royal Doulton figurine 'Patricia' HN 3365, won 'Figure of the Year' in 1993, 22cm high.

$450 - $490   **Kings Park Antiques & Collectables, SA**

Royal Doulton figure of 'Claire', c1985.

$370 - $410   **Shop 77, Coliseum Antiques Centre, NSW**

Royal Doulton 'Winter Time' figure, produced only in 1985 for collectors club members, 22cm high.

$320 - $360   **Sturt Street Antiques & Art, VIC**

Royal Doulton figure 'Rowena' HN2077, introduced 1951, withdrawn 1955, designer Leslie Haradine, 18cm high.

$850 - $950   **Brae-mar Antiques, NSW**

Royal Doulton figurine HN3838, 'Margaret Tudor', designer P. Parsons, limited edition of 5000 figures only, produced in 1997 from the Tudor Roses series, 16.5cm high.

$850 - $950   **Roundabout Antiques, QLD**

Royal Doulton figurine HN2002 'Bess', in production 1947-1969, designer L. Harradine, 18.5cm high.

$650 - $750   **Roundabout Antiques, QLD**

Royal Doulton 'The Ermine Coat' Reg No. 842488, designed by L. Harradine, c1945, 11cm deep, 13cm wide, 18cm high.

$460 - $500   **Southside Antiques Centre, QLD**

Royal Doulton figurine HN1914 'Paisley Shawl', in production 1939-1949, designer L. Harradine, 16.5cm high.

$550 - $650 Roundabout Antiques, QLD

Royal Doulton figure of 'The Bridesmaid', HN2196, c1975, 13cm high.

NZ$230 - $270 Colonial Heritage Antiques Ltd, NZ

Royal Doulton figurine HN2116 'Ballerina', in production 1953-1973, designer M. Davies, 18.5cm high.

$500 - $600 Roundabout Antiques, QLD

Royal Doulton figurine HN2026 'Suzette', in production 1949-1959, designer L. Harradine, 18.5cm high.

$750 - $850 Roundabout Antiques, QLD

Royal Doulton figurine HN3142 'Mary Queen of Scots', designer P. Parsons, issued in a limited edition of 5000 in 1989 from the series entitled 'Queens of the Realm', 23cm high.

$1150 - $1350 Roundabout Antiques, QLD

Royal Doulton figurine 'Sweet Anne' HN1496, Lesley Harradine 1932-1967, 19cm long.

$480 - $520 Shop 21, Southern Antique Centre, NSW

Royal Doulton 'Camille' HN1586 introduced 1933, withdrawn 1949, designed by Leslie Harradine, 16cm high.

$1800 - $2000 Brae-mar Antiques, NSW

Royal Doulton figurine 'Old Country Roses' HN3482, c1992, 15cm high.

NZ$430 - $470 Alexandra Antiques, New Zealand

Royal Doulton figurine HN3316 'Amy', 1991 Figure of the Year, designer P. Gee. It was the first Royal Doulton Figure of the Year, 20.5cm high.

$1100 - $1300 Roundabout Antiques, QLD

Royal Doulton figurine HN2110 'Christmas Time' in production 1953-1967, designer M. Davies, 16.5cm high.

$680 - $780 Roundabout Antiques, QLD

Royal Doulton 'Elegance' figurine HN2264, c1960, 19cm high.

NZ$255 - $295 Alexandra Antiques, New Zealand

Royal Doulton 'Arabian Nights' bowl, 25cm diameter.

$275 - $315

Paddington Antique Centre Pty Ltd,
QLD

Royal Doulton 'Woodley Dale' dish.

$185 - $205

Shop 3, Coliseum Antiques Centre,
NSW

Royal Doulton 'Candor Castle' tray, 24cm wide,
19cm high.

$105 - $125

Bob Butler's Sentimental Journey,
QLD

Royal Doulton 'Coaching Days' bowl,
15cm diameter.

$600 - $700

Armadale Antique Centre,
VIC

Royal Doulton Coaching Scene Series Ware cake tray,
in production 1905-1955, 22cm wide, 5cm high.

$200 - $240

Vintage Charm,
SA

Royal Doulton coaching scene plate designed by
S. E. Grace, in production 1953-1967, 26cm diameter.

$225 - $265

The Old General Store - Kempton,
TAS

Royal Doulton 'G' series
'Dickens' jug in low relief
'Old London' D6291, in
production 1935-1960,
11cm deep, 20cm wide,
13cm high.

$480 - $580

Roundabout Antiques,
QLD

Royal Doulton 'G' series 'Dickens' jug in low relief 'White
Hart' jug with Poor Jo and Fat Boy D6394, in production
1935-1960, 9cm deep, 20cm wide, 20cm high.

$700 - $800

Roundabout Antiques,
QLD

Royal Doulton 'G' series 'Dickens' tankard in low
relief 'Oliver Twist', Oliver and the Artful Dodger
D6286, in production 1935-1960, 15cm wide,
15cm high, 12cm diameter.

$410 - $450

Roundabout Antiques,
QLD

Royal Doulton 'G' series 'Dickens' jug in low relief
'Oliver Asks for More' D6285, in production 1935-1960,
10cm deep, 20cm wide, 15cm high.

$430 - $470

Roundabout Antiques,
QLD

Dickens series 'Mr Micawber', 6cm deep, 6cm wide, 6cm high.

$135 - $155

Sherwood Bazaar, QLD

Royal Doulton Dickens display plate with embossed images of Sam Weller and Mr Pickwick, c1940, 27cm wide.

$235 - $275

Sturt Street Antiques & Art, VIC

Royal Doulton 'The Fat Boy' tray, 24cm wide, 19cm high.

$125 - $145

Bob Butler's Sentimental Journey, QLD

Royal Doulton 'Dickens' series 'A' teapot 'Mr. Squeers', in production 1912-1950, 11cm deep, 25cm wide, 15cm high.

$650 - $750

Roundabout Antiques, QLD

Royal Doulton Series Ware plate 'Fireside' series D4570, in production 1925-1942, 26cm diameter.

$255 - $295

Roundabout Antiques, QLD

'Historic England' Royal Doulton bowl 'Sir Francis Drake and Plymouth Hoe', 22cm high.

$80 - $100

Rathdowne Antiques, VIC

Royal Doulton 'Historic England' plate 'Queen Elizabeth At Kenilworth Castle', c1948.

$120 - $140

H.O.W Gifts & Collectables, QLD

Royal Doulton Gaffers Series plate 'Zunday Zmocks' by C. J. Noke, in production 1936-1950.

$245 - $285

The Old General Store - Kempton, TAS

Royal Doulton 'The Gleaners' from Old English Scenes series, 19cm wide, 19cm high.

$155 - $175

Yesterday's Gems, NSW

Royal Doulton Shakespearean trio.

$185 - $205

Antipodes Antiques, QLD

Royal Doulton cake plate 'The Greenwood Tree', in production 1914-1967.

$255 - $295

Heartland Antiques & Art, NSW

Royal Doulton cabinet plate of 'The Doctor' from 'The Professionals' series, in production 1909-1949, 27cm diameter.

$230 - $270

The Old Post Office Antiques, VIC

Royal Doulton Series Ware 'Under the Greenwood Tree' comport, introduced 1914 withdrawn 1967, 11cm high, 20cm diameter.

$410 - $450   **Ardeco Antiques & Collectables, WA**

Royal Doulton Series Ware hexagonal 'Robin Hood' bowl, introduced 1914, withdrawn 1967, 22cm wide, 5cm high.

$410 - $450   **Ardeco Antiques & Collectables, WA**

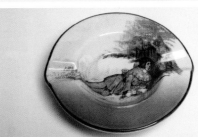

Royal Doulton Series Ware ashtray 'Under the Greenwood Tree', introduced 1914 withdrawn 1967, 12cm diameter.

$130 - $150   **Ardeco Antiques & Collectables, WA**

Royal Doulton charger 'Under the Greenwood Tree', special back stamp, in production 1914-1967, 34.5cm diam.

$430 - $470   **Turn O' The Century, QLD**

Royal Doulton Series Ware bowl 'Under The Greenwood Tree' D3751, 'Robin Hood and Little John', in production 1914-67, 16cm diameter.

$245 - $285   **Armadale Antique Centre, VIC**

Royal Doulton 'Under the Greenwood Tree' cabinet plate, introduced 1914, discontinued 1967, 26cm diam.

$220 - $260   **Thompsons Country Collectables, NSW**

Royal Doulton sandwich tray D6341 'Under the Greenwood Tree' featuring 'Robin Hood, The Friend of the Poor' scene, special backstamp, c1951, 15cm high.

$190 - $210   **H.O.W Gifts & Collectables, QLD**

Royal Doulton Series Ware vase 'Under The Greenwood Tree' D6094 'Little John and John a'Dale', in production 1914-67, 5cm high.

$380 - $420   **Armadale Antique Centre, VIC**

Royal Doulton 'Parson Brown' ash bowl, in production 1939-1960, 7.5cm high.

$185 - $205   **Yanda Aboriginal Art Melbourne, VIC**

Royal Doulton pin dish, 13cm wide.

$20 - $30   **The Restorers Barn, VIC**

Doulton ashtray of 'Farmer John' in production 1934-1960, designer Henry Fenton, 8cm high, 8cm diam.

$260 - $300   **The Mill Markets, VIC**

Royal Doulton kookaburra and wattle bowl, 4cm wide, 20cm diameter.

$340 - $380   **Ancanthe, TAS**

Royal Doulton 'Glanis Thistle' coffee set with six cups and saucers, cream jug, sugar bowl and coffee pot.

$470 - $510   **Copperfield Antiques - NSW, NSW**

Royal Doulton 'Wild Rose' bowl, in production 1940-1959, c1950, 23.5cm wide, 5.5cm high.

$460 - $500   **Chambers & Crosthwaite Antiques, QLD**

'Reynard the Fox' bone china coffee set with hand painted decoration, c1953, 20cm high.

$1100 - $1300   **Brae-mar Antiques, NSW**

Royal Doulton 36 piece tea set in the 'Golmis Thistle' pattern, including six teacups, saucers, plates and six coffee cups, c1950.

$1700 - $1900   **Avoca Beach Antiques, NSW**

Pretty 'Arcadia' pattern tea cup, saucer and plate.

$125 - $145   **Eilisha's Shoppe, QLD**

Royal Doulton 'Poppies in the Cornfield' comport, 11cm high, 21cm diameter.

$480 - $520   **Fyshwick Antique Centre, ACT**

Royal Doulton Australian Bicentenary 'Loving Cup', issued in a limited edition of 350, c1988, 17cm high.

$700 - $800   **Roundabout Antiques, QLD**

Royal Doulton part dinner service ' Carlyle' pattern, c1970.

NZ$470 - $510

Country Charm Antiques, New Zealand

Six person Royal Doulton dinner set in the Seville pattern.

$185 - $205

Cool & Collected, SA

Royal Doulton 'Sonnet' dinner set, 8 place settings, 56 pieces, c1970.

$1300 - $1500

Avoca Beach Antiques, NSW

Royal Doulton 'Wild Roses' jug, in production 1940-1959, c1950, 13cm high.

$430 - $470

Antique Centre of Stonnington, VIC

Royal Doulton miniature salt glaze jug with dark blue rim, applied rural figures, circle mark for Lambeth, production 1902-1956, 3.5cm wide, 4.2cm high.

$340 - $380

Turn O' The Century, QLD

Pair of Royal Doulton 'Wild Rose' jugs, c1948.

$750 - $850

Arleston Antiques, VIC

Royal Doulton 'Toasting Motto's' jug, 15cm high.

$480 - $520

Antique Centre of Stonnington, VIC

Royal Doulton 'Balloon Man' tableware plate, c1980, 26cm wide.

$170 - $190

Western District Antique Centre, VIC

Royal Doulton 'Australian Views C' plate, 'Aborigines in Corroboree Dress', in production 1953-1975, 26cm diameter.

$190 - $210

Roundabout Antiques, QLD

Royal Doulton plate in 'The Parson' pattern, 26cm diameter.

$175 - $195

The Old General Store - Kempton, TAS

Doulton Lambeth jug with initials 'MH' on base, 21cm high, 12cm diameter.

$430 - $470

Pieces, TAS

Royal Doulton Lambeth vase with stylised flowers in relief, 17cm high.

$235 - $275 — **Helen's On The Bay, QLD**

Royal Doulton vase by Florence Barlow with pate-sur-pate birds, 48cm high, 56cm diameter.

$2700-$2900 — **Chelsea Antiques & Decorative Art Centre P/L, QLD**

Royal Doulton hand painted vase, 22cm high.

$450 - $500 — **Antique Centre of Stonnington, VIC**

Royal Doulton plate 'A Brighter day' Children of the World, after an original work by Lisette De Winne, Collectors International, c1978, 21cm diameter.

$560 - $660 — **Avoca Beach Antiques, NSW**

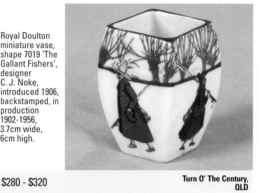

Royal Doulton miniature vase, shape 7019 'The Gallant Fishers', designer C. J. Noke, introduced 1906, backstamped, in production 1902-1956, 3.7cm wide, 6cm high.

$280 - $320 — **Turn O' The Century, QLD**

Boxed Royal Doulton 'Winning Colors', after original work by Le Roy Neiman No.6335. 'Winning Colors' was the race horse who won the Kentucky Derby in 1988, 26.5cm diameter.

NZ$230 - $270 — **Maxine's Collectibles, New Zealand**

Royal Doulton plate 'Poppies', in production 1931-1950, 26cm diameter.

$230 - $270 — **Antique General Store, NSW**

Royal Doulton floral vase, c1950, 15cm high, 15cm diameter.

$360 - $410 — **White Park Antiques, SA**

Royal Doulton limited edition plate 'Journey's End'. Signed by Stobart, c1980, 26.5cm diameter.

$410 - $450 — **C. V. Jones Antiques & Art Gallery, VIC**

Royal Doulton vase, 10cm wide, 21cm high.

$330 - $370 — **Antiques, Goods & Chattels, VIC**

Vase of a young girl on one side and two girls playing with a rabbit on the other, c1960, 18cm long, 26cm high.

NZ$520 - $550 — **Antiques & Curiosities, New Zealand**

Hand painted floral plate by F. Percy, 27cm diameter.

$530 - $630 — **Trinity Antiques, WA**

Royal Winton red roof basket, c1950.

$185 - $205   **Western District Antique Centre, VIC**

Royal Winton cake stand in 'Red Roof' pattern, c1950, 5cm high, 20cm diameter.

$165 - $185   **White Park Antiques SA.**

Royal Winton footed 'gateway' comport with a scalloped edge, c1950, 7cm high, 17cm diameter.

$115 - $135   **White Park Antiques, SA**

Royal Winton 'Bunny's Playtime' trio, c1950.

$40 - $60   **Antiques & Collectables Centre - Ballarat, VIC**

Royal Winton 'Hostess Set' comprising 'Red Roof' cup and saucer, c1950, 14cm deep, 20cm wide.

$85 - $105   **Antiques & Collectables Centre - Ballarat, VIC**

Royal Winton 'Daffodil' pattern trio, c1950, 7cm deep, 13cm wide, 21cm high.

$65 - $85   **White Park Antiques, SA**

Royal Winton 'Romany' demitasse, c1950.

$35 - $45   **Sturt Street Antiques & Art, VIC**

Royal Winton 'Peking' lidded trinket box, Pattern No. 320, c1950, 14cm long, 10cm wide.

$275 - $315   **Armadale Antique Centre, VIC**

Royal Winton matt green glaze segmented serving plate, c1948, 24cm wide, 13cm high.

NZ$40 - $60   **Casa Manana Antiques & Collectables, New Zealand**

Royal Winton lettuce set in the 'Honey Lily' pattern, c1950.

$150 - $190   **Southside Antiques Centre, QLD**

Royal Winton 'Red Roof' jug and bowl, c1950, 10cm wide, 8cm high.

$115 - $135   **Antiques & Collectables Centre - Ballarat, VIC**

Royal Winton yellow 'Petunia' four slice toastrack, c1950, 6.25cm long, 18.75cm deep, 6.25cm high.

$150 - $190   **Windsor Cottage Antiques & Collectables, NSW**

Royal Winton 'Lands End' cruet set, c1940, 21cm wide, 7cm high.

$225 - $265   **Shenton Park Antiques, WA**

Royal Winton green 'Rose Bud' cheese wedge, c1945, 15cm long, 12cm wide.

$165 - $185   **Camberwell Antique Centre, VIC**

Petunia jug and bowl, by Royal Winton, c1950, 9cm high.

$110 - $130   **Days of Olde Antiques & Collectables, VIC**

Royal Winton 'Red Roof' sandwich plate, c1950, 28cm long, 13cm wide.

$60 - $80   **Camberwell Antique Centre, VIC**

Royal Winton 'Red Roof' dish, c1950, 18cm long, 10cm wide.

$60 - $80   **Camberwell Antique Centre, VIC**

Royal Winton green 'Tiger Lily' six cup teapot, c1950.

$380 - $420   **Gumnut Antiques & Old Wares, NSW**

Royal Winton wall pocket in the gateway pattern, c1950, 21cm long, 13cm wide.

$245 - $285   **White Park Antiques, SA**

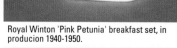

Royal Winton yellow 'Rosebud' Albans teapot, one to two cup capacity, c1945, 11cm high.

$245 - $285   **Camberwell Antique Centre, VIC**

Royal Winton 'Pink Petunia' breakfast set, in producion 1940-1950.

$900 - $1000   **Camberwell Antique Centre, VIC**

Royal Winton 'Tiger Lily' five bar toast rack, c1950, 20cm long.

$190 - $230   **Sturt Street Antiques & Art, VIC**

Royal Worcester trio, in the Chamberlain pattern.

$155 - $175   **The Old General Store - Kempton, TAS**

Royal Worcester double handled vase and cover, hand painted fruit, signed F. Clarke, c1965, 22cm high.

$2850 - $3050   **Austiques Antiques & Collectables, NSW**

Royal Worcester cylindrical vase, hand painted with fruit, signed Hook, c1965, 23cm high.

$2650 - $2850   **Austiques Antiques & Collectables, NSW**

Royal Worcester two handled lidded vase by H. Stinton, c1955, 18cm wide, 25cm high.

$8300 - $8700   **Camberwell Antique Centre, VIC**

Royal Worcester heavily gilded plate with hand painted fruit, signed S. Weston, c1965, 27cm long, 27cm high.

$1180 - $1380   **Austiques Antiques & Collectables, NSW**

Handpainted plate with 'Warwick Castle' by Raymond Poole, c1960.

$600 - $700   **Trinity Antiques, WA**

Hand painted plate with 'Inverloch Castle' by J. Allen, c1950, 26cm diameter.

$480 - $520   **Trinity Antiques, WA**

Royal Worcester vase, signed, c1959, 7cm wide, 8cm high.

NZ$750 - $850   **On Victoria, New Zealand**

Small hand painted and signed Royal Worcester fruit pattern posy vase, 7.5cm wide, 6.5cm high.

$265 - $305   **Richmond Antiques, TAS**

Limited edition Royal Worcester sword fish with certificate by Ruth Van Ruyckevelt, c1960, 45cm long.

$1880 - $2080   **Austiques Antiques & Collectables, NSW**

SHELLEY

Drip glaze Shelley coffee pot, c1950, 23cm high.

$360 - $400   **Antique Centre of Stonnington, VIC**

Shelley 'Melody' pattern trio, c1945.

$130 - $170   **Sturt Street Antiques & Art, VIC**

Shelley 'Old Ireland' trio, c1948.

$100 - $135   **Sturt Street Antiques & Art, VIC**

Shelley 'Crochet' trio, c1950.

$115 - $135   **Yanda Aboriginal Art Melbourne, VIC**

'Violets' tennis cup and saucer, c1950, 20cm long.

$115 - $135   **Brae-mar Antiques, NSW**

Shelley, cup, saucer and plate trio, c1930.

NZ$135 - $155   **Woodville Mart, New Zealand**

Shelley 'Rose Lattice' trio in the Cambridge shape, c1945.

$165 - $185   **Yesterday's Gems, NSW**

Shelley dish, c1950, 12cm wide.

$45 - $65   **Yanda Aboriginal Art Melbourne, VIC**

Shelley trio, c1950.

$100 - $120   **Yanda Aboriginal Art Melbourne, VIC**

Shelley 'Georgian' eight place dinner service, with extras, total 59 pieces.

NZ$2850 - $3050   **Kelmscott House Antiques, New Zealand**

Shelley 'Heather' 21 piece coffee set, including six cake plates, c1950.

$850 - $950   **Gumnut Antiques & Old Wares, NSW**

Shorter & Son 'Anenome' honey pot, c1940, 10cm high, 8cm diameter.

$85 - $105   **Camberwell Antique Centre, VIC**

Shorter & Son green 'Wild Rose' jug, c1940, 16cm wide, 15cm high.

$125 - $145   **Camberwell Antique Centre, VIC**

Shorter & Son honey pot, c1950, 17cm high, 9cm diameter.

$80 - $100   **Camberwell Antique Centre, VIC**

Shorter & Son 'Daffodil' four piece cruet set, c1940, 15cm wide, 5cm high.

$125 - $145   **Camberwell Antique Centre, VIC**

Shorter & Son game dish, c1950, 23cm long, 15cm high.

$85 - $105   **Yanda Aboriginal Art Melbourne, VIC**

Shorter & Son 'Harmony' two tone jug with flowers, Art Nouveau, 19cm high.

$80 - $100   **Treats & Treasures, NSW**

Shorter & Son rose decorated platter, c1950, 34cm high.

$55 - $75   **Timeless Treasures, WA**

Mabel Leigh jardiniere vase, Shorter & Son, hand inscribed, c1933.

NZ$280 - $320\   **Banks Peninsula Antiques, New Zealand**

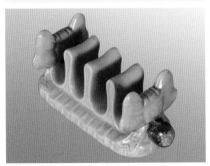

Shorter & Son toast rack with bow decoration, 19cm long, 7cm deep, 7cm high.

$140 - $170   **Sherwood Bazaar, QLD**

Shorter & Son shell vase, 20cm wide.

$65 - $85   **Bob Butler's Sentimental Journey, QLD**

Art Deco vase designed by Mabel Leigh with a scrafitto decoration inspired by a North African tradition, marked 'Period Ware, Handcrafted by Shorter & Sons, Medina', c1945, 24cm high.

NZ$300 - $330   **Blue Moon Antiques, New Zealand**

Hand painted 'Studio Anna' pottery jug, c1960, 13cm high.

$40 - $50 **Western District Antique Centre, VIC**

Studio Anna Aboriginal mug, c1950, 12cm high, 9cm diam.

$30 - $40 **Town & Country Antiques, NSW**

Studio Anna mug, 12cm high, 8cm diameter.

NZ$85 - $105 **Country Charm Antiques, New Zealand**

$30 - $40 **Rose Cottage Antiques, ACT**

Small Studio Anna dish, with Aboriginal motive of a kangaroo, c1960, 7.7cm long, 11.6cm wide.

Hand painted Austin Studio salt and pepper shakers, c1950, 9cm high.

$1850 - $2050 **Yarra Valley Antique Centre, VIC**

Studio Anna cabinet plate with hand decorated streetscape scene in pink tones, c1960, 26cm diameter.

$60 - $80 **Born Frugal, VIC**

Studio Anna wall plaque, c1950, 17cm long, 17cm wide.

$30 - $40 **Marge's Antiques & Collectables, NSW**

Ceramic plate depicting resting Aboriginal with hunting sticks, incised 'Studio Anna Australia' to base, 24cm diam.

$185 - $205 **Chapel Street Bazaar, VIC**

Studio Anna charger, hand painted landscape, c1950, 31cm diameter.

$480 - $520 **Gumnut Antiques & Old Wares, NSW**

Studio Anna 'Nelle Caledonie' vase with native design, c1960, 8cm wide, 5.6cm high.

$30 - $40 **Rose Cottage Antiques, ACT**

Hand painted Studio Anna Aboriginal motif glazed vase, c1950, 22cm high.

$70 - $90 **Yarra Valley Antique Centre, VIC**

Pair of Susie Cooper China cup, saucer and plate sets, one in cantaloupe colour, one in apple green, c1950, 9cm high, 17cm diameter.

$120 - $140   **The New Farm Antique Centre, QLD**

'Star Burst' cup, saucer and biscuit plate, 7cm high.

$90 - $110   **Camberwell Antique Centre, VIC**

Susie Cooper bone china cup and saucer in 'Carnaby Daisy' design, matt black and green glaze, designed for Wedgewood, c1960.

NZ$40 - $60   **Strangely Familiar, New Zealand**

Susie Cooper handpainted demitasse.

NZ$360 - $400   **Banks Peninsula Antiques, New Zealand**

Tea cup, saucer and plate 'Reverie', c1965, 7cm high.

$60 - $80   **Camberwell Antique Centre, VIC**

Susie Cooper 'Katina' coffee can and saucer, c1962.

$40 - $50   **Camberwell Antique Centre, VIC**

Set of six Susie Cooper coffee cups and saucers, 'Crescent Scraffito' design, c1950.

$260 - $300   **Camberwell Antique Centre, VIC**

Large Susie Cooper 'Sunburst' tea pot, Kestral shaped, 17cm high.

$600 - $700   **Camberwell Antique Centre, VIC**

Limited edition silver jubilee Susie Cooper pin dish, limited to 500 pieces, c1977, 10cm diameter.

$110 - $130   **Woodside Bazaar, SA**

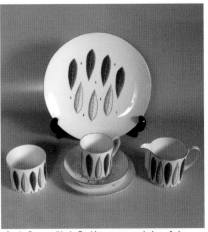

Susie Cooper 'Hyde Park' tea set consisting of six cups and saucers, jug, sugar and cake plate, c1958.

$300 - $340   **Kookaburra Antiques, TAS**

Set of six Susie Cooper 'Carnaby Daisy' coffee cans and saucers, c1960.

$280 - $320   **Camberwell Antique Centre, VIC**

SYLVAC

Two quirky SylvaC dogs impressed '5297' and '5294', made in England, c1950, 3cm long, 9cm high.

$70 - $100   **Chapel Street Bazaar, VIC**

SylvaC matt white figure of a collie dog, c1950, 20cm long, 13cm high.

$85 - $105   **Yanda Aboriginal Art Melbourne, VIC**

SylvaC seated collie dog, model number: 5023, gloss glaze, 14cm wide, 16cm high.

$115 - $135   **Antique General Store, NSW**

SylvaC corgi dog No. 3136 painted in natural colours, c1970, 13cm long, 10cm high.

$65 - $85   **Windsor Cottage Antiques & Collectables, NSW**

SylvaC figure of a dog, 'Monty the Mongrel' in brown, incised number to base 1118 made in England, c1940, 11cm long, 13.5cm high.

$110 - $130   **Windsor Cottage Antiques & Collectables, NSW**

SylvaC frightened cat No.1046, scarce in blue, c1960, 11cm long, 15.5cm high.

$185 - $205   **Windsor Cottage Antiques & Collectables, NSW**

SylvaC foal lying down, No. 1447 in green, c1950, 15cm long, 7.5cm high.

$90 - $120   **Windsor Cottage Antiques & Collectables, NSW**

Pair of SylvaC wall vases, pattern No. 2091, 4cm deep, 13cm wide, 14cm high.

$190 - $210   **Shop 48, Southern Antique Centre, NSW**

SylvaC figure of a koala, 12cm high.

$85 - $105   **Paddington Antique Centre Pty Ltd, QLD**

SylvaC novelty cat No. 5298, c1982, 18cm high.

$100 - $120   **Windsor Cottage Antiques & Collectables, NSW**

SylvaC terrier dog in natural colours, no. 1378, c1982, 8cm wide, 12cm high.

NZ$145 - $165   **Country Charm Antiques, New Zealand**

Wade gnome, 7.5cm high.

$40 - $50   **Helen's On The Bay, QLD**

Wade Pottery

George Wade Pottery was founded in 1810 in Burslem, England and during this early time, produced mostly bottles and related pottery items, then in the early 19th century, ceramics needs for textile mills. In the 1920s and 30's production of figurines with a new 'cellulose' finish were produced. However the new finish proved to turn yellow and peel off with age. At the onset of W.W.II, production of all non-essential ceramic items ceased.

In the early 1950s, George Wade Pottery re-introduced their retail line of pre-War animal figurines, in boxed sets of five, marketed as 'Whimsies', and were very successful. Between 1953 and 1959 Wade produced ten sets of Whimsies for retail sale with the last five sets each having a theme.

During the 1960's Wade produced a new set miniature animals to be included as 'one free', in each box of party crackers or tea bags. And again in 1971, due to their popularity, Wade introduced a new line of Whimsies for retail sale, consisting of 60 animals in twelve sets, which was marketed progressively over the next 13 years in groups of five.

Since the 1950s, Wade has produced several hundred of these porcelain mini figurines in numerous sets. The range includes dogs, cats, birds, snow animals, pets, wildlife, farm animals, dinosaurs, nursery rhyme figures, circus figures, miniature houses, leprechauns, monks and even Disney animals. All these figures are highly collectable and some are very valuable as they are becoming more scarce.

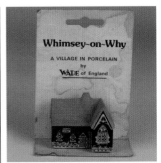

Model of 'Whimsey School' from Wade Potteries 'Whimsey-on-Why' series, mounted on original retailers card, c1986, 4cm wide, 5cm high.

$35 - $45   **Grant & Wendy Brookes, VIC**

Group of Wade characters, 7.5cm high.

$170 - $190   **Helen's On The Bay, QLD**

Group of Wade nursery rhyme characters, 8cm high.

$130 - $150   **Helen's On The Bay, QLD**

Group of Wade nursery rhyme characters, 8cm high.

$130 - $150   **Helen's On The Bay, QLD**

Unusual Wade lustre bowl with a wax-resist design, 20cm long, 13cm wide.

$85 - $105   **The Botanic Ark, VIC**

Large Wade copper lustre mug, c1957.

$55 - $75   **The Botanic Ark, VIC**

Full set of three comic penguin family ceramic figures by Wade bearing base stamp 'England'. Made 1948-1955, c1950, 4cm wide, 9.5cm high.

$410 - $450   **Shop 15, Centenary Antique Centre, NSW**

Large and beautiful Wade heath jug, 25cm high.

$65 - $85   **Myriad Art, NSW**

Wedgwood blue Jasperware candlestick, c1950, 15cm high.

$200 - $240   **Antique Centre of Stonnington, VIC**

Wedgwood green Jasperware jug with a glazed interior, 7cm deep, 9.5cm wide, 10cm high.

$85 - $105   **White Park Antiques, SA**

Small oval Wedgwood platter, c1960, 25cm long.

$165 - $185   **Margaret Sutherland Antiques, VIC**

Wedgwood vase, white with blue raised figures and leaves, 7cm wide, 14cm high.

$55 - $75   **The Exchange Galleries, NSW**

Wedgwood stoneware gilded lustre ware club jug in grapevine pattern, gold resist lustre ware, c1950, 20cm high, 14cm diameter.

$65 - $85   **Fyshwick Antique Centre, ACT**

Wedgwood green Jasperware trinket box, 10cm high, 11.5cm diameter.

$245 - $285   **White Park Antiques, SA**

Blue Wedgwood Jasperware jug with a glazed interior, 13cm high, 11cm diameter.

$135 - $155   **White Park Antiques, SA**

Wedgwood Jasperware kidney shape trinket box with sage coloured body, white jasper, relief decoration and a 'classical' matt finish, c1960, 7.5cm wide, 5cm high.

$40 - $50   **Antique General Store, NSW**

Wedgwood collectors edition 'Sir Francis Drake' plate, c1984, 26cm diameter.

$55 - $75   **Mentone Beach Antiques Centre, VIC**

Wedgwood green coloured jug, c1980, 13cm high, 11cm diameter.

$165 - $185   **Mentone Beach Antiques Centre, VIC**

Wedgwood blue pedestal bowl, c1970, 13cm high, 20cm diameter.

$190 - $210   **Vintage Charm, SA**

Blue Wedgwood Jasperware two handled lidded bowl, 10cm high, 11cm diameter.

$115 - $135   **White Park Antiques, SA**

Wedgwood bone china plate with a centre scene of a sailboat on the sea, turquoise border, 24cm wide.

$150 - $170   **Moorabool Antique Galleries, VIC**

Blue Wedgwood Jasperware teapot, 22cm long, 14cm wide, 13.5cm high.

$380 - $420   **White Park Antiques, SA**

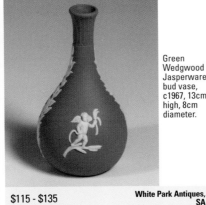

Green Wedgwood Jasperware bud vase, c1967, 13cm high, 8cm diameter.

$115 - $135   **White Park Antiques, SA**

Sand coloured Keith Murray vase made for Wedgwood with a 1941-1951 backstamp, c1945, 15cm wide, 20cm high.

$2400 - $2600   **Kaleidoscope Antiques, VIC**

Three Wedgwood flora pin dishes, c1970, 11cm diameter.

$320 - $360   **Southside Antiques Centre, QLD**

Three fauna pin dishes, c1970, 11cm diameter.

$120 - $140   **Southside Antiques Centre, QLD**

Wedgwood Australia series limited edition plates, set of 4, c1962, 25cm diameter.

$205 - $245   **Yanda Aboriginal Art Melbourne, VIC**

Wedgwood lilac jasper lidded bowl, c1980, 8cm high, 12cm diameter.

$135 - $155   **Southside Antiques Centre, QLD**

Lifelike statue of a magpie by Wembley., c1950, 350cm long, 130cm wide, 190cm high.

$650 - $750

Old World Antiques, SA

Large Wembley Ware koala, designed by John Tribe, c1950, 27cm high.

$1650 - $1850

The Mill Markets, VIC

Australian Wembley Ware pottery koala and cub.

$330 - $370

Deco Down Under, WA

Large Australian Wembley Ware pottery kookaburra holding a snake on a tree stump, 29cm high.

$1350 - $1550

Deco Down Under, WA

Wembley Ware owl lamp, c1950, 15cm wide, 22cm high.

$330 - $370

Vintage Charm, SA

Wembley ware ashtray decorated with a surfer, factory stamp to base, c1950, 13cm wide, 7cm high.

$350 - $390

Jeremy's Australiana, VIC

West Australian Wembley Ware ashtray in the form of a gaming dice, creamy yellow colour, c1940, 7cm deep, 7cm high.

$275 - $315

Colonial Antiques & Tea House, WA

Wembley Ware lustre ashtray decorated with an elephant, c1950, 9cm high, 13cm diameter.

$85 - $105

Shop 16, Southern Antique Centre, NSW

Wembley Ware ashtray depicting Australia surrounded by the sea, decal of a Australian native stockman on the inside, c1950, 16cm wide, 12cm high.

$110 - $130

Mentone Beach Antiques Centre, VIC

Wembley Ware ashtray in the form of an eagle, c1950, 15cm long, 9cm high.

$70 - $90

Settlers Store, NSW

A Wembley Ware lustre ashtray, c1950, 13.5cm wide.

$125 - $145

Sturt Street Antiques & Art, VIC

Wembley Ware lustre glaze ashtray, c1960, 17cm long, 14cm deep, 10cm high.

$115 - $135

Galeria del Centro, NSW

Wembley Ware lustre glaze ashtray, c1960, 12cm deep, 7cm high.

$70 - $90

Galeria del Centro, NSW

Wembley Ware 'Nude Lady' float bowl, c1952, 26cm diameter.

$185 - $205

Antipodes Antiques, QLD

Pair of Wembley vases decorated with fish, 14cm long, 11cm high.

$65 - $85

Treats & Treasures, NSW

Pair Wembley Ware Lily wall vases, c1950, 13cm wide, 26cm high.

$650 - $750

Shenton Park Antiques, WA

Wembley Ware Australian lustre fish vase, c1950, 17cm wide, 28cm high.

$190 - $210

Heartland Antiques & Art, NSW

Wembley Ware vase in an unusual colourway of mauve and green, not an official pattern, possibly experimental, c1950, 22cm high, 15cm diameter.

$250 - $290

Shenton Park Antiques, WA

Blue Bakewell's jug, c1950, 11cm high.

$25 - $35 — Brae-mar Antiques, NSW

Kingsford Smith Limited Edition jug no. 1162/3000 with original box and certificate, c1973, 15cm high.

$160 - $180 — Settlers Store, NSW

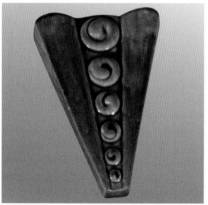

Diana Pottery Art Deco wall vase, c1950, 14cm long, 19cm high.

$50 - $80 — Secondhand Furniture Mart, TAS

Albaware, shell styled vase, c1950, 20cm long, 8cm deep, 10cm high.

$20 - $30 — Galeria del Centro, NSW

Frog on dish

$225 - $265 — Den of Antiquities, VIC

Bendigo Pottery Toby jug of Albert Namatjira with certificate number 1238 of 3000, c1975, 18cm long, 13cm deep, 16cm high.

$60 - $90 — Collectable Creations, QLD

Diana Pottery gumleaf basket, c1950, 25cm long, 14cm deep, 16cm high.

$50 - $110 — Kookaburra Antiques, TAS

'Our Mate Bluey' figure by Bendigo Pottery with certificate No. 226, c1970, 23cm high.

$60 - $90 — Collectable Creations, QLD

Large Bendigo Pottery green glazed frog.

$480 - $520 — Armadale Antique Centre, VIC

Australian pottery wall vase by Diana Pottery, 14cm wide, 19cm high.

$50 - $70 — Nana's Pearls, ACT

Diana Pottery lawn bowls mug with a bowls scene and cars in background, handle is trunk of a palm tree, c1950, 12cm high.

$135 - $155

Carnegie Collectables, VIC

Diana Ware vase with original labels attached, c1950, 15cm high.

$15 - $25

Brae-mar Antiques, NSW

Set of three Diana Pottery spotted wear cannisters, c1960, 17cm high, 15cm diameter.

$215 - $255

Shop 15 Coliseum Antiques Centre, NSW

Australian pottery jug by Ellis with Asian style lettering scraffiti etched and '#41' stamped on bottom, typical Ellis glaze and retro design, some crazing, c1970, 29cm high, 26cm diameter.

$75 - $95

Image Objex, VIC

Ellis Pottery matt black drip glaze vase, scraffito decorated, c1960.

$200 - $240

Chapel Street Bazaar, VIC

Gold and white glaze Ellis Pottery vase, c1950, 25cm high.

$185 - $205

Retro Active, VIC

Ellis Pottery slip cast sitting figural piece in a bright orange glaze, c1964, 22cm high.

$140 - $160

Chapel Street Bazaar, VIC

A small Florenz basket incised 'Florenz', c1955, 12cm wide, 9cm high.

$60 - $80

Sturt Street Antiques & Art, VIC

Florenz Studio pottery vase with wonderful detail of koala on a branch with eucalypt leaves and gum nuts, c1950, 20cm wide, 23cm high.

$275 - $315

Chapel Street Bazaar, VIC

A dry glaze vase incised 'Florenz Sydney', c1950, 14cm high.

$40 - $50

Sturt Street Antiques & Art, VIC

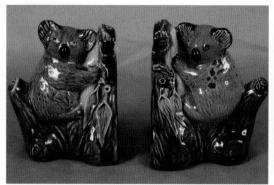

Pair of koala bookends by Florenz Australia, c1950, 13cm high.

$205 - $245

Yanda Aboriginal Art Melbourne, VIC

Pair of Australian ceramic fish vases, 'Kalmar' stamp underneath, c1950, 18cm long, 20cm high.

$75 - $95

Towers Antiques & Collectables, NSW

Ceramic seagull vase by Kalmar, 20cm long, 33cm high.

$60 - $80

Helen's on Discovery Antiques & Decor, QLD

Kalmar Ceramics

Kalmar Ceramics were produced by migrants Julius and Irene Kalmar of Hungary from the early 1950's to mid 1960's. Their first factory was at Lakemba, NSW and they later moved to Punchbowl. Kalmar Ceramics became Australian Art & Ceramic Products (AACP).

Australian ceramic parrot vase by Kalmar, modeled by Irene Kalmar, slip cast parrot on tree stump, all hand painted with Kalmar and V69 impressed mark, pre AACP. c1950, 16cm wide, 22cm high.

$165 - $185

Bower Bird Art & Antiques, QLD

Large lidded ceramic pot with decorative abstract design, signed 'Kevin Boyd' to base. Kevin Boyd is a potter and teacher, c1970, 34cm high, 16cm diam.

$530 - $630

Malvern Antique Market, QLD

Australian pottery bowl, signed Betty McLaren, c1970, 5cm high, 13cm diameter.

$30 - $60

Chapel Street Bazaar, VIC

Handpainted ceramic wall plaque 'Asian Woman' made by Kalmar, c1950, 5cm deep, 16cm wide, 20cm high.

$185 - $205

Retro Active, VIC

Blue ceramic horse signed by Australian potter Gus McLaren, c1970, 22cm long, 6cm wide, 19cm high.

$180 - $200

The Junk Company, VIC

Kalmar lustre glaze vase, c1950, 15cm wide, 20cm high.

$20 - $30

Galeria del Centro, NSW

Large Gus McLaren four legged stoneware abstract vessel with earthy green and brown glazes, signed to base, c1960, 24cm long, 16cm wide, 23cm high.

$340 - $380

Malvern Antique Market, VIC

Pottery salt and pepper shakers by Gus McLaren, 7cm deep, 7cm wide, 26cm high, 7cm diameter.

$175 - $195

The Junk Company, VIC

Sculptured stoneware exhibition centre piece by Gus McLaren, one of the founding members in 1958 of the Potter's Cottage in Warrandyte, Victoria, c1960, 22cm high, 29cm diameter.

$1150 - $1350

Malvern Antique Market, VIC

Australian ceramic vase by MCP with green glaze and stylised Art Deco shape, c1950, 17cm long, 7cm deep, 25cm high.

$115 - $135

Dr Russell's Emporium, WA

Ceramic cow by Betty McLaren. Married to Gus McLaren, Betty worked with Reg Preston and also worked on decorating some of Gus McLaren's items, 16cm long, 9cm deep, 13cm high.

$175 - $195

The Junk Company, VIC

MCP (Modern Ceramic Products) set of three flying wall owls, the largest 8 1/2 in (21cm) wing span, set of three, c1950.

$310 - $350

Olsens Antiques, QLD

Large green ceramic bull signed Gus McLaren. Gus McLaren was a founding member of 'Potters Cottage' and began potting with Reg Preston, c1970, 30cm long, 12cm wide, 19cm high.

$300 - $340

The Junk Company, VIC

Gus McLaren pottery cat, fully marked, c1955, 24cm long, 16cm high.

$155 - $175

Old As The Hills, VIC

CERAMICS

Art koala ornament by Mingay, c1950, 23cm wide, 17cm high.

$275 - $315   **Camberwell Antique Centre, VIC**

MCP blue gravy boat and saucer, c1950, 14cm long, 9cm deep, 8cm high.

$35 - $45   **Galeria del Centro, NSW**

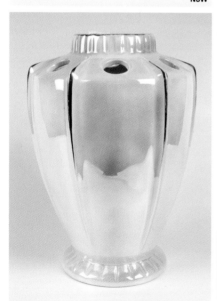

Australian pottery gladioli vase with lustre glaze and impressed mark for 'Mingay' pottery, c1950, 32cm high, 23cm diameter.

$220 - $260   **Shop 10, Centenary Antique Centre, NSW**

Art Deco vase by MCP in a turquoise coloured glaze decorated with a female dancer, 24cm high.

$175 - $195   **Vintage Living, ACT**

Handmade Australian studio ceramic vessel by South Australian master potter Milton Moon. Since 1959 Milton Moon has had approximately seventy exhibitions in Australia and overseas and is the winner of numerous awards, c1980, 16cm high, 19cm diameter.

$1000 - $1200   **Malvern Antique Market, VIC**

Large stoneware casserole dish with lush earthy glazes, signed 'Harry Memmott' to base, an important Queensland potter and author of many books and journals on ceramics. Taught by Merv. Feeney in the early 1950's, he went on to influence many potters including Milton Moon, c1960, 20cm high, 23cm diam.

$275 - $315   **Malvern Antique Market, VIC**

Hand built casserole pot with luscious molten brown glazes, signed to base 'Milton Moon', c1970, 20cm high, 27cm diameter.

$800 - $900   **Malvern Antique Market, VIC**

Australian MCP slipcast swan vase with original sticker 'Mingay', c1950, 20cm wide, 19cm high.

$60 - $80   **Collector's Cottage Antiques, NSW**

Ceramic hand made vase with highly textured surface and drip glazes, Milton Moon's mark to base. Milton Moon is one of Australia's most distinguished living potters, and is represented in all state Public Art Collections and The National Gallery of Canberra. He has worked extensively in Australia and Japan, c1970, 19cm high, 13cm diameter.

$600 - $700   **Malvern Antique Market, VIC**

Wheel thrown stoneware pot with luscious glazes, late 1970s, Milton Moon's mark to base who started with Harry Memmet and learnt the art of wheel throwing from Mervyn Fetney, one of Australia's most distinguished living potters, 18cm high, 9cm diam.

$530 - $630   **Malvern Antique Market, VIC**

Neil Douglas hand painted plate, signed by Neil Douglas and titled 'Early Morning Gibben Plains, Jimboola, Australia', 18cm diameter.

$1250 - $1450   **Antiques On Macquarie, TAS**

Set of three McCallum whisky jugs by Elisher Pottery, 16cm long, 17cm deep.

$135 - $155   **Towers Antiques & Collectables, NSW**

Figure of an Aborigine signed 'Takacs Studio, Australia', 18cm long, 12cm wide, 18cm high.

NZ$70 - $90   **Country Charm Antiques, New Zealand**

Remued Jug, flamed top with original sticker.

$380 - $420   **Den of Antiquities, VIC**

A Remued green glazed basket vase with incised markings, 13cm high.

$630 - $730   **Graham & Nancy Miller, VIC**

Empire Ware figure of a koala, 14.5cm wide, 23.5cm high.

NZ$310 - $350   **Bulls Antiques & Collectables, NZ**

Long and Barden demijohn marked 'The Property of Long and Barden, Sydney', c1950, 33cm high, 18cm diameter.

$100 - $120   **Settlers Store, NSW**

Rose Noble jug with a Kookaburra design, 'Launceston' to the front and a black back stamp to the base, c1950, 7cm wide, 6cm high, 3cm diameter.

$40 - $60   **Mt Dandenong Antique Centre, VIC**

Alan Lowe pottery jug in grey and dark pink, c1950, 10cm high, 11cm diameter.

$40 - $50   **Step Back Antiques, VIC**

Sydney style pottery jug with gum leaves and gum nuts, 22cm high.

$110 - $130   **Western District Antique Centre, VIC**

Delemere Australian pottery basket.

$190 - $210   **Shop 77, Coliseum Antiques Centre, NSW**

Ceramic koala on a gumtree decanter, c1950, 7cm deep, 10cm wide, 22cm high.

$120 - $140   **Galeria del Centro, NSW**

CERAMICS

Johnson of Australia dinner set for six including plates, side plates, cups, saucers and bowls, c1971.

$110 - $130

frhapsody, WA

Johnson of Australia setting for one comprising one dinner plate, side plate, cup and saucer, c1971.

$20 - $30

frhapsody, WA

Plate featuring Sydney Opera House with floral border and Coat of Arms, Woods & Son Ltd. information legend on back, 25.5cm diameter.

NZ$65 - $85

Country Charm Antiques, New Zealand

Matt-black vase by 'Gunda' with enameled decoration and internal glazing, c1954, 25cm high.

$150 - $170

Found Objects, VIC

Large unmarked, fluoro lustre glaze vase, c1960, 18cm deep, 25cm high.

$40 - $50

Galeria del Centro, NSW

Floral design hand painted plate with gloss glaze, signed 'Isobel Aust', c1950, 2cm high, 25cm diameter.

$155 - $175

Hamilton Street Antiques, VIC

Australian studio pottery dish, signed 'ARN Australia', 2cm high, 11cm diameter.

NZ$40 - $60

Country Charm Antiques, New Zealand

Antipasto platter made by Sylha Melbourne with individual multi-coloured segments in cane basket, c1950, 35cm diameter.

$45 - $65

Retro Active, VIC

Australian majolica glaze pottery plate with grape design in relief, signed Olga Williamson, c1940, 18cm diameter.

$150 - $170

Patinations, NSW

Hollywood vase, fluted shape in green and yellow, c1950, 10cm deep, 16cm wide, 20cm high.

$30 - $40

Twice Around, NSW

Australian pottery vase by Daisy in blue metallic drip glass, c1955, 22cm high.

$75 - $95

Helen's On The Bay, QLD

A. M. Bosel pottery vase with internal decoration, c1950, 10cm high.

$120 - $140

Sturt Street Antiques & Art, VIC

Australian pottery hand painted wall plaque by Vande Pottery, Mosman, Sydney, in production 1952-1962, c1955, 14cm wide, 14cm high.

$60 - $80

Shop 15, Centenary Antique Centre, NSW

Austrian ceramic face mask of young boy, c1950, 21cm high.

$150 - $170   **Shop 18, Centenary Antique Centre, NSW**

Killawarra Collection, liquer muscat in duck family decanter, full, 26cm wide, 24cm high.

$140 - $160   **Helen's On The Bay, QLD**

Pair of 'Red-stone' brand glazed portrait heads depicting indigenous people, c1950, 10cm wide, 16cm high.

$275 - $315   **Calmar Trading, VIC**

Ceramic vase signed 'Jackman', c1960, 11cm deep, 19cm wide, 37cm high.

$110 - $130   **The Junk Company, VIC**

Retro kangaroo and palm tree wall hanging or standing vase, c1960, 20cm wide, 14cm high.

$30 - $40   **The Mill Markets, VIC**

Studio pottery unmarked gum nut vase, c1950, 9cm high, 16cm diameter.

$430 - $470   **Antiques & Collectables Centre - Ballarat, VIC**

Hand made Australian pottery shell vase, BF mark to base, c1965, 9cm deep, 24cm wide, 18cm high.

$45 - $65   **Mac's Collectables**

'Monkeys of Melbourne' Luna Park teapot. The pottery is no longer in production, c1988, 26cm wide, 17cm high.

$185 - $205   **Chapel Street Bazaar, VIC**

Daga wall vase of male and female lovers' heads, c1950, 22cm long, 6cm deep.

$65 - $85   **Cool & Collected, SA**

Australian pottery vase, unmarked, c1950, 12cm wide, 17cm high.

$45 - $65   **Galeria del Centro, NSW**

Unmarked Hoffman pottery sponge decorated bread crock, made in Adelaide, c1940.

$140 - $160   **Bower Bird Art & Antiques, QLD**

Hoffman pink pudding bowl, c1950, 14cm high, 21cm diameter.

$40 - $60   **Step Back Antiques, VIC**

Te Rona Potteries agate ware vase, 19cm high, 12cm diameter.

NZ$110 - $130

Bulls Antiques & Collectables, New Zealand

Boot ornament made by Temuka Pottery, c1950, 14cm long, 6cm wide, 10cm high.

NZ$40 - $50

Memory Lane, New Zealand

Temuka pottery boot, c1950, 18cm long, 6cm wide, 9.5cm high.

NZ$40 - $60

Memory Lane, New Zealand

Cactus planter decorated with toadstools, signed Mollie Godsell, c1950, 27cm long, 5cm high.

NZ$230 - $270

Banks Peninsula Antiques, New Zealand

Flower trough designed by Nellie Fulford and manufactured by Te Mata Potteries, Havelock North New Zealand with clay dug from a pit in Waimarama Road and fired to an orange red colour. During the 1950's Nellie Fulford and a Mrs. Hawley, hand-fashioned a range of log vases in various shapes and sizes., c1950, 33cm long, 6cm wide.

NZ$40 - $60

Casa Manana Antiques & Collectables, New Zealand

Maori chief tobacco jar made by Temuka, c1950, 29cm high, 17cm diameter.

NZ$460 - $500

Antiques & Curiosities, New Zealand

Teapot by Stewart Pottery, Auckland, original information tag, 13cm wide, 18cm high.

NZ$70 - $90

Country Charm Antiques, New Zealand

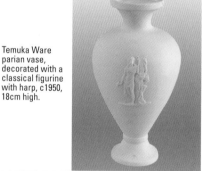

Temuka Ware parian vase, decorated with a classical figurine with harp, c1950, 18cm high.

NZ$270 - $310

Antiques of Epsom, New Zealand

Meneford Tui, New Zealand nature bird figurine, c1960, 18cm high.

NZ$380 - $420

Country Charm Antiques, New Zealand

O. C. Stephens vase, c1950, 6cm wide, 7cm high.

NZ$55 - $75

Oxford Court Antiques Centre, New Zealand

Olive Jones vase, c1960, 11cm wide, 10cm high.

NZ$205 - $245

Oxford Court Antiques Centre, New Zealand

Porcelain Arabia teapot with semi-matt brown glaze cane handle made by Arabia, Finland, designed by Ulla Procope, c1960, 16cm high.

$90 - $110

506070, NSW

Arabia 'Sunflower' teapot with cane handle designed by Ulla Procope, c1950, 16cm high.

$85 - $105

Vintage Living, ACT

Hand painted 'Arabia' coffee pot, retro styling, signed on base by artist, c1970, 18cm high, 10cm diameter.

$25 - $35

Born Frugal, VIC

Aynsley cup and saucer sets in russet and cobalt blue with handpainted roses in bowl, signed Bailey, c1955, 14cm wide, 7cm high.

$340 - $380

The New Farm Antique Centre, QLD

Black, brown and white Ulla Procope Arabia teapots, c1960.

$135 - $155

Design Dilemas, VIC

Aynsley gilded, hand painted cabinet plate, fruit insert, c1950, 27cm diameter

NZ$520 - $620

Country Charm Antiques, New Zealand

Eight 'Ruska' coffee cups and saucers by Ulla Procope for Arabia, Finland, c1965, 8cm high, 7cm diameter.

$110 - $130

Image Objex, VIC

Arabia dish wheel thrown in blue and black, c1960, 17cm diameter.

$65 - $85

Obsidian Antiques, NSW

Arabia hand painted sunflower jug and plate, c1960.

$90 - $110

Cool & Collected, SA

Lorna Bailey 'Somerville' pattern teapot, c1994, 19cm high.

$200 - $240   Decodence Collectables, VIC

Lorna Bailey designed salt and pepper shakers, c1994.

$55 - $75   Decodence Collectables, VIC

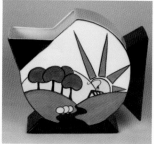

Squat, circular hand painted vase, designed by Lorna Bailey in the 'Apedale Valley' pattern.

$110 - $130   Decodence Collectables, VIC

Belleek small jug and sugar bowl, backstamped with third green mark, shell form, gloss glaze, lustre to intertior, c1970.

$165 - $185   Antique General Store, NSW

Lorna Bailey

Lorna Bailey was born on 10th February 1978 and was brought up in Newcastle-under-Lyme, Staffordshire. She has lived throughout her life in and around the Newcastle-under-Lyme area, and it is this area from which the majority of the names for her designs are taken.

She attended Stoke-on-Trent College leaving with a B.Tec National Diploma in Design (Ceramics). Stoke-on-Trent College is the successor to the Burslem School Of Art where Clarice Cliff, Susie Cooper, Charlotte Rhead and Fredrick Rhead and Mabel Leigh amongst others, all studied.

Her designs are manufactured by L.J.B. Ceramics, where she worked while still studying at college.

Lorna Bailey's bold, striking designs are often compared with those of Clarice Cliff

Lorna Bailey vase with 'Fantasia' pattern c1994, 17cm high.

$240 - $280   Decodence Collectables, VIC

Lorna Bailey designed vase, in the 'Apedale Valley' pattern, c1994, 17cm high.

$175 - $195   Decodence Collectables, VIC

Lorna Bailey designed jug 'Harmony' pattern, c1994, 20cm high.

$230 - $270   Decodence Collectables, VIC

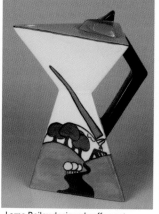

Lorna Bailey designed coffee pot 'Apedale Valley' pattern, c1994, 22cm high.

$190 - $230   Decodence Collectables, VIC

Lorna Bailey vase in the style of Rennie Macintosh, c1994, 21cm high.

$220 - $260   Decodence Collectables, VIC

Belleek lidded sugar bowl and saucer.

$205 - $245   Den of Antiquities, VIC

Belleek teapot in the face and grapes pattern with a second black mark, 13cm high, 20cm diameter.

$1500 - $1700   G & N Miller Antiques, VIC

Belleek beaker with brown mark, 9cm high.

$145 - $165   Bob Butler's Sentimental Journey, QLD

Bing & Grondahl figurine of a fat man on a hot day, 'Den Trstige Mand' by Erik Henningsen, c1960, 21cm high.

NZ$470 - $510   **Tinakori Antiques, New Zealand**

Two piece Burleigh Ware condiment set in the 'Acorn' pattern for salt, pepper, mustard and sugar.

$185 - $205   **Margaret Sutherland Antiques, VIC**

Bing & Grondahl figure of a cellist, No. 2032, c1950, 20cm high.

$330 - $370   **Elizabeth Antiques, NSW**

Plaster wall figure of a kingfisher made by Bossons, UK, c1950, 27cm long, 9cm deep, 16cm wide, 27cm high.

$185 - $205   **Dr Russell's Emporium, WA**

Bust of a Middle Eastern man wearing a fez, 9cm wide, 16cm high.

$220 - $260   **Kings Park Antiques & Collectables, SA**

Coalport hand painted, lidded vase, signed 'Peter Gosling', c1970, 13cm long, 24cm high.

$1400 - $1500   **Armadale Antique Centre, VIC**

Bisque vase, hand painted, 17cm wide, 32cm high.

$230 - $270   **Furniture Revisited, VIC**

Scottish Buchan jug with lid in blue and white, c1970, 19cm wide, 27cm high.

NZ$85 - $105   **Maxine's Collectibles, New Zealand**

Adams 'English' scenic plate, c1950, 31cm diameter.

$60 - $110   **Antiques On Macquarie, TAS**

Small Burleigh Ware teapot in the 'Willow' pattern, 19cm long, 12cm high.

$60 - $80   **Shirley & Noel Daly Antiques, VIC**

Coalport china comport with elaborate gilding and hand painted scene, 24cm wide, 14cm high.

$380 - $420 **Antiques At Birkenhead, NSW**

Coalport plate, depicting Sir Robert Menzies, c1978.

$15 - $25 **Marge's Antiques & Collectables, NSW**

Caolpoart 'Town Crier' figurine, 22.5cm high.

NZ$380 - $420 **Memory Lane, New Zealand**

T. G. Green cream ware mixing bowl, c1950, 12cm high, 28cm diameter.

$60 - $80 **Step Back Antiques, VIC**

Blue and white Cornishware bowl, 26cm diameter.

$155 - $175 **Paddington Antique Centre Pty Ltd, QLD**

Coalport figurine from 'The Age of Elegance' collection, named 'Lavender (sic) Walk', c1994, 19cm wide, 22cm high.

$330 - $370 **Glenelg Antique Centre, SA**

Coalport 'Beefeater' figurine, 22.5cm high.

NZ$380 - $420 **Memory Lane, New Zealand**

Coalport 'Grenadier Guard' figurine, 25cm high.

NZ$380 - $420 **Memory Lane, New Zealand**

T. G. Green Cornishware yellow and white butter container with lid, green mark to base, c1960, 15cm wide, 7cm high.

$135 - $155 **Antiques At Birkenhead, NSW**

T. G. Green Cornishware salt pig, c1940, 8cm deep, 15cm wide, 12cm high.

$230 - $270 **Colonial Antiques & Tea House, WA**

T. G. Green Cornishware pie funnel, from an edition of 500, c1996.

$140 - $160 **Grant & Wendy Brookes, VIC**

T. G. Green Cornishware yellow and white lidded canister, green mark to base, 16cm high, 13cm diameter.

$170 - $190 **Antiques At Birkenhead, NSW**

T. G. Green Cornishware yellow and white flour shaker with screw off lid, green mark to base, c1961, 12cm high, 9cm diameter.

$135 - $155 **Antiques At Birkenhead, NSW**

Dennis China slip trail panther vase, designed by Sally Tuffin. c1995, 23cm high.

$1000 - $1200   **Goodwood House Antiques, WA**

Sally Tuffin

Sally Tuffin came into ceramics from a background in fashion design. In the early 1960's she was the other half of 'Foale & Tuffin', one of the trendiest labels in Carnaby Street, London.

She turned to ceramics in 1972 when her retailing partnership was dissolved and in 1985, with her husband, Richard Dennis, launched The Dennis China Works to make ceramics for collectors.

In 1986, Richard Dennis and a partner purchased the ailing Moorcroft pottery and over the next six years Sally Tuffin's designs injected new life into the pottery.

Sally and Richard Dennis re-started the Dennis China Works in 1993 after reviving Moorcroft pottery for the previous six years.

Sally Tuffin's designs are influenced by the arts and crafts movement and nature. All pieces are signed and numbered.

Denby brown handglazed pottery vase, 40cm high.

$35 - $45   **Myriad Art, NSW**

Denby Pottery 'Cretonne' pattern stoneware vase by Glynn Colledge, c1955, 24cm wide, 15cm high.

$230 - $270   **Vintage Living, ACT**

Gouda globular vase hand painted, made by Royal Goedewaagen, c1980, 15cm high, 18cm diameter.

$255 - $295   **Patinations, NSW**

Dennis China poppy design slip trail technique vase, designed by Sally Tuffin, c1995, 24cm high.

$870 - $920   **Goodwood House Antiques, WA**

Gouda vase numbered 2525/5218, 18.5cm high, 16cm diameter.

$270 - $310   **Furniture Revisited, VIC**

P. Z. H. handpainted Gouda vase in the 'Nadza' pattern, c1925, 18cm high.

$310 - $350   **Northumberland Antiques & Restorations, NSW**

Unusual shaped Art Deco style Gouda jug, c1950, 16cm high.

NZ$185 - $205   **Camelot Antiques, New Zealand**

Dennis China elephant design, slip-trail technique and designed by Sally Tuffin, c1990, 19cm high.

$950 - $990   **Goodwood House Antiques, WA**

Later Gouda vase with transfer decoration, c1970, 16cm wide, 26cm high.

$275 - $315   **Northumberland Antiques & Restorations, NSW**

Goldschneider figurine, c1950, 40cm high.

$1700 - $1900   **Hunters & Collectors Antiques, NSW**

Grimwades 'Maori Ware' lidded tobacco jar with 'Maori Carver' scene, 10cm wide, 11cm high.

NZ$480 - $520   **Bulls Antiques & Collectables, NZ**

Royal Winton Grimwades tray in yellow tiger lily with a moulded relief, 28cm long, 2cm deep, 14cm wide.

$75 - $95

Laidley Old Wares, QLD

Pair of Limoges matching ice buckets.

$480 - $520

Ardeco Antiques & Collectables, WA

Lilliput Lane

Known as 'Cottage Ware', ceramic miniatures of buildings have been manufactured by many potteries including Goss, Beswick and Royal Winton. Lilliput Lane commenced production of their miniature cottages in 1982. David Tate, the founder, opened workshops at Skirsgill, in England's Lake District and the company has remained in the area ever since. The majority of their models are based on real cottages with collections based not only on British Cottages but also American, and in the past German, Dutch and French Cottages.

Most Lilliput Lane Cottages are made on the scale of 1:76. The modellers have more than 200 different tools at their disposal, including dentistry tools, to create a wax model which, is then used to make a mould for the cottage.

The cottages have attracted a worldwide collector following. As new models are launched, older models are retired and become collectable. Subtle variations in models can affect the price, for example changes in colour or design, and with regular retirements and new issues, there is solid demand for earlier and rarer cottages.

The most expensive Lilliput cottage sold is the model of The Royal & Ancient Clubhouse at St. Andrews, Scotland. This exclusive silver-plated sculpture was produced between 1997 and 1999 in a limited edition of only nine models worldwide. The models were usually sold by auction at golf tournaments where they commanded a price of between £2,000 and £5,000. All proceeds from the sale of each model were donated to various charities throughout the U.K.

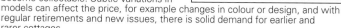

Hand made model of the 'Swan Inn', by Lilliput Lane c1980, 12cm wide, 14cm high.

$225 - $265

Glenelg Antique Centre, SA

Grimwades cereal bowl featuring Maori motif, 4cm high, 17cm diameter.

$290 - $330

Shop 7, Centenary Antique Centre, NSW

Limoges vase in a dark red glaze, c1980, 14cm long, 20cm high.

$250 - $290

Pendulum Antiques, SA

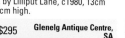

Hand made fantasy piece, 'Secret Garden', by Lilliput Lane, c1980, 13cm wide, 16cm high.

$255 - $295

Glenelg Antique Centre, SA

Lilliput Lane hand made model 'Woodcutters', c1980, 6cm wide, 6cm high.

$65 - $85

Glenelg Antique Centre, SA

Limoges grand piano trinket box, c1970, 13cm long, 9cm wide, 6cm high.

$120 - $140

Helen's On The Bay, QLD

Trio, back stamped 'Haviland, France, Haviland & Co., Limoges'.

$50 - $60

Archer St Antiques & Gallery, TAS

Lilliput Lane hand made model of 'The Croft', c1980, 9cm wide, 7cm high.

$75 - $95

Glenelg Antique Centre, SA

Lilliput Lane hand made model of 'St. Mary's Church', c1980, 16cm wide, 10cm high.

$185 - $205

Glenelg Antique Centre, SA

Limoges powder bowl with ornate blue and gold scene of a boy and girl, signed 'Jragonard', c1960, 15cm long, 4.5cm high.

$50 - $80   **Bendigo Antique Centre, VIC**

Lladro water bird, model number 1599, registered marks to base, gloss glaze, hand made, 11.5cm long, 7.5cm wide, 6.5cm high.

$205 - $245   **Antique General Store, NSW**

Large reclining Lladro figure of a young man reading, 40cm long, 17.5cm high.

$850 - $950   **Poplar Antiques, NSW**

Lladro figurine 'Girl With Lamb', retired 1993, 22cm high, 7cm diameter.

$330 - $370   **Glenelg Antique Centre, SA**

Early Lladro figure of a seated maiden at a large bowl, c1970, 20cm wide, 19cm high.

$430 - $470   **The Bottom Drawer Antique Centre, VIC**

Lladro model no. 4749, 'Small Dog', in production in production 1971-1985, 9cm deep, 8cm high.

$275 - $315   **Glenelg Antique Centre, SA**

Lladro hand painted figurine of a rabbit, 10cm wide, 8cm high.

$135 - $155   **Copperfield Antiques - NSW, NSW**

Large pottery jug by Mason's with raised acorn and oak leaf hand painted decoration, 25cm high.

$255 - $295   **Vintage Living, ACT**

Masons pink and white 'Vista' pattern large lidded soup tureen, c1950, 31.5cm long, 20.5cm deep, 22cm high.

$480 - $520   **Reflections, NSW**

Black and white 'Homemaker' plate by Ridgways, c1950, 25cm diameter.

$40 - $50   **Vintage Living, ACT**

Beautiful understated Royal Dux figure of a seated female, c1950, 25cm long, 15cm high.

$145 - $165   **Fyshwick Antique Centre, ACT**

Royal Dux model of a peacock, c1970, 7.5cm deep, 25cm wide, 18cm high.

$170 - $190   **Galeria del Centro, NSW**

Lifelike Royal Dux figure of a kookaburra, c1980, 18cm wide, 30cm high.

NZ$580 - $680   **Colonial Antiques, New Zealand**

Royal Dux figural group, 30cm high.

$650 - $750   **Paddington Antique Centre Pty Ltd, QLD**

Royal Dux model of a lion, c1950, 24cm long, 6cm deep, 12cm high.

$140 - $170   **Sherwood Bazaar, QLD**

Royal Dux hand painted Venetian carnival group, in rouge colour, c1945, 30cm wide, 47.5cm high.

$4800 - $5200   **Barry McKay, NSW**

Royal Dux white figurine of an owl with pink triangle mark to base, 36cm high.

$480 - $520   **Hamilton Street Antiques, VIC**

Hollinshad & Kirkham Tunstall 'Homestead' set of three jugs, c1950.

$185 - $205   **Yanda Aboriginal Art Melbourne, VIC**

Royal Dux figurine of a nude lady, c1960, 22cm high.

NZ$720 - $770   **Tinakori Antiques, New Zealand**

Royal Dux hand painted and gilded two handled vase, c1980, 12cm long, 30cm high.

$400 - $435   **Antiques & Collectables Centre - Ballarat, VIC**

Large H. K. Tunstall hand painted bowl, 'Viola' pattern, c1950, 85cm deep, 200cm diameter.

$255 - $295   **Old World Antiques, SA**

Tunstall lustre jug with gold decoration by J. Fryer & Sons, 17cm high.

$135 - $155   **Timeless Treasures, WA**

Handpainted Villeroy and Boch ceramic tile, c1950, 15cm wide, 15cm high.

$45 - $65   **Retro Active, VIC**

Pair of 'Acapulco' serving dishes by Villeroy & Boch, Luxembourg, c1960, 37cm long.

$185 - $205   **Found Objects, VIC**

Villeroy & Boch scarlet vegetable dish, 13cm high, 27cm diameter.

$90 - $110   **Cool & Collected, SA**

Zsolnay green Eosin polar bears, c1990, 19cm long, 13cm high.

NZ$330 - $370   **Antiques On Victoria, New Zealand**

Ceramic wall mount Scottie dog head.

$110 - $125   **Munro's Mill Antique Centre, NSW**

Large German porcelain match striker featuring well modelled pigs in a car, 13cm wide, 9cm high.

$185 - $205   **Shop 7, Centenary Antique Centre, NSW**

Ceramic polar bear by Bretby, natural clay colour, stamped to base, 28cm wide, 40cm high.

$600 - $700   **Tarlo & Graham, VIC**

Set of three flying swallows for wall mounting, c1950, 18cm long.

$110 - $130   **Shop 17, Centenary Antique Centre, NSW**

Zsolnay model of an elephant, c1990, 10cm long, 7cm high.

NZ$125 - $145   **Antiques On Victoria, New Zealand**

Russian art pottery stylised giraffe, marked to base 'Made in USSR', c1960, 25cm high.

NZ$100 - $130   **Peachgrove Antiques, New Zealand**

Branksome soup dish, plate and jug with green lid and fawn body. Branksome Ceramics Ltd. in Bournemouth, was founded by two workers from Poole Pottery, c1950, 26cm long, 15cm high.

NZ$60 - $80

Casa Manana Antiques & Collectables, New Zealand

Upsala Ekeby, Sweden, ceramic bowl by Goran Andersson, c1960, 21cm wide.

$40 - $60

frhapsody, WA

Amphora hand painted grape design bowl, c1920, 15cm long, 10.5cm high.

$360 - $400

Bendigo Antique Centre, VIC

Art pottery bowl in black and gold, c1960, 19cm long, 29cm deep, 11cm high.

$90 - $110

Obsidian Antiques, NSW

Stanley rose patterned cup and saucer, c1953, 10cm wide, 6cm high.

$55 - $75

Helen's On The Bay, QLD

French strawberry dish, c1950, 23cm long, 13cm wide, 5cm high.

NZ$480 - $520

Antiques On Victoria, New Zealand

Portmerion 'Phoenix' coffee set, comprising coffee pot, six cups and saucers, jug and sugar basin, designed by John Cuffley, c1960.

NZ$275 - $315

Moa Extinct Stuff, New Zealand

Lustre ware basket by Arthur Wood, c1945, 27cm wide, 19cm high.

$225 - $265

Goodwood House Antiques, WA

Thirteen piece Winterling bone china coffee set, transfer pattern, c1960.

$145 - $165

Chapel Street Bazaar, VIC

Continental vase with floral decoration, c1940, 14cm long, 20cm high.

$60 - $70

Pendulum Antiques, SA

Set of six Calypso pattern trios by Kathie Winkle for Broadhurst, printed and hand painted, c1960.

$300 - $340

frhapsody, WA

Dresden china chocolate cup and saucer with cover, handpainted gilded decoration, 13cm wide, 9cm high.

$240 - $280

Antiques At Birkenhead, NSW

Humorous ceramic figural group by Capodimonte signed by artist 'Defenel', c1970, 26cm wide, 29cm high.

$255 - $295

Glenelg Antique Centre, SA

Paragon figurine of 'Lady Ursula', 18cm high.

NZ$270 - $310

Kelmscott House Antiques, New Zealand

Thomas German dinner set comprising four dinner plates, four bread and butter plates, four entrée plates and four saucers with four soup bowls, c1960.

$200 - $240

Tarlo & Graham, VIC

Hollahaza porcelain girl, kneeling figure in mauve dress, 10cm deep, 10cm wide, 19cm high.

$220 - $260

Yarra Valley Antique Centre, VIC

Art Deco lady figurine, c1940, 15cm long, 30cm high.

$400 - $435

Shenton Park Antiques, WA

A figure designed by Kevin Francis in the 'Pyjama Girl' pattern, limited edition 111/1500, c1998, 22cm high.

$800 - $900

Decodence Collectables, VIC

Paragon fine china figurine of Lady Isobel, c1949, 19cm high.

$200 - $300

Old Bank Antiques, NSW

Schaubach Kunst German figurine 'Girl on Horse', c1955, 22cm wide, 30cm high.

NZ$640 - $740

Country Charm Antiques, New Zealand

Paragon figure of 'Lady Melanie' produced in 1952, 17.5cm high.

$340 - $370

Elizabeth Antiques, NSW

Figure of a Ballerina by Veb Hallendorf, c1964, 20cm wide, 16cm high.

$310 - $350

Furniture Revisited, VIC

Art Deco studio pottery jug, 9cm long, 28cm high.

$50 - $70   **Old Grainstore Antique Market, VIC**

Royal Stanley Jacobean jug, c1960, 17cm wide, 13cm high.

NZ$310 - $350   **Oxford Court Antiques Centre, New Zealandz**

Tall blue amphora water jug, c1950, 28cm high, 14cm diameter.

$275 - $315   **Arleston Antiques, VIC**

Jug and basin set with green floral decoration.

$175 - $195   **Roger Hose Antiques, QLD**

Amphora styled 'Grape and Leaf' pattern squat water jug, c1950, 16.5cm high, 16.5cm diameter.

$310 - $350   **Arleston Antiques, VIC**

Hand decorated Italian drink set, Baldelli, Litia Di Castello, Italy, c1950, 17cm high.

$310 - $350   **Found Objects, VIC**

English 'Trianon Ware' jug and sugar bowl, c1960, 17cm high.

$50 - $80   **Old Grainstore Antique Market, VIC**

Art Deco Toronto jug, handpainted red, yellow and green, signed, 14cm wide, 16cm high.

$110 - $130   **Roger Hose Antiques, QLD**

Retro ceramic centrepiece jug, c1970, 35cm high.

$115 - $135   **Helen's On The Bay, QLD**

Lancaster and Sandland mug of 'Sairey Gamp and Weller' with a lamp post handle and the underside impressed with Mr Weller in stocks, c1949, 11cm deep, 14cm wide, 12cm high.

$155 - $175   **White Park Antiques, SA**

David Winter model of Stratford House, finely modeled and hand painted, c1985, 15cm wide, 12cm high.

$275 - $315   **Glenelg Antique Centre, SA**

Moorland wall plaque head of a lady, Art Deco style, c1995, 19cm high.

$85 - $105   **Decodence Collectables, VIC**

Figgjo, Turi design 'Daisy' pattern casserole dish, c1969, 22.5cm wide.

$55 - $75   **frhapsody, WA**

Egg-shaped Fornasetti paperweight with original Milano sticker on underside. Porcelain with transfer glaze of Greco-Roman bust, purchased from the estate of Australian actor Frank Thring, c1950, 10cm long, 7cm wide, 4cm high.

$275 - $315   **Chapel Street Bazaar, VIC**

Pair of French porcelain ice pails, hand painted with battle and coast scenes, 20cm high.

$920 - $970   **Chilton's Antiques & Jewellery, NSW**

French porcelain dog shaped knife rests, c1950.

$205 - $245   **Antiques On Consignment, NSW**

Italian lidded vessel, manufactured by Mancioli, Italy, a lidded vessel in the form of a fantastical female form with a cap, c1950, 30cm high.

$150 - $170   **506070, NSW**

Ceramic flatback ornament in the 'Red Dancer' pattern, from the Brian Wood Collection, limited edition 20/100, c1998, 24cm high.

$550 - $650   **Decodence Collectables, VIC**

Czechoslovakian ceramic bookends, c1950, 12cm wide, 15cm high.

$255 - $295   **Antique Centre of Stonnington, VIC**

Set of eight Gerz beakers with relief pattern, West German backstamps, c1960, 10.5cm high.

$90 - $110   **frhapsody, WA**

Ceramic water fountain with brass tap, white with red and gold banding, 33cm long, 35cm high.

$250 - $300   **Old Bank Antiques, NSW**

Paragon cabinet plate, heavily gilded edges and border with floral arrangement in centre, c1952, 27cm diameter.

$200 - $240 — **Helen's On The Bay, QLD**

Quimper plate, back stamp Henriot Quimper France 1972, c1972, 22cm diameter.

$85 - $105 — **Antiques & Collectables Centre - Ballarat, VIC**

Paragon cabinet plate with heavily gilded edges and border with floral arrangement in centre, c1952, 27cm diameter.

$200 - $240 — **Helen's On The Bay, QLD**

French Longwy plate with abstract floral design and curved ends, c1950, 45.5cm long, 19.5cm wide, 12cm high.

NZ$280 - $320 — **Maxine's Collectibles, New Zealand**

Paragon bone china cabinet plate, c1950, 27cm wide.

$185 - $205 — **Sherwood Bazaar, QLD**

Seven piece Wilkinson's 'Rural Scenes' serving set, c1950.

$150 - $200 — **Yande Meannjin Antiques, QLD**

Earthenware dish made by Upsala - Ekeby, Sweden and hand decorated by Mari Simmulson in 1951, c1950, 21cm long, 21cm deep, 21cm wide.

$200 - $240 — **506070, NSW**

Moorland three piece tea set in the 'N' Lightning design manufactured by Chelsea Works, Burslem, c1995.

$170 - $190 — **Decodence Collectables, VIC**

Tea for two, eight piece set by Salisbury Bone China.

$100 - $150 — **Things 4 U, NSW**

James Kent 'La Rosa' breakfast set for one.

$450 - $490 — **Woodside Bazaar, SA**

BCM Nelson Ware teapot in the 'Lavender Lady' pattern, c1950, 14cm long, 15cm deep, 12cm high.

$340 - $380 — **Southside Antiques Centre, QLD**

Tuscan tea set of fourteen pieces, soft pink background with gold pattern and pink rosebuds, c1960.

$200 - $240

Helen's On The Bay, QLD

Hand painted Egyptian teapot depicting the Sphinx, maker Tony Wood, c1950, 11cm deep, 25cm wide, 16cm high.

$310 - $350

Urbanized, VIC

Price Kensington teapot in the form of an old red mail box, painted red upper half with painted black lower section, marked on base, 'P & K, Made in England', 23cm wide, 25cm high.

$165 - $185

Bower Bird Art & Antiques, QLD

Gibsons octagonal 'Paisley' pattern tea pot, six cup size, registered mark on base, c1920, 16.5cm wide, 14cm high.

$175 - $195

Hamilton Street Antiques, VIC

'Luck and Flan' Maggie Thatcher political cartoon teapot, c1980, 13cm deep, 29cm wide, 21cm high.

$310 - $350

Southside Antiques Centre, QLD

Midwinter Stylecraft 'Red Domino' design teapot by Jessie Tait, c1950, 22cm long, 13cm wide, 13cm high.

$255 - $295

Retro Active, VIC

British Orcadia Ware vase made in Wadenheath, 18cm high, 13cm diameter.

$125 - $145

Home Again, NSW

Polish porcelain vase by Wausel, c1950.

$220 - $260

Found Objects, VIC

Troika square shaped vase, signed 'A. J.', c1960, 6.5cm long, 6.5cm wide, 9cm high.

NZ$310 - $350

Banks Peninsula Antiques, New Zealand

Troika 'Coffin' vase, signed 'C.F', c1950, 18cm high.

NZ$380 - $420

Banks Peninsula Antiques, New Zealand

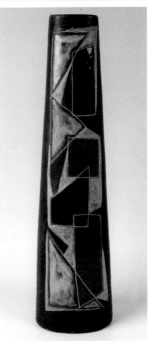

Italian ceramic vase by Marcello Fantoni, c1950.

$1200 - $1400

Gallery Narcisse, NSW

Pair of Paris lidded Medici porcelain vases on square bases with scrolled handles, gilded with a hand painted front panel of a deer in a forest setting and signed by J. Missant, c1950, 23cm long, 48cm high.

$2400 - $2550   **Mentone Beach Antiques Centre, VIC**

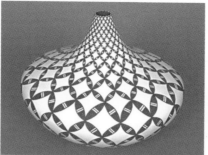

Contemporary Acoma potter Dorothy Torivio vase with a fine black and white geometric design.

$9300 - $9600   **Four Winds Gallery, NSW**

Pair of hand painted lidded urns in Paris porcelain and signed 'J. Missant', c1950, 23cm wide, 47cm high, 15cm diameter.

$2400 - $2600   **Mentone Beach Antiques Centre, VIC**

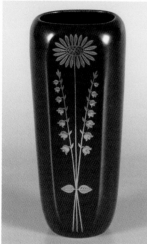

Swedish Gustavberg stoneware and silver inlay vase, Stig Linaberg designer, c1950, 6cm deep, 8cm wide, 19cm high.

$850 - $950   **Antiques & Collectables Centre - Ballarat, VIC**

Pair of Italian ceramic vases with hand decorated underglaze, c1950, 30cm high.

$310 - $350   **Found Objects, VIC**

Carl-Harry Stalhane designed superb blue turquoise glazed vases for Rorstrand, Sweden, the undersides with an incised 'R' surrounded by three crowns, c1950, 12cm high.

$720 - $820   **Kilbarron Antiques and Collectables, VIC**

A vase, in the shape of a woman's head and shoulders, wearing a high collar, c1950, 15cm high.

$275 - $315   **Days of Olde Antiques & Collectables, VIC**

Hand painted lady head vase, c1950, 7.5cm long, 5cm deep, 13cm high.

$170 - $190   **Old King Cole Antiques, NSW**

Hand painted lady head vase, c1950, 10cm long, 17cm high.

$400 - $450   **Home Again, NSW**

Gilded and hand painted amphora vase with two handles, 12cm long, 21cm high.

$350 - $400   **Timeworn Old Wares & Collectables, NSW**

Amphora twin handled vase, c1940, 14cm long, 15cm high.

$140 - $170   **Bendigo Antique Centre, VIC**

Continental K.P.M. glazed vase with floral decoration, c1940, 29cm high, 12.5cm diameter.

$160 - $190   **Pendulum Antiques, SA**

H. A. Kahler stoneware vase decorated in green and brown with stylised fruits and foliage, incised HAK monogram, c1950, 18cm high.

$300 - $340   **Vintage Living, ACT**

Mens 1970's clothing outfit, never worn, comprising pants, shirt, waistcoat, jacket, belt and hat, c1970.

$300 - $340   **The Wool Exchange Geelong, VIC**

Mens 60's-70's Bisley body shirt, in stretch polyester photo print, c1965.

$40 - $60   **River Emporium, NSW**

Strapless ball gown with chartreuse taffeta, black lace and satin. Approximate size 10, no labels, professionally made, c1954.

$280 - $320   **Circa Vintage Clothing, VIC**

Bronze tafetta opera coat with puffed sleeves, size up to 18, professionally made, c1957.

$215 - $255   **Circa Vintage Clothing, VIC**

Pink and green silk dress by Emilio Pucci, approximate size 10-12 (label marked as 16), c1967.

$430 - $470   **Circa Vintage Clothing, VIC**

Black crepe dinner dress, c1950.

NZ$50 - $70   **Country Charm Antiques, New Zealand**

Mens 60's-70's French theme polyester picture shirt, 'Autumn in Paris', Tres Cool, c1965.

$60 - $80   **River Emporium, NSW**

CLOTHING

Cotton shirt by Golden Gate, Sydney, light pink with hot pink bands on sleeves and bottom, and four figures of women in different 1950s clothing, three buttons half way down, c1950.

$90 - $110 **Decades of Fashion, VIC**

Turquoise long gown, with Georgian styling, all rayon XSSW (8) with embroidered bodice, 'Paton Original Melbourne', c1960.

$150 - $170 **Gorgeous, VIC**

Pleated cotton print peasant dress with floral design, size 10, c1973.

$55 - $75 **Gorgeous, VIC**

Beaded top by 'The Lion Knitters', marked 'Made in the British Empire' size 42 (14-16) beaded and sequined top with pearl dropped fringe, c1950.

$70 - $90 **Decades of Fashion, VIC**

Stunning floor length early 1970's gown, unique Art Nouveau print on satin finish, rouching baby doll upper. Size 10-12, c1970.

$100 - $120 **Shappere, VIC**

Electric blue coat dress and belt, in a floral print, Rayon fabric, manufactured by Luana Modes, Melbourne, c1966.

$215 - $255 **Circa Vintage Clothing, VIC**

Burgundy belted dress with sequin trim, c1950.

NZ$60 - $80 **Country Charm Antiques, New Zealand**

Dull gold satin grograin ball gown, a Du Hill original with gathered skirt detail, size 10, c1950.

$275 - $315 **Shag, VIC**

Full length Musquash coat, with lining, approximately size 12, c1930.

NZ$185 - $205 **In Vogue Costumes & Collectables, New Zealand**

Fuzzy wuzzy pink mohair cardigan with pink glass buttons, hand made size 10, c1950.

$40 - $60 **Decades of Fashion, VIC**

Hand made sequined and beaded cocktail dress, size 8, c1970.

$140 - $160 **Decades of Fashion, VIC**

Green velvet dress, Belvera Fashions, c1950.

$185 - $205   **Shop 32, Mittagong Antiques Centre, NSW**

Bronze, silver and grey shortened dress by Grantheums, made from silk and miracle viscose, size 16 (now 12), c1970.

$110 - $130   **Decades of Fashion, VIC**

Vintage hand made mauve dress with chiffon skirt, approximately size 10, c1960.

$65 - $85   **Kenny's Antiques, VIC**

Hand made black rayon dress with large collar and skin of layers of scales on mesh, c1950.

$70 - $90   **Decades of Fashion, VIC**

Blue wool cardigan made by Leedall, pure wool, size 12, c1955.

$40 - $60   **Gorgeous, VIC**

Blonde, well detailed mink jacket with the 'SAGA' label, selected mink from Scandinavia, original length, good detail, c1950.

NZ$550 - $650   **In Vogue Costumes & Collectables, New Zealand**

Long red fox fur shoulder cape, deep back, c1930.

NZ$330 - $370   **In Vogue Costumes & Collectables, New Zealand**

Pink floral kaftan dress with pleats by 'Habe Garments' Sydney, made with polyester satin, size 12, c1960.

$230 - $270   **Gorgeous, VIC**

Speedo black, white and floral long beach dress, light nylon Speedo fabric, c1975, 140cm long.

$700 - $800   **Gorgeous, VIC**

Sheer floral dress made by Danielle D'Amie, polyester chiffon, size 10, c1970.

$65 - $85   **Gorgeous, VIC**

Green wool mohair cape, size 12-16 made by John Crowther, England, sold by Kon Tiki in Melbourne.

$70 - $90   **Decades of Fashion, VIC**

COSTUME & DRESSING ACCESSORIES

Retro skirt, taffeta stripes, grey background with primary coloured multi-stripe, size 12, full flare, designer Nelly de Grab, New York, USA, c1950.

NZ$115 - $135   **Waterfords of Mangaweka Village, New Zealand**

Fine quality, intricately beaded dress, hand made, c1960.

$130 - $150   **Kenny's Antiques, VIC**

Cotton party dress with gold paint, styled by Campua Fashions size SSW (10), c1950.

$110 - $130   **Decades of Fashion, VIC**

Floral kaftan dress by 'Allen Gar' Melbourne, made with poliammide, size 14, c1960.

$265 - $305   **Gorgeous, VIC**

Mint green hand made beaded dress, designed as a stage costume, c1960.

$70 - $90   **Kenny's Antiques, VIC**

Full length, lined dress with exaggerated bat wing sleeves, by 'Madmoiselle' of England, size 16, maker's paper tag with pencil notes sewn into lining, c1968, 147cm high.

$190 - $210   **frhapsody, WA**

Rayon, lace and chiffon evening dress by Patou originals, Melbourne, size SSW (10), c1960.

$70 - $90   **Decades of Fashion, VIC**

Floral paisley print mod dress by 'Gulp', size 10.

$110 - $130   **Gorgeous, VIC**

Daisy print bathing suit, by 'Jantzen Australia', made with cotton, size 8, c1950.

$80 -$100   **Gorgeous, VIC**

Silk fully lined robe, mutli stripe, black satin reveres and cuffs, satin lining, c1950.

NZ$75 - $95   **Waterfords of Mangaweka Village, New Zealand.**

Gold metallic swim suit by 'Corals', adjustable, made with cotton straps and zip, size 14, c1950.

$140 - $160   **Gorgeous, VIC**

Nylon floral print day dress, c1950.

$70 - $90   **Decades of Fashion, VIC**

Gypsy style blue pure wool Prue Acton dress, size 12, measuring bust 85cm, waist 65cm and hips 90cm, with gold metallic braid, glass buttons, ribbon trimmings and patterned sleeves, c1970.

$90 - $110   **Decades of Fashion, VIC**

Blue and white cotton damask day dress with short sleeves and pleated neckline, approximate size 8, no label, homemade, c1956.

$65 - $85   **Circa Vintage Clothing, VIC**

J.M. Martin coral flocked nylon party dress, size 8-10, c1960.

$220 - $260   **Adornments, QLD**

Pale brown fox fur Art Deco cape, c1930.

NZ$180 - $200   **In Vogue Costumes & Collectables, New Zealand**

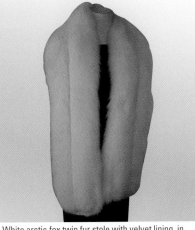

White arctic fox twin fur stole with velvet lining, in mint condition, c1940.

NZ$500 - $600   **In Vogue Costumes & Collectables, New Zealand**

Tulle and tafetta prom dress with appliqued flowers and rhinestones, approximate size 8, bust 82cm, waist 60cm, skirt length 86cm, no label, c1954.

$265 - $305   **Circa Vintage Clothing, VIC**

Red and white candy striped silk shirt with cufflink sleeves, made by 'Renato Nucci' Paris, size 12, c1980.

$40 - $60   **Gorgeous, VIC**

Pink silk cocktail or evening suit with beaded pockets, hand-tailored by Destination Fashions (size 8), c1952.

$170 - $190   **The Botanic Ark, VIC**

Empireline 60's evening dress in William Morris brocade and velvet, size 12, c1967.

$170 - $190   **The Botanic Ark, VIC**

Green silk organza and taffeta dress with pleated and ruched bodice, approximate size 14, styled by Camille Lee of Melbourne, c1954.

$140 - $160   **Circa Vintage Clothing, VIC**

CLOTHING

Wool kaftan dress, design incorporating green apples and multi coloured flowers, from 'The Opera Collection', designer John J. Hilton, c1970, 150cm long, 15cm wide.

$140 - $160

Gorgeous, VIC

'Laura Ashley' 1970's floor length 100% cotton peasant style dress, size 12, c1970.

$75 - $95

Shappere, VIC

Lace, size 10 wedding dress with mutton chop sleeves, veil, pettycoat and original box, c1929.

$500 - $600

Shaws Antiques, NSW

Khaki wool dress with pearl and gold beading, Rondel's, c1960.

$275 - $315

Shop 32, Mittagong Antiques Centre, NSW

House of Merivale red crepe dress in a 1930's style with satin inset, size 8. House of Merivale style W58, colour 2/W4, c1972.

$330 - $370

Circa Vintage Clothing, VIC

Lace dress with ribbon waist tie and embroidered lace insert around neck, c1980.

$40 - $60

Kenny's Antiques, VIC

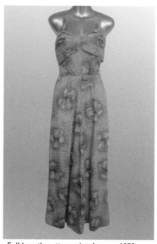

Full length cotton print dress, c1950.

NZ$70 - $110

In Vogue Costumes & Collectables, NZ

Crocheted black and red wool trouser suit, c1960.

NZ$110 - $130

Banks Peninsula Antiques, New Zealand

Black chiffon and lace dress, no label, size 10, c1970.

$190 - $210

Gorgeous, VIC

Lady's two piece 1950's grey ribbed wool suit, approximate size 12-14, c1955.

$175 - $195

Circa Vintage Clothing, VIC

Red, cream and black wool swing coat with burgundy quilted velvet details, c1972.

$330 - $370

Circa Vintage Clothing, VIC

William Drummond & Co 1930's shagreen make-up case with original containers, c1930, 25cm long, 14cm deep, 6cm high.

$480 - $520

De Mille, VIC

Early gold plated manicure set in leather case, 17cm deep, 24cm wide, 10cm high.

$140 - $160

Shop 15, Antiques & Collectables - Hamilton, NSW

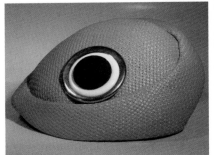

Vintage hat by 'Mr. Individual' of Melbourne, c1960, 78cm diameter.

$65 - $85

frhapsody, WA

Vintage felt and ribbon hat by Robit of Sydney, c1960, 78cm diameter.

$65 - $85

frhapsody, WA

Ladie's musical manicure set, c1900, 20cm long, 24cm wide.

$540 - $640

Angel's Antiques, VIC

Sterling silver ladies belt with buckle and eight sections, hallmarked London 190.

$800 - $835

Rutherford Fine Jewellery & Antique Silver, VIC

Czech glass button with a metal shank, dragon fly decoration, c1980, 3.5cm diameter.

$20 - $30

Buttons Buttons Buttons, NSW

Solid hide overnight bag, made in NSW, c1950.

$140 - $160

Bob & Dot's Antiques & Old Wares, NSW

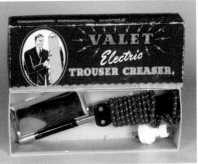

Electric trouser creaser in box, made by 'Reliance', c1950.

$55 - $75

Kingston Antiques, VIC

Pair of authentic Louis Vuition suitcases, c1960.

$1350 - $1550

Barry McKay, NSW

Various plastic belt buckles, priced per item, c1950, 7cm long, 0.5cm deep, 4cm wide, 7cm high.

$14 - $24

Dr Russell's Emporium, WA

HANDBAGS & PURSES

Multi coloured carnival patterned velvet hand bag, c1960, 18cm long, 10cm wide, 15cm high.

$50 - $70 **The New Farm Antique Centre, QLD**

White wicker tourist bag with destination plates, Stylecraft, Miami, c1950, 33cm long, 25cm high.

$160 - $180 **Shag, VIC**

White beaded purse.

$20 - $30 **Paddington Antique Centre Pty Ltd, QLD**

Magnificent shopping bag made from white hessian with velvet flowers, c1960.

$165 - $185 **Chapel Street Bazaar, VIC**

Suede leather hand bag, c1940.

$65 - $85 **Coming of Age Antiques, QLD**

Lucite

Lucite was invented in 1931 by chemists at DuPont. It was crystal clear, resistant to water and UV rays, and was low density yet stronger than previous plastics.

Like Bakelite, Lucite was used extensively in war supplies during WWII.

After the war, the plastics were used for jewellery and other items. Lucite rings were highly popular during the '50s and '60s, as were Lucite handbags.

In 1993, DuPont sold its acrylic resin operations, and the Lucite name now belongs to Lucite International in Southampton, UK.

Rialto lucite handbag c1950, 20cm long, 10cm deep, 10cm high.

$330 - $370 **Chapel Street Bazaar, VIC**

Clear lucite purse from USA, studded with diamante and a huge diamante clasp, c1950, 18cm long, 18cm deep, 4cm wide.

$140 - $160 **Rosebud Antiques, NSW**

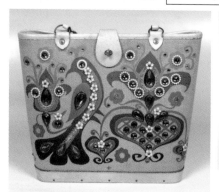

Enid Collins 'Hearts & Flowers' handbag with decorative shopper leather trim, hand painted Hessian and jewels, c1966, 30cm wide, 27cm high.

$60 - $80 **Chapel Street Bazaar, VIC**

Leather handbag with bagpipes motif, by Mantra Manufacturing, Sydney, 15cm deep, 26cm wide, 17cm high.

$55 - $75 **Shop 15, Antiques & Collectables - Hamilton, NSW**

Enid Collins leather and woven bag, with 'Roadrunner' clasp, c1960, 33cm long, 10cm deep, 20cm high.

$70 - $90 **Chapel Street Bazaar, VIC**

Original Lucite purse, 20cm long, 14cm wide.

$310 - $350

Curio Retro, NSW

Original Lucite purse, 17cm long, 10cm wide.

$310 - $350

Curio Retro, NSW

White and silver glass beaded handbag, c1960, 28cm long, 15cm wide.

$65 - $85

Northumberland Antiques & Restorations, NSW

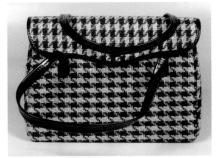

Houndstooth patterned woollen handbag with leather trim and straps, c1960, 33cm wide, 27cm high.

$85 - $105

Chapel Street Bazaar, VIC

Black lucite bag with chevron detail and gold insert, c1955.

NZ$50 - $70

In Vogue Costumes & Collectables, New Zealand

Coffee hessian dilly bag with shell applique, c1950, 25cm wide, 28cm high.

$40 - $60

Shag, VIC

Grain hide Australian handbag, including coin purse, c1960, 18cm wide, 15cm high.

$45 - $65

Southside Antiques Centre, QLD

Snakeskin handbag, c1955.

$200 - $240

Circa Vintage Clothing, VIC

Embroidered bag, wooden bottom canvas top, 'Enid Collins' Texas, c1950, 34cm wide, 21cm high.

$260 - $300

Gorgeous, VIC

Woven metal and lucite box bag, c1950, 23cm long, 8.5cm wide, 8cm high.

NZ$225 - $265

Deborah's Antiques, New Zealand

Clutch purse in black silk with white beaded and diamante trim, c1950.

NZ$30 - $60

In Vogue Costumes & Collectables, New Zealand

COSTUME & DRESSING ACCESSORIES

Oroton

Oroton mesh purses are prized by collectors and prices have risen as a result of increased demand.

Oroton commenced production in the late 1920's in Western Germany, reaching the peak of their mesh production in the 1970's with the supply of a whole range of purses and fashion accessories such as lipstick covers, compacts, glasses, cigarette cases, mesh belts and scarves.

The gold and silver mesh are the fashion, however there are bargains to be had in the coloured mesh range which are presently well undervalued and a good boxed item in excellent condition can still be found for under $40.

Oroton's major competitor is the United States company of Whiting and Davis. Their mesh bags are extremely collectable in the U.S.A. and their older vintages are more readily available in the South Pacific than Oroton due to the intervention of the war years in Europe.

Another notable manufacturer is Glomesh and more recently Sterling Mesh, both Australian companies which have gained a foothold in later years with coloured mesh being one of their most popular lines.

Look out for top condition examples of Oroton's early 1970's range of diamante gold and silver handbags as future heirlooms. Be aware of Chinese copies of mesh purses unless its an early example. If it doesn't have a clear indication of the maker, its probably a copy.

Oroton gold metal diamante evening bag, boxed, c1970.

NZ$310 - $350 — In Vogue Costumes & Collectables, New Zealand

Tan ostrich leather handbag by Riviera Bags, made in England, c1960, 25cm long, 20cm high.

$85 - $105 — Shag, VIC

Coroneite ruby red patent leather handbag, c1950.

$90 - $110 — Shop 32, Mittagong Antiques Centre, NSW

Dark blue handbag, blue silk lining and chased metal clasp with purse, Art Deco style.

NZ$60 - $80 — In Vogue Costumes & Collectables, New Zealand

Beaded multi colour handbag, c1950.

$185 - $205 — Shop 32, Mittagong Antiques Centre, NSW

Butter yellow lizard skin bag with calf skin lining, made by H. Stevens Pty Ltd, c1950, 29cm long, 9cm deep, 19cm high.

$135 - $155 — Northside Secondhand Furniture, QLD

Silver and grey crystal beaded bag with envelope top, c1940.

NZ$40 - $60 — In Vogue Costumes & Collectables, New Zealand

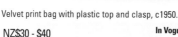
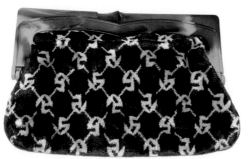

Silver mesh purse, 24cm long.

$140 - $160 — Paddington Antique Centre Pty Ltd, QLD

Velvet print bag with plastic top and clasp, c1950.

NZ$30 - $40 — In Vogue Costumes & Collectables, New Zealand

Hallmarked sterling silver mesh evening purse with original red silk lining.

NZ$275 - $315 — In Vogue Costumes & Collectables, New Zealand

Brown shaped felt hat with mink fur band by 'Mister of Melbourne', c1950.

$35 - $45   **Decades of Fashion, VIC**

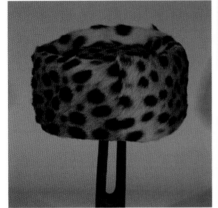

Art Deco design Cheetah hat, c1950.

$650 - $750   **Woollahra Decorative Arts Gallery, NSW**

Bottle green felt hat, c1950.

$45 - $65   **Shop 32, Mittagong Antiques Centre, NSW**

Black shaped stiffened felt hat with diamante brooch, c1945.

$35 - $45   **Decades of Fashion, VIC**

Arctic fox and flock hat.

$85 - $105   **Shop 32, Mittagong Antiques Centre, NSW**

Brown Akubra hat, c1960.

$23 - $33   **Paddington Antique Centre Pty Ltd, QLD**

Lady's brown fur felt with gros grain band marked 'Janifer' made in England, c1950.

$100 - $120   **Baxter's Antiques, QLD**

Red chenile hat with velvet crown, c1950.

NZ$20 - $30   **Country Charm Antiques, New Zealand**

Blue and white hat.

$45 - $65   **Shop 32, Mittagong Antiques Centre, NSW**

New grey felt hat branded Dobbs Fifth Avenue New York, retailed by McLeods Men's Wear, Brisbane and Rockhampton, size 7 1/8, c1960.

$100 - $120   **Baxter's Antiques, QLD**

Green cocktail hat with black rose trim.

NZ$50 - $70   **Country Charm Antiques, New Zealand**

Pair of shoes manufactured by Charles Jourdan, c1960.

$40 - $60

**Southside Antiques Centre,
QLD**

Brown leather shoes with genuine crocodile buckle detail, c1955.

$40 - $60

**Womango,
VIC**

Embroidered lurex round toe chock heel shoes by 'Betta Australia', size 6 1/2, c1950.

$40 - $60

**Shappere,
VIC**

Aqua suede heeled wedge shoes with studded detail over toe, size 7, c1970.

$40 - $60

**Shappere,
VIC**

Flat suede over-the-knee slouch boots, multi coloured panels separated by a zip detail, size 7-8, made by Taxi, c1980.

$185 - $205

**Shappere,
VIC**

Pair of blue leather knee high go go boots with red heels and platform, size 5 1/2, c1960.

NZ$190 - $210

**Banks Peninsula Antiques,
New Zealand**

Zodiac fab brown soft leather tall boots, steel cap on toe, wooden heel, size 6M, c1970.

$220 - $260

**Shappere,
VIC**

Metallic blue square toe ladies' shoes with brogue style detailing, c1965.

$90 - $110

**Shag,
VIC**

Silver leather court shoes with clear acrylic cage heel studded with rhinestones, unusual heel design, size 6, c1965.

$120 - $140

**Shag,
VIC**

Texas made leather cowboy boots depicting an eagle motif on the front, size 10.5.

$205 - $245

**The Bottom Drawer Antique Centre,
VIC**

French shoes, never worn, black and white leather with snaffle front, size 7.

$120 - $140

**Shag,
VIC**

Blue and white two tone reflective sunglasses, c1970.

$25 - $35

Bowhows,
NSW

Vintage French sunglasses with pale pink plastic frames and asymmetrical 'Petit Fleurs', c1950.

$115 - $135

Retro Active,
VIC

Vintage Ray Ban sunglasses with original case, by Bausch & Lomb, c1950.

$55 - $75

Antipodes Antiques,
QLD

French designer Molyneaux striped sunglasses, c1970, 15cm long, 7cm wide.

$50 - $70

Shag,
VIC

Pair of sunglasses in check pattern, oval plastic frames, c1960.

$135 - $155

Curio Retro,
NSW

Pair of white plastic octagonal framed sunglasses, c1960.

$40 - $50

Curio Retro,
NSW

George Bolle sunglasses, green and goldplate, with box, c1950, 12cm long, 12cm deep, 5cm high.

$1600 - $1800

Bowhows,
NSW

Pop sunglasses in red and white plastic, glass lenses, c1960.

$85 - $105

Chapel Street Bazaar,
VIC

Original vintage Ted Lapidus sunglasses, made in France, c1970.

$24 - $34

Fat Helen's,
VIC

Pair of square rimmed green plastic sunglasses, c1960.

$135 - $155

Curio Retro,
NSW

Pair of black plastic sunglasses, fitted with blue UV circular lenses, c1960.

$50 - $70

Curio Retro,
NSW

OTHER

Two butterfly wing objects, one a compact with butterfly wing decoration in a ship motif, the other a silver brooch made with butterfly wing decoration of Dutch children.

$130 - $150

Louisa's Antiques, TAS

Lady's octagonal compact, c1950, 6cm wide.

$115 - $135

Antique Centre of Stonnington, VIC

Lady's compact case in the form of a black satin evening bag, c1945, 13cm long, 3cm deep, 10cm high.

$135 - $155

Rosebud Antiques, NSW

Art Deco powder and rouge compact, complete with powder puff, rouge, powder sifter and finger ring, 5.5cm diameter.

$205 - $245   **Scheherazade Antiques, VIC**

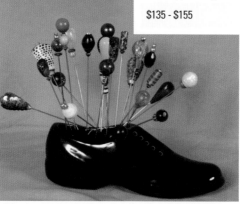

Selection of twenty four large hat pins, circa 1930-1960, 18cm long.

$480 - $580

The New Farm Antique Centre, QLD

Vintage leather kit bag, the locks in working order.

$40 - $60   **Squatters Antiques & Restorations, SA**

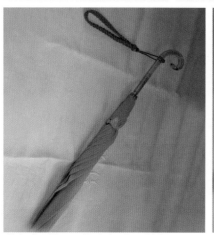

Umbrella with curved lucite handle and nylon cover, c1950.

NZ$30 - $60   **In Vogue Costumes & Collectables, New Zealand**

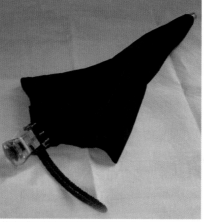

Umbrella with lucite handle, whipped cord handle and nylon cover, c1945.

NZ$55 - $75   **In Vogue Costumes & Collectables, New Zealand**

Three Japanese pagoda cut crystal perfume bottles, c1950.

$40 - $50   **The Botanic Ark, VIC**

Art Deco malachite glass perfume bottle with impressed female faces and flowers and a feather shaped stopper, c1930, 23cm high.

$375 - $415

Wenglen Antiques, NSW

Three perfume flasks and stacking glasses in a leather look case, c1950, 20cm high.

$380 - $420

Antique Centre of Stonnington, VIC

Double cased, red and clear glass scent bottle, signed to base 'Michael Hook', a glass maker from Melbourne, c1990, 9cm deep, 12cm high, 9cm diameter.

$60 - $80

The Junk Company, VIC

Lalique floral perfume bottle, 9cm wide, 9cm high.

$260 - $300

Antique Centre of Stonnington, VIC

Art Deco style Czech perfume bottles, post 1950, with hand cut crystal stoppers, 18cm high.

$480 - $520

Vintage Living, ACT

Belt, intricately beaded in citrus colours, c1965, 6cm wide.

$80 - $100

Shag, VIC

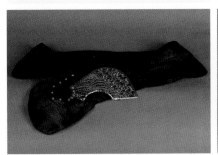

Black leather belt with multi coloured jewelled metal buckle, c1985, 12cm wide.

$40 - $60

Shag, VIC

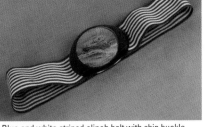

Blue and white striped clinch belt with ship buckle, c1970, 6cm wide.

$30 - $60

Shag, VIC

Black beaded belt on yellow fabric, c1960, 90cm long, 4cm wide.

$30 - $40

Southside Antiques Centre, QLD

Bakelite buckle.

$30 - $40

Southside Antiques Centre, QLD

1920s metal chain belt with Art Nouveau motifs and silver plating, stmped TG silver plated monogram, c1926.

$65 - $85

Circa Vintage Clothing, VIC

Plastic reverse carved brooch, c1940, 3.5cm long, 4cm high.

$40 - $50   **Pedlars Antique Market, SA**

Orange juice Bakelite brooch, c1945, 7.5cm long.

$150 - $170   **Rosebud Antiques, NSW**

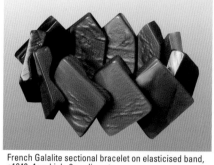

French Galalite sectional bracelet on elasticised band, c1940, 4cm high, 8cm diameter.

$245 - $285   **b bold - 20th Century Furniture & Effects, VIC**

Austrian rhinestone brooch and earring set, c1940, 7.5cm long.

$65 - $85   **Armadale Antique Centre, VIC**

French ivory and Bakelite black and white sectional bracelet, c1940, 3cm high, 8cm diameter.

$240 - $280   **b bold - 20th Century Furniture & Effects, VIC**

French 1940's Bakelite bangle, honeycomb design, c1940, 2.5cm high, 8.5cm diameter.

$200 - $240   **b bold - 20th Century Furniture & Effects, VIC**

Bakelite and lucite figural brooch in the shape of musical instrument with gold card strings, c1945, 10.5cm long, 3.5cm wide.

NZ$205 - $245   **Deborah's Antiques, New Zealand**

Sterling silver marcasite articulated bow brooch, c1940.

$205 - $245   **Costiff Antiques, VIC**

Bakelite and elastic bracelet, c1950.

$120 - $160   **Antique Centre of Stonnington, VIC**

A waterfall effect brooch with texture of crystal, diamantes and pearls set on a plated back with pin. Movement from the individually placed adornments makes it quite individual, 6cm long, 6cm wide.

$90 - $110   **Well Warne, WA**

Plastic brooch of a bird with moving eye, c1950, 3.5cm high.

$5 - $15   **Baimbridge Antiques, VIC**

Plastic brooch of three terrier dogs.

$15 - $25   **Baimbridge Antiques, VIC**

Costume jewellery brooch with large crystal centre surrounded by rhinestones, c1950, 5cm long, 2cm deep, 5cm wide, 5cm high, 5cm diameter.

$65 - $85   **Dr Russell's Emporium, WA**

Fantasy gilt metal horse brooch with blue diamante ears, diamante mane and tail, c1950, 4cm wide, 5cm high.

$35 - $45   **Retro Active, VIC**

Intricate floral design Italian mosaic brooch, gold plated backing, c1950, 3cm long, 3cm wide.

$60 - $80   **Well Warne, WA**

Vintage diamante hair clip made by Simpson, c1950, 9cm long, 2cm wide.

$50 - $70   **Retro Active, VIC**

Post-war aurora crystal brooch of hand soldered construction, c1955, 8.5cm long, 3.5cm wide.

$65 - $85   **Womango, VIC**

Colourful flower brooch and earring set, incorporating pastel paste petals with orange paste centre stone. Brooch has three flowers attached to gold stem, earrings are clip-on. Brooch length: 9cms, width 6.5cms. Earrings: length 3cms, width 3cms, c1950.

$140 - $160   **Well Warne, WA**

Costume jewellery brooch with purple glass stones, c1950, 3cm long, 0.5cm deep, 2cm high.

$40 - $60   **Dr Russell's Emporium, WA**

Large brooch with pale blue diamantes and pink carnival stones, c1959, 6cm long, 5cm wide.

$55 - $75   **The Botanic Ark, VIC**

Simpson original paste brooch and matching earrings, in original box, c1950, 11cm long.

$80 - $100   **Gumnut Antiques & Old Wares, NSW**

Green glass costume jewellery brooch, c1950, 5cm long, 0.5cm deep, 5cm high.

$50 - $70   **Dr Russell's Emporium, WA**

Quality American costume jewellery brooch with blue and green rhinestones, c1955, 7cm wide.

$175 - $195   **Chapel Street Bazaar, VIC**

Celluloid brooch, c1950, 7cm long.

$55 - $75   **Rosebud Antiques, NSW**

1940s & 1950s

Esoteric silver and orange, brown and black four link enamel bracelet by modernist designer Perli, signed, c1950, 18cm long.

$230 - $270   **Chapel Street Bazaar, VIC**

Diamante paste bracelet on silver plate backing with extensions from main strand in a tear drop design, c1950, 18cm long, 3cm wide.

$60 - $80   **Well Warne, WA**

Vintage costume brooch, purple paste, c1950.

$55 - $75   **Shop L21, Mittagong Antiques Centre, NSW**

American diamante bow, with a large centre diamante surrounded by hundreds of smaller stones as petals. Brooch has gold detailing pin across the back and matching clip on earrings. Brooch 11 x 3 cm; earrings 4 x 4 cm, c1950.

$230 - $270   **Well Warne, WA**

American ornate diamante drop down adornments set on a gold link bracelet chain with seven charms in total, shaped like an ice cream cone. American origin, worn as a cocktail style piece, c1950, 19cm long, 2cm wide.

$140 - $160   **Well Warne, WA**

French Lucite bangle, c1950, 7cm deep, 7.5cm wide, 5cm high.

$220 - $260   **b bold - 20th Century Furniture & Effects, VIC**

Lucite and diamante bangle, c1950, 7cm diameter.

$185 - $205   **Rosebud Antiques, NSW**

Paste flower brooch, c1950.

$200 - $240   **Shop L21, Mittagong Antiques Centre, NSW**

Costume jewellery brooch with blue glass stones, c1950, 4cm long, 0.5cm deep, 4cm high.

$40 - $60   **Dr Russell's Emporium, WA**

Stunning blue rhinestone American brooch by 'Arcansas Jewellery', c1955, 6cm diameter.

$155 - $175   **Chapel Street Bazaar, VIC**

Pink lucite rabbit brooch, c1950, 7cm high.

$145 - $165   **Kaleidoscope Antiques, VIC**

French Bakelite carved cat bracelet, c1950.

$145 - $165   **Online Antiques, VIC**

French pop art Bakelite bracelet on elasticised band, c1950, 2cm high, 7cm diameter.

$200 - $240   **b bold - 20th Century Furniture & Effects, VIC**

Aurora crystal rhinestone costume jewellery floral spray brooch, Austrian made, c1955, 8cm wide, 9cm high.

$175 - $195   **Chapel Street Bazaar, VIC**

Marquisite phoenix in foliage brooch, quality marquisite on sterling silver, made in Germany, c1950, 6cm wide, 6cm high.

$230 - $270   **Chapel Street Bazaar, VIC**

Costume brooch decorated with a floral spray multicoloured rhinestones, matching earrings (not photographed), c1950, 10cm wide.

$155 - $175   **Chapel Street Bazaar, VIC**

Clip-on earrings, silver plated settings with light blue diamantes in a flower shape, c1955, 3.5cm diameter.

$50 - $70   **The Botanic Ark, VIC**

Vintage bead clip on earrings with large centre bead and five beaded drops hanging from the centre, c1950, 10cm long.

$25 - $35   **Kenny's Antiques, VIC**

Art Deco style, faux onyx and rhinestone drop earrings, c1950.

$65 - $85   **Antique Centre of Stonnington, VIC**

Clip on earrings made from an early plastic, c1950, 5cm long.

$20 - $30   **Kenny's Antiques, VIC**

Pair of West German clip-on orange lucite earrings, c1950.

$5 - $15   **Savers, VIC**

Pair of clip-on loop earrings, c1950.

$30 - $40   **Rosebud Antiques, NSW**

White plastic and diamante necklace and earrings, c1950.

NZ$115 - $135   **Deborah's Antiques, New Zealand**

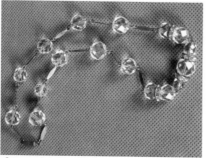

Cut crystal choker with diamante rondells, white metal links, c1950, 42cm long.

$65 - $85   **Womango, VIC**

Diamante and faux cabochan ruby coloured rhinestones with faux grey pearls and leaves, c1952.

$430 - $470   **Chapel Street Bazaar, VIC**

Double strand choker, vintage Venetian pale blue glass beads with silver foil, c1950, 40cm long.

$275 - $315   **Retro Active, VIC**

Two colourful plastic bead necklaces, c1950, 25cm long.

$40 - $60   **Towers Antiques & Collectables, NSW**

Chain and bakelite necklace, c1950, 10cm long.

$260 - $300   **Rosebud Antiques, NSW**

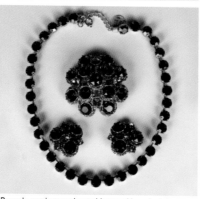

Blue and white diamante necklace, c1953, 38cm long.

$50 - $70   **The Botanic Ark, VIC**

Red and white glass bead necklace, c1950, 42cm long.

$30 - $40   **The Botanic Ark, VIC**

Brooch, earrings and matching necklace in rich garnet coloured rhinestones, c1955.

$275 - $315   **Chapel Street Bazaar, VIC**

Diamante necklace and earrings set, c1950, 6cm long, 20cm high.

$75 - $95   **Towers Antiques & Collectables, NSW**

Green and white diamante cocktail set of choker and earrings, c1960.

$115 - $135

Womango,
VIC

Enamel on copper pendant in blue by Karl Schibensky, Germany, c1960, 6cm high.

$280 - $320

Kaleidoscope Antiques,
VIC

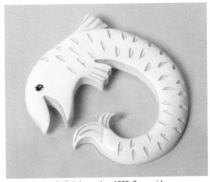

Carved plastic fish brooch, c1960, 8cm wide.

$65 - $85

Kaleidoscope Antiques,
VIC

Plastic gollywog brooches in assorted colours and different faces from Taiwan, c1960, 7cm diameter. Priced per item.

$24 - $34

Shag,
VIC

Plastic gollywog brooch in assorted colours and hair styles all with hoop earrings and moving eyes, from Taiwan, c1960, 4cm diam. Priced per item.

$13 - $23

Shag,
VIC

Magnificent costume jewellery bracelet, earrings, necklace and brooch by 'Coro', c1960.

$275 - $315

Chapel Street Bazaar,
VIC

Pair of brightly coloured plastic earrings, c1960.

NZ$180 - $200

Banks Peninsula Antiques,
New Zealand

Drop hoop earrings consisting of four hoops, c1960, 7cm long.

$20 - $30

Kenny's Antiques,
VIC

Vintage leopard brooch with black enamel spots and diamantes, c1960, 5cm wide, 5cm high.

$85 - $105

Retro Active,
VIC

Vendome necklace and matching bracelet, beautifully detailed, gold plated surround with large aurora crystals, c1960.

$480 - $580

Chapel Street Bazaar,
VIC

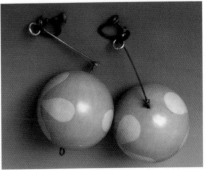

Ping-Pong ball earrings, bought in Carnaby street, London in 1966, c1966, 8cm long, 4cm diameter.

$40 - $50

The Botanic Ark,
VIC

Vintage lucite black and white cuff, with tag on stretch elastic, c1970, 4cm wide.

$30 - $40   **Fat Helen's, VIC**

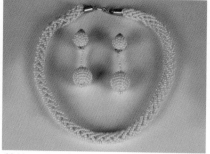

Multi strand pearl necklace and clip on drop earrings, c1970.

$45 - $65   **Kenny's Antiques, VIC**

French Bakelite bangle with Pierrot on two sides, c1970.

$105 - $125   **Online Antiques, VIC**

Bakelite and diamante brooch in shape of a leaf, c1970, 14cm long.

$115 - $135   **Rosebud Antiques, NSW**

Ex factory stock plastic costume jewellery, c1975, 4cm wide.

$23 - $33   **Fat Helen's, VIC**

Huge circular colourful resin earrings, c1970, 4cm diameter.

NZ$65 - $85   **Deborah's Antiques, New Zealand**

Glass and plastic necklace with etched glass beads, c1970, 38cm long.

$85 - $105   **Chapel Street Bazaar, VIC**

Baltic red amber necklace, c1970.

$730 - $830   **Antique Centre of Stonnington, VIC**

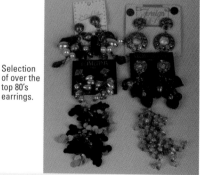

Selection of over the top 80's earrings.

$15 - $25   **River Emporium, NSW**

Stretch costume jewellery bracelet, black with pink scotty dog applied, c1980, 5cm high, 7cm diam.

$215 - $255   **Chapel Street Bazaar, VIC**

Mahjong stretch bracelet and wooden beads, assembled 1990's however, Mahjong tiles are 1950s/60s.

$75 - $95   **Chapel Street Bazaar, VIC**

Coloured lucite brooch in the form of an owl, designed by Lea Stein, limited edition, c1980, 4cm wide, 6cm high.

$120 – $140   **Chapel Street Bazaar, VIC**

'Carmen' brooch marked 'Lea Stein, Paris', c1960, 5cm wide.

$170 – $190   **Kaleidoscope Antiques, VIC**

Purple fox brooch marked 'Lea Stein, Paris', c1960, 9cm high.

$170 – $190   **Kaleidoscope Antiques, VIC**

Lea Stein

A French trained artist who was born in Paris in 1931, Lea Stein began making her whimsical pieces of jewellery in 1969 when her husband, Fernand Steinberger, came up with a process of laminating layers of rhodoid (cellulose acetate sheets) with interesting textures and colours.

The layers were baked overnight with a secret component of his creation and then cut into shapes for various designs of pins, bracelets, earrings and shaped decorative objects. Viewed from the side, as many as 20 layers of cellulose can be seen in some models, bonded together to make these pieces.

The most easily recognizable Lea Stein pin is the 3-D fox, which has been produced in a myriad of colours and designs. Often, lace or metal layers were incorporated into the celluloid, which produced an astounding number of unique textures. The 3-D fox's tail is looped from one piece of celluloid.

Many different styles of cats, dogs, bugs, bunnies, birds, ducks and other creatures were introduced, as well as Deco-styled women, mod-styled children, flowers, cars, hats, purses, gold-encased and rhinestone encrusted designs and lots of little "things" such as stars, hearts, rainbows... even pins resembling John Travolta and Elvis Presley.

These 'vintage' pieces of jewellery were made from 1969 until 1981 and are identified by a v-shaped pin-back which is heat mounted to the back of each piece, as are the pin-backs on her newer pieces. The v-shaped pin back is always marked 'Lea Stein Paris.' The smallest pieces have tiny straight pin-backs which say 'Lea Stein.' Some of the thinner pieces have the clasp glued or heat-mounted on a small plastic disk, but all of them are marked in the same way.

Lea Stein rhodoid penguin brooch.

$180 – $220   **Antique Centre of Stonnington, VIC**

Vintage crocodile brooch by Lea Stein, Paris c1970.

$275 – $315   **Esmerelda's Curios, WA**

Fox brooch by Lea Stein, Paris, c1970, 8cm high.

$205 – $245   **Jennifer Wren Antiques, NSW**

French Lea Stein plastic penguin brooch, c1970, 9cm high, 4cm wide.

$185 – $205   **b bold - 20th Century Furniture & Effects, VIC**

Red cat face brooch marked 'Lea Stein, Paris', c1960, 6cm wide.

$160 – $180   **Kaleidoscope Antiques, VIC**

Boxed set necklace and earings by Lea Stein Paris, unmarked, c1995.

$480 – $520   **Jennifer Wren Antiques, NSW**

Vintage French celluloid bangle by Lea Stein Paris, c1970, 7cm diameter.

$60 – $80   **Retro Active, VIC**

LEA STEIN

Red and Black lucite brooch, Lea Stein designer, limited edition, 7cm long.

$120 - $140
Chapel Street Bazaar, VIC

Autumnal hues form this 'Grenoville' cicada brooch made from lucite, designed by Lea Stein, c1980.

$110 - $130
Chapel Street Bazaar, VIC

Cat brooch, blue with black face, by Lea Stein, Paris, c1970, 5cm deep.

$205 - $245
Jennifer Wren Antiques, NSW

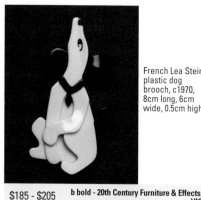

French Lea Stein plastic dog brooch, c1970, 8cm long, 6cm wide, 0.5cm high.

$185 - $205
b bold - 20th Century Furniture & Effects, VIC

French Lea Stein plastic lady bug brooch, c1970, 6cm long, 1cm deep, 5cm wide.

$155 - $175
b bold - 20th Century Furniture & Effects, VIC

Lea Stein Scottie brooch in grey and white plastic, made in Paris, c1960, 4cm long, 3.5cm wide.

$60 - $80
The Botanic Ark, VIC

Brooch depicting a panther in red, orange and black lucite, designed by Lea Stein, limited edition, c1980, 9.5cm long.

$120 - $140
Chapel Street Bazaar, VIC

Tennis lady brooch marked 'Lea Stein, Paris', c1960, 11cm long.

$280 - $320
Kaleidoscope Antiques, VIC

Brooch, pair of cats black and red by Lea Stein, Paris, c1970, 5cm high.

$205 - $245
Jennifer Wren Antiques, NSW

Brooch, cat with red body by Lea Stein Paris, c1970, 8.5cm high.

$205 - $245
Jennifer Wren Antiques, NSW

Tortoiseshell cat brooch by Lea Stein, Paris, c1970, 7.5cm high.

$205 - $245
Jennifer Wren Antiques, NSW

Ceramic trinket box of Barbie in 'Suburban Shopping' outfit, original box included, produced by Mattel, c2001.

$15 - $25   **Chapel Street Bazaar, VIC**

Vintage 'Barbie' doll with original wig, swimsuit 'Fashion Queen', c1962, 30cm high.

$90 - $110   **The Mill Markets, VIC**

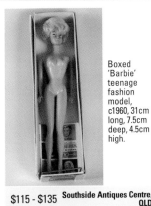

Boxed 'Barbie' teenage fashion model, c1960, 31cm long, 7.5cm deep, 4.5cm high.

$115 - $135   **Southside Antiques Centre, QLD**

Barbie, 'Bubble Cut' edition by Mattel, c1964, 28cm high.

$150 - $170   **Chapel Street Bazaar, VIC**

Japanese all Bisque character doll in red polka dot dress, c1950, 19cm high.

$205 - $245   **Mooney Collectables, NSW**

Black composition AM Dream baby doll, 64cm high.

$750 - $850   **Bank House Antiques, QLD**

Celluloid kewpie doll, sold at the Royal Melbourne show, dressed in pink nylon and lurex lace, all original, c1950, 6cm deep, 38cm wide, 43cm high.

$40 - $60   **The Botanic Ark, VIC**

Celluloid English Bobby Tourist doll, no brand or marketing, nice detail in uniform, c1960, 12cm high.

$30 - $40   **Chapel Street Bazaar, VIC**

Reliable composition doll, Scottish dress, c1950, 40cm high.

$160 - $180   **Chapel Street Bazaar, VIC**

Hedgehog composition made in US Zone West Germany, paper label to base of foot, c1950, 12cm high.

$23 - $33   **Chapel Street Bazaar, VIC**

Steiff 'Puck' character doll, all original clothes, paper label sewn onto jacket, c1960, 20cm high.

$140 - $160   **Chapel Street Bazaar, VIC**

Australian made Maretta composition doll's head, sleeping eyes, moulded hair, masked 331, celluloid arms and legs on a cloth body, original dress and petticoat, c1940, 40cm long, 13cm wide.

$360 - $400   **Isadora's Antiques, NSW**

'Pedigree' walking doll, a bride, original clothes, c1950, 22cm wide, 50cm high.

$370 - $410   **Galeria del Centro, NSW**

'Pedigree' bride walking doll, made out of hard plastic, c1950, 72cm long.

$360 - $400   **The Mill Markets, VIC**

Black 'Pedigree' doll, hard plastic, c1950, 40cm high.

$380 - $420   **Northside Secondhand Furniture, QLD**

Maori 'Pedigree' doll, c1960, 30cm long, 17cm deep, 17cm wide, 30cm high.

$60 - $80   **Dr Russell's Emporium, WA**

'Pedigree' walker doll, c1950, 54cm high.

$230 - $270   **Antiques and Collectables - Port Macquarie, NSW**

Plastic Roddy Doll, with original clothes, wig and make up, c1970, 90cm high.

$185 - $205   **Rare Old Times Antiques & Collectables, SA**

Pedigree Dolls

Pedigree dolls were very popular in Australia during the late forties and through the fifties. They came in many sizes and styles.

They were manufactured by Pedigree Soft Toys Ltd. of the United Kingdom, which had factories New Zealand, South Africa and Australia, and was a subsidiary of the biggest toy company in the world from the 1930s to the 1950s: Lines Brothers Ltd.

Pedigree's Sindy was the great success story of the 1960s toy industry, cleverly catching the mood of the new teenage culture. Sindy, first made in 1962 by the Pedigree Company, is the best-selling 'teenage' fashion doll ever produced in Great Britain.

Pedigree, in financial difficulties, sold the Sindy licence to toy giant, Hasbro in 1986, and her popularity with modern children has now been somewhat eclipsed by her rival 'Barbie'.

'Pedigree' walker-crawler doll c1950, 55cm high.

$380 - $420   **Antiques and Collectables , Port Macquarie, NSW**

Annette Hemstedt 'Barefoot Children' series, German rubber doll in original condition, c1980, 61cm high.

$1100 - $1300   **Mooney Collectables, NSW**

Plastic sleeping and walking doll with legs and head that move when walking and moving eyes and arms, c1960, 12cm wide, 23cm high.

$110 - $130   **Mac's Collectables**

Original 'Gerry Gee' ventriloquist doll with special edition glass eyes, c1960, 61cm high.

$600 - $700   **Chapel Street Bazaar, VIC**

'Big Eye' doll made from stocking, in handmade dress of the era, c1960, 8cm wide, 59cm high.

$115 - $135   **Dr Russell's Emporium, WA**

Ceramic nodder/wobbler doll of a Hawaiian dancer, c1950, 18cm long, 8cm deep, 8cm wide, 18cm high.

$85 - $105   **Dr Russell's Emporium, WA**

Mohair mouse doll with glass eyes and felt feet, c1950, 40cm long.

$130 - $150   **The Bottom Drawer Antique Centre, VIC**

Black doll, original box, clothes and wig, by Ceppi Ratti, Italy, c1960, 38cm high.

$125 - $145   **The Mill Markets, VIC**

Musical wax doll in box, plays music, moving head, c1960, 38cm long, 22cm deep, 20cm.

$480 - $520   **Towers Antiques & Collectables, NSW**

Bridie Thomas dam troll doll, made in Denmark, c1977, 26cm high.

$50 - $70.   **Fyshwick Antique Centre, ACT**

'Roaring 1890's' style stocking doll on wooden stand with original tag, c1960, 12cm deep.

$30 - $40   **Chapel Street Bazaar, VIC**

Boudoir doll, dressed as a 19th century lady in a blue nylon crinoline, c1960, 28cm deep, 28cm wide, 36cm high.

$30 - $40   **The Botanic Ark, VIC**

'Cyclops' childs pram with wicker basket, metal brackets and handles, vinyl green cover, metal spring suspension and rubber wheels on spokes, c1950, 40cm deep, 82cm wide, 77cm high.

$275 - $315

Twice Around, NSW

Mona Lisa ballerina in original condition with tag, hard plastic body and vinyl head, made by Valentine Dolls, New York, c1950, 61cm high.

$275 - $315   **Town & Country Antiques, NSW**

Australian cane doll's pram, c1950, 45cm long.

$55 - $75   **Step Back Antiques, VIC**

Two storey Marx USA painted tin doll's house, c1960, 49cm long, 20cm deep, 44cm high.

$125 - $145   **Patinations, NSW**

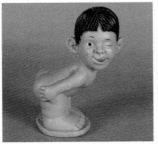

Plastic cheeky naked girl 'Gloobee doll', c1970, 15cm high.

$13 - $23   **Fat Helen's, VIC**

Dolls furniture consisting of a couch and two arm chairs, c1950.

$90 - $110   **Kingston Antiques, VIC**

TEDDY BEARS & OTHER STUFFED TOYS

Plush covered teddy bear pouring a glass of drink, c1950, 11cm wide, 25cm high

$275 - $315   **De Bretts Antiques, VIC**

Vintage teddy bear, c1970, 42cm high.

$65 - $85   **Fyshwick Antique Centre, ACT**

Plush covered teddy bear beating a cymbal, c1950, 11cm wide, 25cm high.

$275 - $315   **De Bretts Antiques, VIC**

$40 - $50   **Chapel Street Bazaar, VIC**

Steiff pig with glass eyes, button in ear, tag torn, c1970

Teddy baby with a black Steiff button, shaved muzzle, flat feet and blond mohair, c1945, 41cm high.

$3100 - $3300   **Quaint Collectables, NSW**

Steiff walrus with blue glass eyes, button and tag on front flipper, c1980, 15cm long, 8cm high.

$70 - $90   **Chapel Street Bazaar, VIC**

Steiff dog named 'Peke', original button and tag in the ear, c1960, 13cm long, 10.5cm high.

$130 - $150   **Chapel Street Bazaar, VIC**

Joy Toy teddy bear with stiff neck and jointed arms and legs, c1950, 62cm high

$330 - $370   **Kingston Antiques, VIC**

Alpha Farnell bear wearing his original waist coat, c1940, 30cm high

$200 - $235   **Chapel Street Bazaar, VIC**

'Bubbles' a soft toy, Michael Jackson's pet monkey from the 'Michaels Pets' series, c1980, 36cm high.

$20 - $30   **Fat Helen's, VIC**

Collection of eight toy 'Steiff' birds, c1950, 6cm high.

$280 - $320   **Kingston Antiques, VIC**

Film Fun 1956 annual edition of 'comics' depicting comedians of the time.

$40 - $60   **Gardenvale Collectables, VIC**

Fibreglass bust of Marilyn Monroe, c1950, 27.5cm wide, 50cm high.

$460 - $500   **Regent Secondhand, VIC**

Figure by Kevin Francis in the 'Marilyn Monroe' pattern, limited edition 418/1500, c1998, 25cm high.

$800 - $900   **Decodence Collectables, VIC**

Austin Powers hard plastic nodding figure of Mike Myers as Austin Powers, released in conjunction with the movie as novelty merchandising, c1997, 7cm wide, 17cm high.

$20 - $30   **Chapel Street Bazaar, VIC**

'Arnold Schwarzenegger T3. Rise of the Machines' worn T-shirt Swatch display, framed with Herb Ritts Terminator photo, c2003, 55cm wide, 75cm high.

$650 - $750   **Memorabilia Gallery, VIC**

Space Productions View Master with three reels of seven pictures from the infamous 'Lost in Space' TV series, still sealed, c1967, 11cm wide, 11cm high.

$140 - $160   **Rockaway Records, QLD**

Unique and numbered 'Star Wars, Return of the Jedi' original 70mm film cel autographed by Anthony Daniels (C3PO) and Kenny Baker (R2D2). The cel depicts the well known scene of C3PO and R2D2 attempting to enter Jabba the Hutts' Palace, numbered 895, c1997, 19cm wide, 7cm high.

$190 - $210   **Rare Memorabilia Gallery, VIC**

Clapper board for 'The Rich Kids', 39cm long, 35cm high.

$40 - $60   **Affordable Collectables & Antiques, VIC**

'Dukes of Hazard' watch, in original box with instructions, c1981.

$25 - $35   **Chapel Street Bazaar, VIC**

'Jurassic Park' original watch, licenced design, unused new old stock, still sealed Universal Studio, c1992.

$25 - $35   **Chapel Street Bazaar, VIC**

Framed handkerchief embroidered with Hollywood superstar Joan Crawford's signature, complete with autographed note donating item to a local charity and second autograph on original envelope, c1965, 4cm deep, 27cm wide, 80cm high.

$380 - $420   **Chapel Street Bazaar, VIC**

'National Panasonic' wrist radio, c1960, 20cm diam.

$55 - $75   **Antiques & Collectables - Hamilton, NSW**

'Astor' plastic cased radio, c1960.

$275 - $315   **Coliseum Antiques Centre, NSW**

Sanyo plastic radio, swivels on its stand, c1970.

NZ$140 - $160   **Maxine's Collectibles, New Zealand**

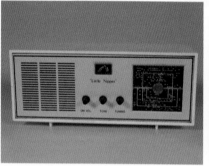

'Little Nipper' mantle radio, c1950.

$115 - $135   **Antiques On Macquarie, TAS**

'Welltron' radio, c1960.

$500 - $600   **The Wool Exchange Geelong, VIC**

'Healing Scales' ivory Bakelite radio, model 404E, c1950.

$1290 - $1490   **Coliseum Antiques Centre, NSW**

Phillips Model 112 Bakelite radio, c1948, 40cm long, 20cm deep, 30cm high.

$480 - $520   **Shop 2, Coliseum Antiques Centre, NSW**

'Fleetwood' radio in the form of a world globe, c1960, 22cm high, 17cm diameter.

$230 - $270   **Cool & Collected, SA**

'Tasma' four valve radio receiver, manufactured by Thom & Smith Sydney, c1948.

$430 - $470   **Laidley Old Wares, QLD**

'HMV Little Nipper' radio in green Bakelite case model A13B, c1949, 29cm long, 11cm deep, 18cm high.

$480 - $520   **Coliseum Antiques Centre, NSW**

Green 'Kreisler' duplex double sided valve radio, c1950, 31cm wide, 20cm high.

$275 - $315   **Gumnut Antiques & Old Wares, NSW**

'Phillips' model 122D cream Bakelite radio, c1952, 25cm long, 12cm deep, 18cm high.

$380 - $420   **Coliseum Antiques Centre, NSW**

STC model A4100 radio in ivory Bakelite case, c1952.

$480 - $520   **Coliseum Antiques Centre, NSW**

Radio cassette deck with red plastic quartz clock, c1960.

$115 - $135   **Bowhows, NSW**

'Kriesler' Bakelite radio, c1950.

$380 - $420   **Coliseum Antiques Centre, NSW**

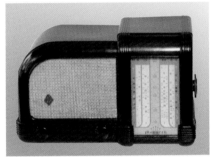

Art Deco 'Peter Pan' Bakelite radio, hard to find model, c1948, 20cm deep, 37cm wide, 25cm high.

$750 - $850   **Resurrection Radio, VIC**

Retro 'Healing' Bakelite radio in green, c1950, 13cm deep, 26cm wide, 16cm high.

$380 - $420   **Resurrection Radio, VIC**

'Philco' model 26 radio in white Bakelite, c1952, 15cm dep, 28cm wide, 17cm high.

$330 - $370   **Gaslight Collectables and Old books, SA**

Combination radio and organ, c1960, 16cm long, 9cm high.

$60 - $80   **Fyshwick Antique Centre, ACT**

AM radio in the shape of a Rolls Royce, the spare tyre as the radio tuner, runs on four AA batteries, perfect in vehicle details, c1980, 20cm long, 9cm wide, 9cm high.

NZ$40 - $50   **Classy Clutter And Collectables, New Zealand**

Crystal 'Eastern Germanium Radio' with diamente inlaid in green plastic, in original box including an earpiece, c1960, 8cm wide.

$115 - $135   **Chapel Street Bazaar, VIC**

'Kriesler' Bakelite radio, c1950.

$480 - $520   **Coliseum Antiques Centre, NSW**

'STC Rambler' plastic, maroon colour electric radio in working order, c1950, 28cm long, 14cm deep, 28cm high.

$135 - $155   **Towers Antiques & Collectables, NSW**

National Panasonic 'Toot A Loop' wrist radio, model R-725 by Matsushita Electric Industrial Co. Ltd, the twistable plastic design allowing the user to wear it on their wrist, takes two AA batteries, has earpohone plug. Designed with the mobile roller skating generation in mind, c1972, 15cm diameter.

$115 - $135   **Image Objex, VIC**

Kitsch 'Adam and Eve' radio with interlocking parts, black plastic and chrome, by Tradepower, c1970, 6cm long, 4cm deep, 6cm wide, 20cm high.

$60 - $80   **Dr Russell's Emporium, WA**

'Panasonic' transistor radio R-70 original box with carrying chain, globe shape in yellow plastic, includes operating instructions, c1970, 12cm diameter.

$75 - $95   **Chapel Street Bazaar, VIC**

'Deskube' transistor radio made by 'Realistic', c1970, 8cm long, 8cm deep, 8cm wide, 8cm high.

$30 - $40   **Rose Cottage Antiques, ACT**

'Tasma' brown mottled Bakelite radio, c1947.

$155 - $175   **Bob Butler's Sentimental Journey, QLD**

Novelty radio in the form of microphone, 'On The Air'.

$75 - $95   **Photantiques, NSW**

'Astor Football' cream Bakelite radio, c1950.

$1100 - $1300   **Coliseum Antiques Centre, NSW**

'S.T.C'. model 141 Bantam radio in brown Bakelite, c1947, 23cm long, 15cm deep, 15cm high.

$200 - $240   **Gaslight Collectables and Old Books, SA**

'STC' timber veneered mantle radio, c1950, 47cm long, 19cm deep, 24cm high.

$135 - $155   **Town & Country Antiques, NSW**

'Astor' Bakelite radio, model JJ, c1947, 44cm long, 23cm deep, 25cm high.

$460 - $500   **Gaslight Collectables and Old Books, SA**

Technico 'Aristocrat' mantel radio of heavy Bakelite construction, cabinet shaped to house an oversize speaker, c1948, 19cm deep, 43cm wide, 24cm high.

$600 - $700   **Resurrection Radio, VIC**

'National 10' transistor radio with leather case complete with earphone and pouch, c1960.

$40 - $50

Chris' Antiques & Collectables, VIC

'AWA Radiola' timber mantel radio, c1949.

$480 - $520

Coliseum Antiques Centre, NSW

'AWA' Bakelite radio, model 500M, c1947, 31cm long, 19cm deep, 20cm high.

$275 - $315   **Gaslight Collectables and Old Books, SA**

Traditional 'Little Nipper' Bakelite radio, c1950.

$210 - $250   **Lancaster's Toowoomba Antique Centre, QLD**

AWA model 510M valve radio, in white Bakelite, c1948, 31cm long, 19cm deep, 20cm high.

$300 - $340   **Gaslight Collectables and Old Books, SA**

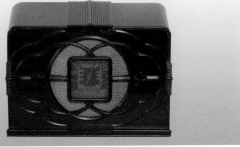

Blaupunkt model 'Riviera' German manufactured timber mantel radio, c1956, 65cm long, 25cm deep, 35cm high.

$480 - $520

Coliseum Antiques Centre, NSW

'Astor Mickey Mouse' radio, Bakelite case, c1940, 13cm deep, 22cm wide, 15cm high.

$1000 - $1200

Resurrection Radio, VIC

'Philco' radio model 26 in brown Bakelite, c1952, 15cm deep, 28cm wide, 17cm high.

$275 - $315   **Gaslight Collectables and Old Books SA**

'Healing' model 401 mantel radio in a 'cappuccino' colour, c1948.

$600 - $700   **Resurrection Radio, VIC**

'STC' brown Bakelite radio with a multi-coloured dial, c1948, 17cm deep, 32cm wide, 23cm high.

$480 - $520   **Resurrection Radio, VIC**

Record, 'Meet the Beatles', c1964.

$40 - $50 — **The Nostalgia Factory, NSW**

Beatles 'A Hard Day's Night' EP.

$35 - $45 — **Gardenvale Collectables, VIC**

Beatles 'Help' EP.

$35 - $45 — **Gardenvale Collectables, VIC**

The Beatles 'Help' album, released by E.M.I. Australia, 32cm long, 32cm wide.

$40 - $60 — **Titles & Treasures, QLD**

The Beatles 'Yellow Submarine Sgt. Peppers Lonely Hearts Club Band' by McFarlange Toys, series 2, c2000, 8cm deep, 21cm wide, 33cm high.

$15 - $25 — **Cardtastic Collectables, VIC**

Beatles 'Yesterday and Today' LP, commonly known as the 'Butcher Cover', withdrawn from sale shortly after release in 1966, mono peeled version Capital T-2533, c1966, 31cm wide, 31cm high.

$2400 - $2600 — **Rockaway Records, QLD**

'Beatles Sgt Pepper', an English pressing of an album that typified the psychedelic sixties. This English pressing comes in a gatefold cover with the original poster of 'cut-outs'. Re-release of original. One of the most important bands in history, their albums are still available on vinyl from Britain, c2004.

$15 - $25 — **Quality Records, VIC**

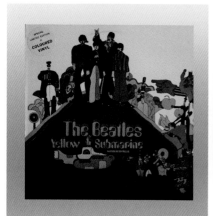

The Beatles - Yellow Submarine, limited release, pressed in the 80's on yellow vinyl, on Parlophone PC80 7070, c1986.

$70 - $90 — **Licorice Pie Records, VIC**

Beatles 'Sgt Peppers Lonely Heart Club Band' LP Record, c1960.

$90 - $110 — **Treats & Treasures, NSW**

'Meet the Beatles' album, their first album, 32cm long, 32cm wide.

$40 - $60 — **Titles & Treasures, QLD**

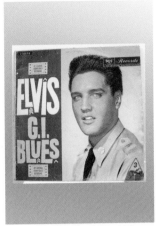

Elvis Presley 'G.I. Blues' 12 inch LP, original soundtrack, c1960.

$2 - $12   **Chris' Antiques & Collectables, VIC**

SPK-Leichenschrei LP, one of the first heavy industrial records from Australia on Thermidor Records T-9, original pressing, c1982.

$90 - $110   **Licorice Pie Records, VIC**

Original Rolling Stones 1966 Australian Tour Program, no creasing or discolouration, 21cm wide, 27cm high.

$850 - $950   **Rockaway Records, QLD**

George Harrison's 'All Things Must Pass' comes boxed in a deluxe three record set with a booklet, superb remastered sound, re-release of original from the Fab Four, c2002.

$40 - $50   **Quality Records, VIC**

Superlative release from US Classic Records of the classic Dave Brubeck 'Time Out' album. Jazz's first million selling record, 'Time Out' featured the hypnotic 'Take Five' which made jazz acceptable to all, c2005.

$70 - $90   **Quality Records, VIC**

Bob Dylan, superlative release from US Classic Records of the concert at Philharmonic Hall, 'Bob Dylan Live 1964 - the Bootleg Series Volume 6'. A three record set with booklet in box on 200 gram vinyl. Among the most famous bootlegs of all time, Bob Dylan's concert performances are gradually being released on record with volumes 4 to 6 in print, c2004.

$135 - $155   **Quality Records, VIC**

Final instalment in the Nick Drake legend, 'Made to Love Magic' includes a few rarities. An addition to 'Treasury' and the three studio albums already released. Re-release of original. Immensely influential artist whose early death meant that he sold few records, making these re-issues very desirable, c2003.

$30 - $40   **Quality Records, VIC**

The Lively Ones - Surf City LP. Classic surf music brought back into vogue by Tarantino, on Del-Fi Records DFLP-1237, original pressing, near mint, c1963.

$50 - $70   **Licorice Pie Records, VIC**

'Brigitte Bardot Show' LP. Quirky album of music and songs taken from her short-lived television series, on disc AZ STEC-41, original pressing, near mint, c1968.

$140 - $160   **Licorice Pie Records, VIC**

Johnny Cash - Greatest! LP. Johnny Cash's seventh album release on the legendary Sun Record Company. Original US pressing on the label made famous by Elvis Presley's first release, Sun Record Company SLP-1240, c1959.

$50 - $70   **Licorice Pie Records, VIC**

Zeppelin's third album, 'Led Zeppelin Three', re-release, c2002.

$40 - $60   **Quality Records, VIC**

ENTERTAINMENT

ALBUMS

Offenbach 'Gaite Parisienne'. Performed by the Boston Pops Orchestra and conducted by Arthur Fiedler, re-release of original 1953 release, c2001.

$40 - $60
Quality Records, VIC

Dvorak Cello Concerto, performed by Janos Starker, re-issue from Germany's Speakers Corner maintains the superlative quality of the previous Bach Cello Sonata issue. Speakers Corner have won numerous Audiophile awards, c2005.

$45 - $65
Quality Records, VIC

'The Best of Revue' 1961 record LP of an early 1961 ATN Television show introduced by Digby Wolfe, pressed in Melbourne, c1961.

$20 - $30
Yarra Valley Antique Centre, VIC

Joe Harriott - Hum-Dono LP. Incredible session featuring the cream of British jazz artists of the 60's, on EMI Columbia Records SCX6354, original pressing, c1969.

$550 - $650
Licorice Pie Records, VIC

John Lee Hooker LP. Hooker's only release for Impulse! Records - 'It Serves You Right To Suffer'. Incredible recording with great production, on Impulse! Records A-9103 (mono pressing), c1966.

$90 - $110
Licorice Pie Records, VIC

The Flying Circus - Prepared in Peace LP. Great pop psych LP from this Australian band, on EMI Columbia, SCXO-7925, c1969.

$35 - $45
Licorice Pie Records, VIC

Limited edition Rolling Stones 1983 original sound recording made by Promotone BV. A: side 'She was Hot'. B: side 'I think I'm Going Mad'. Produced by Chris Kinsey and the Glimmer Twins, c1983, 27cm long, 23.5cm high.

$40 - $60
Nicki's Collection, NSW

Sonic Youth-Dirty LP. Australian release, an edition of 1000 on orange coloured vinyl, encased in a printed cloth sleeve, on Geffen Records - DGC-24485 includes inserts. Limited Australian pressing, c1992.

$90 - $110
Licorice Pie Records, VIC

Khan original 1972 progressive album with Steve Hillage (pre Gong) and Dave Stewart (Egg) on Australian Deram SDL-11. Gatefold cover, record, c1972, 31cm wide, 31cm high.

$65 - $85
Rockaway Records, QLD

John Coltrane's 'Blue Train' album is another re-issue from audiophile Masters Classic Records, with 200 gram vinyl and superb sound, c2002.

$40 - $60
Quality Records, VIC

Main Source - Breaking Atoms LP. From the 'Golden Age' of Hip Hop, on Wild Pitch Records WPL-2004, original pressing,, c1991.

$70 - $90
Licorice Pie Records, VIC

We're The Banana Splits LP, sound track from the 60's psychedelic children's program - Tra la la la, tra la la la, on Decca Records DL-75075, original pressing, c1968.

$70 - $90   Licorice Pie Records, VIC

'C is for Cookie!' LP. One of the most sought after Sesame Street records, on the Childrens' Records of America Inc. 643-0565, original pressing, c1974.

$25 - $35   Licorice Pie Records, VIC

Assorted records, c1970.

$2 - $12   The Wool Exchange Geelong, VIC

Flower Power cover compilation, dated 1967, still in Batman's sleeve with playable recording, c1967.

$2 - $9   Savers, VIC

Framed INXS 'Listen Like Thieves' LP, 20cm x 20cm photo of the time, ticket to concert held in Brisbane, Australia, promotional FM104 radio station sticker for concert and a backstage pass, c1985, 59cm wide, 145cm high.

$650 - $750   Rockaway Records, QLD

'Hendrix Experience', deluxe 8 record set with booklet in silk covered box brings together most of the Jimmy Hendrix alternate and live versions that were previously unreleased. Although he only recorded a few studio albums, Jimi Hendrix's habit of recording and re-recording meant that the record company was able to release albums for many years after his death, c2001.

$165 - $185   Quality Records, VIC

Caetano Veloso - Self Titled LP. One of many of Veloso's self-titled records, this one from 1967 is a stand-out and one of the finest of all Tropicalia albums from Brazil, on Philips Records 6328 497, original pressing, c1967.

$90 - $110   Licorice Pie Records, VIC

Elvis Presley, Jailhouse Rock, 7 inch EP, c1958.

$5 - $10   Chris' Antiques & Collectables, VIC

Dirty Three - Sad and Dangerous LP, their first LP released in a limited pressing, hand printed sleeve, on Poon Village Records, c1993.

$40 - $60   Licorice Pie Records, VIC

Billy Thorpe and The Aztecs, mono 12 inch LP, c1959.

$15 - $25   Chris' Antiques & Collectables, VIC

John Lennon 'Wings Over America' three record set plus poster, E.M.I. Australia, 32cm long, 32cm wide.

$40 - $60   Titles & Treasures, QLD

Karin Krog - 'We Could Be Flying' LP. One of the most extraordinary voices in jazz, this is by far Krog's rarest record, on Polydor Records 2382 051, original pressing, c1975.

$480 - $520

Licorice Pie Records, VIC

Original combined Who/Small Faces Australian Tour program, c1967, 22cm wide, 28cm high.

$750 - $850

Rockaway Records, QLD

INXS French Record Award for Platinum Sales of the album 'Kick', certified by S.N.E.P. in October 1988, 20cm deep, 30cm wide, 50cm high.

$2900 - $3100

Rockaway Records, QLD

Sun Ra - Disco 3000 LP, mid-period Sun Ra. Handmade sleeve and labels, on El Saturn Records CMIJ78, original pressing, near mint, c1978.

$380 - $420

Licorice Pie Records, VIC

Bob Dylan's 1978 Australian Pressing of 'Masterpieces' three CD set. The artwork was not sanctioned by Columbia USA and is different to its overseas counterpart, it was withdrawn from sale.

$90 - $110

Rockaway Records, QLD

Dock Boggs LP, a collection of seminal banjo player Dock Boggs' 78's of the 20's and 30's. This is the first collection of his songs, on Folkways Records FA-2351 including inserts, c1964.

$70 - $90

Licorice Pie Records, VIC

'Dr No' Sound Track LP, sound track to the first James Bond film. On United Artists Records UAS-5108, original pressing, c1962.

$50 - $70

Licorice Pie Records, VIC

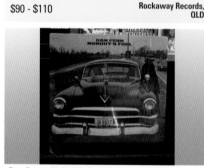

Dan Penn - Nobody's Fool LP, better known as a song writer for many soul smash hits of the 60's, this was Penn's debut solo record, on Bell Records Bell-1127, original pressing, c1973.

$90 - $110

Licorice Pie Records, VIC.

Original WEA 1988 'Travelling Wilburys' Australian LP with Bob Dylan, Tom Petty, Roy Orbison, Jeff Lynne and George Harrison, unavailable on CD due to copyright issues, c1988, 31cm wide, 31cm high.

$40 - $60

Rockaway Records, QLD

Aztecs - Live LP, classic Thorpie recorded live in Melbourne, on Havoc HST-400 1, c1971.

$40 - $60

Licorice Pie Records, VIC

Lobby Lloyde - Summer Jam LP, incredible live recording from Sunbury '73 featuring legendary guitarist Lobby Lloyde, on Mushroom Records L-25073, original pressing, c1973.

$140 - $160

Licorice Pie Records, VIC

'Ramones Raw', DVD cover and outer sleeve, both autographed by band member and music legend, Marky Ramone, also signed by 'Ramones Raw' director, John Cafiero, c2004, 14cm wide, 19cm high.

$140 - $160   **Rare Memorabilia Gallery,**
                                                        VIC

Zoviet France-Norsch with handmade masonite sleeve from the cult avantgarde band Zoviet France-Norsch, on Red Rhino Records, c1983.

$70 - $90   **Licorice Pie Records,**
                                                VIC

'Rolling Stones' first E.P. record.

$40 - $50   **Treats & Treasures,**
                                            NSW

'Chu Bops' miniature albums, contain bubblegum in the shape of a record plus printed lyrics, distributed in Australia by Scanlens, c1980, 7cm wide, 7cm high.

$110 - $130   **Secondhand Furniture Mart,**
                                                            TAS

The Loved Ones' - Magic Box LP, classic Australian 60's garage rock record from Melbourne, on W&G records WG-S-25/5127, original pressing.

$40 - $60   **Licorice Pie Records,**
                                                VIC

Kenny Burrell - 'Blue Lights' LP, sought after Blue Note session from guitarist Burrell, as a bonus cover design by Andy Warhol, on Blue Note Records 1597 Vol.2, original pressing, c1958.

$190 - $210   **Licorice Pie Records,**
                                                    VIC

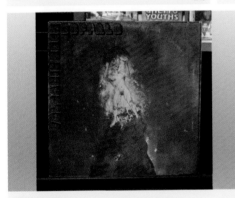

'Buffalo - Volcanic Rock' LP. Classic heavy progressive rock record from Australia's answer to Black Sabbath, on Vertigo Records 6357 101 includes insert (spiral label), original pressing, c1973.

$190 - $210   **Licorice Pie Records,**
                                                    VIC

Norah Jones 'Feels Like Home' album, has a slight jazz feel and is available as a 200 gram release or (cheaper) normal release. Original release, c2004.

$40 - $60   **Quality Records,**
                                            VIC

King Tubby - 'The Roots of Dub' LP. Considered one of the all time great dub reggae records, on Total Sounds Recording Co. Ltd. TSL-105, original Jamaican pressing, c1975.

$140 - $160   **Licorice Pie Records,**
                                                    VIC

'Into Action with Troy Tempest', mini album by 21 Century Records, single 45 rpm, c1960.

$20 - $30   **The Wool Exchange Geelong,**
                                                        VIC

Original 45 record with promotional photograph featuring Danny Robinson and The Maori Hi Fi's, c1965.

$20 - $30   **Savers,**
                                    VIC

Ten original rock badges from various concerts from the 1980s.

$40 - $60   **Rockaway Records, QLD**

DJ desk manufactured in England, c1978, 57cm deep, 92cm wide, 62cm high.

$1400 - $1600   **Retro Relics, VIC**

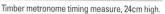

Timber metronome timing measure, 24cm high.

$150 - $170   **Laidley Old Wares, QLD**

Japanese mirrored musical jewellery box with gilt edging and padded tapestry top and sides, c1955, 20cm long, 12cm wide, 7cm high.

$50 - $70   **Helen's On The Bay, QLD**

ABS plastic PAAM tube record player manufactured by BSR. The speakers can be pulled out from the ends of the tube to act as satellites, c1970, 61cm long, 27cm diameter.

$420 - $460   **506070, NSW**

Huon pine heart shaped musical jewellery box made in Sydney, c1950, 16cm long, 5cm deep, 175cm wide.

$115 - $135   **Shop 26, Antiques & Collectables - Hamilton, NSW**

Marine Bind harmonica made by M. Hohner, Germany (Number 1896) with original box and instructions, c1950, 10cm long, 2cm deep, 3cm wide.

$50 - $70   **Mt Dandenong Antique Centre, VIC**

Grundig 'Phono Boy' portable phonograph in red plastic, designed by Mario Bellini 1969, c1969, 23cm high.

$310 - $350   **506070, NSW**

Needles (Styli) for record players all with diamond tip 1910 to current, c1990.

$5 - $15   **Chris' Antiques & Collectables, VIC**

English child's portable Gramophone record player made by Decca, the leatherette clad case decorated with colourful panel of nursery rhymes after Dora Roderick, 35cm deep, 25cm wide, 15cm high.

$360 - $400   **Past Connections Antiques & Decorative Arts, NSW**

'Kingsley' portable record player, c1960, 25cm deep, 30cm wide.

$65 - $85   **Secondhand Furniture Mart, TAS**

Atari 2600 video computer system in original box with instructions and games, released by Atari Corp in 1987, plugs into TV, 29cm long, 18cm wide, 13cm high.

$55 - $75   **Image Objex, VIC**

'Sega Mega Drive' computer game console in original box and arcade power stick, released in 1991, 40cm long, 14cm wide, 40cm high.

$75 - $95   **Image Objex, VIC**

Nintendo 'Entertainment System' in original box with zapper light gun, controllers and Mario Bros. game, Mattel version, c1988, 54cm long, 30cm wide, 13cm high.

$65 - $85   **Image Objex, VIC**

Uncommon Nintendo (NES) games, 'Castlevania', 'Zeld', 'Bubble Bobble', c1988.

$125 - $145   **Image Objex, VIC**

National reel-to-reel tape recorder, good working condition, c1960, 33cm long, 33cm wide, 12cm high.

$115 - $135   **Chapel Street Bazaar, VIC**

Table speaker for transistor radio, made by Matsushita Electric Industries, c1970, 14cm high, 21.5cm diameter.

$65 - $85   **Rose Cottage Antiques, ACT**

G.E.C. Weltron 2007 stereo system 'space-ship' design complete with G.E.C. 2006 speakers and detachable pedestal, includes record player, cassette tape player and AM/FM radio, auxillary input for one player, replacement perspex lid and re-sprayed pedestal, c1970, 70cm high, 56cm diameter.

$1150 - $1350   **Image Objex, VIC**

Plajet microphone, c1970, 6cm long, 7cm high, 3cm diameter.

$110 - $130   **Bowhows, NSW**

'Videoscope', two part acrylic lens filled with oil, steel strap frame, rubber seal to lens parts, hand painted 'Videoscope' logo with patent and dated 1957, made simply to enlarge an early TV screen, 120cm high, 88cm diam.

$3400 - $3600   **Industria, VIC**

Black and white 'JVC' orange videosphere television set, c1970, 30cm high.

$500 - $600   **The Wool Exchange Geelong, VIC**

'Sweathogs' badge, metal, c1976, 7cm diameter.

$30 - $60   **Chapel Street Bazaar, VIC**

Original metal 'Charlie's Angels' lunch box, c1978, 20cm long, 10cm deep.

$115 - $135   **Chapel Street Bazaar, VIC**

Art Deco style Tasmanian oak leadlight kitchen cabinet, made by 'Coogans Furniture Maker Launceston Tasmania', c1940, 40cm deep, 140cm wide, 160cm high.

$550 - $650

Secondhand Furniture Mart, TAS

Art Deco cocktail bar with a maple fiddle back veneered front, centre rotating door, side doors, restored and French polished, c1930, 35cm deep, 92.5cm wide, 95cm high.

$1100 - $1300

River Emporium, NSW

Art Deco cocktail mirrored cabinet the interior with revolving bottle holder, c1940, 40cm deep, 90cm wide, 120cm high.

$950 - $1050

Marrick's Furniture, VIC

Queensland walnut leadlight Art Deco convex display cabinet, c1940.

$1600 - $1800

Seanic Antiques, VIC

French Art Deco display cabinet with a fitted cupboard and sliding glass doors, c1940, 90cm long, 40cm deep, 105cm high.

$2000 - $2300

Andrew Price Antiques, VIC

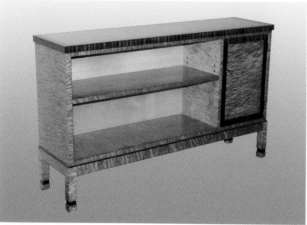

Swedish flame birch Art Deco cabinet with palisander cross banding, c1940, 150cm long, 40cm deep, 75cm high.

$1900 - $2100

Virtanen Antiques, VIC

Queensland walnut and maple Art Deco cocktail cabinet. A high tech piece of furniture locally made from local material with local expertise. Froth and bubble to satisfy the times, c1950, 124cm long, 43cm deep, 118cm high.

$1350 - $1550

Garry Auton Antiques, NSW

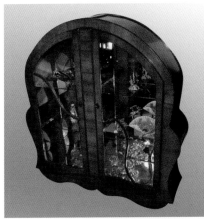

Walnut veneered Art Deco shield shaped display china cabinet with mirrored interior, c1950, 34cm deep, 120cm wide, 130cm high.

NZ$1400 - $1600   **Antiques Centre of Wellington, New Zealand**

Painted kitchenette cabinet, light weight, functional and decorative in the Art Deco manner, 139cm long, 42cm deep, 177cm high.

$410 - $450   **Garry Auton Antiques, NSW**

Art Deco mirror in the shape of a yacht, c1950, 37cm long, 43cm high.

$65 - $85   **Burly Babs Collectables/Retro Relics, VIC**

Art Deco style smokers stand, chrome and black glass, c1950, 75cm high.

$110 - $130   **Chapel Street Bazaar, VIC**

French Art Deco walnut sideboard with marble top, c1930, 50cm deep, 150cm wide, 100cm high.

$1550 - $1750   **Marrick's Furniture, VIC**

Art Deco style inlaid coffee table, c1950, 49cm high, 59cm diameter.

$275 - $315   **Antipodes Antiques, QLD**

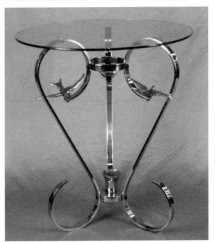

Art Deco chrome and brass bluebird table.

$520 - $620   **Paddington Antique Centre Pty Ltd, QLD**

Australian Art Deco dressing table, light wood bird's eye veneer, three drawers down one side, three shelves on other side, long mirror in middle, original celluloid handles, c1935, 46cm deep, 130cm wide, 165cm high.

$1050 - $1250   **Scheherazade Antiques, VIC**

Art Deco tea trolley with frosted motif on glass door, c1950, 75cm long, 45cm deep, 74cm high.

$330 - $370   **Stumpy Gully Antiques, VIC**

Pair of leather upholstered T4 design single chairs, designed by Fred Lowen for Tessa, c1970, 81cm high.

$480 - $520

Rose Cottage Antiques, ACT

Leather and teak swivel armchair, designer Fred Lowen for Tessa. Tessa was previously known as 'Twen', this chair is the 'Twen-T-One' model, c1970, 85cm deep, 72cm wide, 82cm high.

$380 - $420

The Junk Company, VIC

Pair of 'Fler' swivel saucer chairs designed by Fred Lowen and Ernest Rodeck, founders of 'Fler', c1960, 78cm deep, 88cm wide, 68cm high.

$370 - $410

The Junk Company, VIC

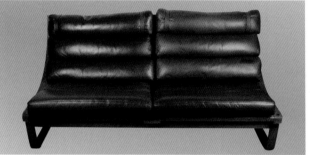

Tessa T4, heat moulded timber, brown leather, net base, made in Victoria, designed by Fred Lowen, c1972, 2.7cm long, 2cm deep, 1.2cm high.

$1700 - $1900

Bowhows, NSW

Twen T2 three seater lounge, designed by Fred Lowen, with velvet cowhide design upholstery and teak arms and base, c1970, 180cm long, 90cm deep, 90cm high.

$1000 - $1200

Retro Active, VIC

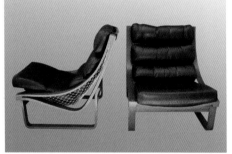

Black leather Tessa T4 lounge chairs, c1975, 82cm deep, 80cm high.

$940 - $1040

Tiffany Dodd Antique & 20th Century Furniture, QLD

Leather upholstered laminated timber frame stool, a Fred Lowen design for Tessa, c1970, 53cm deep, 64cm wide, 35cm high.

$85 - $105

Rose Cottage Antiques, ACT

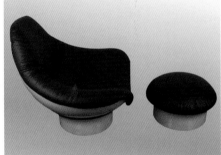

Grant Featherston 230H TV chair, c1950.

$5600 - $6000

Vampt, NSW

Tessa Furniture, Fred Lowen

Tessa Furniture company was founded by Fred Lowen, who was a co-founder of Fler furniture with Ernest Rodeck. Fler was a major influence of Australian design in the 20th century in its own right.

Fred Lowen later founded Twen which was later renamed Tessa, after a friend of his daughter, in the late 1960s.

The Tessa T4 lounge introduced to the public at the Cologne fair in 1971 became an instant design icon with its hammock influence and it is still a design produced by Tessa.

Tessa furniture has had great international success and even after the recent passing of Fred Lowen still continues to be a major influence of modern design today.

Leather 'T8' Tessa chaise lounge, designer Fred Lowen for Tessa, design the 'T8' chaise lounge c1970, 135cm long, 68cm wide, 85cm high.

$850 - $950

The Junk Company, VIC

Elanora E1 suspension chair by designer Grant Featherston, manufactured by Grant Featherston, Emerson Bros., E & F Industries, date 1951 - 55, made of plywood, fibre, horsehair, wadding, rubber, hardwood and upholstery fabric. This chair was part of the 'Contour' range of chairs c1954, 62cm deep, 108cm wide, 82cm high.

$6800 - $7200

506070, NSW

Grant Featherston (1922 – 1995)

Grant Featherston has designed many of the furniture classics of Australian Modernism. From his iconic Contour Series of the 1950s to the plastic Stem Chairs and the polyurethane foam of the Obo chairs of the 1960s and 70s, Featherston was always a pioneer of modern materials and technology.

The most widely recognised designs, the Contour Series, was produced from 1951-1955. They made use of moulded plywood - a technology perfected during World War II. The visually light organic shapes of this series was a contrast to the heavy often uncomfortable furniture of pre-war Australia and have come to be iconic representatives of a new positive forward looking modern Australia.

As well as furniture Grant Featherston also designed jewellery, lighting and glass. In recent years there has been a steady increase in interest in Featherston items from overseas markets reflecting an increasing price over the board for Featherston items.

It is also worth noting that Grant's wife Mary Featherston has been an influential identity in her own right in the history of Australian design.

Two Grant Featherston R160 contour chairs, c1955, 82cm deep, 72cm wide, 91cm high.

$5100 - $5500

Tiffany Dodd Antique & 20th Century Furniture, QLD

Armchair in original condition, designed by Grant Featherston, c1950, 52cm deep, 67cm wide, 75cm high.

$850 - $950

The Junk Company, VIC

Grant Featherston designed R160 rocker, produced 1954, 90cm deep, 66cm wide, 88cm high.

$3800 - $4000

Tarlo & Graham, VIC

Grant Featherston chair, chrome and wool, stamped to base 'Featherston Industries', c1960, 60cm deep, 66cm wide, 82cm high.

$370 - $410

The Junk Company, VIC

Retro Grant Featherston tub chair with white vinyl upholstery, c1950, 70cm long, 65cm deep, 80cm high.

$900 - $1000

Towers Antiques & Collectables, NSW

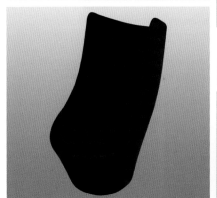

Expo Mark II soundchair, designer Grant Featherston, manufacturer Aristoc in 1967, made from polystyrene, poly urethane foam, Dunlopillo foam rubber, Pirelli webbing, fibreglass, hardwood and upholstery fabric, c1967, 85cm deep, 70cm wide, 115cm high.

$5800 - $6200

506070, NSW

Settee designed by Grant Featherston, fabric upholstery not original, Australian hardwood legs. Model RS161, c1951, 86cm deep, 120cm wide, 91cm high.

$5000 - $5400

Plasma, VIC

FURNITURE

Set of four 'Parker' vinyl upholstered teak chairs, c1960, 84cm high.

$480 - $520   **Rose Cottage Antiques, ACT**

Set of six retro Parker dining chairs with black vinyl upholstery, c1970, 50cm long, 46cm deep, 80cm high.

$550 - $650   **Towers Antiques & Collectables, NSW**

Classic Parker velour armchair, c1960, 79cm deep, 82cm wide, 75cm high.

$940 - $1040   **506070, NSW**

Teak stool by Parker with zippable upholstered seat, c1960, 55cm long, 39cm wide, 50cm high.

$125 - $145   **Vintage Living, ACT**

Large size Parker coffee table in teak, c1965, 107cm wide.

$650 - $750   **Tiffany Dodd Antique & 20th Century Furniture, QLD**

Teak 'Parker' single leaf extension table, c1960, 213.5cm long, 106.5cm deep, 72cm high.

$480 - $520   **Rose Cottage Antiques, ACT**

'Moderntone' teak sideboard by Pattison & Co. Victoria, Australia, c1964, 40.5cm deep, 182cm wide, 66cm high.

$750 - $850   **Tiffany Dodd Antique & 20th Century Furniture, QLD**

Sideboard by T. H. Brown of Adelaide. Roller doors, all teak, craftsman built, shows influence of TV styling., c1964, 170cm long, 46cm wide, 154cm high.

$3400 - $3600   **Vintage Living, ACT**

Set of three 'Sleepy Hollow chairs', in green vinyl, c1965, 87cm deep, 75cm wide, 87cm high.

$840 - $940   **Tiffany Dodd Antique & 20th Century Furniture, QLD**

Robyn Day style white stem tulip chair constructed from fibre glass and metal, c1960, 53cm deep, 57cm wide, 80cm high.

$370 - $410   **The Junk Company, VIC**

Medium height Aristoc laboratory chair from mid 60's, the fabricated steel frame with double curve ply seat and back rest. Commercial prop for schools, universities and laboratories, c1965, 40cm deep, 40cm wide, 84cm high.

$110 - $130   **Industria, VIC**

Harry Betoia style diamond chairs of metal and plastic, c1960, 83cm deep, 83cm high.

$480 - $520   **Chapel Street Bazaar, VIC**

Black plastic-coated wire dining chair designed by Harry Bertoia with black vinyl seat and black pads with vertical stitched detail, c1953, 44cm deep, 53cm wide, 77cm high.

$420 - $460   **506070, NSW**

Cantilever form bent plywood leather upholstered two-seater, probably manufactured by Danish Deluxe, c1970.

$940 - $1040   **506070, NSW**

Rocker recliner chair with original black and white houndstooth velvet velour fabric, 'David Jones' like, made for and featured at the Australian Pavilion at Expo 70, Osaka Japan, c1970, 100cm deep, 77cm wide, 100cm high.

$1350 - $1550   **Vintage Living, ACT**

Old roll top oak desk by B. Fallshaw & Sons of Melbourne with central locking mechanism, 73cm deep, 123cm wide, 117cm high.

$950 - $1150   **Old Bank Corner Collectables, NSW**

Australian red cedar set of drawers with oval mirror on Queen Ann feet and high gloss finish, by Dineen Sydney, c1965, 86cm wide, 175cm high.

$750 - $850   **Helen's On The Bay, QLD**

Three tables of graduated size in ABS plastic manufactured by Advance Industries under license from Kartell Italy, c1970, 41cm high, 46cm diameter.

$70 - $90   **506070, NSW**

Sculptural coffee table by Paul Kafka, c1950, 90cm long, 62cm wide, 47cm high.

$3100 - $3300   **Vampt, NSW**

Smoked glass and black vinyl fondue table stamped 'T. H. Brown & Sons', South Australia, c1965, 42cm high, 85cm diameter.

$650 - $750   **Tiffany Dodd Antique & 20th Century Furniture, QLD**

Pair of bedside tables of teak veneer on plywood manufactured by Chiswell, c1970, 52cm long, 37.5cm deep, 63cm high.

$350 - $390   **506070, NSW**

Seven piece dining suite comprising an extension table and six chairs, made of veneered and solid Queensland walnut with new upholstery. Made in Melbourne by European company Zoureff, designed by Dario Zoureff. Zoureff furniture was made to order and no two pieces are alike, c1960.

$2300 - $2500   **Plasma, VIC**

Nesting teak dining setting comprising an extension table and six chairs, by Hansen, Melbourne, c1960, 120cm diameter.

$2100 - $2300   **Found Objects, VIC**

'Guiramand & Coulent' French bar comprising five insulated cabinets, two sinks in stainless steel and ash from a bar in Marseille, c1950, 330cm long, 210cm deep, 240cm high.

$9750 - $10150 — **Cote Provence, VIC**

Classic dining table designed by Charles Rennie Mackintosh with drop sides in blackened ashwood, a later reproduction of an original 1915 design, c1980, 175cm long, 125cm deep, 75cm high.

$1300 - $1500 — **Le Contraste, VIC**

Djinn sofa, stretch fabric covered polyurethane foam upholstered, bent tubular steel frame, manufactured by Airborne International, France, designed by Olivier Mourgue in 1965, 120cm long, 69cm deep, 66cm high.

$7800 - $8200 — **506070, NSW**

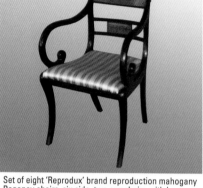

Set of eight 'Reprodux' brand reproduction mahogany Regency chairs, six side, two armchairs with brass inlay. Surrey, c1960, 82cm high.

$1350 - $1550 — **Roys Antiques Pty Ltd, VIC**

English custom made oak drinks cabinet, c1950, 40cm deep, 72cm wide, 126cm high.

$850 - $950 — **Paddington Antique Centre Pty Ltd, QLD**

English 'G Plan' teak sideboard, c1968, 183cm long, 45cm deep, 74cm high.

$750 - $850 — **Tiffany Dodd Antique & 20th Century Furniture, QLD**

Rodica Chair designed by Mario Brunn for Comfort Italy 1968, fibre glass leather, 110cm deep, 98cm wide, 77cm high.

$4400 - $4600 — **Mondo Trasho, VIC**

UP 5

The UP 5 was designed in 1969 by Italian designer Gaetano Pesce and manufactured by 'C&B Italia'. The Up 5 Chair is a design from a series of seven in the 'Up' range.

An icon of the 1960's Pop Art movement, the chair is constructed from moulded polyurethane and stretch fabric upholstery. Upon purchase, the chair came compressed and vacuum packed in PVC wrapping within a cardboard box, a fraction of their eventual size. Once unwrapped, Up 5 bounced into life and within an hour the full sized chair had grown. Designer Gaetano Pesce described the series as 'transformation furniture'. It turned the act of purchasing a chair into a 'happening'. The purchaser watched the transformation from 'flat pack to 3 dimensional form'.

Up 5 and matching ball shaped footstool 'Up 6' are the Up series' more famous members. Also known as 'La Mamma', Up 5 + 6 represent mother, the chair, and child, the footstool.

Up 5 has now been reissued by B&B Italia, however it no longer comes in flat pack form.

*Gaetano Pesce is a legend of 20th design having extended his talent to a multitude of design disciplines.

'UP 5' chair designed in 1968 by Gaetano Pesce for B & B Italia Italy, stretch fabric upholstered over moulded polyurethane, c1968, 117cm deep, 110cm wide, 110cm high.

$3900 - $4100 — **Mondo Trasho, VIC**

Rodica Chair

The Rodica Chair was designed in 1968 by Italian designer Mario Brunu and manufactured by 'Comfort' Italy.

The Rodica Chair consists of two separate fibreglass sections, a hollow cylindrical base and egg-cup shaped seat, comprising a layer of polyurethane and dacron, under leather upholstery. The seat rests upon the base allowing it to move freely into an unlimited number of positions, transforming it from lounge chair, to recliner, to chaise lounge.

This chair epitomizes 1960's space age, pop design through its organic shape, high gloss finish and rebellious demeanour.

Rodica was available in a choice of colours and upholstery finishes. An optional footstool was also available.

Brown leather chair with separate cushions on a chrome five star base, c1960, 80cm long, 80cm deep, 100cm high.

$650 - $750   **Le Contraste, VIC**

White moulded plastic 'Casala' chair, c1975.

$110 - $130   **Bowhows, NSW**

Pair of green leather and chrome cantilever chairs, c1970, 56cm wide, 87cm high.

$225 - $265   **Chapel Street Bazaar, VIC**

Clear acrylic chair, on chrome legs, c1975.

$115 - $135   **Bowhows, NSW**

Retro vinyl swivel chair on aluminium base, c1960, 78cm wide, 95cm high, 78cm diameter.

$380 - $420   **Rock N Rustic, SA**

Pair of metal and plastic bar stools, c1950, 33cm deep, 98cm high.

$185 - $205   **Chapel Street Bazaar, VIC**

Stainless steel and aluminium hospital bedside cabinet and drawers, of typical pre 1970 Namco design with rear castors, 39cm deep, 51cm wide, 94cm high.

$360 - $400   **Industria, VIC**

Metal desk with glass top and eight drawers, c1970, 76cm deep, 142cm wide, 77cm high.

$3100 - $3300   **Mondo Trasho, VIC**

Chrome 'Zig Zag' chair with vinyl cushions, c1970, 50cm deep, 50cm wide, 80cm high.

$630 - $730   **Mondo Trasho, VIC**

METAL, GLASS & PLASTIC

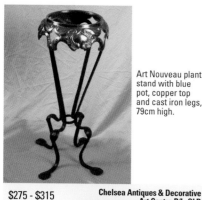

Art Nouveau plant stand with blue pot, copper top and cast iron legs, 79cm high.

$275 - $315

Chelsea Antiques & Decorative Art Centre P/L, QLD

Green plastic injection moulded stool, c1970.

$65 - $85

Bowhows, NSW

Funky orange phone table with unusual glass top and vinyl seat, c1960, 90cm long, 38cm deep.

$75 - $95

Vintage Living, ACT

'Framac' teak and painted metal Dining Suite, c1965, 153cm long, 71cm wide, 91cm high.

$900 - $1000

Tiffany Dodd Antique & 20th Century Furniture, QLD

Six seater dining suite with original polka dot vinyl and red laminex tabletop, c1950, 152cm long, 92cm wide, 74cm high.

$500 - $600

Northside Secondhand Furniture, QLD

Warren Platner table, nickel-plated steel construction with black plastic terminations, 16mm glass top, c1960, 75.5cm high, 121.5cm diameter.

$1880 - $2080

506070, NSW

Stainless steel ex-hospital trolley on castors, ubiquitous plain design, 80cm long, 46cm deep, 95cm high.

$360 - $400

Industria, VIC

Metal and glass top chess table, 43cm high, 40cm diam.

$85 - $105

Chapel Street Bazaar, VIC

Chrome and smoke glass tea wagon, c1950, 80cm long, 45cm wide, 60cm high.

$330 - $370

The New Farm Antique Centre, QLD

Set of three black leather Siesta chairs, designed by Ingmar Relling, c1970, 92cm high.

$840 - $940

Tiffany Dodd Antique & 20th Century Furniture, QLD

Two seater sofa with arms from the '1, 2, 3 System' by Verner Panton, manufactured by Frite Hansen Denmark, c1960, 130cm long, 77cm deep, 70cm high.

$4300 - $4500

506070, NSW

'Falcon' chair and footstool, designed in 1970 by Sigurd Ressell in Norway, chocolate leather on suspended canvas sling on laminated rosewood coloured timber supports, 80cm deep, 76cm wide, 100cm high.

$1350 - $1550

Plasma, VIC

Johannes Andersen designed teak sofa table, c1950, 150cm long, 60cm deep, 53cm high.

$420 - $460

Mid Century Modern, SA

Pair of Saarinen style swivel stools, c1970.

$800 - $900

Vampt, NSW

'Tulip' chair in black leather and steel designed by Kastholm & Fabricius, made by Alfred Kill in Germany, by Danish designers made by the original manufacturer, now being made by a different company, c1960, 59cm deep, 73cm wide, 107cm high.

$2100 - $2300

Plasma, VIC

Tulip Chair

Designed in 1964 by the Danish duo Jorgen Kastholm and Preben Fabricius, the 'Tulip', or 'Bucket', chair is a classic example of the Danish postwar Modern style. Along with Designers such as Arne Jacobsen (The 'Egg', and 'Swan' chairs), and Poul Kjaerholm ('PK', series), Kastholm and Fabricius pioneered the use of modern materials and production techniques to realize complex and previously unattainable forms.

The Tulip is an example of this new chapter in Danish design history. Made of moulded fiberglass with a leather upholstered latex 'jacket', cover, and perched on a single piece cast base, it has a delicate, insectile quality.

Their attention to detail and precise specifications were, however, not at all new to Danish Furniture manufacturing. The great Danish tradition of cabinet making had before the war produced pared back, elegant and curvaceous designs in timber. The modern invent of synthetics such as fiberglass and high tensile, lightweight aluminium merely allowed a new generation of designers to produce an almost limitless array of 'plastic', designs whilst keeping one foot rooted firmly in tradition.

The Tulip chair is now manufactured by Walter Knoll with various bases available. Older examples by Alfred Kill with the 3 legged base are the ones to search out. Original variations include castor wheels, height adjustable stem and high or low backs.

Set of eight Hans J Wegner design teak dining chairs, c1955, 52cm long, 43cm deep, 78cm high.

$1400 - $1550

Mid Century Modern, SA

Armchairs by Swedfurn, c1970.

$2100 - $2300

Flashback, VIC

Danish gentleman's chair made from rosewood and beech, designed by Fin Juhl, c1950, 55cm deep, 49cm wide, 75cm high.

$1750 - $1950

Vampt, NSW

FURNITURE

Danish wingback armchair, designed by Svend Skipper, new upholstery, c1950.

$5050 - $5450

Vampt, NSW

Original Saarinen tulip chairs, c1950.

$810 - $910

Vampt, NSW

Modernist arm chair designed by Danish born Jens Risom produced by Latchford (under license from Knoll Furniture, New York), upholstered in berber and sitting on a black-bean skid base.

$870 - $910

Mondo Trasho, VIC

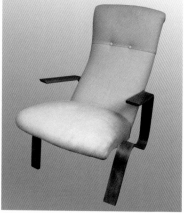

'Grasshopper Chair 61', designed by Eero Saarinen for Knoll, laminated bentwood birch frame, c1950, 88cm deep, 72cm wide, 99cm high.

$800 - $900

The Junk Company, VIC

Dining chair, model 3107 designed by Arne Jacobsen in Denmark 1955 and later made by Fritz Hansen, Denmark, formed ash plywood and chromed metal legs. A much copied chair, but never copied well, c1986, 51cm deep, 46cm wide, 75cm high.

$300 - $340

Plasma, VIC

Teak chest of drawers with shaped handles, c1950, 44cm deep, 82cm wide, 122cm high.

$550 - $650

Mid Century Modern, SA

Small Danish rosewood three drawer chest of drawes, c1960, 150cm long, 29cm deep, 52cm wide, 60cm high.

$410 - $450

Vampt, NSW

Teak sideboard with cabinet and six drawers, c1950, 43cm deep, 120cm wide, 148cm high.

$750 - $850

Mid Century Modern, SA

Danish rocking chair, c1970, 117cm high.

$410 - $450

Tiffany Dodd Antique & 20th Century Furniture, QLD

Teak chest of drawers with fitted handles, c1950, 45cm deep, 100cm wide, 102cm high.

$480 - $520

Mid Century Modern, SA

Pair of Danish teak bedside tables, c1960, 36cm deep, 49cm wide, 50cm high.

$1400 - $1600

Vampt, NSW

Teak retro sideboard, typical of Australian made pieces with Scandinavian influences, c1960, 153cm long, 46cm deep, 127cm high.

$700 - $800

Garry Auton Antiques, NSW

Retro style four drawer teak chest of drawer on splayed legs, c1960, 45cm deep, 75cm wide, 82cm high.

$130 - $150

Secondhand Furniture Mart, TAS

Danish teak storage cupboard on oak base, c1960, 175cm wide, 118cm high.

$900 - $1000

Found Objects, VIC

Three drawer Danish rosewood cabinet, c1960, 30cm deep, 71cm wide, 62cm high.

$730 - $830

Vampt, NSW

Danish five drawer desk in rosewood, consisting of two drawers on each side, c1950, 140cm long, 70cm deep, 75cm high.

$2500 - $2700

Three Quarters 20th C Furnishings, VIC

Lounge suite, with two single seats and one two seater lounge, upholstered in brilliant green wool, with teak frame, c1960.

$480 - $520

Bowhows, NSW

Scandinavian teak credenza with shaped doors, c1950, 210cm long, 44cm deep, 116cm high.

$750 - $850

Mid Century Modern, SA

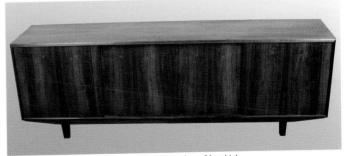

Danish rosewood sideboard, 196cm long, 44cm deep, 64cm high.

$3350 - $3550

Vampt, NSW

Danish wall mirror with teak frame, c1960, 59cm high.

$125 - $145   **Tiffany Dodd Antique & 20th Century Furniture, QLD**

Danish silver birch dressing table with wing mirrors flanking central mirror, glass shelving to centre, side drawers plus two matching bedside cabinets, ex-Dutch Embassy 1950's, c1935, 162cm high.

$650 - $750   **Vintage Living, ACT**

Custom made teak chess table with slide-out reversable top and plain teak on other side and storage compartment, c1960, 62cm long, 45cm wide, 56cm high.

$255 - $295   **Retro Active, VIC**

Teak chest with six graduated drawers, c1960, 61cm long, 45cm deep, 132cm high.

$330 - $380   **Secondhand Furniture Mart, TAS**

Pair of Scandinavian leather and timber framed armchairs, c1970, 80cm deep, 95cm wide, 70cm high.

$500 - $600   **20th Century Furniture & Effects, VIC**

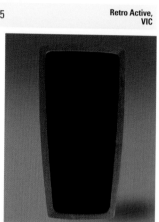

Scandinavian teak frame, amoeba form wall mirror, c1960, 38cm wide, 75cm high.

$85 - $105   **Cool & Collected, SA**

Two tiered teak sofa table with a slide out end, c1950, 167cm long, 60cm wide, 48cm high.

$380 - $420   **Mid Century Modern, SA**

Moon shaped teak sofa table, c1955, 150cm long, 70cm deep, 50cm high.

$370 - $420   **Mid Century Modern, SA**

Danish rosewood sofa table with wicker shelf, c1950, 150cm long, 50cm deep, 49cm high.

$1350 - $1550   **Vampt, NSW**

Danish modern style, long teak coffee table, c1960, 150.5cm long, 45cm deep, 48cm high.

$500 - $600   **506070, NSW**

'Americal' aluminum height adjustable office chair by Shaw Walker, U.S.A., c1950, 60cm wide, 85cm high.

$1150 - $1350

Barry McKay, NSW

'Hat Trick' chair, designed by Frank Gehry, manufactured by Knoll, USA, made of laminated hard white maple strips, c1990, 51cm deep, 58cm wide, 86cm high.

$1500 - $1700

506070, NSW

Chair, back and arms upholstered in black vinyl, the seat in black wool, on teak legs with Bakelite feet, c1965.

$40 - $50

Bowhows, NSW

Rosewood veneered Eames lounge chair with moulded plywood seat and back on a chromed metal frame, designed by Ray and Charles Eames in 1946, c1970, 57cm deep, 56cm wide, 69.5cm high.

$2100 - $2300

50,6070, NSW

Daf chair with seat shells of molded reinforced plastic, fixed back and a black leather seat cushion, base of curved tubular steel, designer George Nelson, manufacturer Herman Miller, USA, c1958, 56cm deep, 73cm wide, 78cm high.

$1500 - $1700

506070, NSW

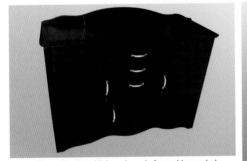

French oak parquetry top sideboard, c1950, 180cm long, 50cm deep, 90cm high.

Australian red cedar sideboard, made from old recycled timber, c1950, 132cm long, 42cm deep, 96cm high.

$580 - $680

Town & Country Antiques, NSW

$2600 - $2800

Seanic Antiques, VIC

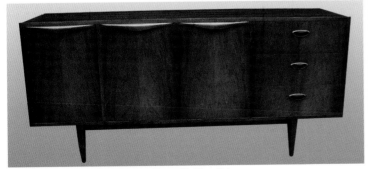

Wooden magazine rack, c1970, 25cm wide, 40cm high.

Walnut sideboard, c1965, 46cm deep, 182cm wide, 70cm high.

$750 - $850

Tiffany Dodd Antique & 20th Century Furniture, QLD

$30 - $40

Chapel Street Bazaar, VIC

Set of six French dining chairs on cabriole legs, original upholstery curved cameo back, c1950.

$3000 - $3200

French Heritage Antiques, VIC

Victorian ash, three door communications cabinet used to house communication equipment on some Melbourne platforms. Manufactured at Spotswood workshops and used at platforms where the main station is above the platforms - Malvern, Toorak, Armadale and Hawksburn, c1947, 42cm deep, 72cm wide, 165cm high.

$1600 - $1800

Victorian Railway Workshops Art & Antiques, VIC

Timber framed office chair with red vinyl upholstery, c1950.

$270 - $310

Doug Up On Bourke, NSW

Silky oak swivel office chair, c1935.

$275 - $315

Paddington Antique Centre Pty Ltd, QLD

Black and white cord saucer chair, c1950, 65cm deep, 70cm wide, 70cm high.

$60 - $80

The Junk Company, VIC

Set of two maple arm chairs with washable covers, c1960, 60cm long, 60cm deep, 85cm high.

$480 - $520

Towers Antiques & Collectables, NSW

Bombo style fibreglass chair and stool, c1970.

$1550 - $1750

Vampt, NSW

Swivel tub chair with new upholstery, c1960, 63cm wide, 76cm high.

$800 - $900

Vampt, NSW

Child's 'Bear' chair, 47cm high.

$45 - $65

Paddington Antique Centre Pty Ltd, QLD

French Louis XV style walnut carved armchair/fauteuil with new upholstery, c1950, 58cm deep, 75cm wide, 105cm high.

$2850 - $3050

Antiques On Consignment, NSW

Leather armchair with rosewood arm rests, c1950, 80cm deep, 77cm wide, 95cm high.

$380 - $420

Mid Century Modern, SA

Upholstered round chair, c1950.

$320 - $360

20th Century Antiques & Collectables Market, QLD

Orange vinyl office chair, c1955.

$115 - $135

Bowhows, NSW

Vintage cane hanging chair, c1970.

$420 - $460

Design Dilemas, VIC

Maple day bed, boasting original fabricoid upholstery, c1955, 71cm deep, 190cm wide, 72cm high.

$650 - $750

Tiffany Dodd Antique & 20th Century Furniture, QLD

Pair late 50's ladies boudoir chairs, diamond button back upholstery, one in tourquise, one in green, c1950, 49cm deep, 58cm wide, 81cm high.

$205 - $245

Kenny's Antiques, VIC

Child's bentwood chair with ebony finish, c1964.

$140 - $170

Step Back Antiques, VIC

French plastic flower chair, c1974, 91cm high.

$185 - $205

Tiffany Dodd Antique & 20th Century Furniture, QLD

Five piece outdoor setting with square table and four armchairs, c1950.

$2350 - $2550

Antiques On Consignment, NSW

Rosewood sideboard cabinet with drawers to back, c1950, 53cm deep, 190cm wide, 125cm high.

$1100 - $1300

Mid Century Modern, SA

Kartel round unit made of hard plastic, c1970, 65cm high, 44cm diameter.

$140 - $160

Chapel Street Bazaar, VIC

All original 1950's ash TV chair with grey fleck vinyl, c1955, 65cm deep, 58cm wide, 85cm high.

$130 - $150

Vintage Living, ACT

Silver ash dentist cabinet with ebonised trim, a black vitrolite top and segmented drawers, c1950, 132cm high.

$780 - $880

Tiffany Dodd Antique & 20th Century Furniture, QLD

Brown velvet bentwood foot stool back supports, teak legs with timber frame, c1955, 35cm wide, 55cm high.

$135 - $155

Bowhows, NSW

Rosewood chest of drawers with fitted handles and slight bow front, c1950, 45cm deep, 84cm wide, 115cm high.

$750 - $850

Mid Century Modern, SA

French Art Deco auto trolley, original glass and fixtures, c1920, 78cm long, 47cm deep, 69cm high.

$635 - $735

Urbanized, VIC

Kitchen dresser featuring lino backing and bench, shaped glazed doors to top and unusual shape, c1950, 37cm deep, 135cm wide, 175cm high.

$630 - $730

44 Brooke Street, VIC

Tasmanian oak leadlight kitchen cabinet, c1940, 135cm long, 40cm deep, 165cm high.

$450 - $500

Secondhand Furniture Mart, TAS

Room divider, Queensland maple and laminated plywood doors and shelving, A-frame form cabinet and shelving that is self-supporting, c1950, 97cm long, 46cm deep, 196cm high.

$940 - $1040

506070, NSW

French cherry wood parquetry top, draw leaf table with cabriole legs, c1950, 150cm long, 100cm wide, 75cm high.

$2850 - $3050

French Heritage Antiques, VIC

Comfortable and stylish outdoor table and two chairs made of plasticised wire, c1970.

$255 - $295

506070, NSW

Rosewood draw leaf table with a set of six matching rosewood chairs, c1950.

$1100 - $1300

Mid Century Modern, SA

Australian hardwood stool with webbing upholstery, c1950, 47cm long, 39cm deep 15cm high.

$85 - $105

Rose Cottage Antiques, ACT

Australian Queensland maple tea trolley with cutlery drawer, c1950, 74cm long, 40cm wide, 74cm high.

$340 - $380

The Exchange Galleries, NSW

Whitefriar's English art glass bowl in the purple bubbles pattern by Baxter, c1956, 16cm wide, 18cm diameter

NZ$240 $280   **Peachgrove Antiques, New Zealand**

Large Whitefriars vase in smokey grey, c1950, 23cm wide, 31cm high.

$600 - $700   **Obsidian Antiques, NSW**

A vintage Whitefriars vase of beaker form, spiral decoration in blue on pale green body, original paper label on base, c1950, 12.5cm diameter

NZ$180 - $200   **Anticus Antiques, New Zealand**

Whitefriars banjo vase, in tangerine tone, c1950, 35cm wide.

$310 - $350   **Woollahra Decorative Arts Gallery, NSW**

Deep red Whitefriars vase, c1960, 15.5cm high, 10cm diameter

$110 - $130   **The Botanic Ark, VIC**

Whitefriars 'Knobbly' art glass vase, c1960, 23cm high.

$85 - $105   **Chapel Street Bazaar, VIC**

Whitefriars textured cylinder vase, c1970, 22cm high, 6cm diameter

$100 - $120   **Obsidian Antiques, NSW**

English glass vase by Whitefriars, designed by Godfrey Baxter, c1967

$1900 - $2100   **Gallery Narcisse, NSW**

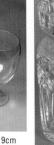

Set of eight brandy balloons, c1910, 13cm high, 9cm diameter

$125 - $145   **Shaws Antiques, NSW**

Crystal biscuit barrel by Waterford, c1950, 13cm wide, 17cm high, 13cm diameter

$250 - $290   **Mentone Beach Antiques Centre, VIC**

Blue glass float bowl with fish centrepiece, c1950, 29cm long, 22cm high.

$250 - $300.   **The Mill Markets, VIC**

Pink art glass centrepiece, c1950, 46cm long, 25cm deep, 17cm high.

$170 - $210.   **Obsidian Antiques, NSW**

Whitefriars 'Knobbly' bowl, c1960, 5cm high, 14cm diam.

$40 - $60   **Chapel Street Bazaar, VIC**

Clear textured glass cube vase, 'Marguerite' by Frank Thrower for Dartington glass, c1970, 11.5cm high.

$40 - $50

Frhapsody, WA

Okra English studio glass vase in ruby with swirled iridescence, c1990, 18.5cm high, 7.5cm diameter

$200 - $230

Pendulum Antiques, SA

Emerald green, art glass 'splash' vase, c1970, 15cm wide, 29cm high

$75 - $95.

Armadale Antique Centre, VIC

Stuart Crystal decanter, c1950, 26cm high.

$110 - $130.

Western District Antique Centre, VIC

Webb & Corbett crystal decanter with six glasses, c1950.

NZ$145 - $165

Gregory's of Greerton, New Zealand

Edinburgh crystal decanter with six matching glasses, signed, c1950, 10cm wide, 25cmhigh.

$275 - $315

Helen's On The Bay, QLD

Caithness paperweight 'Framboise' LE 554/560 by Philip Chaplain, signed on base, c1997, 8cm diameter

$410 - $450

Pastimes Antiques, NSW

Peter McDougall LE paperweight with two blue lamp worked flowers set over a translucent amethyst ground with six side and one top facet. LE ≤ signature cane in base, c2003, 6cm diameter

$520 - $620

Pastimes Antiques, NSW

Signed and dated Mayauel Ward cylindrical paper-weight with a double-sided burst of orange flowers over a sand and pebble ground, limited edition of 25, c1998,11cm high, 7cm dia.

$2850 - $3050

Pastimes Antiques, NSW

Clear cut crystal claret jug by Stuart Crystal, c1975, 26cm high, 14cm diam

$380 - $420

Glenelg Antique Centre, SA

Moon crystal paperweight from Caithness, Scotland, c1980, 5cm high.

$55 - $75

Brae-mar Antiques, NSW

Art glass basket, 23cm long, 21cm wide

$75 - $95

Shop 21, Southern Antique Centre, NSW

Art Deco set of three toilette bottles in prismatic shapes, designed in 1936 by Rudolf Eschler for Moser, made in Czechoslovakia in 1957 on the 100th Anniversary of the Moser glassworks, c1957.

$1150 - $1350.   **Retro Active, VIC**

French Daum crystal salt and pepper dishes with matching spoons, in their original box, c1950, 6cm wide, 4cm high, 6cm diameter

$330 - $370   **Mentone Beach Antiques Centre, VIC**

A conical Waterford crystal decanter, c1980, 27cm high.

NZ$230 -$270   **Gregory's of Greerton, New Zealand**

Russian crystal centrepiece in the form of a conical bowl on a circular footed base, c1990, 28cm high, 24cm diameter

NZ$275 - $315   **Gregory's of Greerton, New Zealand**

Czechoslovakian glass comport, orange overlay, 14cm high, 24cm diam eter

$260 - $300.   **Tarlo & Graham, VIC**

German cut crystal wine glass with a green flared top and hand and wheel-cut decorations, c1950, 20cm high

$115 - $135   **Armadale Antique Centre, VIC**

German cut crystal wine goblet, c1950, 20cm high.

$105 - $125   **Armadale Antique Centre, VIC**

Pair of Rhyton glass Springbok ornamental ceremonial cups, c1970, 15cm long, 8cm high.

$230 - $270   **Chapel Street Bazaar, VIC**

Four Stuart Crystal goblets with bird etching, c1950, 16cm high

$80 - $120   **Adornments, QLD.**

German cut crystal, blue wine glass with a flared top, c1950, 21cm high.

$105 - $125.   **Armadale Antique Centre, VIC**

Ruby red Bavarian glass wheel etched goblet with Masonic symbols, for ceremonial purposes, c1960, 18cm high, 8cm diameter

$650 - $750   **Pieces, TAS**

Polish hand blown aqua marine drinks set, 15cm wide, 26cm high.

$65 - $85

Cool & Collected, SA

'Reveil', opalescent glass figurine of a nude with flowing hair, incised signature 'Sabino, France', c1950, 7cm wide, 17cm high.

$600 - $700.

Armadale Antique Centre, VIC

Crystal Hummel figure of a girl 'Visiting an Invalid', c1990, 10cm high.

NZ$310 - $350

Collector's Choice, New Zealand

Millefiori glass jug, c1950.

$85 - $105.

Victory Theatre Antiques, NSW

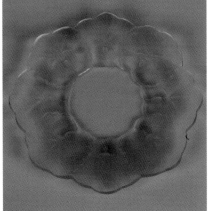

A small Lalique plate, 'Honfluer' design, c1965, 15cm diameter

$120 - $140.

Shirley & Noel Daly Antiques, VIC

Mid 20th century triple layered Bohemia flash glass vase, c1960, 26cm high.

$155 - $175

The Junk Company, VIC

Czechoslovakian cobalt blue crystal vase, 32cm high.

$500 - $600.

The BottomDrawer Antique Centre, VIC

Rene Lalique vase with doves, acid-etched signature to base, c1950, 10cm wide, 12cm high.

$1050 - $1250.

Galeria del Centro, NSW

Set of four steel-moulded vases by Jiri Ripacek for Bohemia Glass Company, c1970

$420 - $460

Found Objects, VIC

GLASS

Signed green Holmegaard bowl, c1960, 26cm diam

$220 - $260   **Vampt, NSW**

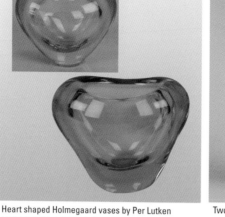

Heart shaped Holmegaard vases by Per Lutken

$185 - $225   **Vampt, NSW**

Two Holmegaard vases by Per Lutken, c1960.

$290 - $330   **Vampt, NSW**

Two green Holmegaard gull vases, c1960

$870 - $970   **Vampt, NSW**

Holmegaard art glass vase, blue overlay over milk glass, c1950, 35cm high.

NZ$55 -$75   **Peachgrove Antiques, New Zealand**

Green Holmegaard vase, c1960, 26cm high.

$240 - $280   **Vampt, NSW**

Sommerso vase in amber and blue by Vicki Lindstrand for 'Kosta', c1960, 17cm high.

$500 - $600   **Virtanen Antiques, VIC**

Set of three signed Vicki Lindstrand vases, in rich amber colouring,designed for 'Kosta', c1960.

$1000 - $1200   **Virtanen Antiques, VIC**

Signed double cased Kosta bowl, the outer casing with a thick clear glass and the inner a deep red glass, c1960, 19cm deep, 6cm high, 19cm diam

$175 - $195   **The Junk Company, VIC**

'Fishermen', a Kosta crystal and engraved vase designed by Vicki Lindstrand, c1955.

$1550 - $1750   **Gallery Narcisse, NSW**

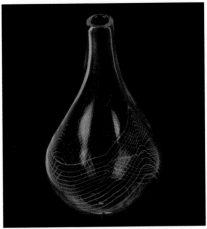

'Arabesque', a Kosta vase designed by Vicki Lindstrand, Sweden, c1950.

$1850 - $2050

Gallery Narcisse, NSW

Sommerso vase in amber and blue, by Vicki Lindstrand for 'Kosta', signed and numbered, c1960, 24cm high.

$700 - $800

Virtanen Antiques, VIC

White and green hand blown Scandanavian art glass bowl, c1970, 24cm deep, 14cm high.

$370 - $410

The Junk Company, VIC

Swedish tear drop glass bowl, c1960, 24cm long, 12cm wide, 6cm high.

$75 - $95

The Junk Company, VIC

Red Swedish glass bowl, c1960, 21cm wide, 7cm high, 21cm diameter

$175 - $195

The Junk Company, VIC

Festiva glass candlesticks, designed by Timo Sarpaneva, Finland 1967, c1970, 41.5cm high.

$20 - $30.

506070, NSW

Green Swedish art glass vase, paper label attached 'Made in Sweden', attractive sculptured form, 1960, 29cm high, 9cm diameter.

$55 - $75.

Image Objex, VIC

Aseda glass vase 'Svenska', by Bo Borgstrom, Sweden, 24cm high, 85cm diameter.

$150 - $170

Shop 26, Antiques & Collectables - Hamilton, NSW

A set of Stromberg Shyitan vases in clear and purple, designed by Gunnar Nylund, c1950.

$230 - $260

Le Contraste, VIC

SCANDINAVIAN

Swedish signed Orrefors glass bowl, c1970, 6cm high, 17cm diameter.

$220 - $260   **Towers Antiques & Collectables, NSW**

Large purple coquille bowl by Paul Kedelv, made by Flygfors, Sweden, c1960.

$500 - $600   **506070, NSW**

Oiva Tokkia bowl made by 'Arabia', Finland, c1970, 13cm wide, 12cm high, 13cm diameter.

$110 - $130   **The Junk Company, VIC**

'Pala' vase designed by Helena Tynell for Riihimaen Lasi of Finland, in clear textured glass with sticker, c1968, 7cm high.

$40 - $50.   **frhapsody, WA**

'Faces', an Orrefors ariel technique vase, designed by Ingelborg Lundin, c1970.

$11000 - $12000   **Gallery Narcisse, NSW**

Swedish Art glass vase, c1960, 16cm high, 8cm diameter

$135 - $155   **Antiques & Collectables Centre - Ballarat, VIC**

Swedish Pukeberg vase, mould blown with protruding circular pattern, c1960, 9cm high.

$30 - $40   **frhapsody, WA**

A variety of Finnish glass vases by Riihimaen, c1970, 22cm high.

$65 - $85   **Design Dilemas, VIC**

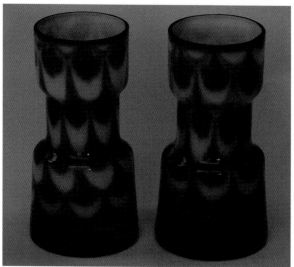

Pair of handblown Swedish vases, c1960, 25cm high.

$85 - $105   **Eclectica, TAS**

Blue glass candlestick by Kaj Franck Nuutajarvi Works Finland Notsjo 63, c1900, 17.5cm high.

$205 - $245   **Yanda Aboriginal Art Melbourne, VIC**

Exceptional aquatic bird by Seguso Arte Vetri, Murano. Each bird or animal from this series being a typical one of a kind mastership of Archimede Seguso c1970, 40cm long, 15cm high

$2400 - $2600   **Kilbarron Antiques and Collectables, VIC**

Archimede Seguso (1909 - 1999)

Archimede Seguso was born in 1909. He belonged to a Murano family with centuries of ancient glass-making traditions going back to the Middle Ages.

Archimede Seguso was apprenticed to his father, Antonio, in the glass-house La Vetreria Artistica Barovier where his father was a partner. Working alongside the designers Vittorio Zecchin and Flavio Poli, Archimede Seguso acquired impressive manual skills at the furnace resulting in a vibrant glass-house.

By twenty, Archimede Seguso was a true glass maestro and by 1945 had established his own glass-house.

In 1957 he revived his earlier models of animals in opalescent glass with delicate stripes.

By birth, by training, by his working life, by the way in which he lives the art of glass, he embodies the qualities that have characterised Murano culture and that over the centuries have determined the professional and social prestige of the master glass worker (Rosa Barovier Mentasti, I Vetri Di Archimede Seguso, 2002).

Murano glass fish, 'Seguso', c1980, 44cm high.

$600 - $700   **Gorgeous, VIC**

Pair of Murano Seguso figures, c1950, 36cm high.

$1050 - $1250.   **Ritzy Bits - ACT, ACT**

A Flavio Poli double sommerso dog figurine for Seguso Vetri d'Arte, c1950, 13cm wide, 24cm high.

$550 - $650   **Armadale Antique Centre, VIC**

Glass Seguso Duck, c1950, 30cm high.

$380 - $420   **Antique Centre of Stonnington, VIC**

Murano red glass vase attributed to Seguso, c1950, 17cm high.

$280 - $310   **Elizabeth Antiques, NSW**

Antonio da Ros Cenedese & Co. glass Goede bowls, c1960, 22cm wide.

$155 - $175   **Design Dilemas, VIC**

Murano glass sommerso cockatoo, by Antonio deRos for Cenedese & Co. using the sommerso technique, c1950, 14cm wide, 20cm high.

$1650 - $1850   **Armadale Antique Centre, VIC**

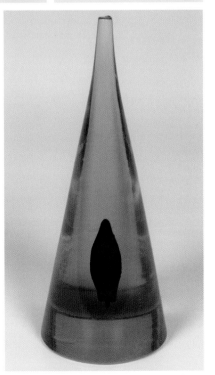

Murano glass bowl signed on label 'Pietro Tosso', unusual colour, c1950, 14cm long, 12cm wide, 7cm high

$300 - $340   **Armadale Antique Centre, VIC**

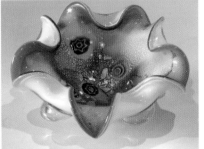

Large Fratelli Toso Murano glass bowl by A.V.E.M, c1955, 32cm wide.

$155 - $175   **Design Dilemas, VIC**

Antonio da Ros sommerso obelisk paperweight, for Cenedese & Co, c1950, 6cm wide, 17cm high.

$360 - $400   **Armadale Antique Centre, VIC**

Large vase designed by Dino Martens for Aureliano Toso with superb Murrine pinwheels set in the clear glass exterior against the white interior. Value is added to this item by the size, clarity, colour variation and sharpness of the pinwheels and the item's size. c1950, 30cm high, 16cm diameter.

$3650 - $3850   **Kilbarron Antiques and Collectables, VIC**

Dino Martens (1894 - 1970)

In the 1950s Dino Martens was one of the leading innovative glass artists in Murano, Italy.

He was born in Venice in 1894 and studied painting at the Accademia di Belle Arti in Venice from c1918 - 1924.

After completing his painting studies, he worked freelance for more than 10 years as a painter and designer of hollow glass and mosaics for a number of companies including S.A.L.I.R. and Salviati.

Late 1930s he was appointed artistic director and head designer of Aureliano Toso glassworks in Murano.

His design creativity in composition and use of colour was set free. By 1948 he had already designed his first patchwork Zanfirici in subtle colours as well as the Oriente in strong colours. His pieces were often characterised by striking asymmetric form. He continued designing for Aureliano Toso until the early sixties.

A Fasce vase designed by Dino Martens for Aureliano Toso, Murano, c1958.

$2700 -$2900   **Gallery Narcisse, NSW**

Six cased glass bowls by Carlo Moretti, c1970, 14cm wide

$430 -$470   **Design Dilemas, VIC**

Labelled Dino Martens ewer, for Aureliano Toso, c1950, 19cm wide, 36cm high.

$2350 - $2550   **Armadale Antique Centre, VIC**

Murano glass rooster by Dino Martens, c1953, 25cm high

$1750 - $1950   **Ritzy Bits -ACT, ACT**

Barbini (left) and Cenedese (right) Italian glass paperweights, c1960, 10cm wide, 15cm high.

$275 - $315   **Chapel Street Bazaar, VIC**

Art glass vase signed Molina blue, yellow and green in colour, c1960, 130cm wide, 90cm high.

$140 - $160   **Chris' Antiques & Collectables, VIC**

Murano glass figure of a cat, signed V. Nason, c1950, 22cm high.

$520 - $620.   **Elizabeth Antiques, NSW**

Green decorative jug by Opalina Florentina, c1960, 32cm high, 16cm diameter

$115 -$135   **The Botanic Ark, VIC**

Alfredo Barbini double Sommerso Bullicante & Aventurine bowl, c1950, 15cm wide, 7cm high.

$205 - $245   **Armadale Antique Centre, VIC**

Turquoise and red decorative bottle by Opalina Florentina, 45cm high, 11cm diameter

$175 - $195   **The Botanic Ark, VIC**

Large blue and green Murano glass bird signed V. Nason and C. Murano, c1960, 26cm long.

$1900 - $2100   **Alan Syber's Antiques Antiquarian, VIC**

A large and complex Mezza Filigrana vase, attributed to Carlo Scarpa for Venini & Co.,c1920, 16cm wide, 28cm high.

$2350 - $2550	Armadale Antique Centre,VIC

Sommerso vase with abstract twists, by Luciano Gaspari for Salviati & Co., c1950, 11cm wide, 26cm high.

$1350 - $1550.	Armadale Antique Centre, VIC

Louredan Rosin

Loredano Rosin was an Italian master craftsman and sculptor in glass who died in 1991.

Studio Rosin was founded in 1992 to perpetuate the styles of Loredano Rosin,and is headed by his brother Dino Rosin

Contemporary Italian glass figure in Sommerso technique, naturalistic clear glass case, signed Loredano Rosin, c1970, 38cm wide, 16cm high.

$5750 - $6150	Philip Cross Antiques, NSW

Unsigned Arto Vetraria Murano vase, c1950, 13cm high, 11cm diam

$1900 - $2100	Alan Syber's Antiques Antiquarian, VIC

Italian glass vase by Alfredo Barbini, for Gino Cenedese. Murano, c1950.

$11500 - $12500	Gallery Narcisse, NSW

Carlo Moretti beaker vase for Fratelli Toso, Murano, c1960, 25cm high, 15cm diameter

$650 - $750	Pastimes Antiques, NSW

A shortened teardrop shaped vase by Aldo Nason from the Yokohama series with white, blue, gold bullseye murrine and latticino inclusions on a red, gold and silver ground, c1960, 16cm wide, 26cm high

$6750 - $7150	Kilbarron Antiques and Collectables, VIC

Barbini glass vase, pink with mauve banding, internal bubbles and etched signature, Murano Italy, c1975, 25cm wide, 25cm high.

$800 - $900	Tarlo & Graham, VIC

'Tutti-Frutti' vase by Ansolo Fuga for Arte Vetri Murano (A.Ve.M), c1950, 10cm wide, 15cm high.

$1100 - $1300	Armadale Antique Centre, VIC

Hartil Latticino glass vase, c1950, 8cm long, 15cm high.

$90 - $120.	Southern Antique Centre, NSW

Venetian glass vase by Van Zanfinco, c1950, 26cm high.

$600 - $700	Malvern Antique Market, VIC

Pair of 'Arte Murano' Italian vases, c1980, 20cm high, 13cm diameter

$135 - $155	Antique Effects, VIC

Glass vase in rich emerald green, cobalt and clear, c1950, 18cm high.

$275 - $315 **Collectique, VIC**

Three interlocking vases by Alfredo Barbini, Murano, c1970, 23cm high.

$330 - $370 **Found Objects, VIC**

Murano glass clown ashtray, c1940, 10cm deep, 15cm wide, 19cm high.

$225 - $265 **Angel's Antiques, VIC**

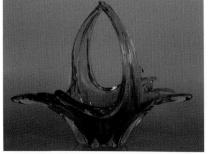

Murano glass basket with air bubbles design, c1970, 27cm long, 24cm high.

$75 - $95 **Towers Antiques & Collectables, NSW**

Murano art glass bowl, 27cm long, 17cm high.

$90 - $100 **Marrick's Furniture, VIC**

Murano glass pheasant, c1940, 33cm long, 24cm high.

$275 - $315 **Angel's Antiques, VIC**

Murano glass basket shaped bowl, c1950, 11cm wide, 12cm high.

$65 - $85 **Galeria del Centro, NSW**

Heavy, five pointed blue glass bowl, pulegoso technique, c1950, 9.5cm high.

$110 - $130 **frhapsody, WA**

Orange decorative bottle by Opalina Florentina, c1960, 23cm high, 17cm diameter.

$110 - $130 **The Botanic Ark, VIC**

Purple art glass fruit bowl made in Italy, c1960, 24cm long, 24cm deep, 24cm wide, 9cm high, 24cm diameter

$70 - $90 **Dr Russell's Emporium, WA**

Murano art glass bowl, deep red background, c1950, 54cm long, 15cm high.

$180 - $200 **Ardeco Antiques & Collectables, WA**

Murano multi-coloured glass bowl, c1950, 23cm long, 18cm high.

$115 -$135   **Towers Antiques & Collectables, NSW**

Murano Sommerso bowl, c1955, 280cm wide, 8cm high

NZ$190 - $230   **Oxford Court Antiques Centre, New Zealand**

Blue glass organic vase, c1950, 19cm deep, 19cm wide, 27cm high, 19cm diameter

$135 - $155   **The Junk Company, VIC**

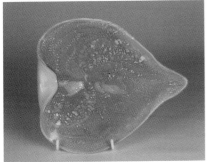

Cased Murano glass dish in the shape of a leaf, c1960.

$55 - $75   **Grant & Wendy Brookes, VIC**

Murano glass lipped bowl incorporating black, blue and silver, c1950, 11.5cm deep, 13.5cm wide, 5cm high.

$115 - $135   **Southside Antiques Centre, QLD**

Triple cased green, white and aventurine glass Murano shell shaped bowl, c1950, 19cm long, 11cm deep, 13cm high.

$350 - $390   **Pastimes Antiques, NSW**

Green art glass bowl, Italian made, c1960, 16cm long, 16cm deep, 16cm wide, 4cm high,16cm diameter

$60 - $80   **Dr Russell's Emporium, WA**

Murano glass scalloped bowl, c1950, 19cm deep, 11cm high.

$105 - $125   **Galeria del Centro, NSW**

Cranberry Murano glass bowl, c1950, 20cm long, 14cm high

$60 - $70   **Hollyhock Antiques, QLD**

Murano art glass cased bowl in blue, milk and clear, c1960, 18cm long, 15cm wide

$110 - $130   **Obsidian Antiques, NSW**

Murano glass bowl, 15cm high

$60 - $70   **Marrick's Furniture, VIC**

Amber cut art glass bowl with red base and scalloped edges, c1960, 15cm wide, 25cm high.

$115 - $135   **Helen's On The Bay, QLD**

Murano glass centrepiece bowl in blue and pink, c1950, 32cm long, 14cm deep, 12cm high.

$60 - $70   **Newport Temple Antiques, VIC**

Green and blue double layered Murano glass bowl, c1950, 16cm wide, 5cm high.

$85 - $105   **The Junk Company, VIC**

Retro glass comport, orange with yellow barley twist stem and base, Italian cased glass, c1970, 25cm high, 14.5cm diameter

$170 - $190   **Avoca Beach Antiques, NSW**

Red Murano glass bowl, c1950, 21cm long, 13cm deep, 24cm high.

$80 - $100   **Galeria del Centro, NSW**

Murano glass two colour, three sided bowl, c1950, 15cm wide, 8cm high.

$85 - $105   **Armadale Antique Centre, VIC**

Retro Italian cased glass comport, red bowl with red barley twist stem and base, c1970, 27cm high, 13.5cm diameter

$170 - $190   **Avoca Beach Antiques, NSW**

Murano candle stick, c1970, 100cm wide, 22cm high

NZ$185 - $205   **Oxford Court Antiques Centre, New Zealand**

Murano glass with dolphin stem, c1950, 25cm high

$205 - $245   **Antique Centre of Stonnington, VIC**

Art glass bowl in soft orange with clear glass edges, c1960, 16cm high, 24cm diameter

$110 - $130   **Helen's On The Bay, QLD**

Double cased Murano glass bowl, c1950, 28cm long, 17cm wide, 9cm high.

$215 - $255   **The Botanic Ark, VIC**

Hand blown green glass decanter with turquoise spiral and stopper, c1960, 41cm high, 16cm diameter

$140 - $160   **Retro Active, VIC**

Murano glass clown decanter, c1950, 34cm high

$410 - $450   **Sherwood Bazaar, QLD**

Murano green glass decanter with six glasses, gilded with hand painted enamel floral decoration, 26cm high.

$125 - $145.   **Kings Park Antiques & Collectables, SA**

Double layered green and blue Murano glass vase, c1950, 23cm deep, 23cm wide, 29cm high.

$175 - $195.   **The Junk Company, VIC**

Murano gilt and enamel glass goblet, c1950, 21cm high.

$275 - $315   **Armadale Antique Centre, VIC**

Italian art glass Murano clown, c1950, 12cm long, 9cm deep, 9cm wide, 19cm high

$275 - $315   **Dr Russell's Emporium, WA**

Zany pale blue and aventurine Murano glass bird with red crest, c1950, 19cm long, 12cm

$135 - $155   **Pastimes Antiques, NSW**

Murano art glass shell in clear to hazy white, pale peach inner colour on gilt speckled base portraying swirling water, c1945, 33cm wide, 22cm high

$330 - $370   **Heartland Antiques & Art, NSW**

Italian yellow cased decanter with amber stopper, c1960, 15cm wide, 23cm high

$130 - $150   **Obsidian Antiques, NSW**

Murano glass colourful clown, c1950, 9cm long, 7cm deep, 21cm high.

$185 - $205   **Towers Antiques & Collectables, NSW**

Pair of multi coloured Murano glass roosters with millefiori eyes, c1950, 14cm long, 12cm deep, 17cm high.

$500 - $600   **The Junk Company, VIC**

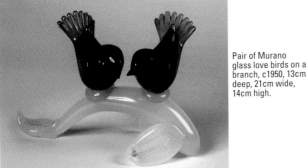

Pair of Murano glass love birds on a branch, c1950, 13cm deep, 21cm wide, 14cm high.

$225 - $265   **The Junk Company, VIC**

Large blue glass and gilt decorated decanter with spired stopper, 200cm wide, 600cm high.

$700 - $800.   **Tooronga Hall Antiques & Caulfield Antique W'house, VIC**

Murano glass bird in pink, c1950, 18cm long, 10cm deep, 30cm high

$480 - $520   **Towers Antiques & Collectables, NSW**

Murano angel fish, the speckled underbelly decorated with included glass beads, c1960, 19cm wide.

$380 - $420   **Shenton Park Antiques, WA**

Murano glass figurines, c1950, 12cm wide, 20cm high.

$470 - $510   **Richmond Antiques, TAS**

Murano glass duck figurine, c1950, 30cm high.

$330 - $370   **South Perth Antiques & Collectables, WA**

Murano bird figurine, c1950, 18cm wide, 35cm high.

$310 - $350   **Antiques & Collectables Centre - Ballarat, VIC**

Murano glass duck, c1950, 32cm long, 35cm wide, 25cm high

$330 - $370.   **Days of Olde Antiques & Collectables, VIC**

Pair of Murano glass figurines, c1950, 17cm high

$460 - $500   **Antiques & Collectables Centre -Ballarat, VIC**

Venetian glass rooster, c1960, 28cm high.

$200 - $240   **Burly Babs Collectables/Retro Relics, VIC**

Murano glass figure with gold inclusions, c1950, 19cm high

$370 - $420   **Past Connections Antiques & Decorative Arts, NSW**

Murano glass clown figurine, c1950, 26cm high.

$205 - $245   **Sherwood Bazaar, QLD**

Turquoise hand blown water set comprising a jug and six tall glasses, c1960.

$65 -$85   **Retro Active, VIC**

Murano glass lamp, white with gold fleck and a cream silk shade.

$480 - $520   **Chelsea Antiques & Decorative Art Centre P/L, QLD**

Murano glass tree made up of glass balls and leaves, c1950, 40cm wide, 48cm high.

NZ$410 - $450   **Antiques & Curiosities, New Zealand**

Murano glass dolphin lamp base, 17cm wide, 35cm high.

$380 - $420   **Nicki's Collection, NSW**

$120 - $160   **Pedlars Antique Market, SA**

Murano glass laticino vase, c1950, 18cm high, 7cm diameter.

Murano sommerso glass bird vase, c1960, 32cm high.

$175 - $195   **Yanda Aboriginal Art Melbourne, VIC**

Murano cased art glass vase in orange and salmon tones, c1960, 10cm long, 23cm high.

$120 - $135   **Obsidian Antiques, NSW**

Blue and green Murano glass vase, 30cm high.

$100 - $135   **Munro's Mill Antique Centre, NSW**

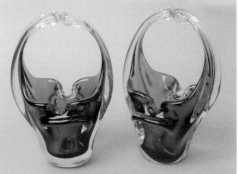

Pair of Murano glass vases in green with clear glass overlay, c1950, 12cm long, 9cm deep, 18cm high.

$160 - $200   **Towers Antiques & Collectables, NSW**

Double-cased red and yellow glass vase, c1960, 5cm deep, 10cm wide, 23cm high.

$245 - $285   **The Junk Company, VIC**

Italian Art glass vase, c1960, 20cm long, 20cm deep, 45cm high.

$250 - $280   **Le Contraste, VIC**

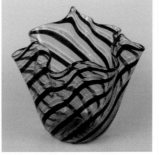

Acid etched Venini vase, c1950, 11cm diameter.

$330 - $370   **Antique Centre of Stonnington, VIC**

Miniature latticino two handled vase, 7cm high, 3cm diameter.

$270 - $310   **Chapel Street Bazaar, VIC**

Murano glass vase, 17cm high.

$180 - $200   **Marrick's Furniture, VIC**

Blue Murano glass vase, 30cm high.

$110 - $150   **Munro's Mill Antique Centre, NSW**

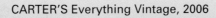

Murano vase, c1950, 64cm long, 22cm wide.

$175 - $195

Furniture Revisited, VIC

Clear glass and red 'Wave' design Murano glass vase, c1980, 30cm high.

$330 - $370

The Bottom Drawer Antique Centre, VIC

Murano cased art, glass vase in yellow, c1960, 31cm high, 16cm diameter.

$100 - $120

Obsidian Antiques, NSW

Long clear, red and orange Murano glass vase, c1980, 27cm high.

$440 - $480

The Bottom Drawer Antique Centre, VIC

Murano glass paperweight aquarium with original sticker. c1950, 9cm high, 7cm diameter.

$480 - $520

Mt Dandenong Antique Centre, VIC

Venetian/Murano Glass

Murano is a small group of islands lying on the edge of the Adriatic Sea in the lagoon of Venice. Murano is about 3,000 metres north of the larger group of islands making up the city of Venice.

In 1291 glass furnaces were banned from the central islands of Venice and relegated to Murano. This move significantly isolated the glassblowing masters preventing them sharing their knowledge with foreigners. The island of Murano became a true industrial area and the capital of glass production in the world.

In Murano today, you will note little change in the furnace structures of the past. The master glass blowers attachment towards centuries-old tradition is maintained. The importance of a glass master's signature on a truly unique item only generally came about in modern times, after WWII. Much of the Murano glass items sold to tourists carry a paper or foil label and not a glass master's signature.

Mottled or cloud glass ball shaped jug vase, c1950, 34cm high, 24cm diameter.

$110 - $130

Cool & Collected, SA

Italian blue art glass vase, c1970, 18cm high, 12cm diameter.

NZ$115 - $135

Maxine's Collectibles, New Zealand

Double cased purple and clear glass vase, c1960, 4cm deep, 11cm wide, 25cm high.

$225 - $265

The Junk Company, VIC

Royal blue cased glass bottle vase, c1960, 37cm high.

$120 - $140

Design Dilemas, VIC

Murano green glass vase, unusual design with chrome base, c1950, 50cm long, 15cm deep, 40cm high.

$155 - $175

Towers Antiques & Collectables, NSW

Murano glass vase, 19cm high.

$70 - $80

Marrick's Furniture, VIC

Murano glass vase, unusual design, purple colours, c1950, 40cm long, 23cm deep, 30cm high.

$220 - $260

Towers Antiques & Collectables, NSW

Double cased black and clear glass vase with clear hole near centre, c1960, 8cm deep, 12cm wide, 26cm high.

$370 - $410   **The Junk Company, VIC**

Venetian glass vase with gilding and hand enamelled decoration, c1950, 30cm high.

$235 - $275   **Bob Butler's Sentimental Journey, QLD**

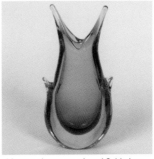

Murano glass vase, signed Salriatisco, c1972, 20cm high.

$300 - $340   **Malvern Antique Market, VIC**

Triple layered glass Murano vase in blue, amber and clear, c1960, 4cm deep, 14cm wide, 22cm high.

$265 - $305   **The Junk Company, VIC**

Murano glass vase, 43cm long, 23cm wide.

$270 - $310   **Furniture Revisited, VIC**

Orange, gold and white Murano glass vase.

$80 - $100   **Munro's Mill Antique Centre, NSW**

Blue bio-morphic shaped Murano art glass vase, 30cm wide, 18cm high.

$75 - $95   **The Junk Company, VIC**

Orange Murano glass vase, of bio-morphic shape, c1950, 30cm wide, 18cm high.

$75 - $95   **The Junk Company, VIC**

Red and yellow Murano glass cased vase, c1950, 13cm deep, 37cm high.

$90 - $110   **The Junk Company, VIC**

Murano sommerso yellow glass vase, c1950, 21cm high.

$275 - $315   **Elizabeth Antiques, NSW**

Murano green and clear glass vase, c1950, 11cm long, 5cm deep, 29cm high.

$160 - $200   **Le Contraste, VIC**

Green and violet Murano glass vase, c1960, 15cm long, 9cm deep, 18cm high.

$80 - $100   **Newport Temple Antiques, VIC**

Filigrana vase, c1965, 120cm wide, 30cm high.

NZ$265 - $305   **Oxford Court Antiques Centre, New Zealand**

Blue-grey and clear Venetian glass stemmed vase, c1960, 26cm high, 15cm diameter.

$65 - $85   **The Botanic Ark, VIC**

Murano glass vase, orange background with splashes of gold and blue, c1950, 26.5cm high.

$160 - $180   **Nicki's Collection, NSW**

Blue and ruby art glass vase, c1960, 23cm high, 10cm diameter.

$115 - $135   **Southside Antiques Centre, QLD**

Murano glass vase with white specks on pink glass, c1950.

$180 - $200   **Towers Antiques & Collectables, NSW**

Murano art glass vase, c1960, 8cm deep, 16cm wide, 37cm high.

$135 - $155   **Antiques & Collectables Centre - Ballarat, VIC**

Murano vase, c1955, 90cm wide, 21cm high.

NZ$165 - $185   **Oxford Court Antiques Centre, New Zealand**

Tall, heavy vase with opalescent interior, cased glass clear over yellow and purple with gold inclusions, c1960, 24.5cm high.

$100 - $120   **frhapsody, WA**

Cased glass ewer vase with clear twist handle and amber body, c1970, 26cm high, 11cm diameter.

$60 - $80   **Born Frugal, VIC**

Murano art glass vase in purple and blue, c1960, 16cm diam.

$65 - $85   **Obsidian Antiques, NSW**

Fenton white glass epergne, 17cm high, 20cm diameter.

$205 - $245

Kookaburra Antiques, TAS

Fenton glass basket, 28cm high, 30cm diameter.

$255 - $295

Antiques & Collectables Centre - Ballarat, VIC

Fenton milk glass bowl with frilled edge, c1950, 10cm high, 17cm diameter.

$85 - $105

Northside Secondhand Furniture, QLD

Amythyst coloured Fenton glass basket, hand painted and signed by S. Hopkins, 21cm high.

$100 - $120

Woodside Bazaar, SA

Retro coffee pot with warmer, Inland Glass, USA, 30cm high.

$30 - $60

Shop 26, Antiques & Collectables - Hamilton, NSW

Glass water bottle and brass bracket holder, c1950, 26cm high, 18cm diameter.

$330 - $370

Bob & Dot's Antiques & Old Wares, NSW

British Syphon Manufacturing Co. Ltd. blue glass soda syphon, made for Woodroofe Norwood South Australia with acid etched logo, 30cm high, 31cm diameter.

$115 - $135

Bower Bird Art & Antiques, QLD

Pair of 'Fenton' milk glass candlesticks, c1950, 9cm high.

NZ$75 - $95

Woodville Mart, New Zealand

Heritage Anniversary American carnival glass bowl, c1967.

$140 - $160

Ardeco Antiques & Collectables, WA

Light blue iridescent carnival glass bowl, 9cm high, 19cm diameter.

$110 - $130

Settlers Store, NSW

Carnival glass punchbowl, marigold colour, grape leaf design with matching cups, hooks and ladle, c1950, 17.5cm high, 31cm diameter.

$165 - $185

Northside Secondhand Furniture, QLD

Art Deco pattern amber glass vase and insert by Crown Crystal Co, 12cm high, 16cm diameter.

$55 - $75

Antiques & Collectables Centre - Ballarat, VIC

Mel Simpson hand blown art glass bowl, c1984, 14.5cm high, 28cm diameter.

NZ$205 - $245

Moa Extinct Stuff, New Zealand

Art glass scent bottle, signed 'De-flute, NZ', c1990, 10cm high.

NZ$55 - $75   **Peachgrove Antiques, New Zealand**

Crown Crystal glass light base, marketed by Gaylife with original sticker, c1960, 47cm high.

NZ$170 - $190   **Banks Peninsula Antiques, New Zealand**

Soda syphon by Lane & Co. Dunedin & Oamaru - New Zealand, 29cm high, 9.5cm diameter.

NZ$105 - $125 **Country Charm Antiques, New Zealand**

New Zealand made layered glass vase, white under clear with turquoise scallop patterned overlay by Crown Crystal, c1960, 59cm high.

NZ$100 - $120   **Waterfords of Mangaweka Village, NZ**

Milk glass basket with clear glass fluted frill to lip, c1960, 20cm high, 30cm diameter.

$185 - $205   **Collectique, VIC**

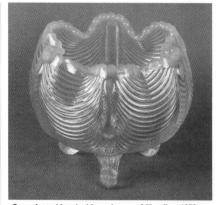

Beraneil bowl, c1960, 190cm wide, 17cm high.

NZ$410 - $450   **Oxford Court Antiques Centre, New Zealand**

Swag footed bowl with opalescent frill to lip, c1950, 13cm wide, 11cm high, 13cm diameter.

$165 - $185   **Collectique, VIC**

Cut glass cocktail shaker with chrome top and black lid, battery operated. 'Cocktail Shaker' is cut into decorated design, c1960.

$15 - $25   **Savers, VIC**

Sherry set comprising decanter, six glasses on round tray, blue with silver trim, c1950, 19.5cm wide, 23cm high.

$65 - $85   **Treats & Treasures, NSW**

Stylised clear art glass figure of an owl perched on a sphere, c1960, 30cm high.

$160 - $180   **North Sunshine Bazaar, VIC**

Large green and blue art glass bowl, c1960, 10cm high, 27.5cm diameter.

$65 - $85

Northside Secondhand Furniture, QLD

Cut crystal dishes in the form of swans, sterling silver wings and mount, c1950, 10cm high.

$480 - $580

Philip Cross Antiques, NSW

Set of six retro tumblers in metal stand, c1960, 18cm high, 21cm diameter.

$45 - $65

Town & Country Antiques, NSW

Blue glass 'Apple', paperweight, c1970, 8cm high.

$40 - $50

Brae-mar Antiques, NSW

Seven piece water set, c1950.

$115 - $135

Furniture Revisited, VIC

Six small, half frosted set of glasses, each a different colour, in original box, clear top half, gold rim, c1950, 30cm long, 2.5cm wide, 7.5cm high.

$40 - $50

River Emporium, NSW

Orange flower tea set, painted glass, stainless steel handles, c1970.

$55 - $75

Bowhows, NSW

Green, silver, white and black hooped clear glass water set comprising jug and five glasses, c1960.

$65 - $85

Kings Park Antiques & Collectables, SA

Set of six red floral drinking glasses, c1970, 45cm high, 6.5cm diameter.

$50 - $70 — **Chapel Street Bazaar, VIC**

Seven piece green glass cordial set with a pressed diamond pattern, c1950, 18cm long, 18cm high.

$90 - $120 — **Newport Temple Antiques, VIC**

Noble glass vase with fluted opalescent edge, c1930, 15cm high.

$85 - $105 — **New temple Antiques, VIC**

Seven piece water set, c1950.

$115 - $135 — **Furniture Revisited, VIC**

Set of six black glass goblets, textured and patterned, c1960, 12cm high.

$60 - $80 — **frhapsody, WA**

Swirled art glass vase, c1950, 18cm high, 29cm diam.

$155 - $175 — **The Mill Markets, VIC**

Set of six Harlequin cocktail glasses with ball detail to stem, c1950, 13.5cm high, 9cm diameter.

$115 - $135 — **Womango, VIC**

Japanese handkerchief style art glass bowl in purple, c1960, 30cm wide, 26cm high.

$185 - $205 — **b bold - 20th Century Furniture & Effects, VIC**

Set of four hand painted ballet scene water glasses, gilt lipped, c1950, 12.5cm high, 6.5cm diameter.

$50 - $70 — **Womango, VIC**

Heavy glass battery casing for industrial power backup and storage, approximately 12-19mm thick green tinged glass. Many sizes were manufactured and this is possibly the largest, 59cm long, 37cm wide, 55cm high.

$410 - $450 — **Industria, VIC**

Purple glass insulator, 12cm high.

$13 - $23 — **Newport Temple Antiques, VIC**

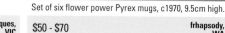

Set of six flower power Pyrex mugs, c1970, 9.5cm high.

$50 - $70 — **frhapsody, WA**

Red art glass paperweight with swivel pen holder top and Parker ballpoint pen, in retro 1960's design, c1955, 7.6cm high, 8cm diameter.

NZ$90 - $110 — **Anticus Antiques, New Zealand**

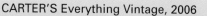

Citrine or uranium glass vase decorated with nude figures in relief, c1960, 15cm high.

| $1050 - $1250 | **Graham & Nancy Miller, VIC** |

Glass vase with fish, 24cm high.

| $40 - $50 | **Serendipity - Preston, VIC** |

Art glass retro bottle vase, turquoise coloured with long narrow neck, hand blown, c1960, 40cm high, 12cm diameter.

| $50 - $70 | **Born Frugal, VIC** |

Opalina Florentina red jug vase with candy cane infusions, 38cm high, 15cm diameter.

| $65 - $85 | **Cool & Collected, SA** |

Citrine coloured lidded glass jar, c1970, 19cm high.

| $20 - $30 | **Shop 23, Centenary Antique Centre, NSW** |

Pair of geometrical glass vases with three layers of cased glass clear red and white, outer layer textured, c1960, 6cm wide, 20cm high.

| $105 - $125 | **Born Frugal, VIC** |

Blue glass vase with bands of darker blue, white interior, c1965, 18cm wide, 16cm high.

| NZ$50 - $70 | **Casa Manana Antiques & Collectables, NZ** |

Art glass vase with swirled decoration, c1950, 12cm wide, 31cm high.

| $80 - $100 | **The Mill Markets, VIC** |

Modernist red spiral glass vase, c1950, 14cm high, 13cm diameter.

| $75 - $95 | **Brae-mar Antiques, NSW** |

Australian studio glass vase by Richard Morrell, signed on base, c1978, 36cm high, 20cm diameter.

| $600 - $700 | **Pastimes Antiques, NSW** |

Set of six glasses with dancing girls, in blue, orange, green, yellow, red and black, c1950, 16cm high.

| $45 - $65 | **Retro Relics, VIC** |

Multi-coloured art glass vase, c1960, 25cm wide, 36cm high.

| $100 - $120 | **Rock N Rustic, SA** |

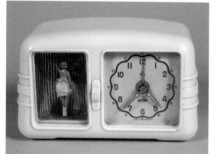

'Peter' cream plastic ballerina alarm clock, c1950, 12cm wide, 8cm high.

$55 - $75   **Secondhand Furniture Mart, TAS**

Original Chinese Chairman Mao alarm clock, nice detail to rim, hand painted enamel design, c1960, 5cm wide, 8cm high.

$40 - $50   **Chapel Street Bazaar, VIC**

Smiths eight day clock in the shape of a bar, c1955, 22.5cm long, 5cm deep, 13.75cm high.

$80 - $100   **Regent Secondhand, VIC**

Perspex rhythm clock, orange lucite with yellow and orange OP art target face, two jewels alarm clock, made in Japan, c1970, 13cm wide, 13cm high.

$155 - $175   **506070, NSW**

Metamec blue plastic electric clock, c1950, 23cm long, 16cm high.

$85 - $105   **Cool & Collected, SA**

Electric globe clock, c1960, 25cm high, 20cm diameter.

$330 - $370   **Ross Agnew, NSW**

Fabulous oversized Pop electric clock in red and white, c1970, 38cm wide, 38cm high.

$100 - $120   **Chapel Street Bazaar, VIC**

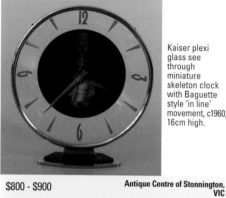

Kaiser plexi glass see through miniature skeleton clock with Baguette style 'in line' movement, c1960, 16cm high.

$800 - $900   **Antique Centre of Stonnington, VIC**

Friesland musical carillion handmade wall clock playing on seven bells with three tunes with complicated calendar indicating day, date, phases of the moon etc. and Huygens single weight style winding on chain, c1970, 25cm deep, 48cm wide, 160cm high.

$7300 - $7700   **Colman Antique Clocks, VIC**

Ceramic clock, red, orange and brown glaze made by Junghams, battery operated, c1960, 30cm diameter.

$110 - $130   **Retro Active, VIC**

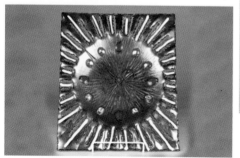

Decorative copper and enamel wall clock with original sticker on reverse, c1970, 2cm deep, 17cm wide, 21cm high.

$115 - $135   **Chapel Street Bazaar, VIC**

Horolavar flying pendulum mantle clock, c1950, 15cm long, 6cm deep, 24cm high.

$930 - $1030   **Dannykay Antiques, NSW**

German one day clock has older movement inside with twenty tooth music box, wooden painted and gilded face, c1980, 45cm long, 35cm wide.

$750 - $850

Helen's On The Bay, QLD

Perspex clock with 'Winter Trees' design, battery operated, c1960, 22cm wide, 40cm high.

$110 - $130

Retro Active, VIC

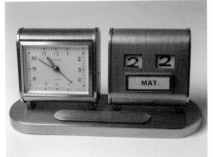

German desk clock with alarm and calendar, c1950.

$500 - $600

Andrew Markerink Master Clockmaker, NSW

'Smiths' electric clock with aluminum star burst decoration, c1960.

$115 - $135

Bowhows, NSW

German purse type timepiece with alarm, c1950, 13cm wide, 6.5cm high.

$330 - $370

Andrew Markerink Master Clockmaker, NSW

Black faced repeater alarm clock in nickled body with luminous numbers and hands, 8cm deep, 13.5cm wide, 18cm high.

$125 - $145

The Evandale Tinker, TAS

Oak cased mantel clock, eight day time and strike with pressed brass face, 28cm long, 27cm high.

$225 - $265

Kings Park Antiques & Collectables, SA

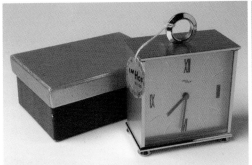

Double dial partners desk clock by Imhof with original tags and box, winding and setting from below, c1950, 8cm wide, 11cm high.

$1000 - $1200

Andrew Markerink Master Clockmaker, NSW

Jaeger Le Coultre Atmos clock, c1955, 16.5cm wide, 22cm high.

$2400 - $2600

Andrew Markerink Master Clockmaker, NSW

Mahogany mantel clock by Committi London, c1950, 18cm wide, 28.5cm high.

$930 - $1030

Andrew Markerink Master Clockmaker, NSW

Simplex bundy clock made in Massachusetts, USA. marked 'Simplex Time Recorder, Gardner Mass USA', 14cm deep, 37cm wide, 105cm high.

$2450 - $2650

Kollectik Pty Ltd, NSW

Unusual 400 day Universe clock by Kaiser with moon phase dial, c1954, 75cm wide, 27cm high.

$1550 - $1750

Alltime Antiques & Bairnsdale Clocks, VIC

Smith 'Sectric' Bakelite wall clock made by Acelec Sydney, 20cm diameter.

$50 - $70

Treats & Treasures, NSW

Triangular shaped and mounted clock from the 'Brian Wood Collection', c1998, 23cm long, 12cm high.

$175 - $195 — **Decodence Collectables, VIC**

Seiko, Japanese gothic style wind up musical clock, c1950, 24cm long, 27cm high.

$70 - $100 — **Helen's on Discovery Antiques & Decor, QLD**

Jaeger Le Coultre Atmos clock, 150th anniversary model with original box and documents, only 3000 made, c1980, 36cm high.

$7700 - $8100 — **Harrington Antiques, QLD**

Art Deco plaster clock with Diana figurine, by Porter Products Aust., c1950, 11cm deep, 37cm wide, 37cm high.

$480 - $520 — **Hamilton Street Antiques, VIC**

Wind up West German 'Lauris' clock, metal with blue porcelain base, c1955, 11cm wide, 17cm high.

$50 - $70 — **Helen's On The Bay, QLD**

Vedette clock, in original box with warranty and receipt, c1977, 19cm diameter.

$180 - $200 — **Obsidian Antiques, NSW**

Timber case Gruen Atmos clock by Jaeger Le Coultre, made for Gruen, c1955, 21.5cm wide, 25cm high.

$2550 - $2750 — **Alltime Antiques & Bairnsdale Clocks, VIC**

Jaeger Le Coultre, Atmos mantle clock, c1950, 16.5cm wide, 22cm high.

$5300 - $5700 — **Andrew Markerink Master Clockmaker, NSW**

The Atmos Clock

The Atmos clock is 'The Clock That Runs on Air'.

For Centuries scientists had experimented with the idea of perpetual motion and watchmakers and clockmakers yearned for a timekeeping device that would work without the need of manual winding; in short a timepiece that would continue to run under its own power.

By the 1920's the closest they had come to this was the 400 day clock. In the late 1920s, Jean-Leon Reutter, a young Paris engineer produced a clock with a timekeeping mechanism designed specifically to consume the smallest possible amount of power to keep the clock running satisfactorily.

As well as changes to the mechanism, Reutter's clock included a mercury and gas filled bellows that would react to the most sensitive changes in temperature and atmospheric conditions, and in so doing, created a gentle rocking motion that gave power to the clock when needed.

The result of Reutter's achievement was an ingenious new clock that could run independently and continuously, and so incredibly sensitive that it could be rewound by the slightest fluctuations in the atmosphere or by the slightest changes in temperature, hence the name 'Atmos Clock'.

In 1930, Jaeger-LeCoultre a world famous Swiss watch-making company, also famous for the 'Reverso Watch' acquired the Atmos Clock Patent from Reutter and has continued to improve the design and manufacture the clocks to the present day.

An Atmos clock takes a month to produce in the factory, then another five weeks of trial and adjustment before it is ready for shipment.

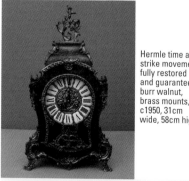

Hermle time and strike movement, fully restored and guaranteed, burr walnut, brass mounts, c1950, 31cm wide, 58cm high.

$2350 - $2550 — **Alltime Antiques & Bairnsdale Clocks, VIC**

Bar movement 800 silver 10 jewel ladies' fob watch with stem wind, open face and engraved back, 3cm diameter.

$275 - $315 **Fyshwick Antique Centre, ACT**

Men's Rolex Oyster Perpetual watch, c1964, 3.9cm long, 1.1cm high, 3.4cm diameter. Steel case with screw down back and screw down crown, Chronometer rated Rolex automatic movement Model #1002, folded steel oyster bracelet.

$2300 - $2500 **Brisbane Vintage Watches, QLD**

The Rolex Oyster

One of the signature design features of Rolex watches is the screw-down crown and water tight cases. It was the development of the screw-down crown by Rolex in 1926, which gave them the final solution to the problem of leaky watch cases. The first ever water and dust resistant case was made by Rolex and named Oyster. As the Rolex Oyster was a sensational watchmaking achievement, the company publicised this feature in advertisements and the watch was worn by Mercedes Gleitz whilst breaking the record for swimming the English Channel.

In 1931, Rolex took the next step in the advancement of its watches with the development of a self winding movement that would eliminate the need for manual daily winding. This style of movement would also eliminate the problem of crowns not being resealed in a moment of forgetfulness when winding. Rolex patented this automatic rotary winding mechanism which it named 'The Rolex Oyster Perpetual'. Only after 1948, when the original patent came to an end were other competitors permitted to introduce their own automatic systems.

Ernest Borel small size chronograph, stainless steel, 2.9cm diameter.

NZ$1700 - $1900 **Lord Ponsonby Antiques, NZ**

Swiss Rolex, engined turned dial. VGC, c1920.

$1900 - $2100 **Colman Antique Clocks, VIC**

Buren 75 lever bar mut, c1903.

$545 - $645 **Colman Antique Clocks, VIC**

Rolex Oyster watch, manual winding, stainless case, c1940, 3.1cm diameter.

NZ$1800 - $2000 **Lord Ponsonby Antiques, New Zealand**

Omega Chronostop watch with tachymetric scale and stainless steel bracelet, c1972, 4.1cm diameter.

NZ$950 - $1050 **Lord Ponsonby Antiques, New Zealand**

Original Heuer Camaro in steel case, manual wind two register chronograph Valjoix movement, all signed, this watch now being copied in the Tag-Heuer classic series, c1968, 4.3cm long, 1.2cm high, 3.7cm diameter.

$2100 - $2300 **Brisbane Vintage Watches, QLD**

Omega gents quartz pin set, day and date, includes original case and bracelet, c1966.

$480 - $520 **Shop 17, Southern Antique Centre, NSW**

Rado watch made by Compu-Chron (Hughes Aircraft Corps), one of the holy grails for Rado collectors, c1970.

$630 - $730 **Chapel Street Bazaar, VIC**

Bulova gent's wrist watch, c1950.

$430 - $470 **Steven Sher Antiques, WA**

10ct gold, small size 'bubble-back' Rolex watch, 2.8cm diameter.

NZ$4700 - $4900 **Lord Ponsonby Antiques, New Zealand**

'Breitling Nanitimer' automatic chronograph, c1970, 4.8cm diameter.

NZ$1800 - $2000 **Lord Ponsonby Antiques, New Zealand**

Omega Constellation watch, stainless steel gold capped, with gold bezel, 3.4cm diameter.

NZ$900 - $1000 **Lord Ponsonby Antiques, New Zealand**

Men's Movado three register chronograph, in steel case with a screw back, manual wind signed 95M movement and white and black Movado signed dial with round pushers, c1950, 4.2cm long, 1.3cm deep, 3.5cm high.

$2600 - $2800 **Brisbane Vintage Watches, QLD**

Men's Omega triple date moonphase watch in gold plated case with fancy lugs, seventeen jewel manual movement signed Omega with day, date, month and moonphase functions, c1950, 4.7cm long, 1.2cm deep, 3.8cm diameter.

$2400 - $2600 **Brisbane Vintage Watches, QLD**

White 18ct gold Cyma bracelet watch with diamond surface, c1950.

$3000 - $3300 **Cavendish Antiques, WA**

Bulova Accutron watch with rotating inner bezel tuning fork movement, c1972, 4.2cm diameter.

NZ$800 - $900 **Lord Ponsonby Antiques, New Zealand**

'Edox Geoscope' amazing new 'old stock' world time wrist watch with multi colour dial and revolving bezels, c1970, 4.8cm diameter.

NZ$2300 - $2500 **Lord Ponsonby Antiques, New Zealand**

Lady's vintage watch in working order, c1950.

$105 - $125 **Antique Centre of Stonnington, VIC**

Breitling 'Super Ocean Professional' automatic diving watch to 5000 ft, c2003, 4.4cm diam.

$NZ2300 - $2500 **Lord Ponsonby Antiques, New Zealand**

Lady's 18ct gold Rolex watch with square dial, c1955.

NZ$1100 - $1300 **Lord Ponsonby Antiques, New Zealand**

Hamilton 14ct gold presentation watch in new condition with both original boxes, c1955.

NZ$1800 - $2000

Lord Ponsonby Antiques, New Zealand

Lucien Fauroud Cubist gold plated pendant with Swiss watch and original chain, c1970, 6.5cm long, 5cm wide.

NZ$165 - $185

Deborah's Antiques, New Zealand

Omega 9ct gold watch with black textured dial, manual winding, original box, c1950, 3.6cm diameter.

NZ$900 - $1000

Lord Ponsonby Antiques, New Zealand

Men's Rolex 'Submariner' with no date, steel case with black dial and bezel, a screw down crown, automatic movement, Rolex steel oyster bracelet and perspex glass, c1967, 4.7cm long, 1.4cm high, 3.9cm diameter.

$3800 - $4000

Brisbane Vintage Watches, QLD

Omega stainless steel 'marine' early waterproof watch with two part case.

NZ$2700 - $2900

Lord Ponsonby Antiques, New Zealand

Omega 'Seamaster Cosmic' automatic with day and date, c1970, 3.5cm diameter.

NZ$480 - $520

Lord Ponsonby Antiques, New Zealand

Platinum and 18ct white gold, diamond set lady's wristwatch with Tudor (Rolex) movement, c1950.

$4000 - $5000

The Goods (House of Fine Jewellery), QLD

Manual gents wrist watch in stainless steel dust resistant case, restored, c1960.

$410 - $450

Antique Centre of Stonnington, VIC

Watch in 14k gold case, manual movement, c1965.

$480 - $520

Antique Centre of Stonnington, VIC

Miniaturised Pac-Man game watch by Halion in original box. Official Namco product, c1980.

$90 - $110

Image Objex, VIC

Smiths Astral English made wrist watch in gold plated case, c1955.

$165 - $185

Philip Cross Antiques, NSW

'Omega Dynamic' in steel on original Omega steel bracelet, a retro funky watch of famous 60s styling with oval form case and bracelet, c1969, 3.6cm long, 4.2cm wide, 1cm high.

$600 - $700 **Brisbane Vintage Watches, QLD**

Gents 'Omega Seamaster' automatic classic stainless steel monoblock (1-piece) case with pearl white dial, black batons and date at '3'. Hi-grade Omega 24 jewel automatic movement, c1970.

$1100 - $1300 **Colman Antique Clocks, VIC**

Rolex 'Air King' automatic black D.A. stainless steel watch with Oyster bracelet, c1960, 3.4cm diameter.

NZ$1900 - $2100 **Lord Ponsonby Antiques, New Zealand**

Smash design '4th Dimension Pyramid' watch, c1990.

$65 - $85 **Chapel Street Bazaar, VIC**

Manual 'Drimex Toptime' watch, c1970.

$115 - $135 **Obsidian Antiques, NSW**

Tissot automatic stainless steel watch with inner revolving bezel, c1970, 4.4cm diam.

$NZ850 - $950 **Lord Ponsonby Antiques, New Zealand**

Smash design deep space voyager watch, c1990.

$65 - $85 **Chapel Street Bazaar, VIC**

Rolex Oyster perpetual date chonometer with stainless heavy Oyster bracelet, c1975, 3.4cm diameter.

NZ$2500 - $2700 **Lord Ponsonby Antiques, New Zealand**

Rolex Oyster date, blue dial manual wind stainless steel watch with Oyster bracelet, c1976, 3.4cm diameter.

NZ$1900 - $2100 **Lord Ponsonby Antiques, New Zealand**

Movado triple calendar, day-date-month moonphase small 'boys size' wrist watch, c1950, 3cm diameter.

NZ$1700 - $1900 **ord Ponsonby Antiques, New Zealand**

'Rolex Oyster Royal' manual winding watch, stainless steel, c1950, 3.2cm diameter.

NZ$1700 - $1900 **Lord Ponsonby Antiques, New Zealand**

Paketa watch with new red leather band, turning compass bezel, c1960.

$115 - $135 **Chapel Street Bazaar, VIC**

Seiko watch with rotating day and date, quartz, c1980

$200 - $240   **Obsidian Antiques, NSW**

Lamy super automatic watch, twenty five jewel with date, gold filled, c1970

$130 - $150   **Obsidian Antiques, NSW**

Classic automatic Omega Seamaster #562 with 18ct gold cap on stainless steel solid lug case, pearl white dial with batons and date at '3', 24 jewels, shock protected movement, EOC, c1962.

$1200 - $1400   **Colman Antique Clocks, VIC**

Rolex Oyster Submariner watch, model 16610 with date, current model stainless bracelet with fliplock, c2001, 4cm diameter.

NZ$4800 - $5000   **Lord Ponsonby Antiques, New Zealand**

Tissot gents manual watch engine turned dial, space age, 2873466 278-21, c1950.

$850 - $950   **Colman Antique Clocks, VIC**

Rado Diastar' superb jewelled dial watch, with scratch proof top, automatic movement, original band, c1970.

$480 - $520   **Chapel Street Bazaar, VIC**

Men's 'Tudor Prince Oyster' date watch, steel case signed by Rolex, screw down Rolex crown, automatic movement with seconds and date, silver dial with baton hour markers, c1960, 4cm long, 1cm high, 3.4cm diameter

$640 - $740   **Brisbane Vintage Watches, QLD**

A.J.C. Swiss made stop watch, c1964, 1.5cm wide, 5cm diam

$110 - $130   **Bowhows, NSW**

Henglebert' 18ct chronograph, large sized rose gold case, gilt dial with gilt hands, sweep seconds and 45 minute chronograph recorders, two rectangular pushers, manual wound seventeen jewel 'Landeron calibre 48' movement, restored, c1950.

$1700 - $1900   **Colman Antique Clocks, VIC**

Military or flight influenced stainless steel Longines watch, the case radial spoked, two tone silver dial and blue steel hands, Longines #12.68Z as in some military and pilots watches, yellow gilt seventeen jewel movement, restored, c1936

$950 - $1050   **Colman Antique Clocks, VIC**

Enicar rotormatic watch, c1960.

$115 - $135   **Shop 17, Southern Antique Centre, NSW**

Jaeger Le Coultre Reverso stainless steel watch, c2004.

NZ$2700 - $2900 **Lord Ponsonby Antiques, New Zealand**

Specialist 'Excelsior Park' chronograph, stainless steel case with two hour rotating bezel, black pulse dial with three separate recorders, superb 17 jewel Girard Perregaux chronograph movement, restored, c1975.

$1200 - $1400 **Colman Antique Clocks, VIC**

Classic Omega black dial Seamaster watch with 18ct gold cap on stainless steel solid lug case, black dial with batons and date at 3,' Omega automatic No. 562, 24 jewel shock protected movement, c1962.

$1300 - $1500 **Colman Antique Clocks, VIC**

Gents Swiss Lanco chronograph in an 18ct warm gold case, pearl dial with gilt hands, sweep seconds and 45 min chronograph recorders, two rectangular pushers, manual 17J 'Landeron 481' shock protected movement. EOC, c1960.

$1200 - $1400 **Colman Antique Clocks, VIC**

Tudor Prince Oyster date by Rolex, 'Rolex Oyster' stainless steel case, white dial with black and red date at '3', on Swiss manual base and Rolex added auto and calendar mechanism. c1953

$1900 - $2100 **Colman Antique Clocks, VIC**

Omega Geneva gent's windup watch, c1960

$340 - $380 **Shop 17, Southern Antique Centre, NSW**

Rolex steel and gold 'Submariner' watch, c2005, 4cm diameter.

NZ$8300 - $8700 **Lord Ponsonby Antiques, New Zealand**

Rolex precision watch, c1960.

$1350 - $1550 **Victory Theatre Antiques, NSW**

Omega stainless steel gent's wristwatch, calibre 283 manual wind with Omega buckle and box, c1951

$400 - $445 **The New Farm Antique Centre, QLD**

Opening front braille manual watch by CYMA, model CYMA flex stainless steel cast, c1960, 4cm diameter

$110 - $130 **Glenelg Antique Centre, SA**

Omega 14ct gold wrist watch with 14ct flexible strap with original box, c1960, 18.5cm long.

NZ$2150 - $2350 **Kelmscott House Antiques, New Zealand**

14ct pendant watch with gold and enamel face, c1980.

$1400 - $1600 **Steven Sher Antiques, WA**

Red and white plastic fan with soft plastic blade, by Philips, c1960, 15cm high.

$35 - $45

Baseless metal fan by 'Elcon', c1950, 25cm high, 18cm diameter

Bowhows, NSW

$50 - $70

Electric heater decorated with an emu, kangaroo and Australian flora in the casting.

Bowhows, NSW

$500 - $600

Dannykay Antiques, NSW

Glow log' chrome and steel heater, glass inner core, manufacturered by STC, c1945, 55cm high, 15cm diameter.

$195 - $235

Bowhows, NSW

Gilford Australian 'Bail-O-Matic' electric jug, automatic, original box, c1950, 22cm high, 15.5cm diameter.

$150 - $170

Avoca Beach Antiques, NSW

Fine coffee pot by Antti Nurmesniem, Finland, designed in 1957 with classic mid 20th century design, enamel granite ware with heavy gauge base, c1975, 15cm wide, 19cm high

$140 - $160

Image Objex, VIC

Orange 'Atomic' coffee machine with 'Bon Trading Label', unusual colour, c1960, 20cm deep, 17cm wide, 23cm high.

$540 - $640

The Junk Company, VIC

Automatic 'Sunbeam' brand toaster, c1950, 24cm wide, 17cm high

$75 - $95

Barry McKay, NSW

Speedy' brand toaster, c1950, 16cm long, 13cm high.

$45 - $65

Barry McKay, NSW

Everest' chrome toaster with original box and warranty card, c1950, 12cm deep, 17cm wide, 20cm high.

$40 - $50

Treats & Treasures, NSW

Model K100 'Health Glo Sauna Steam Bath', electric, fibreglass made with vinyl padded seat and floor mat, 240 volts, c1950, 30cm deep, 65cm wide, 112.5cm high.

$460 - $500

Regent Secondhand, VIC

Green painted cast iron bean slicer with screw clamp, for use on table or bench, marked ' Spong & Co., No. 633', c1965, 26cm long, 11cm wide.

NZ$15 - $25

Casa Manana Antiques & Collectables, New Zealand

Richardson's Yorkshire cream pot, with pictorial of a cow on transfer print, c1900, 7.5cm high.

NZ$55 - $75   **Peachgrove Antiques, New Zealand**

Nutmeg grater, US patent, unusual design, c1920, 8cm long.

$75 - $95   **Antique Centre of Stonnington, VIC**

Cast aluminium pot and percolator with bakelite handles, Vesuviana, c1930

$220 -$260   **Bowhows, NSW**

'Kwikmix' brand vitamiser, 38cm high.

$85 - $105   **Barry McKay, NSW**

Wall mounted can opener in original box, c1960, 25cm long

$75 - $95   **Glenn StevensAntiques, VIC**

Bel Jubilee model cream maker, complete in original box with instructions, c1950, 17cm high.

$55 - $75   **The Exchange Galleries, NSW**

Wall mounted ceramic Koffie grinder, 'Pe De' brand, c1950, 35cm high

$85 - $105   **Newport Temple Antiques, VIC**

Anodised aluminium fan by 'Magic', c1960, 30cm long, 33cm high

$100 - $135   **Victory Theatre Antiques, NSW**

Atomic cast aluminium coffee maker with Bakelite handles and milk frother, c1945.

$225 - $265   **Bowhows, NSW**

Braun desk fan, HL70 designed by Reinhold Weiss, 1961, 13.5cm long, 7cm deep, 14cm high.

$200 - $240   **506070, NSW**

EC folding yellow and black fan, all rubber, c1960, 30cm diameter.

$45 - $65

Chapel Street Bazaar, VIC

'Ice Pet' ice shaver/crusher with rubber bench holder, in box, c1980, 23cm high.

$50 - $70

Bowhows, NSW

Harper food mincer No. 3181, 'Beatrice' model, c1950.

NZ$20 - $30

Strangely Familiar, New Zealand

'Ice-O-Mat' metal ice crusher, c1950, 13cm deep, 19cm wide, 22cm high.

$90 - $110

Cool & Collected, SA

Mixer with four plastic yellow cups and four mixing arms, by General Electric, c1975

$40 - $50

Bowhows, NSW

'Clem' travelling electric iron, plugs into a light fitting, all original including the box, c1954, 11cm long, 6cm deep, 9cm high.

$75 - $95

The Botanic Ark, VIC

Braun bakelite juicer, electric bench style with suction cup feet and safety switch, c1955, 25cm high, 20cm diameter

$110 - $130

Regent Secondhand, VIC

'Sunbeam Mixmaster', c1950, 34cm long, 35cm high.

$135 - $155

Towers Antiques & Collectables, NSW

Sunbeam 'Mixmaster' kitchen mixer, 30cm long, 22cm wide, 34cm high.

$75 - $95

Barry McKay, NSW

General Electric mixer with bowl, juice extractor glass, c1970.

$110 - $130

Bowhows, NSW

Early original hand operated meat or bread slicer with table clamp, original Engels Messe mark, c1950, 33cm long, 14cm wide, 20cm high.

$110 - $130

Mac's Collectables

Hecla chrome water urn with Bakelite handles and tap, slogan 'By Hecla It's Good', 42cm high, 73cm diameter.

$65 - $85

Treats & Treasures, NSW

KITCHENALIA

Set of five anodised canisters by Jason, c1960.

$85 - $105

**Chapel Street Bazaar,
VIC**

Five 'Kleen' canisters (1 – 4 pints) and milk jug, c1950.

$190 - $210

**Step Back Antiques,
VIC**

Set of six multi-colour anodised beakers in chrome carry frame, 23cm long, 17cm deep, 18cm high.

$50 - $70

**Cool & Collected,
SA**

Insulated anodised food container, the 'Hot-N-Cold Apple' by Lemar Industries, c1960, 24cm high, 20cm diam.

$65 - $85

**Antiques & Collectables Centre - Ballarat,
VIC**

Anodised egg cup set on silver plated stand, c1950, 12cm long, 12cm deep, 15cm high.

$85 - $105

**Towers Antiques & Collectables,
NSW**

Red anodised aluminium ice bucket, c1965.

$45 - $65

**Victory Theatre Antiques,
NSW**

Red anodised soda syphon, c1950, 32cm high, 11cm diameter

$65 - $85

**Northside Secondhand Furniture,
QLD**

Set of six anodised beakers in a plastic holder, c1960, 20cm long, 14cm wide

$30 -$40

**Mooney Collectables,
NSW**

Boxed amber plastic three piece eggcup set, c1950, 6.5cm deep, 11cm wide, 4cm high.

$25 - $35

**Southside Antiques Centre,
QLD**

Bakelite vacuum flask, c1970, 20cm high, 12cm diam.

NZ$13 - $23

Woodville Mart, New Zealand

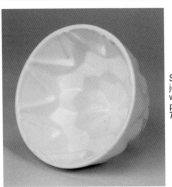

Small ceramic jelly mould with diamond pattern, c1880, 7cm high.

$34 - $44

Temple Antiques, VIC

Dome Master ice bucket by Nicholas Angelakos for Colony, c1970, 30cm high

$45 - $65

The Wool Exchange Geelong, VIC

Insulated plastic cup featuring comic strip of Bazza McKenzie, c1971, 10cm high.

$13- $23

Chapel Street Bazaar, VIC

'Capri' set of five orange plastic white lids, Australian made by B. X. Plastics, stackable within the largest canister, c1960, 17.5cm deep, 12.5cm wide, 25cm high.

$50 - $70

River Emporium, NSW

Baby blue Bakelite vacuum flask made by The Britsh Vacume Flask Co Ltd., London, 25cm high.

$60 - $80

Treats & Treasures, NSW

Circular tray and six coasters with chrome plated rims and windmill designs on perspex bases, c1960, 24cm diameter

$45 - $65

Mooney Collectables, NSW

Fourteen piece Bakelite picnic set, c1950.

$115 - $135

Victory Theatre Antiques, NSW

Plastic and vinyl ice bucket, decorated in a paisley pattern, c1975, 20cm wide, 38cm high.

NZ$55 - $75

Maxine's Collectibles, New Zealand

Speckled red Bakelite Art Deco canisters by Duperite, c1940.

$180 - $200

Treats & Treasures, NSW

Bakelite

Bakelite was the first completely synthetic man-made substance. Bakelite was invented in 1909 by an independent New York chemist Leo H. Baekeland. It was called the "material of a thousand uses" and used to make everything from car parts to jewellery. We often think of the colour of Bakelite items as dark brown, but it was manufactured in various colours including yellow, butterscotch, red, green and brown. Bakelite could also be transparent, or marbleised by mixing two colours. Coco Chanel featured bakelite items in her accessories collection and the material was praised frequently in Vogue magazine.

Manufacture of some consumer Items were suspended in 1942 in order to concentrate manufacturing on the war effort. Bakelite pieces are now valuable collectables. Andy Warhol was an avid collector, and when he died in 1987, his pieces sold for record prices at Sotheby's.

KITCHENALIA

Retro Guzzini plastic ice bucket, c1970, 20cm diameter

$55 - $75

**Collector's Cottage Antiques,
NSW**

Cream Bakelite 'Wardonia' shaving set, complete in good original condition, c1945, 13cm wide, 9.5cm high

$65 - $85

**Coming of Age Antiques,
QLD**

Set of five Avon measuring plastic duck cups, c1980, 8cm long, 10cm high

$45 - $65

**Helen's On The Bay,
QLD**

Colourful plastic retro cannister set, c1950

$75 - $95

**Towers Antiques & Collectables,
NSW**

Retro black and white spice set by 'Nally Ware' with original plastic hanging rack, c1950, 33cm long, 6cm deep, 10cm high

$65 - $85

**. Mt Dandenong Antique Centre,
VIC**

Art Deco Bakelite cake stand with four removable plates, c1955, 24cm wide, 78cm high.

$200 - $240

**Burly Babs Collectables/Retro
Relics, VIC**

Red Bakelite salt and pepper set, c1950.

$30 - $40

**Victory Theatre Antiques,
NSW**

Black plastic 'Kartel' magazine rack, Italian design, c1970, 40cm wide, 34cm high.

$80 - $100

**Born Frugal,
VIC**

Nylex corporation, Bessemer 'Europa' pattern, seven part serving set in melamine, c1970, 35cm long.

$45 - $65

**frhapsody,
WA**

Set of five original hard plastic canisters marked 'Duperite', c1950.

$60 - $80

**Maryborough Station Antique Emporium,
VIC**

Iplex, Adelaide spice set with four canisters in cream and green, labelled pepper, ginger, cinnamon and cloves, made of industrial plastic,, c1950, 8cm high, 6cm diam.

$30 - $60 **Antique General Store, NSW**

Ruhrtix, Bakelite and plastic egg beater and juicer, the juicer has a removable handle, the plastic pouring jug has a handle and quarter litre measures, c1950, 25cm high, 15cm diam.

$50 - $70 **Regent Secondhand, VIC**

Stainless steel serving fork, designed by Jens Quistgaard and manufactured by Dansk, c1960, 22.5cm long.

$90 - $110 **506070, NSW**

Artemide plastic pencil holder, c1970, 8cm high, 9.5cm diameter.

$55 - $75 **Rose Cottage Antiques, ACT**

Fun plastic ice buckets in the form of fruit, c1960, 28cm high.

$60 - $80 **506070, NSW**

Red plastic ice bucket with handle, c1960, 25cm diam.

$15 - $25 **Bowhows, NSW**

Bakelite kitchen style handles, c1950, 9cm long.

$5 - $10 **Twice Around, NSW**

'Triumph' steel apple peeler and corer, c1950, 28cm long, 34cm wide.

NZ$65 - $85 **Collectamania, New Zealand**

Triple level Bakelite cake stand, c1950, 27cm high.

$50 - $70

Rosebud Antiques, NSW

KITCHENALIA

Set of six Rusnorstain knives with their original box.

$30 - $40

Enamelled steel Kobenstyle cookware, for Dansk International Design by Jens Quistgaard, c1954, 20cm wide, 10cm high.

$200 - $240

Enamel Silit cookpot with a steel lid, c1960, 13cm high.

$5 - $15

Three casserole dishes which stack to create a female torso, made in England, marked 'Stoke on Trent', c1970, 24cm deep, 34cm wide, 43cm high.

$600 - $700

Metter's cream and green enamel bread bin, c1945, 32cm high, 32cm diameter.

$115 - $135

Original set of five enamel cannisters, c1920

$430 - $470

Set of six green and cream enamel kitchen canisters, c1930

$540 - $640

Set of six retro heirloom design cannisters by Hornsea England, c1976.

$65 - $85

Set of five red and black tin cannisters, c1950.

$85 - $105

German porcelain kitchen canisters, blue and white, five large (20cm), six small (10.1cm)

$380 - $420

Set of five white and gold metal spice tins with individual labels and fitted lids, paper label 'Waratah Deluxe Genuine Aluminium', c1960

$15 - $25

Set of plastic kitchen canisters, c1960, 15cm long, 15cm deep, 20cm high

$40 - $50

Bowhows,
NSW

Set of five 'Nally' multi coloured canisters, 24cm high

$65 - $85

Treats & Treasures,
NSW

Set of five retro orange coloured 'Capri' canisters, c1960.

$45 -$65

Treats &Treasures,
NSW

Art Deco sixteen piece canister set with wood grained finish, c1950.

$175 - $195

The Evandale Tinker,
TAS

Enamelled sugar canister, c1950

$85 - $105

Marge's Antiques & Collectables,
NSW

Set of five 'Nally' canisters, in original box with swing tag, c1950.

$220 - $260

Regent Secondhand,
VIC

Octagonal tin biscuit with geometrical Art Deco pattern, c1950, 15cm high, 10cm diameter

$5 - $15

Mooney Collectables,
NSW

Kitchen triple stack and bread bin by Waratah, 28cm high, 27cm diameter

$60 - $80

Treats & Treasures,
NSW

Australian Diana Ware kitchen ceramics, comprising one mixing bowl and three jugs in various colours, c1950, 15cm deep, 15cm wide, 12cm high.

$85 - $105

Chapel Street Bazaar,
VIC

Set of four Australian 'Willow' tins, red rose on white background pattern, stackable, side show prize items in South Eastern Queensland and Northern NSW, c1950, 20cm high, 20cm diameter.

$55 - $75

River Emporium,
NSW

Set of four Art Deco blue canisters with gold lettering

$80 - $100

Treats & Treasures,
NSW

European cream, brown and blue enamel bread tin, c1950, 26cm deep, 46cm wide, 15cm high.

$265 - $305

Step Back Antiques, VIC

Enamelled steel Krenit bowl, designed by Herbert Krenchel and manufactured by Torben Orskov, Denmark, c1953.

$280 - $320

506070, NSW

Belgian stove made to look like a piece of French Art Deco furniture, c1950, 99cm wide, 105cm high.

$1850 - $2050

Kaleidoscope Antiques, VIC

Ten weights in a wooden box, ranging from 1gm - 200gm, c1960.

$85 - $105

Chris'Antiques & Collectables, VIC

Family scales, green vinyl, steel construction, adjustable dial, height to weight ratio, c1970, 30cm deep, 40cm wide, 10cm high.

$35 - $45

Bowhows, NSW

Ricketts, clothes washing blue bag, laundry linen whitener.

$5 - $15

Tyabb Hay Shed, VIC

Set of six plus one large Bessemer barbeque serving plates, brightly coloured retro designs, c1970, 9.5cm wide.

$110 - $130

Image Objex, VIC

Zulu bar decoration, c1970, 8cm deep, 16cm wide, 30cm high

$55 - $75

Southside Antiques Centre, QLD

Georg Jensen stainless steel retro style cutlery, c1970.

$40 - $60

Antique Centre of Stonnington, VIC

Corning Ware stove top coffee percolator, six cup capacity, c1960, 21cm high.

NZ$25 - $35

Strangely Familiar, New Zealand

Oval ceramic jelly mould with leaf pattern, 9cm high.

$55 - $75

Newport Temple Antiques, VIC

T. G. Green Cornishware ceramic rolling pin with painted wooden handles., c1940, 46cm long.

$205 - $245
Kings Park Antiques & Collectables, SA

Ice cream scoop from Regent Cinema produced by National Sydney, c1950, 20cm long, 6cm deep, 4cm high

$40 - $60
Southside Antiques Centre, QLD

Coffee grinder with blue and white windmill scene, tiles to four sides and porcelain top, c1960, 15cm wide, 23cm high.

$60 - $80
Helen's On The Bay, QLD

Six multi coloured 'Pyrex' dishes with box, c1965, 12cm deep, 12cm wide, 5cm high.

$35 - $45
Bowhows, NSW

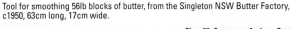

Tool for smoothing 56lb blocks of butter, from the Singleton NSW Butter Factory, c1950, 63cm long, 17cm wide.

$90 - $110
Shop 77, Centenary Antique Centre, NSW

Thermos flask by Aldotura of Turin, Italy, made of lacquered vellum or parchment, c1950, 26cm high.

$200 - $240
506070, NSW

Tea pot, white enamel on steel with teak handles, c1950.

$15 - $25
Bowhows, NSW

Stelton stainless steel small jug and sugar bowl, designed by Arne Jacobson, c1950.

$75 - $95
Rose Cottage Antiques, ACT

Hand painted plaster bride and groom wedding cake topper, c1930, 5cm wide, 9cm high.

$25 - $35
Mt Dandenong Antique Centre, VIC

Koala and baby tea cosy with glass eyes, leather nose and paws, c1920, 26cm wide, 24cm high.

NZ$185 - $205
Bulls Antiques & Collectables, New Zealand

Pine rolling pin c1950, 46cm long.

$40 - $50
Step Back Antiques, VIC

Set of four graduated copper and brass measuring cups, 1/4, 1/2, 3/4, 1 cup, various sizes from 7 cm to 11 cm, c1940

$110 - $130

Antiques At Birkenhead, NSW

Vinyl covered tray with plastic rafia edges and sides, c1950, 52cm long, 31cm wide.

$130 - $150

Cool & Collected, SA

American flower salt and pepper shakers, c1950, 10cm wide, 13cm high

$30 - $40

Antiques, Goods & Chattels, VIC

Stainless steel tea pot, c1975.

$155 - $175

Bowhows, NSW

Large aluminium 'Swan' brand colander, c1950, 15cm high, 35cm diameter.

$30 - $60

Step Back Antiques, VIC

Set of four pyrex tableware bowls, c1970.

NZ$40 - $60

Woodville Mart, New Zealand

Retro Mexican styled cocktail platter with red and green plastic handle, c1960

$5 - $10

Savers, VIC

Servex Chef pie funnel made in Holland, c1950, 12cm high, 5cm diameter

$165 - $185

Mt Dandenong Antique Centre, VIC

Fondue set, includes forks and recipe book.

$30 - $40

Paddington Antique Centre Pty Ltd, QLD

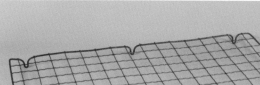

Wire cake cooling rack, c1950, 25cm deep, 52cm wide.

$25 - $35

Step Back Antiques, VIC

Dress fabric, screenprint on cotton border, featuring Japanese tea party by Selwyns, c1960, 300cm long, 110cm wide

$90 - $110

Flashback, VIC

Fortex screen print fabric, approximately 2 x 2m in two sections, design is called 'Fabric', c1968, 223cm wide, 222cm high.

$110 - $130

frhapsody, WA

Framed vintage fabric, Australian designed and manufactured, features bark print, c1955, 45cm wide, 60cm high.

$65 - $85

Chapel Street Bazaar, VIC

Scandinavian blue fabric, silk and linen, c1960, 120cm wide.

$90 - $110

Tarlo & Graham, VIC

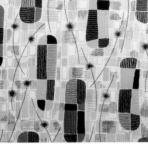

Framed vintage 50's fabric, Australian designed and manufactured, c1952, 45cm wide, 60cm high

$65 - $85

Chapel Street Bazaar, VIC

Dress fabric screenprint on cotton pique by Sekers, c1960, 500cm long, 112cm wide.

$140 - $160

Flashback, VIC

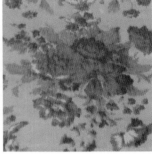

Four metres of vintage cotton with a floral pattern, 400cm long.

$145 - $165

Back Antiques, VIC

Dress fabric with crysanthemums, in the style of Margaret Macdonald, 1920's revisited, c1975, 350cm long, 88cm wide

$115 - $135

Flashback, VIC

Dress fabric, screenprint on cotton, featuring Chianti bottles, c1955, 500cm long, 86cm wide.

$140 - $160

Flashback, VIC

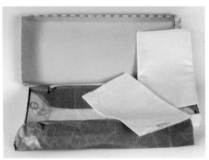

Boxed set of Irish linen with damask tablecloth and six serviettes, never used, c1930, 274cm long, 183cm deep.

$140 - $160

Southside Antiques Centre, QLD

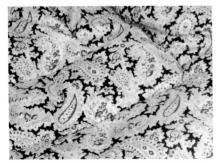

Vintage paisley eiderdown, c1950, 1.6cm long, 1.4cm wide

NZ$130 - $150

Strangely Familiar, New Zealand

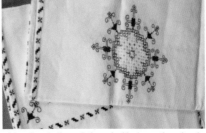

A hand made linen cloth worked in drawn thread and black work, c1950, 108cm long, 108cm wide

$35 - $45

The Bottom Drawer Antique Centre, VIC

Soft furnishing fabric, screenprint on 50% cotton and 50% polyester, 'Aquarius' by Sheridan, priced per metre, c1975, 120cm wide.

$60 - $80

Flashback, VIC

SOFT FURNISHINGS & WALLPAPER

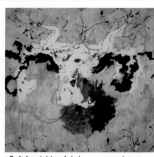

Soft furnishing fabric, screenprint on cotton, 'Scherazade' by Otto Nielsen, c1975, 120cm wide.

$155 - $175

Flashback, VIC

Soft furnishing fabric, screenprint on cotton, geometric design, priced per metre, c1965,120cm wide.

$60 - $80

Flashback, VIC

Soft furnishing fabric, screenprint on cotton, priced per metre, 120cm wide

$70 -$90

Flashback, VIC

Soft furnishing fabric, screenprint on cotton/rayon blend, priced per metre, 120cm wide.

$70 - $90

Flashback, VIC

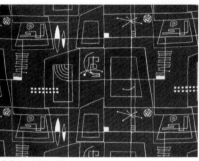

Soft furnishing fabric, screenprint on cotton/polyester blend, price per metre, c1955, 150cm wide

$70 - $90

Flashback, VIC

Wallpaper featuring French posters, c1970, 100cm long, 52cm wide

$165 - $185

Flashback, VIC

Vinyl black and white wallpaper, charcoal drawn style of girls' faces, c1960, 100cm long, 53cm wide.

$165 - $185

Flashback, VIC

Wallpaper featuring hand drawn girls in garden, c1950, 100cm long, 46cm wide.

$165 - $185

Flashback, VIC

Flock wallpaper, orange floral, c1960, 100cm long, 50cm wide.

$205 - $245

Flashback, VIC

Buying fabrics from the 1950s-1960s-1970s

Post war fabrics are becoming increasingly popular due to the unending variety of designs that were made. Soft furnishing, dress and upholstery fabrics are sought after for their unique patterns, weaves and quality. Popular designs for each period follow.

1950s: Industrialism, freedom and optimism inspired designers to create patterns that had never been seen before. Abstraction merged with nature and science to produce atomic designs which were printed onto cotton barkcloth. Traditional formality made way for organic shapes featuring brighter colour palettes.

1960s: With an experimental approach to pattern design, psychedelic patterns were the new trend. Large scale flower prints were popular from interiors to fashion. Optical designs, once popular in modern art, were now being printed onto fabric.

1970s: Geometric designs were essential for the modern interior and fashion trends. A revival of the Art Nouveau era saw stylised florals and picture or photoprint designs emerge. Conversational designs are also sought after and include cowboys, racing cars, cocktails, feathers, surfers, horses, people, space themes, robots, music, aeroplanes, nautical, homewares, travel and children's prints.

Soft furnishing fabric of trees and leaves screenprint on cotton, by Pacific Prints, c1977, 300cm long, 120cm wide

$155 - $175

Flashback, VIC

Red telephone box

$1900 - $2100   **Wooden Pew Antiques, VIC**

ABS Plastic Boby phone, in two tone green, c1970

$430 - $470   **506070, NSW**

Retro red plastic telephone, c1970, 12cm long, 18cm deep, 15cm high

$65 - $85   **Towers Antiques & Collectables, NSW**

Twenty cent coin operated public 'Red Phone' telephone, c1970, 20cm long, 25cm deep, 32cm high.

$275 - $315   **Rare Old Times Antiques & Collectables, SA**

Black Bakelite wall phone, made in Australia for P.M.G. workshops, c1960, 13cm deep, 16cm wide, 23cm high.

$135 - $155   **Mt Dandenong Antique Centre, VIC**

Large early Telecom Australia mobile phone, Traveller-P model designed to plug into a car cigarette lighter or back-pack and weighs 4.2 kgs, c1988, 11cm long, 20cm wide, 21cm high.

$125 - $145   **Image Objex, VIC**

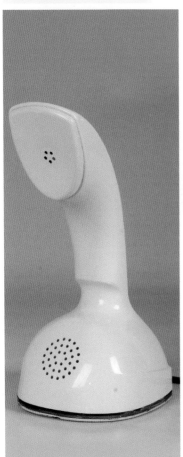

White plastic 'Erica Phone' telephone with thumb grip, c1970, 25cm high, 10cm diameter

$185 - $205   **Bowhows, NSW**

Black Bakelite telephone, c1950

$55 - $75   **Antipodes Antiques, QLD**

Bakelite black extension telephone, c1950, 15cm long, 23cm high.

$85 - $105   **Towers Antiques & Collectables, NSW**

HOUSEHOLD & WORKSHOP

Apprentice model house, made by technical school students, c1960, 42cm deep, 83cm wide, 55cm high.

$240 - $280

Tarlo & Graham, VIC

A pair of oil cans with long spouts and caps, c1950, 40cm high.

$140 - $160

Granny's Market Pty Ltd, VIC

'Martin' taxi meter manufactured by 'Taximeters' Australia Melbourne Pty Ltd, registering in dollars and cents, c1960, 25cm deep, 18cm wide, 18cm high.

$155 - $175

Lydiard Furniture & Antiques, VIC

'Wayne' 605 Shell bowser petrol pump with variable octane rating switch, c1960, 65cm wide, 200cm high.

$1900 -$2100

The Mill Markets, VIC

'Golden Fleece' imperial pint oil bottle, H.C. Sleigh Limited, with a 'Golden Fleece' ram embossed on bottle, tin pourer.

$900 - $1000

Yarra Valley Antique Centre, VIC

Embossed 'Castrol Oil' bottle with tin top, large one-quart size, c1950, 9cm long, 9cm deep, 38cm high.

$170 - $190

Northside Secondhand Furniture, QLD

One imperial quart 'Golden Fleece' H. C Sleigh oil bottle with tin pourer, c1950, 38cm high

$190 - $210.

Kings Park Antiques & Collectables, SA

'Ampol' petrol pump manufactured by 'Wayne', c1945.

$3400 - $3600

The Mill Markets, VIC

Retro blue Olivetti plastic typewriter in black plastic case, c1970, 35cm long, 35cm deep.

$75 - $95

Towers Antiques & Collectables, NSW

Pump action insecticide sprayer with floral painted decoration to the barrel and drum, c1960, 36cm long, 9cm wide.

$30 - $60

Obsidian Antiques, NSW

'Gestetner Duplicator No. 70, c1950, 44cm long, 40cm deep, 12cm high.

$70 - $110

Victory Theatre Antiques, NSW

Concrete garden statues of a pair of Aboriginal children, signed, registered design, c1950, 25cm long, 25cm deep, 60cm high.

$255 - $295

Towers Antiques & Collectables, NSW

Early brass door knocker featuring crowned lion head, c1950, 12cm long

$30 - $60

The Bottom Drawer Antique Centre, VIC

Silvercross pram, c1950, 120cm long

$550 - $650

The Restorers Barn,
VIC

Dutch travelling tea cosy.

$135 - $155

Den of Antiquities,
VIC

Black lady fruit bowl with beaded basket,
made of plaster, complete with earrings,
c1950, 25cm wide, 30cm high.

$270 - $310

Regent Secondhand,
VIC

Kathi Chakla beadwork and applique satin wall hanging, Gujerat, c1980, 88cm long,
85cm wide.

$185 - $205

The Rug Shop,
NSW

Caucasian rug, to celebrate Lenin's 100th birthday, c1970, 274cm long, 146cm wide.

$1300 - $1500

The Rug Shop,
NSW

Woollen pictorial rug of the Sydney skyline featuring Sydney Harbour Bridge,
Opera House not shown indicating rug was completed prior to erection of the
Opera House, c1965, 140cm long, 68.5cm wide.

$185 - $205

Gorgeous,
VIC

Green shag-pile rug, c1960, 190cm long, 125cm wide.

$720 - $820

506070,
NSW

A felt carpet, pieced and applique woven selvedges and fringes, pure dyed wool,
c1960, 350cm long, 150cm wide.

$1150 - $1350

The Rug Shop,
NSW

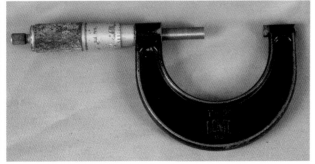

Micrometer, 1-2 inch.

$30 - $60

Paddington Antique Centre Pty Ltd, QLD

Norris coffin-shaped smoothing plane with rosewood infill and patent adjuster, original iron, c1950, 23cm long.

$2100 - $2300

Sheridan Brown Antiques, VIC

A set of hand operated hedge clippers, c1950, 52cm long.

NZ$110 - $130

Woodville Mart, New Zealand

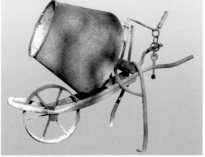

Record plane 070 box scraper, made in England, c1950, 32cm long.

NZ$115 - $135

Ikon Antiques, New Zealand

Hand painted concrete mixer, 115cm long, 60cm wide.

$120 -$140

Wooden Pew Antiques, VIC

'Blow' butter churn, six imperial quarts, British registered design No. 856612, c1950, 18cm wide, 38cm high.

Blue Lloyd Loom laundry basket, c1930, 24cm deep, 40cm wide, 52cm high.

A small French Billot butcher's table, the thick and heavy chopping-block top with upward-facing end grain, c1950, 50cm long, 30cm deep, 82cm high.

NZ$150 - $170

Casa Manana Antiques & Collectables, New Zealand

$165 - $185

Step Back Antiques, VIC

$900 - $1000

Miguel Meirelles Antiques, VIC

Bookends in the form of metal stick-figure men, 20cm long, 7cm deep, 20cm high

$40 - $50

Cool & Collected, SA

Brass tooled jardiniere stamped 'Daalderop', monogram KMD made in Holland, c1950, 23cm high, 28cm diameter.

$145 - $165

Maryborough Station Antique Emporium, VIC

Galvanised iron small watering can 1½ gallons, c1950, 33cm high, 20cm diameter.

$40 - $60

Step Back Antiques, VIC

Cardboard periscope, c1950, 46cm high.

NZ$40 - $60 **Collectamania, New Zealand**

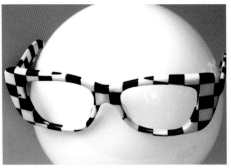

Italian black and white plastic frames, c1960

$85 - $105 **Retro Active, VIC**

Japanese celestial globe, c1960, 32cm high, 26cm diameter.

$370 - $410 **Mondo Trasho, VIC**

A green pressed glass eye bath, 'Ophthlamic Optabs' on glass, c1950, 3cm high

$50 - $70 **Grant & Wendy Brookes, VIC**

Six panel fluorescent lamp, ex hospital x-ray viewer, separately switched panels, 110cm long, 25cm deep, 104cm high.

$500 - $600 **Industria, VIC**

Japanese made inflatable terrestrial globe with aluminium strap frame, c1950, 45cm high, 30cm diameter.

$85 - $105 **Industria, VIC**

Small plastic coated cast metal medical mannequin with multiple parts (about 30) not as high quality as large scale German models but quite accurate, hand painted, unnamed and undated, 5cm deep, 8cm wide, 26cm high.

$90 - $110 **Industria, VIC**

Cardboard packet 'Wet-Chek' condoms with sealed contents, c1979.

$20 - $30 **Wooden Pew Antiques, VIC**

Steriliser for medical instruments, chrome plated, 'Vaxhaull' brand, 35cm long, 20cm deep, 25cm high.

$230 - $270 **Towers Antiques & Collectables, NSW**

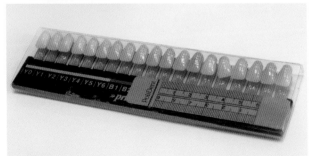

Dentist sample set of front teeth made by Polident, including original colour check display pack by Primodent, c1960.

$25 - $35 **Wooden Pew Antiques, VIC**

Sample dentist's teeth set in Bakelite case, c1950, 38cm long, 32cm deep, 100cm high.

$360 - $400 **Antique Effects, VIC**

SCIENTIFIC & TAXIDERMY

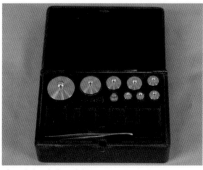

Set of chemist's weights

$65 - $85   **Paddington Antique Centre Pty Ltd, QLD**

Child's microscope set in original box, COC brand, c1960

$25 - $35   **Kingston Antiques, VIC**

Amber glass apothecary bottle, with faceted stopper, 8cm wide, 18cm high.

$85 - $105   **Retro Active, VIC**

Large laboratory desiccator with ceramic plate, ground lid to base surface.

$260 - $300   **Industria, VIC**

Typical large scale (10L) boiling vessel, with multiple outlets 'Quik Fit' fittings, 42cm high, 30cm diameter.

$110 - $130   **Industria, VIC**

'Ohio' brand circular dial, wall mounted thermometer measuring in farenheit, c1950, 31cm diameter

$155 - $175   **Kenny's Antiques, VIC**

Tasmanian wood hen mounted on wood block, c1960, 46cm high.

$85 - $105   **Rose Cottage Antiques, ACT**

Bantam's duplicator with rollers, inks and instructions, c1950, 45cm wide.

$100 - $120   **Timeless Treasures, WA**

Billy goat's head and neck with horns and glass eyes, mountable on wall, 45cm long.

$205 - $245   **Wooden Pew Antiques, VIC**

Taxidermied small crocodile, 60cm long.

$220 - $260   **Settlers Store, NSW**

Mounted turkey, c1980, 50cm deep, 60cm wide, 70cm high.

$700 - $800   **Tarlo & Graham, VIC**

Peridot set, 15ct gold bracelet, c1990.

$2100 - $2300 — **Munro's Mill Antique Centre, NSW**

Retro 18ct yellow gold bracelet, rare example of period, c1940, 200cm long

$3100 - $3300 — **Martin of Melbourne - Fine Jewels, VIC**

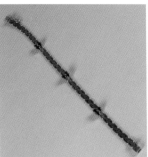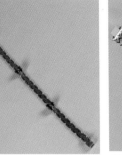

14ct white gold bracelet set with sapphires, c1980.

$400 - $440 — **Imogene, VIC**

18ct gold retro herringbone bracelet, 38 grams, c1960, 20cm long.

$800 - $900 — **Paddington Antique Centre Pty Ltd, QLD**

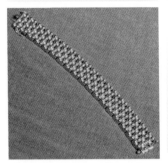

18ct hand made wide gold bracelet, c1940.

$4850 - $5050. — **Carillon Antiques, WA**

Good quality 14ct gold bracelet, European, maker's mark 'S.K.', with flip-over safety catches, weight approx 97 grams, c1950, 19.5cm long, 3cm deep.

NZ$2100 - $2300 — **. Anticus Antiques, New Zealand**

Vintage Indian metal bracelet with chunky dangly charms, c1960, 20cm long.

$75 - $95 — **Retro Active, VIC**

Vintage Mexican silver bracelet with amethysts, c1960, 19cm long.

$380 - $420 — **Kaleidoscope Antiques, VIC**

Herbert Kitchener Currie

Kitch Currie was the maker of this wide silver and amazonite bangle which belies the heaviness of the silver by the fineness of the Australian fern motif giving the effect of laciness. The bangle carries the influences of the Arts and Crafts period that carried through to the 1950's. The bangle is secured by a fine pin through the side hinge so that it is discreetly disguised. The inside panel of the bangle is inscribed KC for Kitch Currie and stamped Sterling Silver

Herbert Kitchener Currie was born in Perth in 1915.

Silver and amazonite bangle, by Kitch Currie of Western Australia c1950.

$3500 - $3700 — **Mary Titchener Antique Jewels, VIC**

Danish sterling silver and amethyst bracelet by H. Siersbol, c1960

$480 - $520 — **Steven Sher Antiques, WA**

After his education at Wesley College, Kitch Currie attended the Perth Institute of Art. There he worked part time as an assistant for jeweller J.W.R Linton but received no formal apprenticeship until 1936 when he joined Linton's workshop in the evenings learning the art of jewellery making and silversmithing. For over a decade, Kitch Currie joined his brother on a gold refinement plant in Wiluna before returning to Perth in 1945 to resume his position with James Linton until Linton's death in 1947.

Kitch Currie continued the skills taught to him by Linton, and with his sister Betsy, moved to Greenmount. He joined the Fremantle Technical College as a teacher of jewellery and design founding a new generation of prolific jewellers.

The work of Herbert Kitchener Currie is displayed in the Art Gallery of Western Australia.

Israeli sterling silver bracelet with Eilat cabachons and faux pearl decoration, c1950, 18cm long, 3cm wide.

$135 - $155 — **Shop 15, Antiques & Collectables Hamilton, NSW**

Silver brooch with eleven cultured pearls, c1950, 4cm long.

$310 - $350   **Margo Richards Antiques, NSW**

Marquisite brooch with sterling silver floral arrangement, quality German made, larger than normally found, c1950, 7cm wide, 9cm high.

$500 - $600   **Chapel Street Bazaar, VIC**

9ct Mizpah brooch, features detailed inscription and ivy leaves.

$230 - $270   **H.O.W Gifts & Collectables, QLD**

18ct gold cameo pendant/brooch, c1950, 3cm high.

$480 - $520   **Antipodes Antiques, QLD**

Cultured pearl brooch stamped 14k, c1960

$275 - $315   **Antipodes Antiques, QLD**

Sterling silver and enamel brooch.

$280 - $320   **Alan's Collectables, NSW**

Sterling silver brooch of a baby in a pot. Baby moves in and out of pot by pressing the back of brooch, c1950, 4cm long.

$125 - $145   **Baimbridge Antiques, VIC**

Butterfly wing brooch

$75 - $95   **Den of Antiquities, VIC**

A 14ct gold multi-wire brooch, set with four graduated cultured pearls and three diamonds, of European origin, c1960, 4cm wide, 3.7cm high.

NZ$420 - $460   **Anticus Antiques, New Zealand**

18ct gold filigree emerald brooch, c1970

$430 - $470   **Steven Sher Antiques, WA**

Opal and white metal brooch in the form of a scorpion, c1950.

$430 - $470   **Steven Sher Antiques, WA**

Sterling silver, marquesite and enamel brooch, c1950.

$280 - $320   **Alan's Collectables, NSW**

18ct white gold brooch set with 21 partly-coloured sapphires, c1968, 4cm long, 3.5cm wide.

$1150 - $1350   **Scheherazade Antiques, VIC**

Yellow 18ct gold flower brooch with a nine diamond cluster to the centre, 15 grams, c1960, 5cm diameter

$1850 - $2050   **Rutherford Fine Jewellery & Antique Silver, VIC**

Finnish sterling silver brooch, c1960

$275 - $315   **Steven Sher Antiques, WA**

9ct gold peridot and seed pearl brooch, 4cm wide.

NZ$205 - $245   **Right Up My Alley, New Zealand**

Italian brooch, le giore del cuore, 10cm long

$125 - $145   **Rosebud Antiques, NSW**

Norwegian silver gilt and enamel flower brooch, c1950, 6cm long

$185 - $205   **Armadale Antique Centre, VIC**

Sterling silver enamelled fish brooch by David Andersen of Norway, enamel in yellow and shades of green, bubbles on fish, c1950, 5.5cm long.

$275 - $315   **Armadale Antique Centre, VIC**

9ct gold and silver lined shell cameo brooch, c1940

$120 - $160   **Chambers & Crosthwaite Antiques, QLD**

Danish sterling silver brooch, designer 'John L', c1950, 8.5cm long.

$115 - $135   **Armadale Antique Centre, VIC**

Shell cameo brooch/pendant by Donadio, set in sterling silver, c1950, 3cm long, 2cm wide.

$110 - $130   **Rare Old Times Antiques & Collectables, SA.**

Italian mosiac brooch, 4cm diameter

$110 - $130   **Antiques, Goods & Chattels, VIC**

GENERAL

Assorted pewter jewellery from Denmark, c1970.

$40 - $60

Design Dilemas, VIC

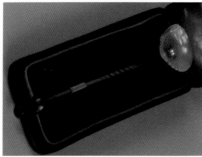

15ct yellow gold mother of pearl stick pin with centre pearl.

$275 - $315

Chilton's Antiques & Jewellery, NSW

Set of boxed English made cufflinks and dress studs, c1940.

NZ $65 - $85

In Vogue Costumes & Collectables, New Zealand

Albert Scharning of Norway, enameled sterling silver necklace, bracelet and earrings, the bracelet and necklace can be joined to form one long necklace, c1950.

$500 - $600

Armadale Antique Centre, VIC

Masonic jewel in enamel and iron pyrites (marcasite)

NZ$950 - $1050

Anthea's Antiques Ltd, New Zealand

Demi-parure 15ct gold pendant brooch and drop earrings with garnets set in flower design, with new ear loops, c1890, 7cm long.

$4695 - $4895

Antique Complex, VIC

GEORG JENSEN

Danish sterling silver grape brooch by Georg Jensen, c1950, 3cm wide, 5cm high.

$750 - $850 **Kaleidoscope Antiques, VIC**

Pair of Danish silver clip-on earrings by Georg Jensen, c1960, 4cm wide

$750 - $850

Kaleidoscope Antiques, VIC

Pair of Georg Jensen Danish silver earrings for pierced ears, c1950, 5cm high.

$670 - $770

Kaleidoscope Antiques, VIC

Georg Jensen sterling silver brooch by Henning Keppel, c1960

$500 - $600

Steven Sher Antiques, WA

Sterling silver Georg Jensen ring, designed by Henning Kopell, c1960

$430 - $470

Marian's Collection, NSW

Tiffany 18ct gold mesh ear drops, c1981.

$740 - $840

**Imogene,
VIC**

18ct blue and green enamel diamond earrings, c1980.

$650 - $750

**Imogene,
VIC**

Pair of tri-colour 18ct gold earrings, c1990.

$225 - $265

**Imogene,
VIC**

Art Deco onyx and diamond pendant, hand made, 14ct, c1950.

$3400 - $3600

**Carillon Antiques
WA**

Edwardian 9ct gold fob chain with shark's tooth charm on a gold mount, c1905.

$380 - $420

**Timeless Treasures,
WA**

9ct gold chain with 17 suspended coloured natural tourmalines, c1960, 50cm long.

$1580 - $1780

**Pendulum Antiques,
SA**

Sterling enamel pendant, c1950, 2.5cm wide.

$140 - $160

**Malvern Antique Market,
VIC**

Victorian swivel locket, 18ct yellow gold set with an onyx cameo, depicting Hades and Carnelian gemstone on obverse, c1970, 4cm long, 2.3cm wide.

$1300 - $1500

**Blake & Angel,
NSW**

Very large Peruvian pendant hand made of brass and malachite. Provenance: Frank Thring 1926-1994, Australian actor and filmstar, 11cm long, 7.5cm wide.

$500 - $600

**Scheherazade Antiques,
VIC**

Pendant, 18ct gold, South Sea pearl and diamonds, 1.5cm wide

$1500 - $1700

**Malvern Antique Market,
VIC**

Miniature painted scene on a pearl shell, silver bound

$115 - $135

**Windsor Bridge
Antiques, NSW**

Lapis lazuli ring set with diamonds and corded gold work, c1980, 2.5cm long, 2.5cm high

$2000 - $2300 — **Mary Titchener Antique Jewels, VIC**

Sterling silver and alexandrite ring, 2cm long, 1cm wide.

$200 - $240 — **The Botanic Ark, VIC**

Hand-crafted sterling silver and turquoise ring, c1966.

$170 - $190. — **The Botanic Ark, VIC**

18ct white gold diamond 'Butterfly' cocktail ring, total diamond weight approximately 1.30 carats, c1940.

$7300 - $7700. — **Carillon Antiques, WA**

Sterling silver ring with 19 natural rubies in a cluster setting, c1960

$360 - $400 — **Womango, VIC**

18ct ruby and diamond ring, c1950

$3400 - $3600 — **Blackheath Antiques & Jewellery, NSW**

Dress ring of 18ct gold with an oval amethyst of approximately 26 carats,

$2400 - $2550 — **Antiques & Heirlooms, WA**

14ct white gold Art Deco style diamond ring featuring a flower centrepiece, c1980.

$750 - $850 — **The Bottom Drawer Antique Centre, VIC**

Superb large acquamarine ring of fine colour, set in 18ct gold, c1940.

$4850 - $5050 — **Carillon Antiques, WA**

Superb French aquamarine ring set in 18ct gold with hand made mount bearing maker's stamp and French standard marks, c1940.

$9750 - $10150 — **Carillon Antiques, WA**

18ct yellow and white gold opal ring, the Lightning Ridge opal 7.7cts, c1970.

$7300 - $7700 — **Steven Sher Antiques, WA**

Superb quality large citrine ring, surrounded with claw set diamonds on side and in basket, 18ct yellow and white gold, c1940.

$5300 - $5700 — **Carillon Antiques, WA**

Knot lamp by Giovani Banci, Italy, c1960, 72cm high

$2800 - $3000   **Mondo Trasho, VIC**

Pair of well-proportioned, in the Neo-Classical style, carved, fretted and painted urn-shaped table lamps, the off-white paint finish distressed and crackled, c2000, 40cm high.

$1300 - $1500   **Miguel Meirelles Antiques, VIC.**

French adjustable arc lamp on marble base with perspex shade and dimmer switch, arc made from beech, c1960, 200cm high.

$1850 - $2050   **b.bold - 20th Century Furniture & Effects, VIC**

Art Deco style table lamp, chrome and bakelite, c1950, 169cm high.

$215 - $255   **Chapel Street Bazaar, VIC**

Art Deco Hicks Bakelite standard lamp with hand painted parchment shade, c1950.

$275 - $315   **Antipodes Antiques, QLD**

Chromed brass ring lamp with original mottled/cloud glass shade and D.H. 'Comet' aeroplane, re-wired, 35cm high.

$700 - $800   **Prism Original Lighting, VIC**

Art Deco German black and white lamp, c1970, 8cm deep, 11cm wide, 17cm high.

$230 - $270   **Southside Antiques Centre, QLD**

Art Deco style, chrome, three branch ark light, c1970, 100cm wide, 230cm high.

$850 - $950   **Chapel Street Bazaar, VIC**

ABS Plastic

ABS is responsible for the sharp shiny look of the 1960s. Acrylonitrile Butadiene Styrene was used extensively by the Italian furniture and light manufacturers Artemide and Kartell. It is a hard inflexible plastic that cracked easily but allowed for furniture in all the colours of the rainbow.

ABS was replaced by polypropylene which was more flexible and not prone to cracking and chipping. In the sixties plastics appeared to have a bright future but the oil crisis in the 1970s led to a revival of traditional crafts and materials.

Yellow ABS plastic stackable light, KD27 designed by Joe Colombo 1967, manufactured by Advance Industries Australia under licence from Kartell, Italy. C1967, 25cm high, 25 cm diameter.

$260 - $300   **506070, NSW**

Pop art wooden crayon lamp, c1970, 120cm high

$380 - $420   **Trasho, VIC**

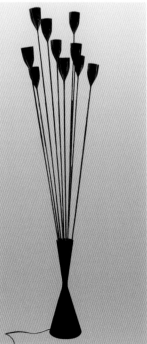

Floor lamp, black metal base with ten brass prongs each containing a separate light, c1950, 60cm wide, 212cm high.

$4400 - $4600   **Tarlo & Graham, VIC**

CANDLESTICKS

Pair of Italia candlesticks, 'Ice' design, c1970, 15cm high, 7cm diameter.

$23 - $33   **Antique General Store, NSW**

'Black lady' plaster candle holder, c1950, 33cm high.

$135 - $155   **Newport Temple Antiques, VIC**

Two piece signed, 'Stuart' English tall crystal candleholder, c1948, 25cm high.

NZ$115 - $135   **Peachgrove Antiques, New Zealand**

Pair of brass church candle holders, c1950, 4.5cm high, 17.5cm diameter.

$85 - $105   **Maryborough Station Antique Emporium, VIC**

Pair of candle holders made in Finland, marked GOG/LH, c1960, 5.2cm high, 75cm diameter.

$30 - $40   **Rose Cottage Antiques, ACT**

Ceramic candlesticks, Jersey pottery, c1960, 10cm long.

$110 - $130   **Obsidian Antiques, NSW**

Pair of candelabra, silver plate on copper, c1950, 12cm deep, 30cm wide, 30cm high.

NZ$700 - $800   **Antiques Centre of Wellington, New Zealand**

Basket of white porcelain flowers with removable centre to convert to a candle holder, c1950, 9cm wide, 6cm high.

$45 - $65   **Helen's On The Bay, QLD**

Pair of sterling silver candlesticks, hallmarked Birmingham, 1976, 5cm wide, 12cm high.

$330 - $370   **Maryborough Station Antique Emporium, VIC**

Italian Rococo candelabra of hallmarked silver with ebonised stems, c1950, 38cm high.

$2350 - $2550   **Kollectik Pty Ltd, NSW**

Retro light, chrome plated frame with molten clear and amber glass shades, c1965, 52cm deep, 60cm wide, 96cm high, 120cm diameter.

$1530 - $1730
Nextonix, VIC

V.P. globe designed by Verner Panton and manufactured by Louis Poulsen, c1970, 60cm diameter

$2600 - $2800
506070, NSW

Retro hot pink molten glass shades connected to gold gilt frame, unusual and aesthetic, c1960, 60cm wide, 100cm high, 22cm diameter

$1550 - $1750
Nextonix, VIC

Scandinavian four pendant light, tinted glass, hand chrome, c1970, 195cm long.

$380 - $420
Tiffany Dodd Antique & 20th Century Furniture, QLD

Retro light, molten amber glass panels fixed to a chrome frame with six light globes on gold structure, c1960, 68cm wide, 80cm high, 18cm diam

$1850 - $2050
Nextonix, VIC

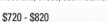

Pendant starburst light in brass and black enamel made by Ritelite Australia, c1950, 62cm diameter

$720 - $820
506070, NSW

U.F.O. horizontal banded glass pendant light, the shade with vertical banding, c1950, 23cm high, 38cm diameter

$140 - $160
Cool & Collected, SA

20th century French off-white, painted pressed tin three-light chandelier, in the shape of a posy comprising stems with leaves and pink-coloured flowers, retaining the original chain and rosette, c1950, 40cm wide, 55cm high

$550 - $650
Miguel Meirelles Antiques, VIC

Hand cut five light lead crystal chandelier, silver plated arms and concealed wiring, c2000, 60cm diameter

$850 - $950
Glenelg Antique Centre, SA

Eight light hand cut lead crystal chandelier, silver plated arms and concealed wiring, c2000, 69cm diameter.

$1500 - $1700
Glenelg Antique Centre, SA

Six light hand cut lead crystal ruby and gold chandelier, c2000, 63cm diameter.

$1500 - $1700
Glenelg Antique Centre, SA

Vintage Czechoslavakian crystal and brass chandelier, 50cm long, 40cm high, 50cm diameter.

$430 - $470
Towers Antiques & Collectables, NSW

LAMPS

Pair of ceramic lamps, one with bird and the other with fish motif, original plastic blue shades, c1950, 15cm long, 41cm high.

$225 - $265   **Towers Antiques & Collectables, NSW**

M.I. Hummel table lamp 'Happy Days', backstamp 'TMK 2B. W.Goebel', c1954, 24cm long, 24cm high.

NZ$580 - $680   **Collector's Choice, New Zealand**

Retro 'black lady' lamp, c1950, 40cm high.

$230 - $270   **FyshwickAntique Centre, ACT**

Very unusual black 'Egyptian head' lamp, c1950, 13cm wide, 28cm high.

$240 - $280   **Rock N Rustic, SA**

Pair of 'Aladdin' black lady bust television lamps, c1950, 14cm wide, 29cm high

$840 - $940   **Vampt, NSW**

Italian ceramic table lamp with vintage shade, c1970, 80cm high.

$170 - $190   **Found Objects, VIC**

Hand decorated slip cast Australiana table lamp with aborigine in hunter stance. Original basket weave shade, c1960, 53cm high, 20cm diameter

$155 - $175   **Born Frugal, VIC**

Black lady lamp with original shade, c1940, 23cm long, 50cm high.

$205 - $245   **Ardeco Antiques & Collectables, WA**

'Budgie' ceramic bird lamp with original shade, c1950, 40cm long, 20cm deep, 40cm high.

$135 - $155   **Towers Antiques & Collectables, NSW**

Pair of Royal Doulton 'Flambe' lamps, octagonal with black marble pattern, c1950, 49cm high.

$2350 - $2550   **Toowoomba Antiques Gallery, QLD**

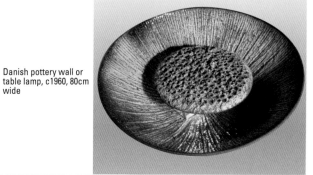

Danish pottery wall or table lamp, c1960, 80cm wide

$1200 - $1400   **Design Dilemas, VIC**

Brass student's desk lamp converted to electricity, c1950, 43cm high.

$480 - $580   **Ardeco Antiques & Collectables, WA.**

Italian glass and chrome table lamp, c1970, 60cm high

$480 - $520   **Mondo Trasho, VIC**

Italian pink glass night lamp with brass base, c1950

$145 - $165   **Towers Antiques & Collectables, NSW**

Alabaster and chrome lamp, c1950, 26cm long, 42cm high, 26cm diameter

$410 - $450   **Urbanized, VIC**

Adjustable metal desk lamp in red, black and chrome by Mar-Mac, c1968, 60cm high.

$110 - $130   **frhapsody, WA**

Pair of tri-colour 'plastic' lamps in the shape of a flaming candle, c1950, 9cm wide, 33cm high.

$255 - $295   **Calmar Trading, VIC**

Original 1950s desk lamp, with aluminium shade and metal base, c1950, 30cm long, 30cm deep, 40cm high.

$145 - $165   **Towers Antiques & Collectables, NSW**

Large table top, teak and brass lamp with original glass shades, c1965, 74cm high.

$480 - $520   **Tiffany Dodd Antique & 20th Century Furniture, QLD**

'Tessere' (patchwork) lamp by Ercole Barovier for Barovier & Toso, c1950, 16cm wide, 32cm high.

$2850 - $3050   **Armadale Antique Centre, VIC**

Acrylic table lamp, c1970, 21cm wide, 46cm high.

$60 - $80   **Rock N Rustic, SA**

Funky chrome frame table lamp with glass ball up-light, c1970, 44cm high, 26cm diameter.

$200 - $240   **Cool & Collected, SA**

Handkerchief style glass table lamp on chrome base, 20cm wide, 28cm high.

$190 - $210   **Shop 48, Southern Antique Centre, NSW**

Green pressed metal, extendable arm desk lamp, c1970, 10cm deep, 16cm wide, 60cm high.

$65 - $85   **Bowhows, NSW**

Desk lamp with a white glass globe, a two setting dimmer, on a gray timber base, c1970, 55cm high, 35cm diameter.

$110 - $130   **Bowhows, NSW**

TABLE & DESK

Desk lamp with white plastic shade and stand, chrome steel frame, c1970

$65 - $85   **Bowhows, NSW**

Pair of mushroom shaped plastic table lamps with scalloped edges, c1960, 40cm high, 35cm diameter

$50 - $70   **The New Farm Antique Centre, QLD**

'Bendix' desk lamp, stainless steel and chrome, glass fibre optics, changes colour every five seconds, c1970, 55cm high, 30cm diameter.

$190 - $210   **Bowhows, NSW**

Twin table lamp of black painted steel and chrome construction with individual switches, c1975, 40cm high.

$40 - $50   **Bowhows, NSW**

Mushroom shade plastic table lamp, c1970, 43cm high, 37cm diameter.

$190 - $210   **Cool & Collected, SA**

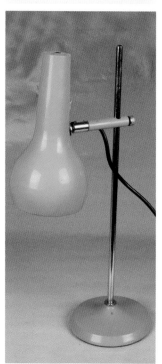

Green pressed metal desk lamp on stainless steel pole, c1970, 35cm high, 10cm diameter.

$60 - $80   **Bowhows, NSW**

Modernist enamelled metal desk lamp, after Arteluce, c1950, 32cm wide, 36cm high.

$380 - $420   **Armadale Antique Centre, VIC**

White plastic and chrome mushroom table lamp, c1970, 32cm high.

$70 - $90   **506070, NSW**

Clear black and red acrylic desk lamp, c1960, 15cm deep, 15cm wide, 43cm high.

$160 - $180   **Bowhows, NSW**

Desk lamp shaped as a white acrylic cube on chrome stand, c1970, 15cm deep, 15cm wide, 35cm high.

$40 - $50   **Bowhows, NSW**

'Twin Gold' standard lamp with twin spots, adjustable height, 360 degrees rotation, separate switches, c1975.

$115 - $135   **Bowhows, NSW**

Original Art Deco plaster figural lamp, c1910, 105cm high.

$900 - $1000   **The Mill Markets, VIC**

Blue annodised aluminium desk lamp with a flexible brass stem, c1950, 35cm high, 18cm diameter.

$50 - $70   **Bowhows, NSW**

Hanimex yellow plastic, adjustable stem desk lamp, c1970.

$30 - $40   **Bowhows, NSW**

Single chrome ball standard lamp, adjustable 360 degrees, chrome steel, black plastic cover on flexible arm, c1975.

$135 - $155   **Bowhows, NSW**

Art Deco chromed brass ring lamp with decorative cedar insert and original glass shade, re-wired, c1930, 25cm wide.

$500 - $600   **Prism Original Lighting, VIC**

Original double Diana lamp, c1930, 50cm high.

$1050 - $1250   **Three Quarters 20th C Furnishings, VIC**

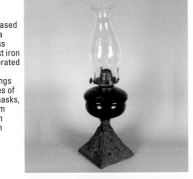

Cast iron based lamp with a purple glass font on cast iron base, decorated with cast foliage, wings and a series of demonic masks, c1900, 12cm deep, 12cm wide, 42cm high, 15cm diameter

$445 - $485   **Lydiard Furniture & Antiques, VIC**

Early 20th century floral decorated metal lamp with slat glass panels, c1920, 39cm high.

$475 - $515   **Wenlen Antiques, NSW**

Art Deco table lamp in burr elm and mahogany, telescopic height and adjustable shade, the table section filled with a drawer, c1930, 157cm high, 58cm diameter

$2200 - $2400   **Virtanen Antiques, VIC**

LAMPS

An original Barsony ceramic black lady lamp, c1950, 57cm high.

$225 - $265

Rose Cottage Antiques, ACT

Black lady lamp by Barsony Ceramics with original shade, plastic, yellow and black, c1950, 21cm wide, 51cm high.

$275 - $315

Chapel Street Bazaar, VIC

Large Barsony black lady lamp, in the form of a bikini clad girl, original shade, c1950, 72cm high, 20cm deep,.

$380 - $420

Dr Russell's Emporium, WA

Black lady lamp made by Barsony Sydney with original plastic ribbon shade, c1950

$330 - $370

Retro Active, VIC

Barsony black lady ballerina lamp with original shade, c1950, 27cm wide, 55cm high

$185 - $205

Brae-mar Antiques, NSW

Barsony

Founded by George Barsony, the factory operated from Guildford in Sydney between the 1950s and 1970s, and produced slip mould products such as figural and abstract lamp bases, vases, bowls, candlesticks, figurines, ashtrays, wall hangings and bookends.

However, Barsony are mostly associated with the black figural lamp bases, which have become highly collectable over the last ten years. Some of the lamp bases even had built in ash trays but the inclusion of the ashtray was a monetary not a design consideration. At that time a high sales tax was levied on ornamental items, while utilitarian items such as cups, plates and ashtrays attracted a reduced sales tax.

Genuine Barsony can be identified by the numbering system on the base of the item: 'H' indicated head, 'V' indicated vase', and 'L' indicated 'lamp'. Thus 'FL' indicated a figural lamp and 'HL' indicated a head lamp. These letters are followed by the model or mould number.

Many of the lamps and figures are named models, such as 'Drumbeat of Trinidad' (FL-41), 'Beauty of the Beach' (F-19) and 'Sitting Black Lady' (FL39)

The price of a lamp will be boosted if it has the original shade which, often were of plastic ribbon and raffia trimmed with thin velvet ribbon.

Original 'George Barsony' black lady lamp, signed under 'George Barsony', with original shade, c1950, 15cm long, 50cm high.

$275 - $315

Towers Antiques & Collectables, NSW

Black Barsony lamp signed to base, no shade, the light comes out of the vase, c1955, 25cm high, 17.5cm diameter.

$280 - $320

Regent Secondhand, VIC

Brass kerosene ship's lantern, c1970, 17cm deep, 17cm wide, 37cm high.

$155 - $175

The New Farm Antique Centre, QLD

Tall upright figural lamp, c1950, 50cm high.

$190 - $210   **Coming of Age Antiques, QLD**

Cast aluminium anodized working lighthouse lamp, c1950, 18cm long, 19cm deep, 34cm high.

$430 - $470   **Philicia Antiques & Collectables, SA**

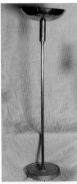

Stainless steel and chrome standard lamp, three bulb turret, c1965.

$65 - $85   **Bowhows, NSW**

Chrome and steel bedside lamps, c1970, 45cm high, 25cm diameter.

$100 - $120   **Bowhows, NSW**

Australian coachwood floor lamp, c1950, 114cm high.

$225 - $265   **RoseCottage Antiques, ACT**

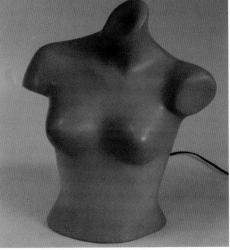

Original 1960's hard plastic lady's bust lamp, c1960, 43cm long, 23cm deep, 52cm high.

$275 - $315   **Towers Antiques & Collectables, NSW**

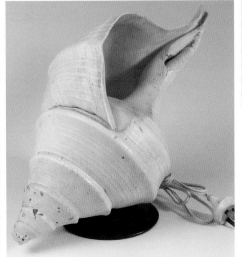

Australia made shell lamp, c1960, 43cm wide, 30cm high.

$280 - $320   **506070, NSW**

Tulip lamp with original glass shades and fittings, c1965, 173cm high.

$275 - $315   **Tiffany Dodd Antique & 20th Century Furniture, QLD.**

Aluminium reading lamp, stamped 'Day Dream' on base, c1950, 15cm long, 50cm high.

$165 - $185   **Towers Antiques & Collectables, NSW**

Fenton fairy light, in selenium glass, used as altar light, c1945, 11.5cm high, 9cm diameter.

$175 - $195   **Kookaburra Antiques, TAS**

Italian blue swirl glass lamp, c1960.

$155 - $175

Retro Active, VIC

Brown ballerina lamp and shade, unusual colour, c1950, 15cm long, 21cm high.

$255 - $295

Towers Antiques & Collectables, NSW

Handpainted black plaster 'lady lamp', c1950, 55cm high.

$185 - $205

Newport Temple Antiques, VIC

Brass and wood light with wooden base and two copper brass bulb covers, c1965, 45cm high, 15cm diameter.

$100 - $120

Bowhows, NSW

Australian timber lamp, c1930, 38cm high.

$800 - $900

Antique Centre of Stonnington, VIC

Vintage plaster hand painted lady lamp with original shade.

$130 - $150

Squatters Antiques & Restorations, SA

Pair of teak 'rocket' lamps, c1970, 22cm wide, 67cm high, 22cm diameter.

$150 - $170

Rock N Rustic, SA

Italian zebra lamp with pleated shade, c1950, 26cm high.

NZ$330 - $370

Maxine's Collectibles, New Zealand

Pair of teak and fibre glass lamps, c1970, 26cm wide, 79cm high, 26cm diameter

$170 - $190

Rock N Rustic, SA

Nursery lamps made of moulded plastic, c1982, 25cm high.

$23 - $33

Chapel Street Bazaar, VIC

Retro fibre optics lamp, 'Cinderella's Coach and Horses', or 'Crown', c1960, 23cm deep, 45cm wide, 36cm high.

$235 - $275

Galeria del Centro, NSW

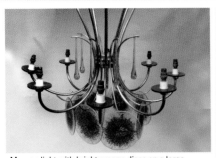

Murano light with bright orange discs on a large chrome frame that hold eight lights, very chic, c1960, 60cm wide, 70cm high, 120cm diameter

$1550 - $1750

Nextonix, VIC

Murano glass fish design lamp with glitter inclusions and a silk shade, c1950, 23cm wide, 38cm high.

$330 - $370

Thompsons Country Collectables, NSW

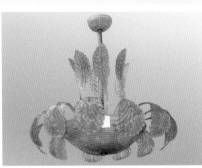

Pink Deco Murano glass chandelier with eighteen leaves, c1950, 70cm high, 70cm diameter.

$1400 - $1600

Chapel Street Bazaar, VIC

Pair of green and clear double cased glass matching Murano lamps, c1960, 15cm deep, 15cm wide, 40cm high.

$175 - $195

The Junk Company, VIC

Murano glass, blue and yellow pyramid lamp base, c1950, 7.5cm deep, 9.5cm wide, 37cm high.

$360 - $400

PRICE: Southside Antiques Centre, QLD.

Pair of very ornate Venetian glass candlesticks featuring grape and vine leaf decoration, artist Toso, c1950, 14cm deep, 25cm wide, 20cm high.

$2100 - $2300

Hermitage Antiques - Geelong Wintergarden, VIC

Italian Murano glass lamp of grapes and leaves, c1950, 42cm wide, 42cm high.

$2100 - $2300   **True Blue Antiques, NSW**

Murano lamp, c1950, 52cm high.

$200 - $240 **Days of Olde Antiques & Collectables, VIC**

Sommerso table lamp by Luciano Gaspari for Salviati, Murano, c1960, 48cm high.

$750 - $850

Found Objects, VIC

Murano glass lamp with gold leaf and original shade, c1960, 11cm wide, 37cm high.

$300 - $340

. Obsidian Antiques, NSW

Italian Murano glass mushroom lamp, c1970, 24cm wide, 36cm high.

$2350 - $2550

Vampt, NSW

Murano glass cased mushroom lamp, c1970, 25cm high.

$220 - $260

Design Dilemas, VIC

Retro light with with brass bendable arms, shelf and magazine rack, c1960, 175cm high.

$100 - $120

Vintage Living, ACT

Reproduction lamp with shade and double dimplex burner, 65cm high

$600 - $700

Green Gables Collectables, NSW

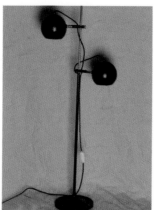

Twin Black Ball Spot with adjustable lamps, wine glass base, matt black and chrome, c1975.

$135 - $155

Bowhows, NSW

Side table with light, of wood, steel and aluminium construction, an orange plastic shade, and ray lamp style legs, c1965.

$200 - $240

Bowhows, NSW

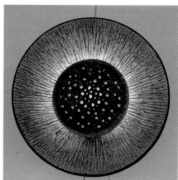

Ceramic glazed Danish wall light, made in Denmark, c1960, 18cm deep, 55cm diameter

$500 - $600

Tarlo & Graham, VIC

Plastic and metal 'Boalum' tube form light that can be placed on any surface as it falls or arranged as desired, designed in 1971 by Gianfranco Frattini and Livio Castiglione, manufactured by Artemide Italy , c1970, 194cm long, 7cm diameter.

$420 - $460

506070, NSW

Polished aluminium flower pot lights by Verner Panton, c1960, 22cm wide, 16cm high

$275 - $315

Tarlo & Graham, VIC

Plastic night light in the form of a pelican, the beak can be pushed into the body of the lamp, c1970, 22cm high.

$150 - $170

506070, NSW

Autographed Elvis Presley Sun Record sleeve, framed with a limited edition gold vinyl LP, an original concert ticket from 1977 scheduled prior to his death and a 1993 Gracelands postmarked 1st day cover, 58cm wide, 126cm high.

$4400 - $4600   **Rockaway Records, QLD**

Australian Open 1999 Womens Doubles Championship match used tennis ball, framed with autographs of winners Anna Kournikova and Martina Hingis and a photo of them holding the Championship Trophy. Championship ball, unable to locate another from this match. Autographs are limited to 500 each worldwide, 50cm wide, 85cm high.

$1890 - $2090   **Rare Memorabilia Gallery, VIC**

Lleyton Hewitt autograph and match worn T-shirt swatch, framed with Australian Open photo and plaque, the autograph and swatch both very limited. Autograph to only 500 worldwide. Both are authenticated by the benchmark in authentic tennis cards and memorabilia, Netpro, c2004, 55cm wide, 85cm high.

$1000 - $1200   **Rare Memorabilia Gallery, VIC.**

Bo Diddley framed original UK pressing of LP 'Rides Again', inset with an autograph from his visit to Brisbane, Australia in 1989, 59cm wide, 104cm high.

$1200 - $1400   **Rockaway Records, QLD**

Elvis Presley memorabilia display consisting of an unused Elvis Concert ticket, a swatch of Elvis worn scarf, various career photos, all framed together with a plaque. Original concert ticket unused for a show one month after Elvis passed away. Scarf from Las Vegas Hilton shows, includes documentation from 'Elvis Archives' and 'Elvis-Arama Museum' in Las Vegas, 90cm wide, 80cm high.

$2190 - $2390   **Rare Memorabilia Gallery, VIC**

Cilla Black framed early New Zealand pressing of LP 'Cilla Sings a Rainbow', inset with an autograph obtained in Brisbane Australia in mid 80's, in stylish grey and black frame, 58cm wide, 119cm high.

$650 - $750   **Rockaway Records, QLD**

George Thorogood framed self titled LP with a set in autograph from his 1983 visit to Brisbane, Australia, c1983, 59cm wide, 120cm high.

$480 - $520   **Rockaway Records, QLD**

Michael Hutchence's shirt, framed with a set of autographs of Michael plus three other band members, a 12" LP, three guitar picks (Kirk, Garry & Tim) and a pair of drumsticks from the 'Elegantly Wasted Tour', c1990, 6cm deep, 130cm wide, 96cm high.

$2400 - $2600   **Rockaway Records, QLD**

Autograph of John Pertwee, now deceased, of 'Dr Who', c1990.

$230- $270   **Cat's Cradle Comics, VIC**

'My Fair Lady' souvenir magazine autographed by cast members: Robin Bailey, Bunty Turner, Richard Walker, Kenneth Laird and Ailsa Grahame., c1959.

$55 - $75   **Yarra Valley Antique Centre, VIC**

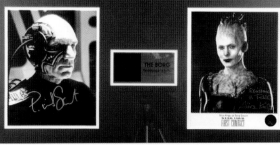

'The Borg' Star Trek display, consisting of a Patrick Stewart autographed photo as Locutus of Borg, Alice Krieg autographed photo as the Borg Queen and a unique Borg emblem plaque, 80cm wide, 45cm high.

$800 - $900   **Rare Memorabilia Gallery, VIC**

Father Christmas night light made of ceramic and metal, c1930, 7cm wide, 16cm high.

$75 - $95   **Chapel Street Bazaar, VIC**

Beswick cabinet Christmas plate, 'Christmas in Holland', stamped underneath 'Registered by the Royal Doulton Group. Beswick Collectors International John Beswick Royal Doulton Group 1976. This is number 8914 of an edition of 15,000', c1976, 21cm long, 21cm high.

$130 - $150   **Towers Antiques & Collectables, NSW**

'Jewelbrite' brand American made Christmas decorations in original box, c1950

$5 - $10   **Savers, VIC**

Father Christmas figure made of plastic and felt, c1960, 7cm wide, 19cm high

$20 - $30   **Chapel Street Bazaar, VIC**

Father Christmas show dome made of hard plastic and filled with water, c1960, 7cm wide, 15cm high.

$30 - $40   **Chapel Street Bazaar, VIC**

Six papier mache Nativity figures, c1910, 10cm high.

$40 - $60   **De Bretts Antiques, VIC**

Hard plastic Father Christmas figure, c1960, 6cm wide, 12cm high.

$15 - $25   **Chapel Street Bazaar, VIC**

Christmas plate depicting an angel with a harp, beautifully decorated and gilded, designed by Bjorn Wiinblad and produced by Rosenthal Germany, c1978, 28.5cm diam

$380 - $420   **Toowoomba Antiques Gallery, QLD**

Father Christmas with nodding head, plastic and felt, c1965, 6cm wide, 17cm high.

$25 - $35   **Chapel Street Bazaar, VIC**

Hard plastic figure of Father Christmas, c1950, 8cm wide, 15cm high.

$20 - $30   **Chapel Street Bazaar, VIC**

Father Christmas in a sleigh pulled by a Reindeer, hard plastic, c1960, 22cm long, 8cm high

$25 - $35   **Chapel Street Bazaar, VIC**

Royal Cauldon rack plate, commemorating Shopshire Federation of Women's Institutes 1956, transferred to rear of plate, c1956, 26cm diameter

$115 - $135   **Ardeco Antiques & Collectables, WA**

Commemorative amethyst Wedgwood goblet issued for the 25th anniversary of the conquest of Everest, c1978, 16cm high

Limited edition Wedgwood commemorative bowl, specially commisioned by NCR Ltd. America (number 667 of 2,000), c1984, 25cm diameter.

$700 - $800   **Tooronga Hall Antiques & Caulfield Antique W'house, VIC**

Royal Copenhagen plate, produced to commemorate Independence Day in Papua New Guinea 1975, 18cm diameter

$55 - $75   **Fyshwick Antique Centre, ACT**

NZ$90 - $110   **Colonial Heritage Antiques Ltd, New Zealand**

Limited edition glass tankard produced for the 200th anniversary of the Trent & Mersey Canal by Wedgwood, c1977, 10cm high, 10cm diameter

$65 - $85   **North Sunshine Bazaar, VIC**

Wedgwood American Bicentennial mug, 1976 first edition, from the Fathers Day series,12cm high.

$275 - $315   **Brae-mar Antiques, NSW**

Commemorative stein for the XIVth Commonwealth Games, Auckland, New Zealand 1990 Diamond Jubilee, V. M. Murray artist, hand screen-printed limited edition 142/400 manufactured by Isis Decora Designs Limited, Auckland, New Zealand.

It is believed that a range of cups, saucers and plates etc. produced in 1990 for the XIV Commonwealth Games in Auckland New Zealand didn't sell well and couldn't even be sold at auction. It is said that 90% of the range was destroyed, c1990, 14cm high, 9cm diameter.

NZ$75 - $95   **Casa Manana Antiques & Collectables, New Zealand**

Wade whisky decanter with Prince Andrew and Sarah Ferguson, c1980, 25cm high, 15cm diameter

$30 - $40   **Chapel Street Bazaar, VIC**

Royal Doulton character jug 'Sir Francis Drake' D6660, issued in 1980 to commemorate the 400th anniversary of the first circumnavigation of the world, c1980, 11cm wide, 23cm high.

$380 - $420   **Glenelg Antique Centre, SA**

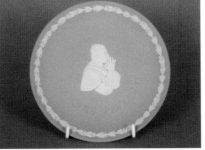

Wedgwood plate commemorating the visit of Pope John Paul to Melbourne in 1982, 17cm diameter

$115 - $135   **Camberwell Antique Centre, VIC**

Commemorative plate depicting Sydney Harbour Bridge, c1981, 26cm diameter.

$15 - $25   **Marge's Antiques & Collectables, NSW**

Souvenir 78 rpm record to commemorate the 1952 Royal Tour featuring the Gay Gordons City of Edinburgh Pipe Band, map and pictures of Australia Side A; photo of Queen Elizabeth II and Duke of Edinburgh Side B and a recording of Queen Elizabeth speaking to the British Empire, c1952, 24.5cm diameter.

$30 - $40   **Abra Card Abra Roycroft, VIC**

Queen Elizabeth II Coronation teapot, June 1953, c1953, 18cm long.

$40 - $60   **Antipodes Antiques, QLD**

Wedgwood Queensware commemorative jug or pitcher, blue on white bas-relief 1953 Coronation of Queen Elizabeth II with Duke of Edinburgh on obverse, laurel leaf border, c1953, 13.5cm high, 13cm diameter.

$65 - $85   **Fyshwick Antique Centre, ACT**

Charles and Diana wedding beaker by Fosters Pottery, c1981, 12cm high.

$20 - $30   **Fat Helen's, VIC**

Aynsley 'Coronation of Elizabeth II' cup, saucer and plate, dated 1953, photograph portrait of Queen Elizabeth II the central feature of cup and plate, c1953.

$45 - $65   **Antique General Store, NSW**

Crystal commemorative glass, for The Queen Mother's 80th birthday, c1980, 22cm high.

$185 - $205   **Tony Barons, VIC**

Coca-Cola commemorative 250ml bottle, Royal Wedding 1981, 18cm high.

$255 - $295   **The Glass Stopper, NSW**

Royal Doulton jug commemorating the coronation of Queen Elizabeth II, c1953, 16cm high, 12cm diameter.

$460 - $500   **Arleston Antiques, VIC**

Bushells tea tin commemorating Coronation, c1952, 15cm high.

$75 - $95   **Shop 9, Centenary Antique Centre, NSW**

Limited edition Charles and Diana portrait Wolf Blass port, number 626 of 1000 boxed and unopened.

$750 - $850   **Unique & Antique, VIC**

Wedgwood glass commemorative goblet for Princess Anne and Mark Phillip with original box and certificate, produced in limited edition of 500, c1973, 14cm high.

$130 - $150   **North Sunshine Bazaar, VIC**

Guiness bottle with raised motif of unicorn and lion, for the coronation of Queen Elizabeth II, full and sealed, c1953, 21cm high.

$190 - $210   **Settlers Store, NSW**

Wedgwood 'Royal Wedding' collection, limited edition white terra-cotta and black jasper tankard, c1981, 15cm high.

$275 - $315   **Camberwell Antique Centre, VIC**

Wedgwood cameo goblet, produced in a limited edition of 300 to celebrate 25th anniversary of the coronation of Queen Elizabeth II, c1953, 15cm high.

$90 - $110   **North Sunshine Bazaar, VIC**

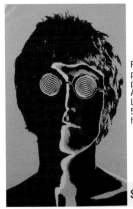

Famous psychedelic poster by Richard Avedon of John Lennon, c1960, 56cm wide, 78cm high.

$430 - $470 **506070, NSW**

Beatles Monthly No 20.

$90 - $110 **Gardenvale Collectables, VIC**

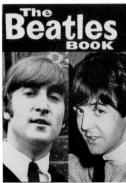

Beatles Monthly No 21.

$90 - $110 **Gardenvale Collectables, VIC**

Three Beatles figurines, the Russian versian of Beatles, where only traditional musical instruments were permitted to be shown, c1967.

NZ$165 - $185 **Colonial Antiques, New Zealand**

Set of four original 1977 Mego Corporation Kiss action figures, no boxes, complete with all accessories, c1977, 35cm high.

$550 - $650 **Rockaway Records, QLD**

Series one Kiss badges, guitars Paul and Gene, unopened box, c2003.

$13 - $23 **Fat Helen's, VIC**

Kiss record player, released in late 1978 for Christmas period but was pulled off shelves after a few weeks, made by Tiger Electronics Toys, model 7-411, c1978, 35cm wide.

$800 - $900 **Go Figure Collectables, VIC**

Kiss 'On Tour' board game, Aucoin 1978 produced by American Publishing Corporation, c1978, 47cm long, 5cm deep, 24cm wide.

$275 - $315 **Rockaway Records, QLD**

Michael Jackson colorform dress up set by MJJ Productions, complete in box, c1988, 3cm deep, 20cm wide, 31cm high.

$60 - $80 **Rockaway Records, QLD**

Michael Jackson figure singing doll with changeable music chip, c1997, 9cm deep, 20cm wide, 34cm high.

$55 - $75 **Cardtastic Collectables, VIC**

Collection of five original Beach Boys unused backstage passes, c1990, 8cm wide, 12cm high.

$50 - $70 **Rockaway Records, QLD**

Plastic guitar by Selcol, England 1957, with a facsimile raised signature of Elvis Presley on the body, missing photo on neck and original Selcol sticker inside, 27cm wide, 78cm high.

$650 - $750 **Rockaway Records, QLD**

SOUVENIR WARE - AUSTRALIAN

Souvenir of Sydney Harbour Bridge, 9.5cm high.

$25 - $35   **Antipodes Antiques, QLD**

Souvenir plate, Flinders St. Melbourne, English Buckfast Potteries, c1950, 23.5cm diameter.

$65 - $85   **Womango, VIC**

Souvenir cup and saucer of Sydney Harbour Bridge, c1950.

$65 - $85   **Victory Theatre Antiques, NSW**

Souvenir of 'The Look Out Range' Toowoomba by Willow Art China, 9.5cm high.

$25 - $35   **Antipodes Antiques, QLD**

Australian pottery dish with aboriginal motif, c1950, 16cm long, 10cm deep.

$40 - $50   **Settlers Store, NSW**

Red Cross flag for the Royal Tour by the Queen in 1954, c1954, 25cm wide.

$25 - $35   **The Wool Exchange Geelong, VIC**

Sydney Harbour Bridge girl, 13cm long, 10cm high.

$225 - $265   **Margo Richards Antiques, NSW**

Glass ashtray with photograph 'Parliament House Canberra, ACT', c1950, 15cm long, 9.5cm deep, 3cm high.

$30 - $40   **Rose Cottage Antiques, ACT**

Baby emu mounted on mulga wood stump, c1950, 40cm long, 60cm high.

$1500 - $1700   **Hunters & Collectors Antiques, NSW**

Cast aluminium, copper finished aboriginal head wall display, c1960, 11.5cm wide, 15cm high.

$75 - $95   **Womango, VIC**

A souvenir bowl made from Tasmanian timbers with original 'West Tamar Woodcrafts' paper label to base, manufactured by Sovereign, c1980, 29cm diam.

NZ$15 - $25   **Collector's Choice, New Zealand**

Carved emu egg on silver base, the egg 1985 Australia, the base c.1900 England, 30cm high.

$530 - $630   **The Restorers Barn, VIC**

Aboriginal wire figurines, 16cm high.

$25 - $35   **Paddington Antique Centre Pty Ltd, QLD**

Australiana desk calendar, c1960.

$10 - $20   **Treats & Treasures, NSW**

A religious certificate 'Souvenir of First Holy Communion', printed by Pellegrini & Co, c1950, 18cm wide, 26cm high.

$10 - $20   **Shirley & Noel Daly Antiques, VIC**

Mulga wood serviette ring stand, decorated with a kangaroo, 15cm long, 7.5cm deep, 10cm high.

$40 - $50   **Tyabb Hay Shed, VIC**

Olive wood decorative hand mirror with Australia motif to reverse, 45cm high.

$120 - $140   **Paddington Antique Centre Pty Ltd,**

Hand spun wool and hand woven wall hanging featuring a vase of flowers, c1972, 60cm wide, 86cm high.

$65 - $85   **Chapel Street Bazaar, VIC**

Japanese made souvenir koala milk jug for 'Jenolan Caves', 10cm high.

$30 - $40   **Brae-mar Antiques, NSW**

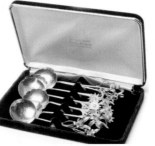

Boxed set of six silver spoons decorated with Western Australian wildflowers, c1950.

$650 - $750   **Trinity Antiques, WA**

Glass ashtray with a photograph adhered to base of Aboriginals whistling with eucalypt leaves, c1940, 10cm wide.

$75 - $95   **Chapel Street Bazaar, VIC**

Souvenir date/desk set with a mulga wood base and a metal kangaroo, c1950, 15cm long, 6.5cm deep, 9cm high.

$35 - $45   **Galeria del Centro, NSW**

Souvenir plaque from Jenolan Caves decorated with a hand painted kookaburra, 25cm diameter.

$115 - $135   **Bob Butler's Sentimental Journey, QLD**

Hand painted Australian ceramic salt and pepper shakers with aboriginal silhouttes in rich glazes by CVGP Australia, c1950, 8cm long, 8cm deep, 8cm wide, 8cm high, 8cm diameter

$85 - $105   **Dr Russell's Emporium, WA**

SOUVENIR WARE - NEW ZEALAND

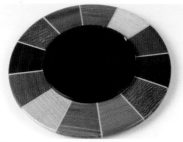

Circular souvenir cheese board made from different New Zealand timbers, original paper label for 'Sovereign Woodworkers Ltd' to base, c1980, 19cm diameter.

NZ$15 - $25 — Collector's Choice, New Zealand

New Zealand wood and paua box, c1950, 9.5cm long, 5cm high.

NZ$40 - $50 — Strangely Familiar, New Zealand

Carved wooden souvenir corkscrew, c1960, 9cm long.

NZ$40 - $50 — Collectamania, New Zealand

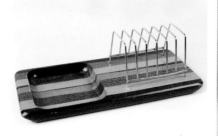

Nickel plated toast rack, the base made from specimen New Zealand timbers, c1970, 31cm long.

NZ$20 - $30 — Collector's Choice, New Zealand

Maori wood carving, c1970, 6cm wide, 14cm high.

NZ$35 - $45 — Oxford Court Antiques Centre, New Zealand

New Zealand native timber bowl with lid, 11.5cm high, 16cm diameter.

NZ$185 - $205 — Bulls Antiques & Collectables, New Zealand

New Zealand rewa/honeysuckle desk blotter, c1950, 6cm deep, 14cm wide, 8cm high.

NZ$30 - $60 — Country Charm Antiques, New Zealand

Maori souvenir of a tiki carved from chipboard on a woven covered masonite board, c1970, 31cm wide, 33cm high.

NZ$30 - $40 — Collector's Choice, New Zealand

Totara burr inlaid clock edged with black marie, burr totara face, kauri numerals and brass hands, c1950, 30cm long, 23cm high.

NZ$370 - $410 — Elmwood Antiques, New Zealand

'Sovereign' desk calendar made from native timber of New Zealand, marked 'Sovereign Woodworkers Ltd', c1950, 4cm deep, 15cm wide, 7cm high.

NZ$20 - $30 — Maxine's Collectibles, New Zealand

New Zealand souvenir box, the various timbers named on the interior of the lid, c1970, 16cm long, 9cm deep, 4cm high.

NZ$20 - $30 — Collector's Choice, New Zealand

Carved Maori canoe on a stand, carved in Hamilton, New Zealand, c1970, 73.5cm long, 7.5cm wide.

NZ$280 - $320

Maxine's Collectibles, New Zealand

Wooden box by 'Sovereign', inlaid in New Zealand native timbers, c1950, 13cm long, 5cm high, 9cm diameter.

NZ$20 - $30

Woodville Mart, New Zealand

Kiwi designed clock with shell overlay, c1960, 19cm wide, 15cm high.

$85 - $105

Rose Cottage Antiques, ACT

Good luck horseshoe of paua shell set in acrylic, c1970, 10cm high.

NZ$5 - $15

Collector's Choice, New Zealand

Glass and silver metal Kiwi brooch, c1960, 5.5cm long.

NZ$40 - $50

Deborah's Antiques, New Zealand

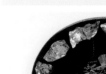

Souvenir dish of paua shell, set in black acrylic with images of New Zealand birds to centre, c1970, 14cm diameter.

NZ$10 - $20

Collector's Choice, New Zealand

Tin manufactured for Wellington College Centenary, c1967, 9cm high, 23cm diameter.

NZ$30 - $40

Memory Lane, New Zealand

Souvenir sea horse with pacca shell, set in clear and black acrylic, c1970, 30cm high.

NZ$30 - $40

Collector's Choice, New Zealand

Paua shell letter rack with brass support, c1970, 9cm long, 9cm high.

NZ$10 - $20

Collector's Choice, New Zealand

Small souvenir tray of paua shell, set in acrylic with brass handles, c1970, 21cm long.

NZ$20 - $30

Collector's Choice, New Zealand

Maori match box holder, c1950, 8cm long, 5.5cm wide, 8cm high.

NZ$85 - $105

Maxine's Collectibles, New Zealand

Sterling silver mounted paua shell brooch, c1950, 4cm long, 2cm wide.

NZ$75 - $95 — **Memory Lane, New Zealand**

Titian Studio souvenir tankard with a New Zealand fantail on one side of the tankard and Kia Ora with a fern on the other side, made for Sargoods. In the native bird series there was a tui, fantail and a kiwi, c1956, 9cm wide, 12cm high.

NZ$80 - $100 — **Casa Manana Antiques & Collectables, New Zealand**

Souvenir of the first New Zealand Easter Show in Auckland, in the form of a copper hat, c1953, 14cm diameter.

NZ$55 - $75 — **Collectamania, New Zealand**

Sterling silver and paua brooch in form of a kiwi, c1950, 2cm wide, 3cm high.

NZ$55 - $75 — **Memory Lane, New Zealand**

Carved mural of Maori guide, Sofia, c1963, 22cm wide, 27cm high.

$25 - $35 — **Habitat Antiques, NSW**

Plastic Tiki thermometer, c1960, 14cm long.

NZ$30 - $40 — **Collectamania, New Zealand**

Sterling silver and paua tie clip with silver fern motif, c1960, 7cm long, 1cm wide.

NZ$40 - $50 — **Memory Lane, New Zealand**

Pair Hukaback Rotorua spa towels, 62cm wide, 96cm high.

NZ$140 - $160 — **Country Charm Antiques, New Zealand**

Silver plated set of three fire tools, on stand with Kiwi motif, 50cm high.

$40 - $50 — **Paddington Antique Centre Pty Ltd, QLD**

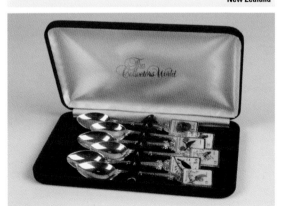

Box set of six teaspoons with New Zealand native birds depicted on handles, silver plate, 12cm long.

NZ$125 - $145 — **Country Charm Antiques, New Zealand**

Chrome plated bottle opener in shape of a Maori 'mere', c1970, 8cm long, 3.5cm wide.

NZ$3 - $13 — **Memory Lane, New Zealand**

Melbourne Football Club, VFL member's badge depicting the famous 'Demons' mascot, c1963, 2.4cm wide, 2.6cm high.

$40 - $50

At The Toss of A Coin, SA

Football card. This high quality football portrait was issued as a set of 30 cards given with 'Golden Flap Jacks'. A booklet was issued to house the set and provide relevant information, c1982, 3.7cm wide, 5cm high.

$25 - $35

At The Toss of A Coin, SA

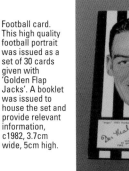

'Argus Card', a printed coupon issued with 'The Argus' newspaper which could be exchanged for one of these high quality football portraits. There were 72 cards in the set and they are now keenly collected. Prices for these cards have trebled in the last two years, c1953, 11.3cm wide, 19.2cm high.

$45 - $65

At The Toss of A Coin, SA

'Coles' card. 'Coles' chain stores issued these rather hideous football cards in conjunction with the National Football league in 1976. The images used are taken directly from a television screen, c1976, 8.8cm wide, 10.8cm high.

$10 - $20

At The Toss of A Coin, SA

'Mobil' card featuring Bob Shearman of West Torrens S.A., part of a set of 40 issued by 'Mobil' petrol stations. A special album to house the cards was available for a shilling. 'Mobil' issued sets of 40 cards in 1964, 1965 and 1971, c1964, 8.2cm wide, 13.2cm high.

$10 - $20

At The Toss of A Coin, SA

'Amscol' card, issued in pairs and found in 'Amscol' ice cream half-gallon tins. They were available for only four months and never found in quantity. These cards are the rarest by far of all cards issued in the last 40 years, c1968, 7.5cm wide, 10cm high.

$190 - $210

At The Toss of A Coin, SA

VFL membership medallions celebrating the opening of VFL Park, priced each, c1970.

$10 - $20

Wooden Pew Antiques, VIC

Six Port Adelaide Football Club S.A. members' badges, running consecutively from 1954 to 1959 inclusive. These are the years of Port's 'Golden Era' where they won six S.A.N.F.L. premierships in a row which is still an Australian record. Made by A.J. Parkes of Brisbane, 2.9cm wide, 2.4cm high.

$700 - $800

At The Toss of A Coin, SA

'Mobil' card showing John Williams of Essendon Football Club VFL in action pose. One of 40 cards given by 'Mobil' service stations with this last series the hardest to complete. This card is from the third and last series of 'Mobil' cards, c1971, 8.2cm wide, 13.2cm high.

$10 - $20

At The Toss of A Coin, SA

'Mobil' card depicting Mike Patterson of Richmond Football Club VFL from high quality series of 40 cards given with any petrol purchase at 'Mobil' service stations, c1964, 8.2cm wide, 13.2cm high.

$10 - $20

At The Toss of A Coin, SA

Souvenir 'Football Record', Grand Final edition, Hawthorn versus St Kilda, 21cm wide, 28cm high.

$50 - $70

Chapel Street Bazaar, VIC

Plastic football team pin issued by 'Milo Tonic Food Drink' in 1964 in the 14oz size tins. A series of 12 were issued in Victoria, 10 in South Australia and 8 in Western Australia featuring team mascots, c1964, 3.4cm wide, 2.1cm high.

$20 - $30
At The Toss of A Coin, SA

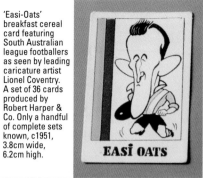

'Easi-Oats' breakfast cereal card featuring South Australian league footballers as seen by leading caricature artist Lionel Coventry. A set of 36 cards produced by Robert Harper & Co. Only a handful of complete sets known, c1951, 3.8cm wide, 6.2cm high.

$70 - $90
At The Toss of A Coin, SA

A.F.L. Bombers tin which originally contained fruit cake, sold in Franklins Stores 1998, 7cm deep, 21cm wide.

$20 - $30
Burly Babs Collectables/Retro Relics, VIC

Wembley Ware footballer in South Fremantle colours, c1950.

NZ$3900 - $4100
Colonial Antiques, New Zealand

Original die cast copies of VFL football club badges, c1960.

$40 - $60
Wooden Pew Antiques, VIC

Australian VFL 1964 Scanlons football card, Darrel Baldock, St. Kilda, c1964, 8cm long, 5.5cm wide.

$190 - $210
Camberwell Antique Centre, VIC

Michael Voss autographed Brisbane Lions training guernsey, fully framed, 80cm wide, 100cm high.

$650 - $750
Rare Memorabilia Gallery, VIC

Weg poster, c1968.

$1400 - $1600
Gardenvale Collectables, VIC

Argus VFL card for Bill Hutchison, Essendon, c1953, 20cm long, 12cm wide.

$25 - $35
Camberwell Antique Centre, VIC

National Football league match souvenir program from the Sturt vs West Perth night game played at football park S.A. on Monday June 14th, 1976. A series of 15 matches were played at football park, Norwood Oval S.A. and Subiaco Oval W.A., all under lights. A very popular series and keenly collected, c1976, 14cm wide, 20cm high.

$15 - $25
At The Toss of A Coin, SA

VFL Coles card, Alan Aylett, North Melbourne, c1953, 9cm long, 6cm wide.

$5 - $15
Camberwell Antique Centre, VIC

Grand Final 'Football Record', VFL Melbourne v Essendon, 1959.

$165 - $185   **Camberwell Antique Centre, VIC**

Vintage Collingwood Football Club photo of Western Australian Touring Party on cardboard frame, with drawing pin marks and wear, but a scarce item, c1951, 30cm long, 25cm wide.

$30 - $40   **Image Objex, VIC**

Wembley Ware figurine of coach 'John Todd' produced in 1974 to commemorate East Fremantle's grand final, 9cm wide, 13cm high.

$1700 - $1900   **Dr Russell's Emporium, WA**

Melbourne Football Club VFL membership ticket for 1959, a year in which they were premiers, c1959.

$280 - $320   **Camberwell Antique Centre, VIC**

Carlton VFL membership ticket 1971.

$15 - $25   **Camberwell Antique Centre, VIC**

Australian football VFL membership ticket for Collingwood, 1956.

$165 - $185   **Camberwell Antique Centre, VIC**

Bound volumes AFL/VFL Football Records for the 1985 Final Series.

$115 - $135   **Camberwell Antique Centre, VIC**

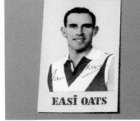

A card from the third series of 'Easi-Oats' breakfast cereal featuring South Australian league footballers with a superimposed signature across the players' portrait. A very elusive card to get in top condition, c1954, 4.6cm wide, 7.6cm high.

$115 - $135   **At The Toss of A Coin, SA**

Football Card from a series of 64 Victorian footballers issued in 1950 by 'Kornies' breakfast cereals. This card is from one of ten different sets issued from 1948 to 1959, c1950, 4cm wide, 6cm high.

$20 - $30   **At The Toss of A Coin, SA**

'Kornies' football card from a series of 64 featuring 'Victorian Footballers' found in 'Kornies' breakfast cereal. All 'Kornies' cards have risen sharply in value in recent times, c1952, 4.8cm wide, 7.3cm high.

$25 - $35   **At The Toss of A Coin, SA**

Five signed Mobil AFL footy cards, c1971, 8cm wide, 13cm high.

$35 - $45   **Secondhand Furniture Mart, TAS**

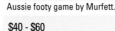

Aussie footy game by Murfett.

$40 - $60   **Gardenvale Collectables, VIC**

Vintage Collingwood Football Club pennant flag, c1970, 55cm long, 24cm high.

$55 - $75

**Image Objex,
VIC**

A playing card sized card, featuring VFL footballers issued in a set of 56 cards by 'Coles' stores. 'Coles' issued three different sets in a two year period in the 50's, c1954, 5.6cm wide, 9.4cm high.

$35 - $45

**At The Toss of A Coin,
SA**

'Jim Beam' whisky decanter in the form of a magpie, c1977, 20cm long, 26cm high.

$115 - $135

**Settlers Store,
NSW**

Heinz poster of footballer Ian Bryant.

$90 - $110

**Gardenvale Collectables,
VIC**

Coca-Cola football bottle tops.

$5 - $15

**Gardenvale Collectables,
VIC**

Two aluminium beer cans made by Cooper & Sons, Essendon and Richmond, c1984, 13cm high.

$40 - $60

**Secondhand Furniture Mart,
TAS**

'Courage' footy stars can, 1972, from set of twelve players, this one, Wayne Richardson, Collingwood, c1972, 13cm high.

$430 - $470

**Carnegie Collectables,
VIC**

Football patches, c1964.

$40 - $60

**Gardenvale Collectables,
VIC**

Scanlen's football cards depicting a variety of clubs and players, c1978.

$10 - $20

**Wooden Pew Antiques,
VIC**

South Melbourne Football Club 'Greigs Honey' glass, released in 1957, c1957, 12cm high.

$125 - $145

**Carnegie Collectables,
VIC**

Richmond Football Club jug with four cups in team colours, by Diana Pottery, c1950, 22cm high.

$600 - $700

**Carnegie Collectables,
VIC**

Fitzroy Football Club 'Greigs Honey' glass, released in 1957, c1957, 12cm high.

$125 - $145

**Carnegie Collectables,
VIC**

Hawthorn Football Club Premiership trophy, Hawthorn's first premiership in the Victorian Football League, 1961, a magnificent piece of football memorabilia. Only issued to premiership team players and club officials, c1960, 17cm wide, 16cm high.

$2400 - $2600   **Carnegie Collectables, VIC**

Nodding head Essendon footballer, the porcelain head on a spring with plaster body, released in the late 50's, 16cm high.

$330 - $370   **Carnegie Collectables, VIC**

Grand Final 'Record', 1944, Fitzroy's last premiership, c1944, 13.5cm wide, 22cm high.

$480 - $580   **Carnegie Collectables, VIC**

Carlton Grand Final pennant 1968, with players names, c1968, 43cm long.

$230 - $270   **Carnegie Collectables, VIC**

Original 1973 'Herald' poster, issued after the grand final for Richmond's Premiership, c1973, 148cm wide, 166cm high.

$500 - $600   **Carnegie Collectables, VIC**

Grand Final 'Record', 1961. Hawthorn defeated Footscray to give Hawthorn their first Premiership victory, c1961, 11.5cm wide, 20cm high.

$800 - $900   **Carnegie Collectables, VIC**

Grand Final 'Record', 1966 for St Kilda's only Premiership victory when they defeated Collingwood by one point. This is the first year that the VFL introduced the large football records for the finals, c1966, 21cm wide, 28cm high.

$310 - $350   **Carnegie Collectables, VIC**

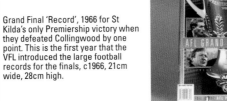

Grand Final 'Record', 2001 when Brisbane defeated Essendon, 21cm wide, 28cm high.

$15 - $25   **Carnegie Collectables, VIC**

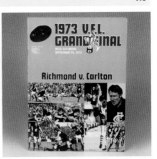

Souvenir 'Football Record' Grand Final edition, Richmond versus Carlton, c1973, 21cm wide, 28cm high.

$50 - $70   **Chapel Street Bazaar, VIC**

Footy decals, unused giveaways at petrol stations, c1970.

$50 - $70   **Chapel Street Bazaar, VIC**

Grand Final 'Record', 1990. Collingwood's first Premiership since 1958, c1990, 21cm wide, 28cm high.

$35 - $45   **Carnegie Collectables, VIC**

Football badges, c1964.

$15 - $25   **Gardenvale Collectables, VIC**

St Kilda Football Club Card 2005 Dynasty, Andrew McQualter, platinum picks, die cut AFL draft card, No. 91 of 130, 5.5cm wide, 9cm high.

$85 - $105

Carnegie Collectables, VIC

Carlton 2005 Signature Card Dynasty, draft pick card of Adam Hartlett, issued with the second series of football cards by Select, 6.5cm wide, 9cm high.

$40 - $50

Carnegie Collectables, VIC

Hall of Fame card, Ted Whitten Senior, 1996, No. 67 of 110, 6.5cm wide, 9cm high.

$5 - $10

Carnegie Collectables, VIC

John Coleman, Essendon Football Club card, one of the first series in 1954 issued by Coles, 6cm wide, 9cm high.

$165 - $185

Carnegie Collectables, VIC

Footscray Football Club membership ticket, 1954. This was Footscray's only premiership, 6cm wide, 8cm high.

$550 - $650

Carnegie Collectables, VIC

Hall of Fame card, 1996, Peter Burns No. 5 of 110, 6.5cm wide, 9cm high.

$1 - $5

Carnegie Collectables, VIC

Set of Geelong Coca-Cola Bottlers cards issued in 1957, mounted in an album, 24cm wide, 32cm high.

$500 - $600

Carnegie Collectables, VIC

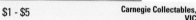

Football Record for the 1967 Grand Final.

$90 - $110

Gardenvale Collectables, VIC

St Kilda Social Club badge for 1967.

$70 - $90

Gardenvale Collectables, VIC

Geelong and District Football Association cap, awarded to members of the premiership team in 1910.

$600 - $700

Carnegie Collectables, VIC

Football decals.

$50 - $70

Gardenvale Collectables, VIC

AFL team coach, St. Kilda's Fraser Gehrig 'Wild Card', c2005, 6.3cm wide, 8.9cm high.

$60 - $80   **Cardtastic Collectables, VIC**

Argus football card, c1953.

$80 - $100   **Gardenvale Collectables, VIC**

Argus football card, c1953.

$80 - $100   **Gardenvale Collectables, VIC**

Cigarette card from a series of forty nine South Australian league footballers, produced by Dungey Ralph, makers of 'Sweet Nell' cigarettes, c1906, 4.1cm wide, 6.6cm high.

$140 - $160   **At The Toss of A Coin, SA**

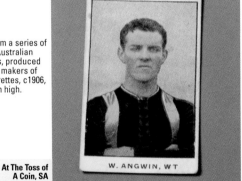

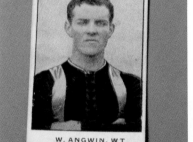

Cigarette card by J. J. Schuh, makers of 'Magpie' cigarettes, who issued a set of 60 cards, 30 featuring V.F.L. footballers and a similar number of S.A. players, c1925, 3.8cm wide, 6.7cm high.

$35 - $45   **At The Toss of A Coin, SA**

Football ticket for South Melbourne, 1961.

$170 - $190   **Gardenvale Collectables, VIC**

Card depicting South Australian league footballer and dual Magarey medallist Bruce McGregor of West Adelaide, distributed free with the boys' magazine 'Pals' and is one of two S.A. footballers included in the series, c1924, 4.3cm wide, 6.6cm high.

$25 - $35   **At The Toss of A Coin, SA**

Football ticket for St Kilda, 1956.

$230 - $270   **Gardenvale Collectables, VIC**

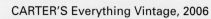

Complete set of 50 Cricketers Series cigarett cards for 1934, issued by John Player & Sons.

$210 - $250   **Kings Park Antiques & Collectables, SA**

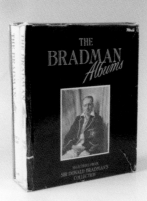

Bradman Albums, Volumes 1 & 2 in slip case 1925-34, 1935-49. 1989 reprint, 20cm wide, 19cm high.

NZ$185 - $205 **South Auckland Antiques & Collectables, NZ**

Don Bradman original photograph, taken after his retirement, c1955, 17.5cm wide, 20cm high.

$90 - $110   **Sport Memorabilia, NSW**

'The Bulletin' newspaper, with Donald Bradman on the cover, c1961.

$20 - $30   **The Nostalgia Factory, NSW**

Miniature size cricket bat with printed autographs of the 1964 Australian team, 28cm long, 3.5cm wide.

$115 - $135   **Abra Card Abra Roycroft, VIC**

Miniature cricket bat souvenir for the 1961 touring series, 42cm long.

$175 - $195 **G & N Miller Antiques, VIC**

Signed miniature collectors bat, 'Australia's Finest Cricketers 1979-80', 27.5cm long, 3.5cm wide.

$40 - $50 **Alan's Collectables, NSW**

Cricket board game.

$35 - $45   **Gardenvale Collectables, VIC**

Ceramic coloured plate showing three rabbits playing cricket and rabbits to rim, 17cm diameter.

$65 - $85   **Abra Card Abra Roycroft, VIC**

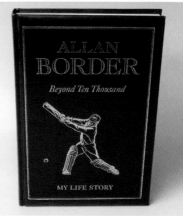

'Beyond Ten Thousand, My Life Story' by Alan Border, special edition of 10,123 copies equal to his test runs scored, this is No. 3150 and signed by Border, c1993.

$430 - $470   **Antiquariat Fine Books, NSW**

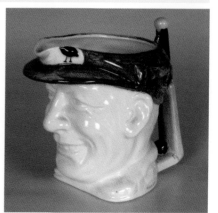

Bradman jug issued in 1930s by Marutomo Ware, Japan, a magnificent jug with rim depicting cricket cap and bat forming handle with lovely depiction of Don Bradman, 17cm deep, 11cm wide, 15cm high.

$480 - $520   **Carnegie Collectables, VIC**

Jack Nicklaus golf display consisting of an autographed GTE Classic pamphlet, a worn game shirt swatch and two career photos, 75cm wide, 75cm high.

$750 - $850   **Rare Memorabilia Gallery, VIC**

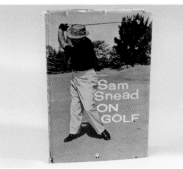

Book, 'Sam Snead on Golf', first edition, c1962.

$20 - $30   **The Nostalgia Factory, NSW**

Spalding advertisement from a magazine, c1956, 12cm wide, 17cm high.

$1 - $5   **The Restorers Barn, VIC**

Mug with golf scenes, the handle forms part of golf bag, by Diana Pottery, comes in two sizes, c1950, 12cm high.

$135 - $155   **Carnegie Collectables, VIC**

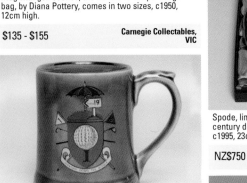

Spode, limited edition golfing series plate, 19th century design ,22 ct gold No. 657 of 2000 worldwide, c1995, 23cm wide.

NZ$750 - $850   **Antiques On Victoria, New Zealand**

Golfing mug, Lord Nelson Ware, c1956, 12cm wide, 15cm high.

NZ$140 - $160   **Antiques On Victoria, New Zealand**

Golfing mug by Wade, c1957, 8cm wide, 10cm high.

NZ$65 - $85   **Antiques On Victoria, New Zealand**

Twentieth century sterling silver pill box, with an enamelled picture on the lid of character cats playing golf, 5cm long, 1cm deep, 4cm wide.

$190 - $230   **Mac's Collectables**

Paperweight golf ball on marble base.

NZ$30 - $40   **Antiques On Victoria, New Zealand**

Spode cup and saucer hand painted, 22 ct gold trim in a 19th century golfing design, c1995.

NZ$550 - $650   **Antiques On Victoria, New Zealand**

Golfers lighter, c1950, 15cm high.

NZ$75 - $95   **Antiques On Victoria, New Zealand**

Westpac money box with the Sydney 2000 mascot, 'Syd', 11cm wide, 23cm high.

$5 - $15

Chapel Street Bazaar, VIC

Fosters Lager Sydney 2000 Olympics bronze medal can, made by CUB Breweries.

$5 - $15

Alan's Collectables, NSW

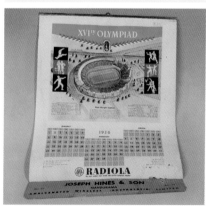

Melbourne Olympic Games Calendar, 1956 with four pages depicting stadiums and parks and an official program distributed by Joseph Hines and Jon Mandurema, 35cm wide, 48cm high.

$10 - $20

Twice Around, NSW

Royal Doulton Bunnykins figure DB28b, 'Australian Olympic Bunnykins'. This is a special colourway that was specifically painted for sale on the Australian market to commemorate our participation in the 1984 Olympics in L.A., 9cm high.

$650 - $750

Roundabout Antiques, QLD

Olympic Games pin lapel badge, with five Olympic rings above a boomerang, c1956, 4cm wide, 5cm high.

$40 - $60

Abra Card Abra Roycroft, VIC

Waterford Crystal Millennium Collection 'Olympian Centrepiece', limited edition of 500. Sands from some of Australia's most famous beaches were gathered and presented by Australian Olympians to Waterford Crystal, Ireland to create a collection for Sydney 2000 Olympic Games.

$1150 - $1350

H.O.W Gifts & Collectables, QLD

Olympic Boxing Association trophy, featuring brass and plated silver, resembling a chinese temple, mounted on a wooden frame, c1950, 10.5cm wide, 13.5cm high.

$85 - $105

Wooden Pew Antiques, VIC

Royal Doulton Bunnykins figure 'Olympic Bunnykins' in Australian green and gold D828, 1983 Golden Jubilee Celebrations, c1984, 4cm deep, 20cm wide, 20cm high.

$830 - $930

H.O.W Gifts & Collectables, QLD

Large souvenir Webb & Corbett original glass, commemorating 1976 Montreal Olympic games in presentation box, 22cm high, 7cm diameter.

$330 - $370

Mac's Collectables,

Melbourne Olympics handkerchief, c1956.

$40 - $50

The Nostalgia Factory, NSW

Australian made all alloy fishing reel by J. J. Crouch and Son, Dunolly Vic, c1950, 9cm diameter.

$275 - $315   **The Evandale Tinker, TAS**

WWE belt, exact replica heavyweight championship, weighs 21kg, made from metal and simulated leather, c2003, 30cm high.

$430 - $470   **Go Figure Collectables, VIC**

On-site fight poster for 'Holyfield vs Tyson II' used at the venue MGM Grand, Las Vegas, to advertise the bout. This is the now notorious 'Bite Fight' in which Tyson bit Holyfield's ear, c1997, 90cm wide, 120cm high.

$840 - $940   **Rare Memorabilia Gallery, VIC**

Coloured action photo of Muhammed Ali and Ken Norton, signed by both in gold pen, 20cm deep, 24.5cm wide.

$480 - $520   **Abra Card Abra Roycroft, VIC**

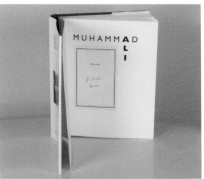

Muhammad Ali Book, 'A Thirty Year Journey' autographed on title page by the great Muhammad Ali and photographer Howard L. Bingham, c1993, 22cm wide, 26cm high.

$550 - $650   **Rare Memorabilia Gallery, VIC**

Piece of basketball court floor where Michael Jordan took his final shot as a Chicago Bull, framed with colour schemed plaque and career photos. Floor piece and photos authenticated from Upper Deck Company where Michael Jordan is on the Board of Directors, c1998, 85cm wide, 50cm high.

$700 - $800   **Rare Memorabilia Gallery, VIC**

'Peter Jackson' shop cigarette packet dispenser of moulded plastic with Seaton/Jones V8 Supercar on top, 10cm deep, 52.5cm wide, 45cm high.

$165 - $185   **River Emporium, NSW**

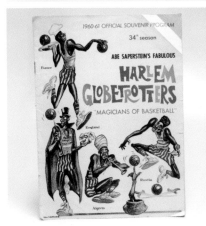

Official souvenir program of the Harlem Globetrotters Australian 1960-61 tour, 27cm long, 19cm wide.

$30 - $60   **Dr Russell's Emporium, WA**

Replica 'Rey Mysterio' leather mask, available in various colours, c2003.

$120 - $140   **Go Figure Collectables, VIC**

Black and white photo postcard of a Ferrari, c1959, 14cm long, 9cm wide.

$20 - $30   **Abra Card Abra Roycroft, VIC**

Royal Doulton character jug in the form of a Manchester United player as part of the football supporters range, modelled by Stanley James Taylor, c1992, 12cm long, 8cm deep, 14cm high.

$145 - $165   **Dr Russell's Emporium, WA**

Caulfield Cup Race Book, 1975.

$25 - $35   **Gardenvale Collectables, VIC**

Melbourne Cup Race Book, 1984.

$35 - $45   **Gardenvale Collectables, VIC**

'Sports Novels' magazine. Melbourne Cup special, c1961.

$10 - $20   **The Nostalgia Factory, NSW**

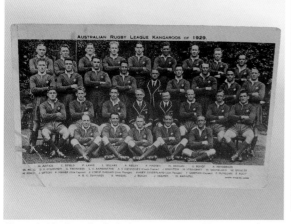

Postcard of the Australian Rugby League test team, c1931.

$55 - $75   **The Nostalgia Factory, NSW**

Western Suburbs Australian Football Club bag, vinyl, c1970, 45cm long, 20cm deep, 30cm high.

$75 - $95   **Towers Antiques & Collectables, NSW**

Melbourne Cup commemorative glass, listing all cup winners to 1979, 24cm high.

$20 - $30   **Antiques & Collectables Centre - Ballarat, VIC**

Adelaide Grand Prix souvenir pewter beer mug from the first Formula 1 Grand Prix held in South Australia, made by Kirra Pewter, c1985, 10.5cm high.

$50 - $70   **Bower Bird Art & Antiques, QLD**

Omega Speedmaster Michael Schumaker model watch, yellow face, automatic, c1998, 4cm diameter.

$1830 - $2030   **Shop 17, Southern Antique Centre, NSW**

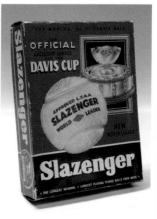

Tennis ball box used to hold twelve white tennis balls, advertising 'Slazenger', c1972.

$40 - $50   **The Bottom Drawer Antique Centre, VIC**

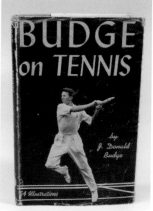

Book, 'Budge on Tennis' by J. Donald Budge, c1949.

$20 - $30   **The Nostalgia Factory, NSW**

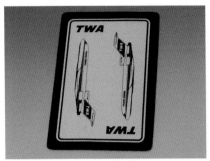

Playing card advertising 'TWA Airlines', c1950, 5cm long, 9cm high.

$5 - $10

Philicia Antiques & Collectables, SA

Australian National Airlines pilot's cap.

$185 - $205

Bill Hayes Antiques, NSW

Apollo XI metal badge, c1969, 4.5cm diameter.

$20 - $30

Chapel Street Bazaar, VIC

Qantas Airways framed travel agents advertising print of a Boeing 707, c1965, 89cm long, 65cm high.

$420 - $460

Kings Park Antiques & Collectables, SA

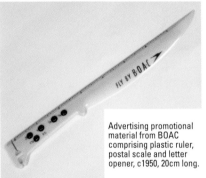

Tan coloured Ansett ANA shoulder bag with white trim. Bags were available at Coles variety stores in the 1950's, 38cm long, 15cm wide, 21cm high.

$125 - $145

Image Objex, VIC

'Air France Globe' poster, artist Plaquet, c1948.

$1400 - $1600

Galerie Montmartre, VIC

Advertising promotional material from BOAC comprising plastic ruler, postal scale and letter opener, c1950, 20cm long.

$55 - $75

Chapel Street Bazaar, VIC

Coloured autographed photo of astronaut John Glenn, c1990, 20cm wide, 29.5cm high.

$225 - $265

Abra Card Abra Roycroft, VIC

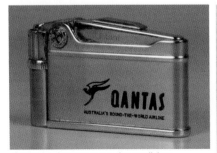

Qantas 1st class passenger cigarette lighter, operating on kero lighter fluid, c1950, 5cm long, 1cm deep, 4cm high.

$65 - $85

Bowhows, NSW

Set of ten Qantas 'Know Your Airline' trade cards, issued by Lever Bros, c1961.

$70 - $90

Abra Card Abra Roycroft, VIC

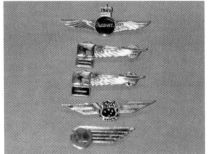

Five assorted airline badges: East West, PAL, Ansett and Qantas, c1970.

$50 - $70

White Hills Antiques & Collectables, VIC

Aluminium advertising plaque for retread equipment, c1950, 30cm high.

$65 - $85

Barry McKay, NSW

A Rolls Royce desk set with flying lady mounts and 'Rolls Royce' engraved to centre, c1950, 17.5cm wide, 27.5cm high.

$2350 - $2550

Barry McKay, NSW

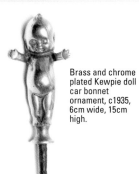

Brass and chrome plated Kewpie doll car bonnet ornament, c1935, 6cm wide, 15cm high.

$75 - $95

Dr Russell's Emporium, WA

Magazine advertisement for 1957 Ford.

$3 - $13

The Time Machine, QLD

Car badge, Automobile Association, Malaya.

$145 - $165

Yarra Valley Antique Centre, VIC

Novelty brass corkscrew, Reg. No. 873.699, c1954, 9cm long.

NZ$135 - $155

Collectamania, New Zealand

'Toyota Sales & Service' advertising sign, c1960, 120cm long, 97cm high.

$330 - $370

Old World Antiques (NSW), NSW

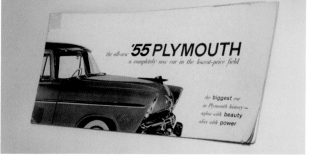

Plymouth sales brochure, c1955, 40cm long, 16cm high.

$100 - $120

Kings Park Antiques & Collectables, SA

Jaguar Mark V leaping cat mascot in chrome, c1960, 20cm long, 8cm high, 11cm diam.

$225 - $265

Wooden Pew Antiques, VIC

Colorado USA number plate.

$25 - $35

Gardenvale Collectables, VIC

Magazine advertisement for Ford motor car, c1950, 54cm wide, 35cm high.

$20 - $30

The Restorers Barn, VIC

Sterling silver Pirelli belt buckle signed lower right by Dali, c1950.

$1400 - $1600

Barry McKay, NSW

Car badge for Queens Royal Visit to Australia, c1954, 6cm wide, 10cm high.

$45 - $65

Dr Russell's Emporium, WA

'Michelin Man' collectable advertising figure playing bagpipes, 5cm wide, 14cm high.

$75 - $95

Chapel Street Bazaar, VIC

'Chevrolet' magazine advertisement, c1956, 21cm wide, 29cm high.

$10 - $20

The Restorers Barn, VIC

'Armstrong Sidley' jet winged sphinx car mascot, c1950, 15cm wide, 10.6cm high.

$380 - $420

Barry McKay, NSW

Mobil Oil Company handy oiler, made of tin, 4 fluid ounces, c1970, 9cm high.

$30 - $40

The Bottom Drawer Antique Centre, VIC

Fold-out sales brochure for the 'Lloyd 600' motor car, c1956, 29.5cm wide, 21cm high.

$25 - $35

The Restorers Barn, VIC

Coloured photo picture postcard of a Nash 'Airflyte' car, c1956, 14cm long, 8.5cm wide.

$20 - $30

Abra Card Abra Roycroft, VIC

Iowa USA number plate.

$25 - $35

Gardenvale Collectables, VIC

'Orient Line' shell pattern design dinner plate, used in the Grill Rooms (first class dining rooms) on their passenger ships. C1950.

$80 - $100 — **Shipping Office, NSW**

P & O Line souvenir ashtray, made by Royal Doulton, featuring incised Royal Doulton and P &O marks, Reg. No. 21022.

$55 - $75 — **Coliseum Antiques Centre, NSW**

Counter display for 'The Blue Funnel Shipping Line' agents, made of cardboard with written information on the back, c1950, 23cm long, 30.5cm wide.

$135 - $155 — **Wooden Pew Antiques, VIC**

Drawing of 'HMAS Kookaburra', A331 built at Cockatoo Island Dockyard, Sydney in 1938-39 as a net class B.D.V. 'Boom Defence Vessel'. Ship sold in 1966. The drawing hung in theSenior Sailors Mess at HMAS Penguin for a time, c1980.

$115 - $135 — **Shipping Office, NSW**

Cruise Line Memorabilia

Mementoes of luxury cruises can give modern collectors a fascinating insight into the golden age of sea travel.

The great ocean liners were matchless symbols of leisurely luxury. Their heyday was in the 1920s and 1930s, before World War II blighted international travel and before the increasing range and sophistication of aeroplanes virtually killed thepassenger trade for ships. Some of the most glamorous destinations were in the Orient, but the journey from Europe to the USA (or vice versa) was the most famous and the most lucrative sea route. The fastest liners took four days to do the Atlantic Crossing, so obviously they could not compete with aeroplanes in terms of speed.

The ocean liners sold souvenirs of the voyage to the passengers, always with the name of the ship prominently displayed. These included posters, prints, photographs and postcards, toys and models, miniature lifebuoys, as well as mugs, ashtrays andpaperweights, all emblazoned with the company's name and badge or a picture of the liner involved.

However, passengers would take their own souvenirs from the voyage, and these unofficial mementoes included anything that could be smuggled off the ship, from pieces of cutlery or crockery, passenger lists, wine lists, concert programs and other pieces of printed ephemera that reflected the glamour and fun of an ocean cruise.

Shipping memorabilia attracts collectors of all ages and from all walks of life, and it is easy to get started, because even those with little money and storage space can collect ephemera.

Bookmark from the 'R.M.S. Oronsay' commemorating its maiden visit to Australia, 1951, 20cm long, 5cm high.

$20 - $30 — **Philicia Antiques & Collectables, SA**

Japanese brass electric ship's lights, port and starboard, in good working order, marked with name plates, c1970, 22cm high, 22cm diameter.

$800 - $900 — **Wisma Antik, WA**

Walker's Excelsior IV ship log, made in England by Thomas Walker & Sons, complete outrigger pattern, 35cm long, 15cm wide, 12cm high.

$410 - $450 — **The Bottom Drawer Antique Centre, VIC**

'Orient Line' Royal Doulton ashtray used on all their passenger ships, mainly in the smoke rooms, c1950.

$80 - $100 — **Shipping Office, NSW**

Wall pennant, from the M.V Kanimbla passenger ship, c1955.

$60 - $80 — **Shipping Office, NSW**

P & O Shipping Line house flag bookmark from the ship's library, c1950, 6cm long, 12.5cm high.

$5 - $15 — **Philicia Antiques & Collectables, SA**

New Zealand Shipping Company bakelite ashtray with metal top, c1955.

$40 - $50   **Shipping Office, NSW**

Australian Coastal Shipping Commission side dish mainly used on the company's Bass Strait Ferry Service, c1970.

$40 - $50.   **Shipping Office, NSW**

Souvenir life bouy from the cruise liner 'Iberia' marked with ports of call, c1963, 13cm diam.

$40 - $50   **Grant & Wendy Brookes, VIC**

New Zealand Steamship Co. wooden cruet set inlaid with enamel logo, in central capstan, 'NZS Co. MV Rangitoto', c1920, 90cm high, 18cm diameter

NZ$185 - $205   **Bulls Antiques & Collectables, New Zealand**

Original ship's air horn marked 'C-Plath WD-18', c1950, 65cm wide, 46cm high.

$1500-$1700   **Wisma Antik, WA**

Port Line pewter mug made as a passenger souvenir, c1965.

$50 - $70   **Shipping Office, NSW**

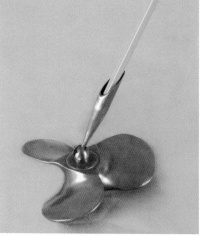

Brass desk pen or quill holder with a base modelled on a boat propeller, 11cm high.

$40 - $60   **Bob Butler's Sentimental Journey, QLD**

Brass porthole with insert photograph of a tug boat, c1970.

$140 - $160   **Shipping Office, NSW**

P & O Lines ship's menu from the 'S.S. Orcades', c1960, 17cm long, 24cm high.

$5 - $15   **Philicia Antiques & Collectables, SA**

Souvenir corkscrew for 'Chandris Shipping Lines', c1960, 11cm long.

NZ$40 - $50   **Collectamania, New Zealand**

'Ampol' garage attendant's enamel hat badge, c1980, 5.2cm long, 4cm wide.

$75 - $95   **Wooden Pew Antiques, VIC**

'Chief Little Wolf' postcard. 'Chief Little Wolf' was a well known wrestler, c1950.

$30 - $40   **The Nostalgia Factory, NSW**

Hooded Singapore trishaw, seats three with baggage compartment, bicycle and timber carriage, 'The Forever Branc' made in Shanghai, China, c1950, 200cm long, 120cm deep, 155cm high.

$1150 - $1350   **Seguin's Antiques & Café, NSW**

'Lucas Batteries' filler bottle, c1960.

$55 - $75   **Victory Theatre Antiques, NSW**

Early New Zealand vehicle registration plate, c1956.

NZ$25 - $35   **Camelot Antiques, New Zealand**

'Rail and Road Service Handbook' 1966-1967, Auckland, N.Z., 13cm long, 11cm wide.

NZ$40 - $50   **Collectamania, New Zealand**

Cast iron railway ticket franking machine, c1950, 14cm wide, 24cm high

$380 - $420   **White Hills Antiques & Collectables, VIC**

An electric wall mounted 'British Railways' clock, c1950, 50cm diameter

$480 - $520   **Granny's Market Pty Ltd, VIC**

New Zealand Rail etched glass, from refreshment rooms, 12cm high, 7.5cm diameter.

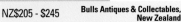

NZ$205 - $245   **Bulls Antiques & Collectables, New Zealand**

Commonwealth Railways trio made by Glove Pottery Co. Ltd, England, c1950, 7cm high, 15cm diameter

$85 - $105   **White Park Antiques, SA**

New Zealand Railways oil can, 'NZR' stamped into body, c1950, 28cm high.

NZ$45 - $65   **Camelot Antiques, New Zealand**

Peters Original Vanilla Ice Cream tin, limited edition 'Toy Story', c1995, 18cm high, 16cm diameter

$15 - $25   **Cardtastic Collectables, VIC**

Rubbery figure of 'Mr Inflation', c1980, 28cm wide, 40cm high.

$900 - $1000   **De Bretts Antiques, VIC**

'Lex Barker Tarzan' metal badge, c1940, 2.5cm diameter.

$20 - $30   **Secondhand Furniture Mart, TAS**

Can of 'Duff Beer' produced by the Razorback Beverages Brewery, Barton, South Australia. Homer Simpson's favourite beer until it was withdrawn from sale due to legal action by Twentieth Century Fox, c1990, 13cm high.

$750 - $850   **Wisma Antik, WA**

Web of Spiderman comic art display framed with comic cover, actual printed page depicting artwork and a unique Spiderman photo plaque. Artist Alex Saviuk finished art Don Hudson, Web of Spiderman #116 - page 20. Spiderman fight scene with Spiderman in every panel of art, plus cover of comic is an interpretation of major panel from page of art, c1995, 90cm wide, 65cm high.

$650 - $750   **Rare Memorabilia Gallery, VIC**

'Alaska' serving tray used for selling chocolates and drinks etc. at cinemas, c1950, 55cm long, 20cm high.

$900 - $1000   **Hunters & Collectors Antiques, NSW**

Coloured photo of Gerald R. Ford, former President of USA, 20cm wide, 25cm high

$185 - $205   **Abra Card Abra Roycroft, VIC**

'How I Raised Shirley Temple' book, c1935, 24cm wide, 26cm high.

$75 - $95   **Shop 7, Centenary Antique Centre, NSW**

Framed collage of antique memorabilia by Stephanie Forsyth entitled 'At the Time of the Kaj', c2003, 10cm wide, 10cm high.

$275 - $315   **Antique General Store, NSW**

An Australian WWII group of five medals comprising 39, 45, Pacific Stars, Defence, War and Australian Service medals. 39/45, PAC, DEF, WM, ASM medals F/S, c1945.

$230 - $270

John Burridge Military Antiques, WA

An Australian Vietnam Service Group of four comprising Active Australian Service, Vietnam medal, National Service medal and Vietnam Campaign Star, c1975.

$1100 - $1300

John Burridge Military Antiques, WA

Belgium 'Croix de Guerre' (Cross of War), c1944.

NZ$65 - $85

Chris' Antiques & Collectables, VIC

An Australian Customs enameled decorative hat badge, c1980.

$75 - $95

Wooden Pew Antiques, VIC

British WWII group of four war medals, comprising 39, 45, Burma and Italy stars, c1945.

$110 - $130

John Burridge Military Antiques, WA

Chrome plated Victorian Police auxiliary force hat badge, numbered, c1950

$50 - $70

Wooden Pew Antiques, VIC

Assorted Red Cross badges and medallions, c1970.

$50 - $70

White Hills Antiques & Collectables, VIC

A replica Boer War and WWI set of medals for family use on Anzac Day. QSA, 14/15, BWM, VIC, c2000.

$140 - $160

John Burridge Military Antiques, WA

National Liberation Front medal from the Vietnam War, c1970, 4cm wide, 6cm high.

$20 - $30

Wooden Pew Antiques, VIC

New South Wales Police badge on timber mount, c1980, 12cm long, 12cm wide.

$40 - $50

Wooden Pew Antiques, VIC

Royal Hong Kong Defence Force sterling silver service medal, c1950, 3.5cm long, 2cm wide.

$40 - $60

Alan's Collectables, NSW

Burmese DHA bayonet of basic design and quality without scabbard, c1960.

$25 - $35 — **John Burridge Military Antiques, WA**

New Zealand Army Officer's mameluke sword with chromed scabbard, etched blade by Wilkinson, gilt fittings and portapee with stores voucher from New Zealand Army, c1990, 94cm long.

NZ$3550 - $3750 — **Ikon Antiques, New Zealand**

Japanese WWII Army Officer's sword complete with scabbard, c1945.

$700 - $800 — **John Burridge Military Antiques, WA**

MIG57 Sig assault rifle bayonet, export version as used by Chile O.A. 14.50, 36.25cm long.

$60 - $80 — **Australian & New Zealand Arms Co Pty. Ltd., VIC**

Replica machine gun is made of steel and resin, all moving parts have been welded and the butt is one centimetre longer to comply with weapon laws, 81cm long.

$1020 - $1220 — **Wooden Pew Antiques, VIC**

Hamilton military watch issued to Australian troops for use in Vietnam, broad arrow marked on back, c1963.

$205 - $245 — **John Summerville Military Antiques, QLD**

English traditional bobby's helmet badged for South Wales Constabulary, c1975, 30cm deep, 23cm high.

$380 - $420 — **Glenelg Antique Centre, SA**

Italian Policeman's cap, once owned by 'Margolfo', c1970, 27cm diameter.

$110 - $130 — **Glenelg Antique Centre, SA**

Lancashire Constabulary bobby's hat.

$360 - $400 — **Tyabb Hay Shed, VIC**

Authentic English Police helmet from Nottinghamshire.

$350 - $450 — **Granny's Market Pty Ltd, VIC**

Russian military cap, c1960

$40 - $50 — **Mooney Collectables, NSW**

Merchant Navy Officer's cap, c1950.

$115 - $135 — **Mooney Collectables, NSW**

Russian Army Officer's cap, c1960

$85 - $105 — **Malvern Antique Market, VIC**

Gilt framed pair of authentic certificates of membership of Saddam Hussein's Fedayeen and Special Forces, received from Senior Officer of US Special Forces, c1990, 52cm wide, 88cm high.

$350 - $390 — **Fyshwick Antique Centre, ACT**

Coloured autographed photo of U.S. Colonel Oliver North seated in military uniform, c1990, 20cm wide, 25.5cm high.

$140 - $160 — **Abra Card Abra Roycroft, VIC**

'Vertex' military wrist watch, English army issue, 3.6cm diameter

NZ$480 - $520 — **Lord Ponsonby Antiques, New Zealand**

Table cast metal cigarette lighter, in the shape of an F-18 Hornet, c1995, 20cm long, 14cm wide.

$110 - $130 — **Fyshwick Antique Centre, ACT**

Victorian Police Force cloth patches.

$30 - $40 — **Wooden Pew Antiques, VIC**

Mess dress, summer uniform to Brigadier Duff DSO, New Zealand Army, comprising white jacket and waistcoat with brigadiers rank, full entitlement of eight miniature medals, dated April 1951 on left breast.

NZ$1150 - $1350 — **Ikon Antiques, New Zealand**

Cast bronze bell from a Russian Soviet diesel electric reconnaissance spy submarine, vessel class and number marked on side of bell, c1960, 20cm wide, 17cm high.

$700 - $800 — **The New Farm Antique Centre, QLD**

Collection of Australian and overseas police patches, c1980.

$20 - $30 — **Wooden Pew Antiques, VIC**

Embroidered Victorian Police 'Mounted Branch' insignia in frame, c1980, 21cm wide, 26cm high.

$155 - $175 — **Wooden Pew Antiques, VIC**

Miniature military 'shirt stud' compass.

$30 - $40 — **Paddington Antique Centre Pty Ltd, QLD**

One Dollar 1969 signature of Phillips and Randall, star replacement issued, c1969.

$2400 - $2600 **John Pettit Rare Banknotes, NSW**

1966 Coat of Arms ten dollar type 1 specimen note, uncirculated.

$14000 - $15000 **The Rare Coin Company, WA**

1974 Australia five dollar type 3 specimen note, uncirculated.

$25000 - $27000 **The Rare Coin Company, WA**

1961 Elizabeth II one pound star replacement note, uncirculated. R34bs Coombs Wilson.

$19000 - $20000 **The Rare Coin Company, WA**

Collection of Australian medallions, 3cm diameter.

$35 - $45 **Newport Temple Antiques, VIC**

1952 George VI Coombs Wilson ten pound note, uncirculated R61.

$13000 - $14000 **The Rare Coin Company, WA**

Royal Life Saving medal, 'The Bronze Star', c1978, 3cm long, 3cm wide.

$10 - $20 **Alan's Collectables, NSW**

Florin George VI Federation Jubilee 1901-1951, c1951.

$1 - $11 **Chris' Antiques & Collectables, VIC**

1963 Perth mint proof penny and halfpenny pair, proof FDC, only 1064 pairs struck.

$1800 - $2000 **The Rare Coin Company, WA**

Art Deco Japanese ceramic vase with three openings, c1920, 19cm wide, 17cm high.

$115 - $135   **Helen's On The Bay, QLD**

Salt and pepper shakers in the shape of a baker and his wife, c1930, 25cm high.

$85 - $105   **Gorgeous, VIC**

Japanese kangaroo and joey, salt and pepper shaker set, c1960, 6cm long, 7cm deep, 12cm high.

$70 - $90   **Galeria del Centro, NSW**

Ceramic stylised cat, c1960, 23cm high.

NZ$135 - $155   **Deborah's Antiques, New Zealand**

Set of three Japanese decorative fish, c1955, 13cm wide, 17cm high.

NZ$410 - $450   **Collectamania, New Zealand**

Set of three flying ducks, c1950, 22cm long, 4cm deep, 22cm high.

$155 - $175   **Kookaburra Antiques, TAS**

Noritake duck in flight, c1960.

$275 - $315   **Brae-mar Antiques, NSW**

Pair of lobster salt and pepper shakers, c1950.

$30 - $40   **Paddington Antique Centre Pty Ltd, QLD**

Novelty ceramic 'Mammy' biscuit barrel with metal handle, c1950, 20cm wide, 20cm high.

$255 - $295   **Chapel Street Bazaar, VIC**

Pair of china pixie figurines, c1980, 12cm long, 10cm high.

$60 - $80   **Chapel Street Bazaar, VIC**

Japanese novelty biscuit barrel in the form of a cat licking its lips, all hand painted and marked on base, c1950, 19cm wide, 18cm high.

$60 - $80   **Bower Bird Art & Antiques, QLD**

Japanese made koala milk jug, c1950, 7.5cm deep, 13cm wide, 13cm high.

$40 - $60   **Southside Antiques Centre, QLD**

Milk jug depicting a ram, c1950, 5cm deep, 15cm wide, 9cm high

$20 - $30 **Southside Antiques Centre, QLD**

Bonzo milk jug, c1950, 7cm deep, 11cm wide, 10cm high

$55 - $75 **Southside Antiques Centre, QLD**

Set of four Kelco Japan porcelain coffee cups and saucers, c1960, 6.5cm high.

$30 - $40 **frhapsody, WA**

Salad set, lobster design, Noritake Japan, plate, bowl and servers, yellow lattice design, c1950.

$100 - $120 **Avoca Beach Antiques, NSW**

Retro coffee pot by Noritake, c1950, 20cm high.

$20 - $30 **Collector's Cottage Antiques, NSW**

'Tutti Fruiti' tea set consisting of teapot, sugar and creamer, c1960, 18cm long, 21cm wide.

NZ$410 - $450 **Deborah's Antiques, New Zealand**

Set of four porcelain Kelco Japan demitasse duos, c1960, 70cm high.

$30 - $60 **frhapsody, WA**

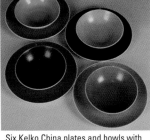

Six Kelko China plates and bowls with multi coloured decoration, c1975, 15cm diameter.

$40 - $50 **Bowhows, NSW**

Japanese Ritz China Meriage saki set, a whistling decanter and six whistling saki cups with matching tray, c1950, 12cm wide, 14cm high, 18cm diameter.

$75 - $95 **Helen's On The Bay, QLD**

Set of six multi coloured Grizelle mugs, c1960.

$70 - $90 **Regent Secondhand, VIC**

Set of four Japanese ceramic egg cups in form of baby birds, 9cm wide, 8cm high.

$45 - $65 **Helen's On The Bay, QLD**

Noritake twenty one piece tea set, c1960

$260 - $300

Antiques &Collectables Centre - Ballarat, VIC.

Imari cup with moulded geisha on base, c1950, 5cm high.

$55 - $75

Margaret Sutherland Antiques, VIC

Japanese ceramic milk jug in form of baby bird, c1960, 11cm wide, 10cm high

$30 - $40

Helen's On The Bay, QLD

Novelty ceramic salt shaker in shape of 'Mammy', c1950, 7cm wide, 12cm high.

$25 - $35

Chapel Street Bazaar, VIC

JFK salt and pepper shakers made in Japan, dated 1962 on the underside, 6cm deep, 6cm wide, 11cm high.

$185 - $205.

Chapel Street Bazaar, VIC

Hayasi Japan tea for two, egg shell china with geisha girl in bottom of cup, c1950, 22cm wide, 16cm high.

$110 - $130

Helen's On The Bay, QLD

Japanese ceramic vase, floral motif and drip glaze, c1960, 30cm long, 9cm deep, 21cm wide, 30cm high.

$55 - $75

Dr Russell's Emporium, WA

Pair of novelty ceramic salt and pepper shakers, c1980, 5cm wide, 9cm high.

$20 - $30

Chapel Street Bazaar, VIC

Japanese ceramic vase for Ikebana, c1960, 20cm wide, 19cm high

$90 - $110

506070, NSW

Ceramic 'lady's head' vase made in Japan, c1955, 11cm deep, 11cm wide, 17cm high.

$185 - $205

Chapel Street Bazaar, VIC

Twin stem Noritake vase, c1950, 14cm wide, 25cm high.

$100 - $120

Vampt, NSW

Ceramic 'lady's head' vase made in Japan, c1955, 10cm deep, 10cm wide, 13cm high.

$115 - $135

Chapel Street Bazaar, VIC

Large hand painted 'lady's head' vase with original pearl earrings and necklace. Original sticker for K-K Japan, c1950, 11cm deep, 13cm wide, 19cm high

$135 - $155   **Shop 15 Coliseum Antiques Centre, NSW**

Glamorous ceramic 'lady's head' vase with pearl jewellery, c1950, 9cm long, 8cm deep, 13cm high.

$330 - $370   **Philicia Antiques & Collectables, SA**

Ceramic 'lady's head' vase made in Japan, c1955, 11cm deep, 11cm wide, 17cm high.

$185 - $205   **Chapel Street Bazaar, VIC**

Spanish style 'lady's head' vase, c1950, 12cm high, 10cm diameter

$155 - $175   **Shop 10, Centenary Antique Centre, NSW**

Glamorous ceramic 'lady head' vase with pearl jewellery, c1950, 10cm long, 8cm deep, 14cm high.

$275 - $315   **Philicia Antiques & Collectables, SA.**

Pair 'black lady' bookends, c1950, 13cm high.

$50 - $70   **Secondhand Furniture Mart, TAS**

China biscuit barrel, c1960, 16cm deep, 15cm wide, 19cm high

$40 - $50   **Maryborough Station Antique Emporium, VIC**

Carved hardstone oriental 'Grotesque' wall mask, c1950, 15cm high.

Set of six multi coloured ramekins in original box, c1950, 41cm long, 6cm deep, 23cm wide.

$50 - $70   **Cool & Collected, SA**

$155 - $175   **Antiques At Birkenhead, NSW**

Chinese red lacquer exhibition vase hand carved cinabar, made into lamp, 58cm high.

$1400 - $1600   **McLeods Antiques, NSW**

Large Japanese original glass and rope buoy, 34cm diameter.

$175 - $195

Collector's Cottage Antiques, NSW

Box of 28 Tagua nuts netsuki, c1950, 27cm long, 20cm wide.

$1900 - $2100

Eagle Antiques, VIC

Hot pink leather punk jacket, by 'Shin & Company', medium size, c1989.

$190 - $210

Gorgeous, VIC

Green glass overlay Chinese snuff bottle decorated with butterflies and flowers with matching glass stopper and spoon, 3cm deep, 6cm wide, 7.5cm high.

$330 - $370

Mac's Collectables

Natural hard stone snuff bottle with matching lid and spoon, flower design, 2cm deep, 4.5cm wide, 6cm high

$280 - $320

Mac's Collectables

Carved ivory gourd shaped snuff bottle with mask handles and rings, people in relief, matching lid with spoon, 2cm deep, 4cm wide, 8.5cm high.

$260 - $300

Mac's Collectables

Chinese hand made and signed ink block, 11cm wide, 18cm high.

$500 - $600

Kollectik Pty Ltd, NSW

Japanese Pretzels tin with multi purpose lid, one bar tray, featuring German helmet.

$65 - $85

Tyabb Hay Shed, VIC

Japanese marquetry picture inlaid puzzle box in the shape of books, c1950, 12cm long, 9cm deep, 10cm high

$140 - $160

Imperial Antiques, VIC

Ivory glove stretchers carved with roses on one side and a village scene on the other, 20cm long.

$100 - $120

Olsens Antiques, QLD

Gourd shape, interior painted glass and cloissone snuff bottle with cloissone lid and spoon, decorated in blossoms and butterflies, 8.5cm high, 4cm diameter.

$280 - $320

Mac's Collectables

Buddha with decorative silver inlay,
c1900, 50cm high.

$800 - $900   **Tarlo & Graham,**
VIC

Pair of Japanese costume dolls, c1950.

$560 - $600   **Victory Theatre Antiques,**
NSW

Japanese wooden hand painted
Kokeshi dolls, c1950, 20cm high.

$85 - $105   **Retro Active,**
VIC

Soap stone engraved plaque on stand,
c1960, 3cm deep, 9cm wide, 16cm high

$80 - $100   **Southside Antiques Centre,**
QLD

Noritake goldfish, c1950, 26cm long.

$75 - $95   **Shaws Antiques,**
NSW

Japanese novelty duster or brush, the handle in the form of a dog, 20cm high.

$14 - $24   **Paddington Antique Centre Pty Ltd,**
QLD

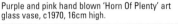

Purple and pink hand blown 'Horn Of Plenty' art
glass vase, c1970, 16cm high.

$65 - $85   **Fat Helen's,**
VIC

Art glass bowl, red colour, made in
Japan, c1960, 24cm long, 24cm deep,
24cm wide, 6cm high, 24cm diameter

$60 - $80   **Dr Russell's Emporium,**
WA

Oriental footed card box with gilded
decoration, containing two sets of
playing cards, 10cm wide, 12cm high.

$110 - $130   **Antiques At Birkenhead,**
NSW

Japanese desk set with musical cigarette
box and ashtray, Mt. Fuji, temple, pagoda,
river and cherry blossom detail, c1950,
14cm deep, 24cm wide, 15cm high.

$85 - $105   **Womango,**
VIC

Hand painted Chinese dragon, 12cm
long, 12cm high.

$70 - $90   **Antiques, Goods & Chattels,**
VIC

MONEY BOXES

Battery powered 'Hole in One' money bank, 21cm wide, 17cm high.

$110 - $130   **The Exchange Galleries, NSW**

Original 'Jolly Nigger' money box made from cast aluminium with original paintwork, c1950, 13cm long, 13cm deep, 16cm high.

$275 - $315   **Towers Antiques & Collectables, NSW**

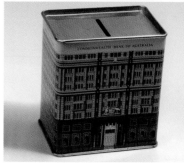

Commonwealth Bank money box, c1980.

$5 - $15   **Furniture Revisited, VIC**

Cast iron Coca Cola Santa money box, 14.5cm high.

$230 - $270   **Alan's Collectables, NSW**

Pig money box, The Lake Domain, Cambridge, New Zealand, 11.5cm long, 4cm wide, 5.5cm high.

NZ$85 - $105   **Country Charm Antiques, New Zealand**

Money bank of 'Miss Piggy', c1980.

$10 - $20   **Cat's Cradle Comics, VIC**

Hull Pottery pig money bank, brown glazed with cream and blue drip glaze on head and ears, made in U.S.A, c1950, 13cm wide, 15cm high.

$65 - $85   **Bower Bird Art & Antiques, QLD**

Frankonia secret coin bank, in working order, c1950, 14cm long, 9cm deep, 5cm high.

$135 - $155   **Towers Antiques & Collectables, NSW**

'Inspector Gadget' money box featuring Penny and Brains, c1990, 6cm deep, 9cm wide, 10cm high.

$10 - $20   **Fat Helen's, VIC**

Plastic money box in the shape of a 1949 Australian penny, 3cm deep, 15.5cm diameter.

$40 - $60   **Abra Card Abra Roycroft, VIC**

'Expo 88' money box, 12cm diameter.

$1 - $11   **Paddington Antique Centre Pty Ltd, QLD**

Genuine polished sperm whale tooth scrimshaw engraved by a Western Australian artist, c1960, 13cm long, 4cm wide.

$550 - $650 — **The Bottom Drawer Antique Centre, VIC**

Pair carved African elephant tusks presented to the Deputy Prime Minister of Trinidad & Tobago by the Government of Nigeria, 1964, 91cm high.

$15500 - $16500 — **McLeods Antiques, NSW**

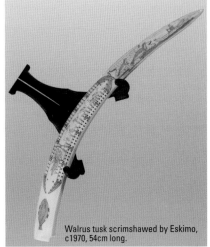

Walrus tusk scrimshawed by Eskimo, c1970, 54cm long.

$1750 - $1950 — **Brisbane Antiques Pty Ltd, QLD**

Italian wooden bottle stopper carved from wood in the form of kissing couple, c1950, 10cm long, 2cm deep, 5cm diameter.

$40 - $60 — **Dr Russell's Emporium, WA**

Small gate being a technical project for mortice and tenon joints for 4th form boys attending Woodwork & Metalwork classes at the Waikato Technical College, c1964, 53cm wide, 53cm high.

NZ$30 - $40 — **Casa Manana Antiques & Collectables, New Zealand**

Carved stand ex Luna Park Sydney, c1950, 77cm high.

$175 - $195 — **The Time Machine, QLD**

Pair of wooden Mexican book ends, 30cm wide, 40cm high.

$23 - $33 — **Myriad Art, NSW**

Original Burmese teak freeform wooden bowls, c1960, 18cm wide, 22cm higha

$40 - $60 — **Design Dilemas, VIC**

Basket made from graduated wooden beads in black and natural colours, c1952, 29cm long, 25cm wide, 21cm high.

$45 - $65 — **The Botanic Ark, VIC**

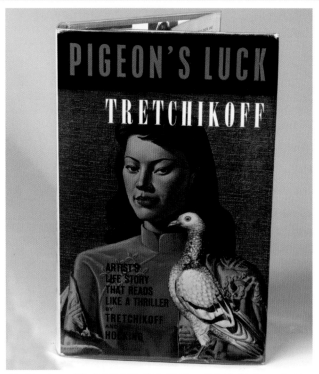

The Adventures of Vladimir Tretchikoff, His Life Story. Tretchikoff is famous for his prints of black women in the 1950s, c1970.

$130 - $150   **Regent Secondhand, VIC**

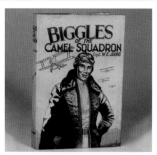

Capt W. E. Johns, 'Biggles of the Camel Squadron', Dean & Sons Ltd, c1960, 2cm deep,13cm wide, 19cm high.

$15 - $25   **Savers, VIC**

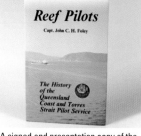

A signed and presentation copy of the book 'Reef Pilots', presented to the former Governor of Queensland, Sir James Ramsay, c1982.

$55 - $75   **Michael Krassovsky**

'Savage Life and Scenes in Australia and New Zealand' by George French Angas. Facsmile of 1846, original, reprinted in 1968

$40 - $60   **Lancaster's Toowoomba Antique Centre, QLD**

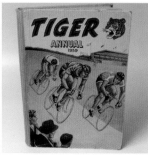

'Tiger Annual' boy's story book, c1959, 20cm wide, 27cm high.

$20 - $30   **Town &Country Antiques,NSW**

Capt W.E. Johns 'Biggles Hunts Big Game', 1955 fourth impression, c1955, 2cm deep, 13cm wide, 19cm high.

$20 - $30   **Savers, VIC**

'The Penny Universal of New Zealand' number 802 of a limited edition of 1000, by G. R. Collins published by The Royal Philatelic Society of New Zealand, c1953,19cm wide, 25cm high.

NZ$40 - $60   **Colonial Heritage Antiques Ltd, New Zealand**

'The Man with the Golden Gun' by Ian Fleming printed by the Chaucer Press, 1st Edition, c1965, 13cm wide, 19.5cm high.

$115 - $135   **Philicia Antiques & Collectables, SA**

'Reference Handbook of Straight Egyptian Horses Vol III', published 1979 by the Pyramid Society, Lufkin Texas.

$140 - $160   **Yarra Valley Antique Centre, VIC**

Design & Living' by E.A. Plishke, Wellington Department of Internal Affairs, New Zealand, 1947, printed by Whitcombe & Tombs Ltd, Wellington. E.A., 28cm long, 21cm wide.

NZ$90 - $110   **Casa Manana Antiques & Collectables, NZ**

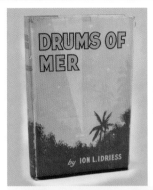

'Drums of Mer' by Ion Idriess, c1951.

$45 - $65

'Gateway to Port Phillip Bay', hardcover book with dustcover, first edition illustrated by Joan Bogunda and written by Leslie M. Moorhead. Jolbo Studio, Victoria 1979.

$65 - $85

'Sydney's First Four Years', by Captain Watkin Tench, a reprint of 1790's narrative of expedition to Botany Bay and complete account of settlement at Port Jackson, c1960.

$85 - $105

Collection of five Australian Songster books, c1955.

$90 - $110

'Birds of the Australian Swamps', two volumes limited edition #94/500 signed by author F. T. Morris, folio 1/2 calf gilt lettering spine, c1981.

$280 - $320

'The Magic Boomerang' Australian magazine, written and illustrated by Syd Nicholls, lovely Australian fairy story, 36cm long, 24cm high.

$65 - $85

Two HMV record catalogues, 1937-39.

$80 - $100

'Zara Holt - An Autobiography My Life and Harry', The Herald, Melbourne 1968, a first edition hardcover version with dust cover, forward by Sir Robert Menzies.

$25 - $35

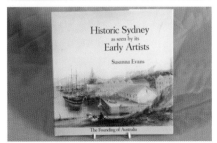

'Historical Sydney as seen by its Early Artists' by Sussanna Evans, Doubleday Australia 1983, first edition hardcover with dust cover, 160 pages with 125 plated maps, drawings and paintings by early artists.

$75 - $95

The works of Ion Idriess, 12 volumes including 'Lasseter's Ride', 'The Desert Column', 'Men of the Jungle', 'Gold Dust and Ashes', 'Drums of Mer', 'The Yellow Joss', 'Man Tracks', 'The Cattle King', 'Forty Fathoms Deep', 'Madman's Island', 'Flynn of the Inland' and 'Over the Range', the national edition, c1941.

$650 - $750

'Robbie's Trip to Fairyland' by Phyllis Johnson and Jean Elder, published by Murfet Pty. Ltd Melbourne, c1946, 27.5cm long, 27.5cm high.

$25 - $35

'Norman Lindsay Pen Drawings' book, c1974, 20cm wide, 27cm high.

$140 - $160   **Treats & Treasures, NSW**

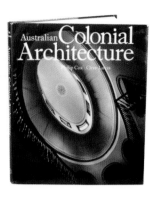

'Australian Colonial Architecture' by Philip Cox and Clive Lucas, 1978, 31.5cm deep, 26.5cm high.

$70 - $90   **Antique Prints and Maps at Full Circle, VIC**

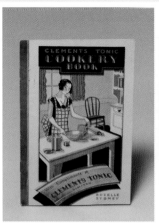

An advertising cook book for Clements Tonic Limited, Rozelle, Sydney produced in the 1940's, 12cm wide, 18cm high.

$10 - $20   **Philicia Antiques & Collectables, SA**

'The Graham Kennedy Story', special edition, soft cover, c1960.

$280 - $320   **Chapel Street Bazaar, VIC**

'More Advertures of Ginger Meggs', Sunbeams book Series 8, original Australian story and art by Bancks with colour cover and interior art, c1931.

$75 - $95   **Comics R Us, VIC**

'More Adventures of Ginger Meggs', Sunbeams book Series 10, original Australian story and art by Bancks, with colour cover and interior art, c1933.

$75 - $95   **Comics R Us, VIC**

'Panel by Panel', an illustrated history book of Australian comics by John Ryan, c1978, 24cm wide, 32cm high.

$20 - $30   **Chapel Street Bazaar, VIC**

'Bony and the Mouse' by Arthur Upfield, Heinmann 1959. A first edition hardcover of 249 pages classical Australian writing.

$60 - $80   **Titles & Treasures, QLD**

'History of Berrima District 1798-1973' by James Jervis, limited edition of 1000 copies.

$40 - $60   **Lancaster's Toowoomba Antique Centre, QLD**

'The Art of Hugh Sawrey' Collectors Edition, created and signed by Hugh Sawrey, published by J. T. Hooper 1981, contains 46 colour plates with commentary, 103 pages.

$65 - $85   **Titles & Treasures, QLD**

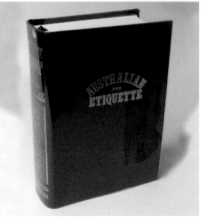

'Australian Etiquette', facsimile edition of original, published in 1885 by the Peoples Publishing Company, deluxe edition, number 35 of 85, c1980.

$185 - $205   **Antiquariat Fine Books, NSW**

'Victorian Splendour, Australian Interior Decoration 1837-1901' by Suzanne Forge, signed copy, published 1981, 240cm wide, 320cm high.

$110 - $130 **Antique Prints and Maps at Full Circle, VIC**

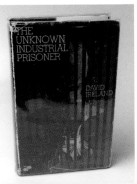

'The Unknown Industrial Prisoner' by David Ireland, first edition hardcover in dust wrapper signed by author, a Miles Franklin Winner in 1972.

$110 - $130 **Antiquariat Fine Books, NSW**

'The Kelly Hunters' by Frank Clune, a brilliant biography of Ned Kelly from his ancestry to his adversity under pioneering conditions and the circumstances that led him to be an outlaw. Published by Angus and Robertson, first edition published 1954.

$50 - $70 **Ainsley Antiques, VIC**

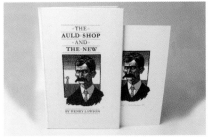

'The Auld Shop and The New' by Henry Lawson, published by Wayzgoose Private Press, Katoomba, quarter leather with wood engraving and lino cut, number 5 of 49 limited deluxe edition, c1992.

$280 - $320 **Antiquariat Fine Books, NSW**

Victorian Railways 'Way and Works Branch Book of Instructions', c1955, 1.5cm deep, 12cm wide, 19cm high.

$20 - $30 **Lydiard Furniture & Antiques, VIC**

'Berger Paints' pricing catalogue with automotive paint samples, c1950, 26cm wide, 20cm high.

$115 - $135 **The Wool Exchange Geelong, VIC**

Eleven Carter's Price Guide to Antiques in Australasia from 1994 to 2004, including two boxed editions 2004 and 2000.

$1300 - $1500 **Seguin's Antiques & Café, NSW**

'Queensland's Sunshine Coast Then and Now 1880-1980', 28cm long, 21cm high.

$20 - $30 **Southside Antiques Centre, QLD**

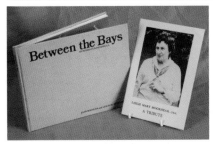

'Between the Bays - Mornington Peninsula' hardcover book number 2 of 250 first edition signed by artist Joan Bognuda and author Leslie Moorhead, Jolbo Studio, Victoria 1979.

$65 - $85 **Titles & Treasures, QLD**

'My Mate Dick', first edition book by Ion Idriess, c1962.

$70 - $90 **The Nostalgia Factory, NSW**

Selection of early 1960's Carter Brown Pulp Fiction novels, first editions printed by Horowitz in Adelaide, Australia, 12cm wide, 18cm high.

$40 - $60 **Born Frugal, VIC**

Australian western 'Red Ryder Comic #14' with colour cover art by Keith Chatto, the contents reprinted from USA comics in black and white, c1963, 25cm deep, 18cm high.

$20 - $30 — Comics R Us, VIC

Book of 'Ginger Meggs' comics, series 5, c1928, 30cm long, 25cm wide.

$115 - $135 — The New Farm Antique Centre, QLD

'Ginger Meggs' comic, c1944.

$65 - $85 — The Nostalgia Factory, NSW

'More Adventures of Ginger Meggs' comic book produced by Bancks and printed in Sydney, c1950, 20cm wide, 27cm high.

$65 - $85 — Philicia Antiques & Collectables, SA

Ginger Meggs Annuals 1951-1956, published by Melbourne Sun Pictorial

$340 - $380 — Chapel Street Bazaar, VIC

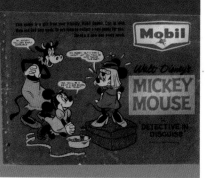

Mickey Mouse 16 page comic distributed by the Mobil Oil Company at garages with the purchase of petrol, c1950, 18cm wide, 13cm high.

$30 - $40 — Philicia Antiques & Collectables, SA

Bluey & Curley Annuals, published in the Melbourne Sun Pictorial, a reprint of the daily comic strip, c1950.

$40 - $50 — Chapel Street Bazaar, VIC

Late 1950's Australian comic featuring the character 'The Lone Avenger' illustrated by Len Lawson who was gaoled for life for murder and rape. Until his death several years ago he was NSW longest held prisoner. Original Australian art and story with colour cover and black and white interior, 17.5cm wide, 25cm high.

$85 - $105 — Comics R Us, VIC

Australian reprint of USA 'Whiz Comics #72' featuring Captain Marvel and Shazam. Colour cover with black and white interior, c1955, 26.5cm deep, 18cm high.

$65 - $85 — Comics R Us, VIC

'More Adventures of Ginger Meggs', Sunbeams Book series 24. Original Australian story, colour cover and interior art by Bancks, c1947, 28cm deep, 20cm high.

$65 - $85 — Comics R Us, VIC

Australian comic featuring the character 'The Lone Avenger' #27 illustrated by Len Lawson. Colour cover with black and white interior, c1956, 17.5cm wide, 25cm high.

$65 - $85 — Comics R Us, VIC

'Amazing Spiderman' comic #13, first Mysterio, c1964, 17cm wide, 26cm high.

$200 - $240   **Cat's Cradle Comics, VIC**

'Amazing Spiderman' comic #300, first full Venom appearance, Todd McFarlane's third issue, c1988, 17cm wide, 26cm high.

$90 - $110   **Cat's Cradle Comics, VIC**

'Amazing Spiderman' comic #15, first 'Kraven the Hunter', first mention of Mary Jane (not shown), c1964, 17cm wide, 26cm high.

$170 - $190   **Cat's Cradle Comics, VIC**

'Amazing Spiderman' comic #14, first Green Goblin, c1964, 17cm wide, 26cm high.

$255 - $295   **Cat's Cradle Comics, VIC**

'Amazing Spiderman' comic #8, 'Fantastic Four' appearance, c1963, 17cm wide, 26cm high.

$410 - $450   **Cat's Cradle Comics, VIC**

'Amazing Spiderman' comic #1, c1963, 17cm wide, 26cm high.

$700 - $800   **Cat's Cradle Comics, VIC**

'Amazing Spiderman' comic #3, first Doctor Octopus, c1963, 17cm wide, 26cm high.

$255 - $295   **Cat's Cradle Comics, VIC**

Comic, 100th issue of 'Amazing Spiderman' comic, 'The 8 Armed Spiderman', c1971, 17cm wide, 26cm high.

$85 - $105   **Cat's Cradle Comics, VIC**

'Amazing Spiderman' comic #40, Green Goblin is revealed as Norman Osborne, c1966, 17cm wide, 26cm high.

$85 - $105   **Cat's Cradle Comics, VIC**

Peter Parker, 'Spectacular Spiderman' comic #1. This was Marvel Comics second regular Spiderman title and signified their expanding fortunes, c1976, 17cm wide, 26cm high.

$65 - $85   **Cat's Cradle Comics, VIC**

Amazing Spiderman' comic #12, 'Doctor Octopus' story, c1964, 17cm wide, 26cm high.

$320 - $360   **Cat's Cradle Comics, VIC**

Ace Comics featuring 'The Phantom', c1948.

$90 - $110   The Nostalgia Factory, NSW

Giant size 'Phantom' No. 14 comic, c1957.

$115 - $135   The Nostalgia Factory, NSW

Giant size 'Phantom' No. 9 comic.

$135 - $155   The Nostalgia Factory, NSW

'Phantom' No. 81 comic, c1954.

$190 - $210   The Nostalgia Factory, NSW

'Phantom' No. 409 comic, printer's proof, one of only two known copies, title 'Fathers & Son', c1969.

$330 - $370   The Time Machine, QLD

'Phantom' No. 52 comic, c1954.

$320 - $360   The Nostalgia Factory, NSW

'Phantom' No. 79 comic, c1955.

$205 - $245   The Nostalgia Factory, NSW

'Phantom' No. 121 comic, c1956.

$90 - $110   The Nostalgia Factory, NSW

USA 'Phantom' #1 comic by Gold Key, 1962, 17cm wide, 26cm high.

$100 - $120   Cat's Cradle Comics, VIC

'Harvey Hits' #36 comic, a showcase title with a different character in each issue. This is one of the early 'Phantom' issues from 1960, in colour. A Falk/McCoy story 'The Secret Of The Lost Treasure City', 17cm wide, 26cm high.

$65 - $85   Cat's Cradle Comics, VIC

Gold Key's 'Phantom' #2, American series, 1963, colour, 17cm wide, 26cm high.

$70 - $90   Cat's Cradle Comics, VIC

First 'Hellboy' comic, four issue mini series, c1994, 17cm wide, 26cm high.

$25 - $35 — **Cat's Cradle Comics, VIC**

'Star Wars' comic No.107, last issue of the 80's series, c1986, 17cm wide, 26cm high.

$40 - $60 — **Cat's Cradle Comics, VIC**

'Dark Shadows' comic No.1 from 1968, 17cm wide, 26cm high.

$40 - $50 — **Cat's Cradle Comics, VIC**

'Brave and the Bold' comic No.36, third Hawkman appearance, c1961, 17cm wide, 26cm high.

$85 - $105 — **Cat's Cradle Comics, VIC**

Comic 'Marvel Tales of Suspense' No.58, c1962.

$190 - $210 — **The Nostalgia Factory, NSW**

'Silver Surfer' comic No.2, c1968.

$140 - $160 — **Cat's Cradle Comics, VIC**

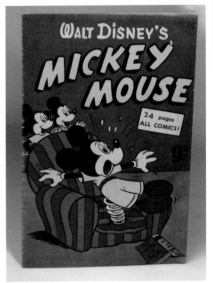

'Mickey Mouse' comic No.5, Australian comic, c1952, 17cm wide, 26cm high.

$110 - $130 — **Cat's Cradle Comics, VIC**

'Iron Fist' comic No.14, the first Sabretooth appearance, c1977, 17cm wide, 26cm high.

$65 - $85 — **Cat's Cradle Comics, VIC**

'Thor' comic 'Journey into Mystery' No.117, Thor goes to Vietnam and fights commies, c1965.

$30 - $40 — **Cat's Cradle Comics, VIC**

'Journey into Mystery' comic No.118, first appearance of Destroyer, c1965, 17cm wide, 26cm high.

$50 - $70 — **Cat's Cradle Comics, VIC**

'Wonder Woman' comic No.48, c1964, 17cm wide, 26cm high.

$40 - $60 — **Cat's Cradle Comics, VIC**

COMICS - OTHER

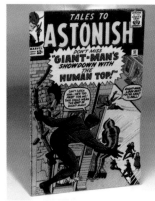

'Tales to Astonish' comic No.51, c1963, 17cm wide, 26cm high.

$6480 - $6880   Cat's Cradle Comics, VIC

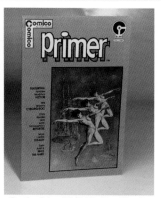

'Comico Primer' No.5 'The First Maxx' MTV story, ten page story by Sam Keith, c1982, 17cm wide, 26cm high.

$40 - $60   Cat's Cradle Comics, VIC

'Batman Annual' 1968 printed in colour, 93 pages, 18cm wide, 27cm high.

$40 - $50   Philicia Antiques & Collectables, SA

'Captain America' comic No.101, 2nd issue in his own title, c1968, 17cm wide, 26cm high.

$30 - $60   Cat's Cradle Comics, VIC

'Prince Namor, The Sub-Mariner' comic No.1, c1968, 17cm wide, 26cm high.

$115 - $135   Cat's Cradle Comics, VIC

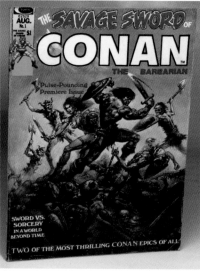

'Savage Sword of Conan' magazine No.1, black and white, c1974, 17cm wide, 26cm high.

$100 - $120   Cat's Cradle Comics, VIC

'Fantastic Four' comic, No.14, c1963, 17cm wide, 26cm high

$140 - $160   Cat's Cradle Comics, VIC

'X-Men' comic No.28, first banshee appearance, c1967, 17cm wide, 26cm high.

$65 - $85   Cat's Cradle Comics, VIC

'Incredible Hulk' comic No.180, first Wolverine appearance, cameo only on last page, c1974.

$60 - $80   Cat's Cradle Comics, VIC

Walt Disney comic No.27, c1948.

$50 - $70   The Nostalgia Factory, NSW

Comic 'Mickey Mouse, Private Eye', c1948.

$50 - $70   The Nostalgia Factory, NSW

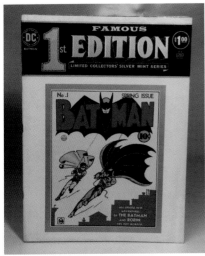

Batman treasury reprint of Batman No.1. This is 'Famous First Edition' No.F-6, 1975 and reprints Batman #1 from 1940, in double sized format, 34cm long, 26cm wide.

$30 - $60   **Cat's Cradle Comics, VIC**

Giant comic war picture library WW2, real pictures and comics, $10 each, c1965, 33cm long, 13cm high.

$5 - $15   **Wooden Pew Antiques, VIC**

'Mandrake the Magician' giant comic album published by 'Modern Promotions', story is 'The Queen of Cats', black and white, c1972, 35cm long, 28cm wide.

$15 - $25   **Cat's Cradle Comics, VIC**

'Werewolf by Night' comic No.32, first Moon Knight appearance, c1975, 17cm wide, 26cm high.

$90 - $110   **Cat's Cradle Comics, VIC**

'Matrix' movie comic. These comics were intended as giveaways to US moviegoers but were recalled and ordered destroyed on the eve of the movie's release, c1999, 17cm wide, 26cm high.

$20 - $30   **Cat's Cradle Comics, VIC**

'My Greatest Adventure' comic No.82, third Doom Patrol appearance, c1963, 17cm wide, 26cm high.

$65 - $85   **Cat's Cradle Comics, VIC**

'Durango Kid' comic No.16, a seven page Frank Frazetta story 'Dan Brand and Tipi, c1952, 17cm wide, 26cm high.

$50 - $70   **Cat's Cradle Comics, VIC**

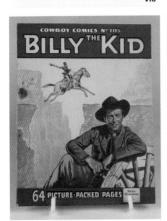

Cowboy Comics 'Billy the Kid', c1950.

$15 - $25   **Gardenvale Collectables, VIC**

Cowboy Comics 'Buck Jones', c1955.

$15 - $25   **Gardenvale Collectables, VIC**

'Brave and the Bold No.82, Batman and Aquaman' comic, Neil Adams art, c1969,17cm wide, 26cm high.

$35 - $45   **Cat's Cradle Comics, VIC**

Cowboy Comics 'Kit Carson', c1955.

$15 - $25   **Gardenvale Collectables, VIC**

'Welcome Back Kotter' double sized comic book treasury contains the unpublished issue 11, photos inside front and back cover, c1978, 34cm long, 26cm wide

$25 - $35   **Cradle Comics, VIC**

'Sgt. Fury' comic No.1, c1963.

$160 - $180   **Cat's Cradle Comics, VIC**

'King Kong' double sized treasury comic adapts the movie, c1978, 34cm long, 26cm wide.

$24 - $34   **Cat's Cradle Comics, VIC**

'I Love Lucy, Lucille Ball' comic, c1961.

$25 - $35   **The Nostalgia Factory, NSW**

'Captain Video' No.2 comic, c1953.

$20 - $30   **The Nostalgia Factory, NSW**

'Gunsmoke' comic, c1969.

$10 - $20   **The Nostalgia Factory, NSW**

'The Flintstones Christmas Party' double sized treasury comic, features Flintstones, Yogi, Snoopy and Blabber, Quickdraw, Augie Doggie and Jetson stories, c1977, 26cm wide, 34cm high.

$24 - $34   **Cat's Cradle Comics, VIC**

'Marvelman' comic No.348 published by L. Miller & Co., London, England, original English art and story, colour cover, black and white interior, c1955, 17.5cm wide, 25cm high.

$65 - $85   **Comics R Us, VIC**

'Mad Magazine' No.155, The Godfather movie cover, c1972, 17cm wide, 26cm high.

$10 - $20   **Cat's Cradle Comics, VIC**

'Vampirella' comic No.4 magazine, c1969, 17cm wide, 26cm high.

$80 - $100   **Cat's Cradle Comics, VIC**

'Vampirella' comic No.2 magazine, c1969, 17cm wide, 26cm high.

$140 - $160   **Cat's Cradle Comics, VIC**

'Justice League' comic No.41, first 'Key Master', c1965, 17cm wide, 26cm high.

$35 - $45   Cat's Cradle Comics, VIC

'Cave Woman' comic No.1, c1994, 17cm wide, 26cm high.

$65 - $85   Cat's Cradle Comics, VIC

'Batman' comic No.183, second Poison Ivy appearance, c1966, 17cm wide, 26cm high.

$40 - $50   Cat's Cradle Comics, VIC

'Green Lantern' No.25, c1963, 17cm wide, 26cm high.

$25 - $35   Cat's Cradle Comics, VIC

Dutch Thunderbirds comic, c1969, 17cm wide, 26cm high.

$10 - $20   Cat's Cradle Comics, VIC

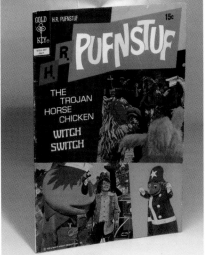

'H.R. Pufnstuf' comic No.8, c1972, 17cm wide, 26cm high.

$35 - $45   Cat's Cradle Comics, VIC

'Incredible Hulk' comic No.105, c1968, 17cm wide, 26cm high.

$40 - $60   Cat's Cradle Comics, VIC

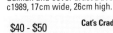

'Sandman' comic No.5 signed by Neil Gaiman and cover artist Dave McKean, c1989, 17cm wide, 26cm high.

$40 - $50   Cat's Cradle Comics, VIC

'Wolverine' comics, No.1 to No.4 mini series, Wolverine in his first solo series in 1982, 17cm wide, 26cm high.

$150 - $170   Cat's Cradle Comics, VIC

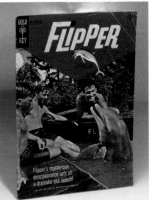

'Flipper' comic No.2 from 1966, 17cm wide, 26cm high

$20 - $30   Cat's Cradle Comics, VIC

D.C. comic 'Bob Hope'

$35 - $45   Gardenvale Collectables, VIC

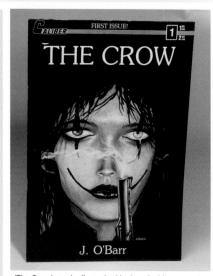

'The Crow' comic, first print black and white, precedes the movie by five years, c1989,17cm wide, 26cm high.

$85 - $105

Cat's Cradle Comics, VIC

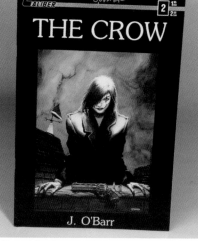

'Second Crow' comic, signed by writer and artist J. O'Barr, c1989, 17cm wide, 26cm high.

$85 - $105

Cat's Cradle Comics, VIC

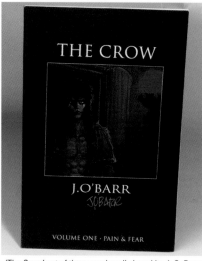

'The Crow' set of three comics all signed by J. O. Barr. This is the first complete printing of The Crow story line, c1992, 17cm wide, 26cm high.

$85 - $105

Cat's Cradle Comics, VIC

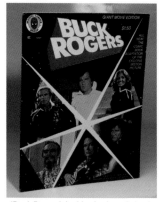

'Buck Rogers' double sized comic book adaptation of the 1979 movie, 34cm long, 26cm wide.

$15 - $25

Cat's Cradle Comics, VIC

'Star Trek Next Generation' comic No.1 from the late 80's, 17cm wide, 26cm high.

$5 - $15

Cat's Cradle Comics, VIC

'Nick Fury, Agent of Shield' comic No.1, with Jim Steranko art and cover, c1968, 17cm wide, 26cm high.

$80 - $100

Cat's Cradle Comics, VIC

'Silver Surfer' comic No.1, c1968, 17cm wide, 26cm high.

$80 - $100

Cat's Cradle Comics, VIC

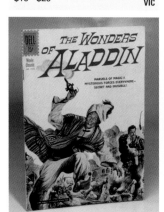

'Wonders of Aladdin' movie comic, c1961, 17cm wide, 26cm high.

$15 - $25

Cat's Cradle Comics, VIC

Buffy number 'Half' mail away comic, 14 page comic story with certificate of authenticity, c1999, 17cm wide, 26cm high.

$14 - $24

Cat's Cradle Comics, VIC

Superman's pal 'Jimmy Olsen' comic No.59, c1962, 17cm wide, 26cm high.

$25 - $35

Cat's Cradle Comics, VIC

'Daredevil' comic No.1, c1964, 17cm wide, 26cm high.

$230 - $270

Cat's Cradle Comics, VIC

'Marvel' comic.

$35 - $45   **Gardenvale Collectables, VIC**

'Marvel' comic.

$35 - $45   **Gardenvale Collectables, VIC**

'Batman' comic No.357, c1966, 17cm wide, 26cm high.

$30 - $40   **Cat's Cradle Comics, VIC**

'Star Trek' comic No.2, c1968, 17cm wide, 26cm high.

$70 - $90   **Cat's Cradle Comics, VIC**

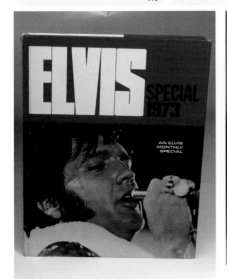

'Elvis Annual', c1973, 26cm long, 21cm wide.

$20 - $30   **Cat's Cradle Comics, VIC**

'Superman' comic No.1 double sized reprint of Superman No.1 from 1939, c1979, 34cm long, 26cm wide.

$30 - $40   **Cat's Cradle Comics, VIC**

'Wonder Woman' comic No.1 reprint double sized comic of Wonder Woman No.1 from 1942, c1975, 34cm long, 26cm wide.

$30 - $40   **Cat's Cradle Comics, VIC**

'Fantastic Four' comic No.15, 'First Mad Thinker', c1963, 17cm wide, 26cm high.

$75 - $95   **Cat's Cradle Comics, VIC**

'Iron Man' comic No.1, c1968, 17cm wide, 26cm high.

$230 - $270   **Cat's Cradle Comics, VIC**

'Banana Splits' comic No.1, c1969, 17cm wide, 26cm high.

$40 - $60   **Cat's Cradle Comics, VIC**

'Captain America' comic, c1963.

$40 - $60   **The Nostalgia Factory, NSW**

'Close Encounters' double sized comic book adapts the movie, c1978, 34cm long, 26cm wide.

$23 - $33   Cat's Cradle Comics, VIC

'Battlestar Galactica Treasury' double comic size adapts television show with articles and interviews in centre pages, c1978, 34cm long, 26cm wide.

$25 - $35   Cat's Cradle Comics, VIC

D.C. comic 'Dean Martin and Jerry Lewis'

$40 - $60   Gardenvale Collectables, VIC

'Fantastic Four' No. 8 comic, c1962.

$80 - $100   The Nostalgia Factory, NSW

'Fantastic Four' No.10 comic, c1962.

$140 - $160   The Nostalgia Factory, NSW

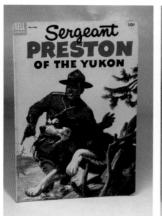

'Sgt Preston of the Yukon' comic No.10 from 1954, 17cm wide, 26cm high.

$20 - $30   Cat's Cradle Comics, VIC

'Warlock' No.1 comic 1972, 17cm wide, 26cm high.

$40 - $60   Cat's Cradle Comics, VIC

'Prince Namor The Sub-Mariner' No.4 comic, c1968, 17cm wide, 26cm high.

$25 - $35   Cat's Cradle Comics, VIC

'Marvel Premiere' No.15 comic the first Iron Fist appearance, c1974, 17cm wide, 26cm high.

$50 - $60   Cat's Cradle Comics, VIC

'X-Men' No.30 comic, c1967, 17cm wide, 26cm high.

$50 - $70   Cat's Cradle Comics, VIC

DC 80 page Giant No.1 'Superman' comic from 1964, 17cm wide, 26cm high.

$85 - $105   Cat's Cradle Comics, VIC

'Playboy' magazines, American editions with centrefolds intact, c1970.

$10 - $20

**Fat Helen's,
VIC**

Playboy Magazine, 1962.

$40 - $60   **Gardenvale Collectables,
VIC**

'Beautiful Britons' magazine produced in England containing photos of women in black and white, 52 pages, c1960, 12cm wide, 18cm high.

$10 - $20

**Philicia Antiques & Collectables,
SA**

'My Home' magazine printed in London containing knitting patterns, cooking, fashion, home improvement ideas and fiction, 72 pages, c1958, 21cm wide, 29cm high.

$10 - $20   **Philicia Antiques & Collectables,
SA**

'Meccano' Magazine March 1957, 180 pages, c1957, 13.5cm long, 20.5cm wide.

$20 - $30   **Philicia Antiques &
Collectables, SA**

'Australian Home Journal' contains three free patterns as displayed on the cover plus recipes, fashion and fiction, 52 pages, c1947, 22cm wide, 27cm high.

$10 - $20   **Philicia Antiques & Collectables,
SA**

Wittner Shoes mail order footware catalogue, 68 pages, c1932, 28cm long, 22cm wide.

$45 - $65   **Secondhand Furniture Mart,
TAS**

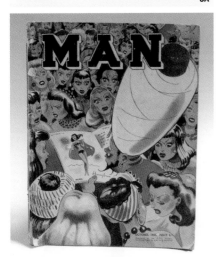

'Man' magazine October 1945, including superb colour Coca-Cola advertisments, c1945.

$20 - $30   **Yarra Valley Antique Centre,
VIC**

'Women's Weekly' March 1962 issue.

$15 - $25   **The Time Machine,
QLD**

'Women's Weekly' July 1976 issue.

$10 - $20   **The Time Machine,
QLD**

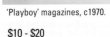

'Playboy' magazines, c1970.

$10 - $20

**Chapel Street Bazaar,
VIC**

'Man Annual' pocket 'Man' magazine printed in Australia, containing glamorous photos, cartoons, facts and fiction, 100 pages, c1955, 13cm wide, 19cm high.

$10 - $20   **Philicia Antiques & Collectables, SA**

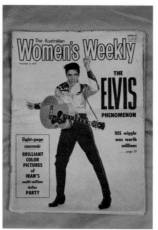

'Women's Weekly' 3 November 1971, Sydney issue only.

$30 - $40   **The Time Machine, QLD**

Movie magazine 'Photo Player', c1941

$20 - $30   **The Nostalgia Factory, NSW**

'Women's Weekly' 1942 issue.

$20 - $30   **The Time Machine, QLD**

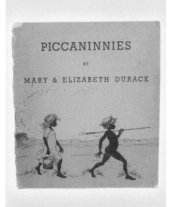

Book 'Piccaninnies' by Mary and Elizabeth Durack, c1945.

$55 - $75   **The Nostalgia Factory, NSW**

Pop music magazines 'Juke', 'Ram' and 'Go-Set', c1970.

$25 - $35   **Chapel Street Bazaar, VIC**

'Women's Weekly' July 1944 issue.

$20 - $30   **The Time Machine, QLD**

'Women's Weekly' 3 November 1971, Melbourne issue only.

$20 - $30   **The Time Machine, QLD**

A weekly Australian magazine that includes fiction and world news, produced 27 August 1955, 40 pages, 20cm wide, 28cm high.

$5 - $15   **Philicia Antiques & Collectables, SA**

'The Australian Women's Weekly' 23 January 1946 giving an insight into the preoccupations, home, family, fashion, emotions of Australian women immediately after World War II, 48 pages, price 4 pence, over 600,000 copies sold every week, 29.5cm wide, 39cm high.

$20 - $30   **Antique General Store, NSW**

'Oz' magazine P. J. Proby, c1965.

$15 - $25   **The Nostalgia Factory, NSW**

'TV Times' magazine featuring Normie Rowe on the cover, c1960.

$45 - $65   **Chapel Street Bazaar, VIC**

'TV Times' magazine, c1960.

$30 - $40   **Chapel Street Bazaar, VIC**

'Man Junior' magazine, c1963.

$10 - $20   **The Nostalgia Factory, NSW**

'New Screen News', vol 14, No. 6, March 18, 1960 with Elvis Presley on the cover, 18cm wide, 24cm high.

$25 - $35   **Lydiard Furniture & Antiques, VIC**

Australian Women's Weekly

The *Australian Women's Weekly* was established in Sydney in 1933 by Sir Frank Packer and E.G. Theodore, a former controversial Labour leader. At that time the publisher was Sydney Newspapers Ltd. forerunner company to today's publisher, Australian Consolidated Press.

The magazine was an immediate success, the first issue selling 120,000 copies in New South Wales. The black and white newspaper selling for twopence,

'Women's Weekly', October 1970 issue.

$30 - $50   **The Time Machine, QLD**

featured articles on "What Smart Sydney Women Are Wearing", knitting patterns for unusual jumpers and women attending the Women's Voters Federation. By the end of the year it was also being sold in Queensland and Victoria. Soon after it was selling in all parts of Australia, and such was its success that it provided the funds for Sir Frank Packer to expand his publishing empire into newspapers and additional magazines.

Circulation continued to grow and by 1939 it had risen to 450,000 and by 1954 when the Queen toured Australia, nearly one million copies of the magazine were sold. Current circulation is around 700,000 copies.

The *Australian Women's Weekly* is an important and valuable contribution to Australian social history from the 1930's to the present day and copies from the 50's, 60's, and 70s provide a blueprint for those interested in the styles of those times.

Magazine 'British Commonwealth Australia and Tasmania' with a beach and surfing theme on the cover, c1950.

$20 - $30   **The Nostalgia Factory, NSW**

'Women's Mirror' 1958-61.

$35 - $45   **The Time Machine, QLD**

Australian comic 'Captain Atom'.

$70 - $90   **Gardenvale Collectables, VIC**

'Wheels' Australia's motoring magazines, c1960.

$30 - $40   **Secondhand Furniture Mart, TAS**

A selection of Australian Womens Weekly magazines from the 1950's, 1960's and 1970's.

$25 - $35   **Thompsons Country Collectables, NSW**

MOVIE POSTERS

Movie poster 'Star Trek II - The Wrath of Khan', c1980, 33cm wide, 68cm high.

$20 - $30 — **Western District Antique Centre, VIC**

Movie daybill for 'Friday the 13th - Part 2' matt finish, printed by M.A.P.S. Litho P/L. distributed by Cinema International Corporation, rated R, c1980, 78cm long, 33cm wide.

$20 - $30 — **Wooden Pew Antiques, VIC**

'Pufnstuf', Australian daybill, c1970, 33cm wide, 76cm high.

$55 - $75 — **Malvern Antique Market, VIC**

'Clockwork Orange' Australian daybill, Stanley Kubrick's classic cult movie, c1971, 33cm wide, 76cm high.

$165 - $185 — **Malvern Antique Market, VIC**

'Bullitt' Australian daybill, a cult movie starring Steve McQueen, c1968, 33cm wide, 76cm high.

$125 - $145 — **Malvern Antique Market, VIC**

'Midnight Cowboy', Australian daybill starring Dustin Hoffman and Jon Voight, c1969, 33cm wide, 76cm high.

$65 - $85 — **Malvern Antique Market, VIC**

'Guns of Navarone' Australian daybill starring Gregory Peck, David Niven and Anthony Quinn, c1961, 33cm wide, 76cm high.

$75 - $95 — **Malvern Antique Market, VIC**

Movie poster for 'Blood Diner' rated 'R', c1987, 68cm long, 33cm wide.

$20 - $30 — **Wooden Pew Antiques, VIC**

Movie poster for 'Black Emanuelle Goes East' rated 'R', c1970, 75cm long, 34cm wide.

$20 - $30 — **Wooden Pew Antiques, VIC**

'Solomon and Sheba' Australian daybill starring Yul Brynner and Gina Lollobrigida, c1960, 33cm wide, 76cm high.

$40 - $60 — **Malvern Antique Market, VIC**

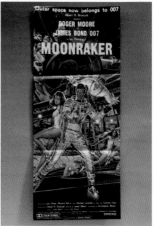

James Bond 007 'Moonraker' movie poster, c1979, 74cm long, 31cm wide.

$20 - $30 — **Wooden Pew Antiques, VIC**

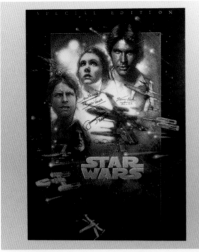

Star Wars special edition poster autographed by eight stars from the movie. Dave Prowse (Vader), Anthony Daniels (C3P0), Kenny Baker (R2D2), Peter Mayhem (Chewbacca), Jeremy Bulloch (Boba Fett), Paul Blake (Greedo), Garrick Hagon (Biggs) and Richard Leparmentier (Motti), c1998, 90cm wide, 115cm high.

$1900 - $2100   **Rare Memorabilia Gallery, VIC**

Australian daybill for 'Rebel Without a Cause', c1956.

$480 - $520   **Chapel Street Bazaar, VIC**

Star Wars original 'Release One' Sheet Sci Fi, c1977.

$330 - $370   **Chapel Street Bazaar, VIC**

'Jaws' original movie lobby card, c1970, 42cm long, 25cm wide.

$30 - $40   **Wooden Pew Antiques, VIC**

Movie poster 'Clash of the Titans', c1980, 33cm wide, 68cm high.

$20 - $30   **Western District Antique Centre, VIC**

Australian daybill for 'Hunted' starring Dirk Bogarde, c1952.

$65 - $85   **Malvern Antique Market, VIC**

Movie poster 'The Legend of the Lone Ranger', c1980, 33cm wide, 68cm high.

$20 - $30   **Western District Antique Centre, VIC**

Australian daybill for 'Rebel Without A Cause' starring James Dean, c1955.

$550 - $650   **Malvern Antique Market, VIC**

Movie poster 'Champion', c1980, 33cm wide, 68cm high.

$20 - $30   **Western District Antique Centre, VIC**

Australian daybill for re-release of 'The day The Earth Stood Still', c1980.

$75 - $95   **Chapel Street Bazaar, VIC**

Australian daybill for Alfred Hitchcock's 'The Birds', c1963.

$120 - $140   **Chapel Street Bazaar, VIC**

Sci Fi One Sheet 'Logans Run', c1970.

$115 - $135   **Chapel Street Bazaar, VIC**

Original Australian daybill for 'Flight to Tangier', c1953.

$65 - $85   **Malvern Antique Market, VIC**

Australian daybill for 'The Red Beret', c1950.

$40 - $60   **Malvern Antique Market, VIC**

Australian daybill for 'The Thief of Venice', c1950.

$30 - $40   **Malvern Antique Market, VIC**

George Formby Australian daybill for 'He Snoops to Conquer', c1944.

$115 - $135   **Malvern Antique Market, VIC**

Original Australian daybill for 'The Caribbean Mystery', c1945.

$35 - $45   **Malvern Antique Market, VIC**

Movie poster 'The Pirate Movie', c1980, 33cm wide, 68cm high.

$20 - $30   **Western District Antique Centre, VIC**

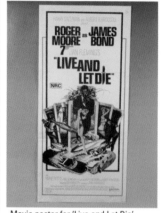

Movie poster for 'Live and Let Die', Australian daybill, starring Roger Moore as James Bond, c1973, 33cm wide, 76cm high.

$145 - $165   **Malvern Antique Market, VIC**

'Harry Potter and the Philospher's Stone' advance movie one sheet poster autographed by the Phelps twins who portray George and Fred Weasley, c2001, 75cm wide, 105cm high.

$900 - $1000   **Rare Memorabilia Gallery, VIC**

George Lazenby autographed James Bond 'On Her Majesty's Secret Service' mini poster, framed with photos from the movie and a unique 007 logo plaque, 90cm wide, 55cm high.

$750 - $850   **Rare Memorabilia Gallery, VIC**

Movie daybill for '20,000 Leagues Under the Sea', matt finish, Greater Union Film Distributors, rated NRC, c1978, 78cm long, 33cm wide.

$40 - $60   **Wooden Pew Antiques, VIC**

'Invisible Boy' movie daybill, c1957, 33cm wide, 75cm high.

$210 - $250

Chapel Street Bazaar, VIC

'When the World's Collide' movie daybill, c1951, 33cm wide, 75cm high.

$400 - $440

Chapel Street Bazaar, VIC

'Taxi Driver' Australian daybill, cult movie classic starring Robert De Niro, c1976, 33cm wide, 76cm high.

$275 - $315

Malvern Antique Market, VIC

Movie daybill for 'Star Wars - The Empire Strikes Back', rated NRC, printed by M.A.P.S. Litho P/L, matt finish, c1985, 78cm long, 33cm wide.

$90 - $110

Wooden Pew Antiques, VIC

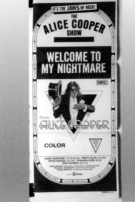

Movie daybill for Alice Cooper in 'Welcome to My Nightmare', released by Filmways, printed by M.A.P.S. Litho P/L., c1975, 78cm long, 33cm wide.

$35 - $45

Wooden Pew Antiques, VIC

Movie daybill for 'Jaws 2', matt finish, printed by M.A.P.S. Litho P/L, rated M, c1970, 78cm long, 33cm wide.

$140 - $160

Wooden Pew Antiques, VIC

'Seminole' movie daybill, c1953, 33cm wide, 75cm high.

$15 - $25

Chapel Street Bazaar, VIC

Movie daybill for 'Hells Angels on Wheels' released by Filmways, printed by M.A.P.S. Litho P/L. Matt finish, c1975, 78cm long, 33cm wide.

$90 - $110

Wooden Pew Antiques, VIC

'Serpico' Australian daybill, starring Al Pacino, c1974, 33cm wide, 76cm high.

$40 - $50

Malvern Antique Market, VIC

The Danish connection movie daybill for 'Forbidden Sex is their Game' rated R, released by Briad Film Productions, printed by Robert Burton Printers P/L, Sydney, c1970, 78cm long, 33cm wide.

$20 - $30

Wooden Pew Antiques, VIC

'Oliver' Australian daybill, hit musical version of the Charles Dickens classic novel, c1968, 33cm wide, 76cm high.

$55 - $75

Malvern Antique Market, VIC

'Tony Rome' Australian daybill, starring Frank Sinatra, c1967, 33cm wide, 76cm high.

$30 - $40 **Malvern Antique Market, VIC**

Movie daybill 'Linda Lovelace for President', matt finish, rated R, a recent release, c1970, 78cm long, 33cm wide.

$15 - $25 **Wooden Pew Antiques, VIC**

Movie poster for 'Alien', Australian daybill for this classic cult movie, c1979, 33cm wide, 76cm high.

$135 - $155 **Malvern Antique Market, VIC**

Movie daybill for 'Evil Dead Can They be Stopped?', released by Filmways, rated R, glossy paper, c1985, 78cm long, 33cm wide.

$15 - $25 **Wooden Pew Antiques, VIC**

Movie poster for 'Apocalypse Now', Australian daybill, directed by Frances Coppolla and starring Marlon Brando, Robert Duval and Martin Sheen, c1979, 33cm wide, 76cm high.

$65 - $85 **Malvern Antique Market, VIC**

Movie daybill for 'Star Wars: Return of the Jedi' Anniversary advance movie, one sheet poster, limited edition, numbered 458, autographed by four stars of the movie, Dave Prowse (Darth Vader), Peter Mayhew (Chew Bacca), Kenny Baker (R2-D2) and Jeremy Bulloch (Boba Fett). 'Revenge of the Jedi' original art 10th Anniversary reprint, c1993, 95cm wide, 130cm high.

$1400 - $1600 **Rare Memorabilia Gallery, VIC**

'The Italian Job' Australian daybill, starring Michael Caine, cult movie, c1969, 33cm wide, 76cm high.

$165 - $185 **Malvern Antique Market, VIC**

Movie poster for 'Butch Cassidy and Sundance Kid', Australian daybill, starring Paul Newman and Robert Redford, c1969, 33cm wide, 76cm high.

$85 - $105 **Malvern Antique Market, VIC**

'Downhill Racer' Australian daybill, starring Robert Redford and Gene Hackman, c1969, 33cm wide, 76cm high.

$45 - $65 **Malvern Antique Market, VIC**

Framed 'The Freedom Fighters' movie bill, c1984, 35cm wide, 90cm high.

$85 - $105 **The Nostalgia Factory, NSW**

Movie poster for 'Barbarella', Australian daybill, classic cult movie starring Jane Fonda, c1968, 33cm wide, 76cm high.

$155 - $175 **Malvern Antique Market, VIC**

'Black Luster' soldier, one of the most powerful cards in the game and the keystone in 'Chaos' decks, c2003, 5.7cm long, 8.5cm high.

$40 - $60

Cardtastic Collectables, VIC

Set of 33 'Home & Away' cards, boxed in blister pack, c1980.

$20 - $30

Cat's Cradle Comics, VIC

'United we stand' in a Yu-Gi-Oh card from Dark Beginnings 1, and is one of the most powerful equip spells in the game, c2005, 5.7cm long, 8.5cm high.

$20 - $30

Cardtastic Collectables, VIC

Cigarette card by the American Tobacco Company from the series of 'Beauties' with a black background, c1900, 3.5cm wide, 6.5cm high.

$3 - $13

Philicia Antiques & Collectables, SA

French fashion dressmaker's catalogue that was available in department stores and dress shops of the day, c1964, 23cm wide, 33cm high.

$65 - $85

Philicia Antiques & Collectables, SA

'End of Anubis' is a secret from AST and very hard to find. This particular example is first edition and misprinted, c2004, 5.7cm long, 8.5cm high.

$30 - $40

Cardtastic Collectables, VIC

'Sanitarium' collectors card books with New Zealand themes, c1946, 28cm wide, 21cm high.

NZ$23 - $33

Memory Lane, New Zealand

A radio QSL card from Elizabethville, Belgian Congo, c1949, 15cm wide, 10cm high.

$10 - $20

Philicia Antiques & Collectables, SA

Multi coloured roll-up school map by Scally, Sydney, of Papua New Guinea, c1960, 120cm wide, 90cm high.

$90 - $110

Industria, VIC

'Neighbours' trading cards, full set in two sealed blister boxes, 66 cards, c1980.

$35 - $45

Cat's Cradle Comics, VIC

Postcards of pin up girls, c1965, 15cm long, 10cm high.

$2 - $6

Chapel Street Bazaar, VIC

An Ilford 35mm colour slide depicting three Hermannsberg Mission Aboriginal women, one with blonde hair, c1950, 5cm wide, 5cm high.

$20 - $30

Philicia Antiques & Collectables, SA

Photograph of a broken down locomotive (523) at Balhannah Railway Station in the Adelaide Hills, c1950, 21cm long, 16.5cm high.

$60 - $70

Philicia Antiques & Collectables, SA

Sheet music for the Beatles 'Ticket to Ride', c1966.

$10 - $20

The Nostalgia Factory, NSW

Sheet music for 'Hello Dolly' as sung by Louis Armstrong, c1966.

$5 - $10

The Nostalgia Factory, NSW

Sheet music for Elvis Presley's 'Separate Ways'.

$10 - $20

The Nostalgia Factory, NSW

Sheet Music.

$5 - $10

Green Gables Collectables, NSW

Clothing ration card issued by the Director of Rationing, Brisbane, 17cm wide, 8cm high.

$5 - $15

Philicia Antiques & Collectables, SA

'Magic the Gathering', complete unglued set, c1998, 6.5cm wide, 8.5cm high.

$130 - $150

Cardtastic Collectables, VIC

'Ranch 57' original certificate to Children's Club, also including original Sheriff's badge, c1950, 8cm wide, 12cm high.

$20 - $30

Chapel Street Bazaar, VIC

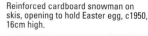

Reinforced cardboard snowman on skis, opening to hold Easter egg, c1950, 16cm high.

NZ$65 - $85

Deborah's Antiques, New Zealand

Five piece skeleton decanter set, c1970, 7cm deep, 8cm wide, 17cm high.

$100 - $120

Southside Antiques Centre, QLD

'Zulu Lulu' tasteless drink stirrers, still carded, c1970, 28cm long, 22cm high.

$10 - $20

Cat's Cradle Comics, VIC

Decorative Italian marbleized decanter, c1965, 17cm deep, 17cm wide, 25cm high.

$85 - $105

Chapel Street Bazaar, VIC

Royal Doulton 'Beam Whiskey' featuring Old Mr Turvey Drop, specially commissioned from Royal Doulton by Jim Beam Bourbon Whisky for the Pickwick collection, c1980, 8cm deep, 12cm wide, 18cm high.

$185 - $205

H.O.W Gifts & Collectables, QLD

Ceramic French brandy container in the form of a dice, the reverse with an ashtray, c1970, 10cm long, 10cm deep, 13cm high.

NZ$30 - $40

Collector's Choice, New Zealand

'Glenfiddich Unblended Scotch Whisky' jug signed William Grout & Sons Ltd, 13.5cm high, 13cm diameter.

$40 - $60

Avoca Beach Antiques, NSW

'John Beggs Scotch Whisky' jug, no base mark, c1950, 15cm high.

$185 - $205

Ardeco Antiques & Collectables, WA

Silver plated bottle pourer with embossed decoration, c1960, 6cm long.

NZ$100 - $120

Collectamania, New Zealand

Turned aluminium champagne bucket advertising Canard-Duchéne Champagne, c1950, 25cm high.

$70 - $90

Miguel Meirelles Antiques, VIC

Beer pull, gold, polished brass, 25cm wide, 50cm high.

$480 - $520

The Mill Markets, VIC

A kitch bar set, with a '19th hole' theme, c1950.

NZ$10 - $20

Antiques On Victoria, New Zealand

PHOTOGRAPHIC – CAMERAS

Russian twin lens reflex camera, 120 format, c1960, 9cm deep, 8cm wide, 12cm high.

$20 - $30

Furniture Revisited, VIC

Bell and Howell 70 DK 16mm hand held camera, collector's item only, c1950, 20cm long, 22cm high.

$350 - $390

Chapel Street Bazaar, VIC

Pathe Webo 16mm movie picture camera with rare film magazine, c1955, 46cm long, 38cm high.

$1050 - $1250

Chapel Street Bazaar, VIC

Miniature spy camera 'Hit' brand, in leather case, made in Japan, c1960, 6cm long, 1cm deep, 6cm wide, 4cm high.

$275 - $315

Dr Russell's Emporium, WA

Nikon F camera No. 6959894 with Nokkor - S auto lens 1.4/50mm No. 492379, c1968.

$1150 - $1350

Kollectik Pty Ltd, NSW

Minolta model 16 P camera, 1960-1965.

$45 - $65

Tyabb Packing House, VIC

Dr Wohler Favor-Saarland shutter camera, c1949, 7cm deep, 14cm wide, 7cm high.

$255 - $295

The New Farm Antique Centre, QLD

Minolta 16 QT Instamatic camera, boxed, c1975, 9.5cm long, 4cm high.

$115 - $135

Chapel Street Bazaar, VIC

Kodak Reinette camera, c1950.

$65 - $85.

Archers Antiques, TAS

Wizard XF 1000 instant Polaroid camera for SX70 Film, c1977.

$40 - $50

Tyabb Packing House, VIC

Kodak box 'Brownie' camera in Bakelite case, c1950, 8cm long, 8cm deep, 8cm high.

$40 - $50

Bowhows, NSW

'Voigtlander Vitamatic IIA' 35mm viewfinder camera with coupled selenium meter match needle readout, top plate and viewfinder, colour skopar F:28/50mm lens, c1959.

$150 - $170

Stumpy Gully Antiques, VIC

'Canon Dial 35' 1/2 frame 35mm camera with spring actuated motor drive and case, unusual meter grid and round spring housing extended to serve as a handle, c1965.

$190 - $210

Stumpy Gully Antiques, VIC

Voigtlander Vitessa T, c1960.

$280 - $320

The Glass Stopper, NSW

Voigtlander Bessamatic camera, c1960.

$230 - $270

The Glass Stopper, NSW

'Olympus Pen F T' camera with case, 35mm 1/2 frame SLR porro-prism allows streamlined design without roof prism, incorporates CDS meter, single stroke lever advance, c1966.

$280 - $320

Stumpy Gully Antiques, VIC

Kodak Tele-Instamatic camera in box with flash and manual, c1970, 20cm long, 3cm deep, 20cm wide, 16cm high.

$20 - $30

Dr Russell's Emporium, WA

Voigtlander Vito Automatic II.

$90 - $110

The Glass Stopper, NSW

Sekonic hand wind 8mm camera, c1970, 14cm long, 6cm deep, 14cm high.

$110 - $130

Bowhows, NSW

Arrow brand hit type mini camera with original box, c1950, 3cm deep, 6cm wide, 3cm high.

$75 - $95

The New Farm Antique Centre, QLD

Kodak bullet camera, c1960, 20cm long, 5cm wide, 12cm high.

$100 - $120

Bowhows, NSW

'Leica' camera manual.

$50 - $70

Photantiques, NSW

Director View Finder, 16mm to 35mm framing with zoom, c1960, 10cm long, 5cm diameter.

$480 - $520

Bowhows, NSW

Camco black and white Bakelite slide viewer, c1964, 10cm long, 8cm deep, 8cm high.

$30 - $40

Bowhows, NSW

Tessina fly strap, tripod adaptor, cassette and case.

$800 - $900

Photantiques, NSW

'Sekonic' light meter, c1960, 5cm long, 4cm deep, 3cm high.

$50 - $70

Bowhows, NSW

Post war Purma Cameras Ltd bloomed lens with box.

$70 - $90

Tyabb Packing House, VIC

A Kodak 25 year service badge with ID card.

$40 - $60

Tyabb Packing House, VIC

Timber and die cast photographic tripod with fluid head system. The Miller Company was the creator of the fluid tripod head system. The Company began selling camera support equipment to leading professional camera operators around the world in 1954, and the fluid head was patented in 1946. Miller is still an industry leader.

$330 - $370

Industria, VIC

Sterling silver Art Nouveau 'frogs and lillies' patterned photo frame, hallmarked Birmingham, 14cm wide, 15cm high.

NZ$340 - $380

Antiques of Epsom, New Zealand

Minature HMSS photo frame.

$205 - $245

Esmerelda's Curios, WA

Solid silver pressed photo frame depicting birds amongst bamboo trees, 13cm wide, 17.5cm high.

$430 - $470

Rare Old Times Antiques & Collectables, SA

Seven willow tree, turned lace bobbins with original glass bead trims, $65 each, 12cm long.

$440 - $480

Angel Cottage, QLD

Singer treadle sewing machine, c1950, 87cm long, 41cm deep, 77cm high.

$460 - $500

Coming of Age Antiques, QLD

'Singer Featherweight' sewing machine, very light, comes with accessories, case and runs on 230 volt power motor and foot control, c1960.

NZ$810 - $910

Classy Clutter And Collectables, New Zealand

'Darn-a-Lile' darning mushroom and needle case made from Bakelite with a tiny torch inside to light the article being darned, c1950, 10cm high, 8cm diameter.

$25 - $35

Mt Dandenong Antique Centre, VIC

Boxed novelty pin cushion with tape measure, in the form of a sewing machine, c1960, 12cm wide, 7cm high.

$40 - $50

Town & Country Antiques, NSW

Wedgwood jasperware 'Royal Wedding' thimble set with Charles and Diana. This model is the most collectable of all jasperware thimbles, c1982, 2.5cm high.

$205 - $245

Needlewitch, ACT

RECREATIONS & PURSUITS

GAMES & PUZZLES

Las Vegas gaming token from the Hotel Fremont, Nevada, USA, c1965, 4cm diameter.

$5 - $10

The Bottom Drawer Antique Centre, VIC

Set of 'Unicorn' darts, c1950, 14cm long.

$30 - $40

Archers Antiques, TAS

Set of twenty eight 'Double Six' dominos in a wooden box, c1950, 6cm deep, 18cm wide, 5cm high.

$55 - $75

Southside Antiques Centre, QLD

Silver chess set, continental silver (800) one side gold plated, boxed with onyx and silver board, c1950, 44cm deep, 49cm wide.

$7300 - $7700

Eagle Antiques, VIC

Slip cast ceramic ashtray, hand decorated bowl with a tribal Aborigine depicted in a hunting stance, c1960, 22cm wide, 3cm high.

$40 - $60

Born Frugal, VIC

Green and yellow plastic ashtray with chrome case, c1970, 15cm diameter.

$20 - $30

Bowhows, NSW

Enamelled ashtray advertising 'Lees Bros Ltd., Ford Dealers of Papakura', c1950, 1.5cm high, 15cm diameter.

NZ$20 - $30

Memory Lane, New Zealand

Gempo 'bronze' and 'black' table lighter and ashtray, quality ceramic pieces with glossy glass like finish, c1960, 7.5cm high.

$55 - $75

Born Frugal, VIC

Italian hand decorated Fantoni era ashtray, c1950, 20cm wide.

$20 - $30

Vintage Living, ACT

Beswick Mallard Duck ashtray no. 755, designer Mr. Watkin, in production 1939-69, 10cm wide, 10cm high.

$85 - $105 **Glenelg Antique Centre, SA**

Wembley Ware ashtray depicting an 'Australian Native Stockman', c1950, 16cm diameter.

$120 - $140

Mentone Beach Antiques Centre, VIC

Carlton Ware 'Friends and Relations' ashtray, c1950, 2.5cm high, 9cm diameter.

$85 - $105

White Park Antiques, SA

An ashtray held in the fingers of a black hand with two smaller trays on the base, 20cm high.

$135 - $155 **Paddington Antique Centre Pty Ltd, QLD**

Glass advertising ashtray for 'Camel' cigarettes, c1980, 2.5cm high, 11cm diameter.

$30 - $40

Rare Old Times Antiques & Collectables, SA

Large 'Camel' advertising ashtray made from melamine by Melel, P107, c1980, 3.5cm high, 20cm diameter.

$55 - $75

Rare Old Times Antiques & Collectables, SA

Ceramic card ashtray with spinning top, c1990, 9cm wide, 19cm high.

$20 - $30   **Chapel Street Bazaar, VIC**

Chrome cigarette box, 15cm long, 6cm wide.

$40 - $60   **Baxter's Antiques, QLD**

Humidore in rosewood and teak, airtight, with moisture pad, by Dunhill, c1970.

$1400 - $1600   **Bowhows, NSW**

Amber cigarette holder in case, 5cm long.

$90 - $110   **Olsens Antiques, QLD**

Ronson novelty pencil lighter, c1960, 13cm long.

$165 - $185   **Chapel Street Bazaar, VIC**

Tape measure in inches made by Zippo Lighters, c1970, 4cm long, 1cm deep, 4cm high.

$25 - $35   **Bowhows, NSW**

Coke bottle lighters, plastic, c1970, 40cm high, 2cm diameter.

$20 - $30   **Bowhows, NSW**

Stratton boxed 'Ronson Variflame' lighter with matching cufflinks, c1960

NZ$65 - $85   **Antiques Centre of Wellington, New Zealand**

Golfers lighter, Panther brand, c1950, 15cm long, 8cm high.

NZ$30 - $40   **Antiques On Victoria, New Zealand**

Gold plated cigarette case with lighter, c1960, 12cm long, 9cm deep, 1.5cm wide.

$25 - $35   **Bowhows, NSW**

Royal Doulton lighter 'The Poacher' D6464, in production 1960-73, 12cm high.

$410 - $450   **Armadale Antique Centre, VIC**

SMOKING RELATED

Gold plated 1960's table lighter by Royal Plaza, 12cm long, 5cm deep, 5cm wide, 12cm high.

$40 - $60

Dr Russell's Emporium, WA

Green Jasperware Wedgwood, 'Ronson' cigarette lighter, c1957.

$55 - $75

Brae-mar Antiques, NSW

Faux tortoise shell table lighter, c1960, 13cm high, 8cm diameter

$50 - $70

AntiqueCentre of Stonnington, VIC

Turkish hookah in blue glass and brass, c1950, 48cm long, 15cm deep, 15cmwide, 48cm high, 15cm diameter.

$115 - $135

Dr Russell's Emporium, WA

Sarome Cruiser cigarette lighter, cream and red enamel, made in Japan, c1950, 8cm long,1cm deep, 3cm high.

$65 - $85

Mt Dandenong Antique Centre, VIC.

Metal kangaroo novelty cigarette lighter, c1960, 13cm wide, 10cm high.

$45 - $65

Chapel Street Bazaar, VIC

Musical Zodiac Globe cigarette holder, holds cigarettes while playing music, a kitch item from 50's era, 15cm long, 15cm deep, 25cm high.

$225 - $265

Towers Antiques &Collectables, NSW

'Photo Flash' table lighter in the style of a camera, in its original box, c1950, 6cm wide, 4cm high.

$85 - $105

Chapel Street Bazaar, VIC

Huon pine timber match box dispenser, a school project from 1955 by M. Howell, c1955, 7cm wide, 25cm high.

$30 - $40

The Bottom Drawer Antique Centre, VIC

Brass lighter, Crown Grace, c1960, 80cm high, 3cm diameter.

$90 - $110

Bowhows, NSW

Match King lighter, side flint, stamped, 'Made in USA', c1950, 4cm long, 1cm deep, 2.5cm wide.

$35 - $45

Bowhows, NSW

Fly line cleaner, c1950.

NZ$30 - $40   **Antiques On Victoria, New Zealand**

Boxed Edgar Sealey twin fishing fly reel, c1950.

NZ$255 - $295   **Antiques On Victoria, New Zealand**

Mucilin line cleaner, Carlton Chemical Works, c1950.

NZ$40 - $50   **Antiques On Victoria, New Zealand**

'Flatfish' fishing lure, x 4 U.S., c1960

NZ$40 - $50   **Antiques On Victoria, New Zealand**

Timber framed tennis racquets, never used, Borg Donnay, McEnroe Maxply plus others, c1980.

$55 - $75   **Wooden Pew Antiques, VIC**

Dunlop golf balls in original wrappers, c1950.

NZ$40 - $50   **Antiques On Victoria, New Zealand**

Alvey wooden side cast fishing reel, c1950.

$25 - $35   **Sport Memorabilia, NSW**

Boxed Spenby exercisers, c1950.

$25 - $35   **Kingston Antiques, VIC**

Pair of lady's black roller skates, unused, size 8, c1980.

$45 - $65   **Fat Helen's, VIC**

Black leather medicine ball with leather stitching, c1975, 45cm diameter

$110 - $130   **Bowhows, NSW**

Red and black women's speed skates, c1980.

$30 - $60   **Fat Helen's, VIC**

Small wooden blotter with inlay to top.

$30 - $40

Bloomsbury Antiques, WA

Onoto 5601 in wine pearl and black marble with plunger filler and 14ct gold nib, c1938,13.8cm long.

$190 - $210

Melbourne Vintage Pens, VIC

Parker Vacumatic in grey pearl, a vacumatic filler with 14ct gold nib, c1939, 13.2cm long.

$200 - $240

Melbourne Vintage Pens, VIC

Sheaffer PFM I pen in burgundy, a snorkel filler with palladium silver nib, c1959, 13.6cm long

$210 - $250

Melbourne Vintage Pens, VIC

Parker 51 pen in teal blue, aeromatic filler with 14ct gold nib, c1956, 13.8cm long.

$115 - $135 **Melbourne Vintage Pens, VIC**

Parker 51

The design for the Parker 51 was completed in 1939, Parker's 51st anniversary, hence the name. There were many unique features to the 51 including the tubular hooded nib and an ink collector separate to the feed. Manufactured in a new plastic material 'Lucite', they were revolutionary.

The first model was released in the USA in 1941, at a price of $12.50 and until 1948 was sold with a 'Vacumatic' filling system.

In 1948 Parker introduced the 'Aerometric Filler'. This series was designated Mk 1 and was manufactured until 1972. Around 1969 a Mk II was introduced with conical ends and a slimmer cap. Later a Mk III was released, similar to the Mk II but now with a metal cap jewel and 'Injection Moulded'.

Production continued until around 1980

Parker 75 pen in matte black epoxy, cartridge/converter filler with 14ct gold nib, c1990, 12.8cm long.

$240 - $280

Melbourne Vintage Pens, VIC

Box of pen nibs for C. Brandauer & Co. Ltd circular pointed pens, c1940, 8cm long, 1.5cm deep, 5.5cm wide.

NZ$10 - $20

Memory Lane, New Zealand

Black Melamine ball on an orange melamine tray, an ashtray that doubles as desk toy for executives, designed by Elenore Peduzi Riva and manufactured by Artemide, Italy, c1960, 22cm long, 22cm deep, 4cm high.

$110 - $130

506070, NSW

'Parker International Duofold' pen, in slate grey marble, cartridge/converter filler with 18ct gold nib, c1995, 13.1cm long.

$400 - $440

Melbourne Vintage Pens, VIC

Sheaffer slim 'Targa' pen, in sterling silver, a cartridge/converter filler with 14ct gold nib, c1980, 13.5cm long.

$330 - $370

Melbourne Vintage Pens, VIC

Conway Stewart 85L pen in rose pearl and black marble, lever filler with 14ct gold nib, restored., c1958, 13.5cm long.

$120 - $140

Melbourne Vintage Pens, VIC

Conway Stewart

In 1905 Conway Stewart began the manufacture of fountain pens in London, and was finally wound up in 1975.

Around 1919, Conway Stewart started producing lever filling fountain pens and although they produced pens with alternative filling systems, the bulk of sales remained lever fillers. A vast number of model number/colour/pattern combinations were made making these pens a popular collectable item.

Today, among those old enough to remember the decades either side of WWII, the name Conway Stewart evokes memories associated with the formative years and the maturing to adulthood.

In 1998, a new company was registered under the name of Conway Stewart to produce pens in designs similar to the originals.

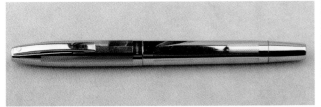

Sheaffer Imperial pen in gold electroplate, a touchdown filler with 14ct gold nib, c1973, 13.7cm long.

$200 - $240

Melbourne Vintage Pens, VIC

Conway Stewart 759 pen in green pearl and black marble, lever filler with 14ct gold nib, restored, c1948, 13cm long.

$110 - $130 **Melbourne Vintage Pens, VIC**

Waterman Man 100 pen, black, cartridge/converter filler with 18ct gold nib, c1990, 14.5cm long.

$230 -$270 **Melbourne Vintage Pens, VIC**

Sheaffer 'Targa' pen in sterling silver, a cartridge /converter filler with 14ct gold nib, c1980, 13.5cm long.

$330 - $370 **Melbourne Vintage Pens, VIC**

Parker 45 Harlequin pen in stainless steel, cartridge /converter filler with octaintium nib, c1980, 13.6cm long.

$100 - $120 **Melbourne Vintage Pens, VIC**

Parker 75 pen in Thuya Laque, cartridge/converter filler with 14ct gold nib, c1990, 12.8cm long.

$220 - $260 **Melbourne Vintage Pens, VIC**

'Parker 75 Flighter' pen in stainless steel, cartridge/ converter filler with 14ct gold nib, c1985, 12.8cm long.

$190 - $210 **Melbourne Vintage Pens, VIC**

Parker 180 'Ecosse' pen, in gold plate, a cartridge /converter filler with 14ct gold nib, c1985, 13.2cm long.

$190 - $210 **Melbourne Vintage Pens, VIC**

Parker Vacumatic in golden pearl, a vacumatic filler with 14ct gold nib, restored, c1946, 12.5cm long.

$180 - $200 **Melbourne Vintage Pens, VIC**

Silver Christofle figural comport, c1950, 25cm high.

$480 - $520

Antique Centre of Stonnington, VIC

Georg Jensen sterling silver bowl, design by Henry Kopel, c1978, 14cm wide, 7cm high.

$3700 - $3900

Antique Centre of Stonnington, VIC

Sterling silver goblet, gilded interior, 16cm high.

$230 - $270

Roys Antiques Pty Ltd, VIC

Set of six sterling silver teaspoons, Lancaster pattern, pattern released 1897, c1950, 15cm long.

$110 - $130

Roys Antiques Pty Ltd, VIC

Georg Jensen 'Acorn' design cutlery set.

$330 - $370

Antique Centre of Stonnington, VIC

Sterling silver whisky label, hallmarked Birmingham 1957, maker T + S, c1957, 16cm long,16cm deep.

$135 - $155

Glenelg Antique Centre, SA

Hand-beaten silver bowl by Juventino Lopez Reyes for Plateria del Recreo, Mexico, c1950, 38cm long.

$360 - $400

Found Objects, VIC

HMSS and mother of pearl stiletto.

$410 - $450

Esmerelda's Curios, WA

Set of six cased enamel and silver coffee spoons by Frigast, Denmark, c1950, 9cm long.

$205 - $245

Steven Sher Antiques, WA

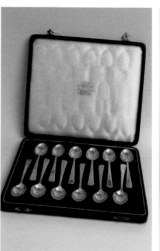

Set of twelve sterling silver spoons hallmarked London 1951, 11cm long.

$275 - $315

Fyshwick Antique Centre, ACT

Sterling silver sugar castor, c1960, 18cm high.

NZ$410 - $450

Kelmscott House Antiques, New Zealand

Forty four piece, six place setting cutlery set, community plate 'Hampton Court' patterned, c1960.

NZ$600 - $700   **Antiques of Epsom, New Zealand**

Boxed French silver plated serving spoon and fork, c1965, 8.5cm long.

$85 - $105   **Womango, VIC**

Silverplated bread fork with boomerang decoration, 21cm long.

$40 - $50   **Nana's Pearls, ACT**

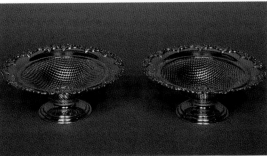

Pair of pierced silver plated dishes with a grape and vine border and a husk wreath in the base, c1950, 18cm wide.

$330 - $370   **Philip Cross Antiques, NSW**

Early Danish engraved silver plated ale mug, 8cm high, 9cm diameter.

$205 - $245   **Copperfield Antiques - NSW, NSW**

Australian 'Renown' silver plate cocktail jug with lid and stopper to spout, c1948, 20cm wide, 26cm high.

$90 - $110   **Womango, VIC**

Miniature silverplated tankard, engraved 'Just a Nip', 4cm high.

$20 - $30   **Nana'searls, ACT**

Silver plated emu serviette ring, mounted with a map of Australia, made by Villiers & Co., c1910, 8cm wide, 6cm high.

$80 - $100   **Secondhand Furniture Mart, TAS**

Art Deco style Walker & Hall silver plated tea set on tray, c1950.

NZ$125 - $145   **Gregory's of Greerton, New Zealand**

EPNS serviette ring with kangaroo and map of Australia base, c1940, 7cm long, 505cm deep, 6.5cm high.

$120 - $140   **Galeria del Centro, NSW**

Silver plated and glass whisky flask with hinged top, made by Mappin and Webb, 13cm high.

$75 - $95   **Nana's Pearls, ACT**

Large wooden model yacht, complete with sails and electric motor, on a wooden stand, c1970, 110cm long, 124cm high.

$650 - $750   **Granny's Market Pty Ltd, VIC**

Pond yacht 'Arctic Star', c1960, 80cm long.

$310 - $350   **Unique & Antique, VIC**

Clockwork 'Sprite Day Cruiser' produced by JW Sutcliffe, England with its original box, c1950, 24cm long, 7.9cm wide, 6.4cm high.

$440 - $480   **Trains Planes & Automobiles, NSW**

A toy battery operated 'Sutcliffe Merlin' speedboat, c1950, 32cm long.

$155 - $175   **Archers Antiques, TAS**

Clockwork 'Jupiter Ocean Pilot' boat produced by J. W. Sutcliff, England with its original box, c1950, 24cm long, 7.9cm wide, 6.5cm high.

$480 - $520   **Trains Planes &Automobiles, NSW**

'The Snipe' electric toy speedboat, boxed, battery operated, made by Bromley, c1960, 35cm long, 9cm deep, 7cm high.

$255 - $295   **Southside Antiques Centre, QLD**

Vintage, handcrafted, fully rigged replica of an 18th century tall sailing ship, 50cm long, 16cm wide, 41cm high.

$125 - $145   **Antique General Store, NSW**

Hand made balsa wood model tall yacht on oak stand, c1950.

$380 - $420   **Rare Old Times Antiques & Collectables, SA**

Model of the Sydney harbour ferry the 'South Steyne' with accompanying framed print, c1930, 53cm long, 9cm wide, 12cm high.

$275 - $315   **Three Quarters 20th C Furnishings, VIC**

Hand made balsa wood model of a tall ship Spanish galleon on an oak stand, c1950, 60cm long, 15cm deep, 50cm high.

Model ship, c1950, 72.5cm long, 12.5cm wide, 16.25cm high

$380 - $420   **Rare Old Times Antiques & Collectables, SA**

$330 - $370   **White Hills Antiques & Collectables, VIC**

Ford Mustang by Nomura, friction drive, metallic red, c1960, 40cm long.

$950 - $1050

Antique Toy World, VIC

Cadillac convertible, with enamel and litho finish, battery powered, Bandai Japan, c1960, 42cm long, 15.2cm wide, 11.5cm high.

$940 - $1040

Trains Planes & Automobiles, NSW

Battery operated Volkswagen mystery action tin toy, with flashing lights in the motor that changes direction when it hits something, c1960, 25cm long, 11cm high.

NZ$380 - $420

Banks Peninsula Antiques, New Zealand

Battery operated toy 'Cadillac' 1955 model tinplate car, c1960, 22cm long, 9cm wide, 7cm high.

$60 - $80

The Junk Company, VIC

Minic Toys, English tin car, c1940, 17cm long, 6.5cm deep, 5.5cm high.

$60 - $80

Leven Antiques - Tasmania, TAS

Lever action tin car, friction operation, made by Modern Toys, c1955, 14cm long, 8cm wide, 11cm high.

$90 - $110

Wooden Pew Antiques, VIC

Tin toy Cadillac four door sedan with battery operated headlights, c1949, 22cm long.

$310 - $350

The Restorers Barn, VIC

Edsel police car with wired controller, c1958, 26cm long.

$410 - $450

The Restorers Barn, VIC

Buick tin toy car, friction driven, c1950, 15cm long.

$195 - $235

The Restorers Barn, VIC

Green Jaguar tin toy car, c1950, 21cm long.

$110 - $130

The Restorers Barn, VIC

Cunningham tin toy car, friction driven, c1960, 18cm long.

$135 - $155

The Restorers Barn, VIC

Dinky Toys Lunar roving vehicle.

$135 - $155   **Unique & Antique, VIC**

Dinky supertoy 'Jones Fleetmaster' crane.

$110 - $130   **Unique & Antique, VIC**

Dinky supertoy 20 tonne lorry-mounted crane.

$100 - $120   **Unique & Antique, VIC**

Dinky forward control tank.

$35 - $45   **Paddington Antique Centre Pty Ltd, QLD**

Dinky 'Mobile Gun' made in England, c1960, 15.5cm long, 7cm deep, 6cm high.

$75 - $95   **Northside Secondhand Furniture, QLD**

Die cast Vickers Viscount Bea with grey wings, made by Meccano Dinky, England, c1965, 12.7cm long, 14.5cm wide, 4.2cm high.

$240 - $280   **Trains Planes & Automobiles, NSW**

'Esso' die cast fuel pumps and sign, number 781 with original box, packing pieces, pump hoses and nozzles, made by Meccano Dinky Toys, England, c1950, 11.5cm long, 3.8cm wide, 11.5cm high.

$255 - $295   **Trains Planes & Automobiles, NSW**

Meccano England, Dinky Supertoys 'Heinz 57 Varieties' 'Big Bedford' truck, c1955, 14.6cm long, 4.5cm wide, 6cm high.

$310 - $350   **Trains Planes & Automobiles, NSW**

'Dinky Toys' boxed station staff, post war O gauge, five people made by Meccano Ltd England, a common item both boxed and unboxed with less paint detail compared to prewar, c1954, 14.2cm long, 5.6cm wide, 2.5cm high.

$155 - $175   **Trains Planes & Automobiles, NSW**

Dinky Supertoys Foden 8 wheel diesel wagon, c1955, 18.5cm long, 5cm wide, 5cm high.

$205 - $245   **Windsor Cottage Antiques & Collectables, NSW**

Dinky toys A.E.C. Monarch Shell Chemicals Ltd, c1954, 15cm long, 5cm wide, 5cm high.

$140 - $160   **Windsor Cottage Antiques & Collectables, NSW**

Three dimension construction puzzle of a castle called 'The Magic Castle', produced by John Sands, Sydney for distribution by the Sun Newspapers Ltd.

$255 - $295

44 Brooke Street, VIC

Wooden 'Clock-Bobs' game, includes six balls and two cues, c1930, 91cm long, 24cm deep, 17cm high.

$205 - $245

Town & Country Antiques, NSW

Children's novelty card games, c1960, 6cm wide, 9cm high.

$3 - $13

Chapel Street Bazaar, VIC

'Barrel of Monkeys' game, c1960, 13cm high.

$20 - $30

Cat's Cradle Comics, VIC

Board game based on the 'Redex Car Trials', c1954, 44cm long, 35cm high.

$50 - $70

P. & N. Johnson, NSW

Enamel chess board by Simpson enamellers, Adelaide, c1920, 36cm wide, 36cm high.

$165 - $185

All In Good Time Antiques, SA

'Magic Robot' child's game, c1960.

$55 - $75

Green Gables Collectables, NSW

Set of Craftsman throwing shoes, also known as ringers, c1920.

$90 - $110

Bob Butler's Sentimental Journey, QLD

Boxed 'Aurora Skittle Pool' board game, picturing Don Adams of the 'Get Smart' television series, c1970.

$25 - $35

Cat's Cradle Comics, VIC

Wooden jig-saw map of the world, a 1950's educational toy, c1955, 29cm long, 23cm wide.

$20 - $30

The Botanic Ark, VIC

'Duperite' carpet bowl set, in original box, complete with set of rules, c1950.

$20 - $30

Savers, VIC

Hornby Meccano Ltd No. 2 turntable, boxed, last series, note Dublo style trademark, green speckled rim, c1957, 34.5cm diam.

$100 - $120

Trains Planes & Automobiles, NSW

Hornby-Meccano Ltd platform crane, post-war last issue, c1951, 9.1cm long, 9.1cm wide,16.8cm high.

$80 - $100

Trains Planes & Automobiles, NSW

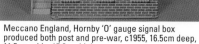

Meccano England, Hornby 'O' gauge signal box produced both post and pre-war, c1955, 16.5cm deep, 11.5cm wide, 15.2cm high.

$200 - $240

Trains Planes & Automobiles, NSW

Meccano Ltd Hornby No. 2 Junction Signal, the last issue with black lamps, c1960, 14.5cm wide, 25.5cm high.

$90 - $110

Trains Planes & Automobiles, NSW

Gauge 0 No.21 passenger set by Hornby, clockwork engine, c1950.

$205 - $245

Wooden Pew Antiques, VIC

Hornby 'Dublo' train carriage, c1950, 8cm long.

NZ$115 - $135

Collectamania, New Zealand

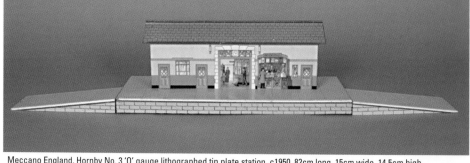

Meccano England, Hornby No. 3 'O' gauge lithographed tin plate station, c1950, 82cm long, 15cm wide, 14.5cm high.

$220 - $260

Trains Planes & Automobiles, NSW

Hornby O guage metal LMS coach set, deep red and black wind up, boxed, c1950.

$500 - $600

The Toy Collector, SA

Hornby O gauge type 501 loco and tender in LMS crimson lake livery, c1949.

$275 - $315

Antique Toy World, VIC

Clockwork engine and three carriers with track, manufactured by Hornby, key wind, c1950, 60cm long, 6cm wide, 8cm high.

$350 - $390

The New Farm Antique Centre, QLD

Hornby 3'6" gauge live steam with Stevenson's rocket and coaches, original boxes, 118.5cm long, 11.5cm wide, 28cm high.

$2000 - $3000

Trains Planes & Automobiles, NSW

Meccano England Hornby series station furniture luggage set, with a 'Sord London' sticker on the wicker picnic basket, 2cm long, 2cm wide, 3cm high.

$200 - $240

Trains Planes & Automobiles, NSW

Bassett-Lowre Northampton 060 electric locomotive, lithographed finish, boxed, c1951, 25cm long, 5.9cm wide, 9.3cm high.

$1330 - $1530

Trains Planes & Automobiles, NSW

Western Special Locomotive, tin, boxed, made in Japan, 34cm long.

$140 - $160

Cat's Cradle Comics, VIC

Robilt Atlantic van made by Rytime, boxed, a classic Australian toy with a short production span, filling the gap for the scarcity of immediate post war toys, c1954,15cm long, 5.3cm wide, 8.6cm high.

$370 - $410

Trains Planes & Automobiles, NSW

Pair of timber liner Gresley teak coaches, all timber construction and metal underframes with hand applied varnish finish, scratch built by a craftsman modeller, c1970, 44cm long, 6.4cm wide, 9.1cm high.

$800 - $900

Trains Planes & Automobiles, NSW

Wren Railways, G and R Wren England, Stanier 2-8-0 8F locomotive including a die cast loco and tender and its original box, c1970, 28.5cm long, 3.4cm wide, 5.3cm high.

$480 - $520

Trains Planes & Automobiles, NSW

Ferris four wheel four sided boxed railway wagon, a classic Australian train, produced by Ferris car radios, c1955, 16.3cm long, 5.3cm wide, 5.5cm high.

$100 - $120

Trains Planes & Automobiles, NSW

Classic O gauge 12 volt DC 'Flying Scotsman' by Bassett-Lowke in BR livery, boxed, c1955, 50cm long.

$3150 - $3350

Antique Toy World, VIC

Bassett-Lowke live steam model in British Rail black, unfired as new, boxed with all accessories, c1955, 45cm long.

$3150 - $3350

Antique Toy World, VIC

TOYS

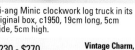

Tri-ang Minic clockwork log truck in its original box, c1950, 19cm long, 5cm wide, 5cm high.

$230 - $270

Vintage Charm, SA

Tri-ang Minic tin clockwork brewery truck in box, c950, 15cm long, 5cm wide, 5cm high.

$330 - $370

Vintage Charm, SA

Tin plate toy 'Esso' gasoline truck by 'Hayasni' of Japan, friction powered, in original box, c1960, 38cm long, 12cm wide, 10cm high.

$1000 - $1200

Wisma Antik, WA

Tin plate fire truck, c1950, 30cm long.

$275 - $315

Antiques and Collectables - Port Macquarie, NSW

Tri-ang Minic 'Green Line' clockwork single-decker bus, 5cm deep, 18cm wide, 7cm high.

NZ$175 - $195

Antiques of Epsom, New Zealand

Britain's covered tender No.1433, 1956-60, boxed, c1956, 16cm long.

$480 - $520

Antique Toy World, VIC

Tri-ang tow truck, Lines Bros, c1957, 45cm long, 14.5cm wide, 29cm high.

$200 - $240

Trains Planes & Automobiles, NSW

Battery operated tinplate fire engine made in Japan by 'Bandai' toys, in original box, c1960, 34cm long, 12cm deep, 16cm high.

$85 - $105

The Junk Company, VIC

Tri-ang Minic tinplate double decker bus advertising 'Tri-ang Pedal Motors' with a clock work motor, 18cm deep, 5cm wide, 10cm high.

NZ$380 - $420

Antiques of Epsom, New Zealand

Tinplate missile launcher made in Japan, c1950, 32cm long.

$85 - $105

Northside Secondhand Furniture, QLD

'Arnott's Biscuits 125th Anniversary Collection' of toy delivery vehicles, by Lledo Toys, c1985, 32cm wide, 8cm high.

$100 - $120

Treats & Treasures, NSW

Beswick England, child's nine piece tea set featuring Disney characters, post-war mark.

$330 - $370

Olsens Antiques,
QLD

Mickey Mouse, Walt Disney tin, c1960, 12.5cm diameter

$35 - $45

Obsidian Antiques,
NSW

Original Walt Disney 'Davy Crockett' jacket, c1950, 58cm long, 40cm wide.

$140 - $160

Western District Antique Centre,
VIC

Set of six Donald Duck skittles, c1955, 4.5cm wide, 19.5cm high.

$115 - $135

Retro Relics,
VIC

Hungry Jack's Mickey Mouse 65th anniversary glass, c1995, 15cm high, 6.5cm diameter

$3 - $13

Cardtastic Collectables,
VIC

'Bambi' cut-out book, uncut, c1950, 24.5cm long, 37cm high.

$40 - $60

Cat's Cradle Comics,
VIC

Paper mache 'Mickey Mouse' ventriloquist doll, c1950, 75cm high.

$750 - $850

Lancaster's Toowoomba
Antique Centre, QLD

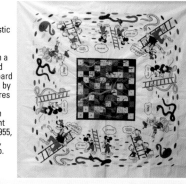

Square plastic Disney tablecloth printed with a 'Snakes and Ladders' board surrounded by Disney figures in various positions, in strong bright colours, c1955, 124cm long, 124cm deep.

$140 - $160

The Botanic Ark,
VIC

Disney character favourites gift pack stereo products mixture of approximately 30 slides made by 'GAF View-Master Stereo Products', c1960.

$75 - $95

Alan's Collectables,
NSW

Retro fibre optic lamp of 'Cinderella's coach and horses, c1960, 45cm long, 23cm deep, 36cm high.

$230 - $270

Galeria del Centro,
NSW

Original children's pre-school bag, c1960, 27cm long, 14cm high.

$75 - $95

Chapel Street Bazaar,
VIC

Mickey Mouse cloth toy by Joy Toys, c1950, 29cm high.

$50 - $70   **Kingston Antiques, VIC**

A Walt Disney 'Mickey Mouse' toy, Mickey mounted on a tricycle with elasticised moving legs, c1977, 13cm high.

$35 - $45   **Grant & Wendy Brookes, VIC**

Walt Disney Mickey Mouse candle, hand painted, c1980, 15cm high.

$23 - $33   **Western District Antique Centre, VIC**

A Walt Disney plastic 'Goofy' toy, Goofy mounted on a tricycle with elasticised moving legs, made by Gabriel Industries, c1977, 14cm high.

$40 - $60   **Grant &Wendy Brookes, VIC**

Tin wind up 'Donald Duck' toy washing machine, c1958, 13cm deep, 13cm wide, 18cm high.

$280 - $320   **Ross Agnew, NSW**

Beswick Walt Disney 'Goofy' plate, c1950, 18cm wide.

$135 - $155   **Archers Antiques, TAS**

Limited edition Wade figure 'The Hat Box Series', No. 4 'Trusty' with original miniature hatbox character from 'The Lady and The Tramp', c1960, 3.5cm high.

$140 - $160   **Chapel Street Bazaar, VIC**

Donald Duck toy manufactured by Bendi, c1960, 17cm high.

NZ$110 - $130   **Banks Peninsula Antiques, New Zealand**

Plastic toy Mickey Mouse with seven pre-recorded messages activated by a pull string, manufactured by Mattel, c1970, 18cm high.

NZ$410 - $450   **Banks Peninsula Antiques, New Zealand**

'Pinocchio' wind up cymbal player in tin and plastic, c1950, 12cm deep, 11cm wide, 30cm high.

$205 - $245   **Southside Antiques Centre, QLD**

Mickey Mouse novelty phone by American Telecommunications Corporation, c1991, 21cm wide, 37cm high.

$255 - $295   **Retro Relics, VIC**

'Jabba The Hutt', Star Wars miniatures rebel storm expansion pack, c2004, 5cm long, 4cm wide, 3.5cm high.

$40 - $60

Cardtastic Collectables, VIC

Star Wars miniatures 'Revenge Of The Sith', c2005, 10cm long, 4cm wide, 6cm high.

$35 - $45

Cardtastic Collectables, VIC

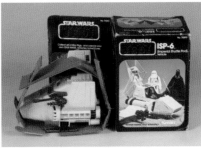

Vintage Star Wars 'Imperial Shuttle Pod' ISP-6 in original box and still in original protective cardboard, c1983, 14cm wide, 10cm high.

$35 - $45

Kenny's Antiques, VIC

Original Star Wars assorted figures, priced each, c1980, 10cm high.

$5 - $7

The Mill Markets, VIC

Selection of Star Wars comics, c1977.

$6 - $10

The Wool Exchange Geelong, VIC

Star Wars No.1 from 1977, 17cm wide, 26cm high.

$65 - $85

Cat's Cradle Comics, VIC

'Star Wars Maths Set' tin, c1977, 18cm long, 7cm wide.

NZ$40 - $50

Collectamania, New Zealand

Vintage boxed 'Yoda' puppet, 'Empire Strikes Back' made by Kenner, c1980, 20cm high.

$45 - $65   **The Mill Markets, VIC**

Star Wars figure, 'Boba Fett'.

$190 - $210   **Gardenvale Collectables, VIC**

Star Wars 'Scout Walker', unopened, c1983.

$200 - $240   **Cat's Cradle Comics, VIC**

Official full size 'Boba Fett' Star Wars helmet autographed by the original Boba Fett, Jeremy Bulloch, c1995, 30cm deep, 25cm wide, 25cm high.

$430 - $470   **Rare Memorabilia Gallery, VIC**

Unopened Star Wars 'Snowspeeder' model kit, 26cm long, 19cm wide, 9cm high.

$35 - $45   **Cat's Cradle Comics, VIC**

Printed card 'Imperial Death Star' from Star Wars, made to go with 3 3/4 inch action figures, c1980, 37.5cm high, 55cm diameter.

$480 - $520   **The Toy Collector, SA**

Star Wars 'Hans Solo' and 'Tauntaun', boxed and unopened, c2000.

$170 - $190   **Cat's Cradle Comics, VIC**

Star Wars Treasury No.1 from 1977, Whitman variant cover, contains the first half of the movie story which is completed in Star Wars Treasury No.2, c1977, 34cm long, 26cm wide.

$40 - $50   **Cat's Cradle Comics, VIC**

Star Wars double sized Comic Book Treasury No.2, adapts the second half of the movie, c1977, 34cm long, 26cm wide.

$30 - $40   **Cat's Cradle Comics, VIC**

'Yoda' from Clone Strike Expansion Pack, Star Wars miniatures, c2004, 2cm high, 2cm diameter.

$40 - $60   **Cardtastic Collectables, VIC**

Star Wars Episode 1 'Queen Amidala' doll, black travel gown, 1999 Portrait Edition box, No. 2 in a series of 3, c1999.

$165 - $185   **Alan's Collectables, NSW**

Small 'Noddy', Combex, c1950, 13cm high.

$45 - $65

Retro Relics, VIC

Late 20th century squeaky 'Noddy' toy, c1970, 12cm high.

$17 - $23

Western District Antique Centre, VIC

Squeaky toy of Noddy in his car, 13cm deep, 7cm wide, 9cm high.

$13 - $17

Treats & Treasures, NSW

Boxed 'Robby the Robot' Forbidden Planet toy with remote control, c1990, 4cm wide, 30cm high.

$230 - $270

Chapel Street Bazaar, VIC

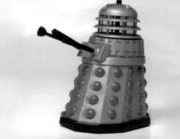

'Talking Dalek' from Dr. Who, battery operated, speaks four phrases including 'exterminate', c1976, 12cm long, 10cm deep, 17cm high.

$65 - $85

The Botanic Ark, VIC

Battlestar Galactica die cast metal galactic cruiser to coincide with the TV series, c1978, 7cm long.

$22 - $28

Go Figure Collectables, VIC

Mechanical TV spaceman by ALPS, Japan, complete with metal antenna, boxed, c1965, 19cm high.

$850 - $950

Antique Toy World, VIC

Star Trek No.5 from 1969, 17cm wide, 26cm high.

$35 - $45

Cat's Cradle Comics, VIC

USS Enterprise Limited Edition model in glass dome, Paramount Pictures Sculpt No. RO 4049, c1994, 10cm long, 10cm wide, 12cm high.

$40 - $50

Alan's Collectables, NSW

Dr. Spock bust, c1990, 27cm high.

$65 - $85

Cat's Cradle Comics, VIC

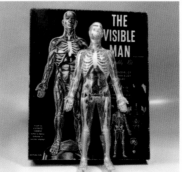

'Visible Man' figure made up with box, c1970, 40cm long, 33cm high.

$35 - $45

Cat's Cradle Comics, VIC

Planet of the Apes, boxed, made by Neca, c2001, 23cm high.

$15 - $25

The Wool Exchange Geelong, VIC

Archie Andrews ventriloquist doll by 'Palitoy', c1960, 35cm high.

$205 – $245   **Retro Relics, VIC**

Mego 'Spiderman' doll, c1970, 20cm high.

$50 – $70   **Cat's Cradle Comics, VIC**

Small 'Humphrey Bear' with squeak, c1970, 20cm high.

$16 – $20   **Cat's Cradle Comics, VIC**

'Humphrey B Bear' musical toy, c1965, 26cm high.

$115 – $135   **True Blue Antiques, NSW**

Doll costume set, 'Red River Floodwaters', boxed, c1970.

$65 – $85   **Cat's Cradle Comics, VIC**

'The Landslide Adventure' costume set for the 1970's 'Lone Ranger' doll, c1970.

$40 – $60   **Cat's Cradle Comics, VIC**

'Lone Ranger's Tonto' doll costume, boxed, c1970.

$40 – $60   **Cat's Cradle Comics, VIC**

Marilyn Monroe collectors doll with box, limited edition of 4,999, c2004, 40cm high.

$230 – $270   **Cat's Cradle Comics, VIC**

Early promotional 'Tomb Raider' statue, c1990, 36cm high.

$190 – $210   **Cat's Cradle Comics, VIC**

Batcraft by L. Marx, U.K., boxed, c1966, 16.5cm high.

$550 – $650   **Antique Toy World, VIC**

Boxed 'Machine Men' set, unopened, c1980, 38cm long, 19cm high.

$85 – $105   **Cat's Cradle Comics, VIC**

'Flintstone' camera, unopened, c1970, 15cm long, 17cm high.

$12 – $18   **Cat's Cradle Comics, VIC**

Donald Trump 12 inch talking doll with 17 phrases such as 'I have no choice but to tell you you're fired', removable clothing, made by Stevenson Entertainment Group and released with the hit TV show 'The Apprentice', c2004, 30cm high.

$40 – $50   **Go Figure Collectables, VIC**

M.A.S.K. Hurricane, small '57 Chevy based from 80's television show, features elevating body, lift up grill, pop out sawblades, shooting spare tyre, an opening sunroof exposing a command box and mini cutting lasers, etc. 20cm long, 7.5cm wide, 5.5cm high.

$40 - $50

The Toy Collector,
SA

M.A.S.K. Rhino, large collectable cab featuring smoke stacks which turn into cannons, front grill which converts into a battering ram, a rear end which detaches to become a small ATV, based on 80's television show, 31cm long, 11cm wide, 15.5cm high.

$55 - $75

The Toy Collector,
SA

'Pink Panther Chatter Chum' toy, c1976, 15.5cm high.

$80 - $100

Retro Relics,
VIC

Plastic 'Astro Boy' toy, c1990, 40cm high.

$65 - $85

Chapel Street Bazaar,
VIC

'Batmobile' model kit, unmade, boxed.

$30 - $40

Cat's Cradle Comics,
VIC

'Incredible Hulk' utility belt, boxed, unopened.

$60 - $80

Cat's Cradle Comics,
VIC

Plastic 'Snoopy' figure with movable parts and cloth ears, in original outfit, c1980, 9cm wide, 22cm high.

$20 - $30

Chapel Street Bazaar,
VIC

'Quarry' brand hot water bottle in shape of Popeye, c1950, 30cm long.

$110 - $130

The Wool Exchange Geelong,
VIC

Original 'Popeye' tin, c1960, 12cm high.

$110 - $130

Western District Antique Centre,
VIC

Blowplastic figure of 'Rainbow Brite' in bright colours, made in Hong Kong, c1984, 18cm high.

$12 - $22   **Fat Helen's, VIC**

Large 18 inch 'Rainbow Brite' doll, includes original dress with hard to find star motif, long clean orange wool hair, polyester stuffed body with hard face, purple star on cheek and painted eyes, c1983, 31cm wide, 45cm high.

$30 - $60   **The Toy Collector, SA**

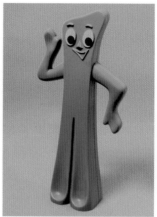

Gumby 12 inch AM/FM table radio, hard plastic moulded with painted face, black dials on side and speaker hidden at rear, operates on a 9V battery, c1985, 5cm deep, 15cm wide, 30cm high.

$35 - $45   **The Toy Collector, SA**

'Dr. Seuss' The Cat in the Hat' made of PVC with a head on a spring, c2003, 7.6cm deep, 7.5cm wide, 19.5cm high.

$25 - $35   **Cardtastic Collectables, VIC**

Plastic 'He-Man' radio, c1987, 10cm long, 4cm deep, 8cm wide, 10cm high.

$90 - $110   **Dr Russell's Emporium, WA**

Pair of 3 inch bendable figures with unique square shaped heads, Blockheads 'G' and 'J' are Gumby's arch rivals, hard to find vintage now, has been re-released overseas, c1980, 4cm wide, 7cm high.

$11 - $21   **The Toy Collector, SA**

14 inch 'Good Luck CareBear' with box, green plush with green hair 'kiss curl', four leaf clover tummy patch, hard plastic nose, winking eye and 'tush heart', c1983, 35cm high.

$45 - $65   **The Toy Collector, SA**

Large Mego 'Batman' doll, boxed, c1970.

$185 - $205   **Cat's Cradle Comics, VIC**

Mego 'Spiderman' doll, large, boxed, c1970, 13cm wide, 35cm high.

$275 - $315   **Cat's Cradle Comics, VIC**

A plush 'Alf' doll with suction stickers on hands, c1980, 20cm high.

$10 - $20   **Western District Antique Centre, VIC**

Limited edition Jonathan 'Coach' Coachman action figure, only 3000 made, exclusive to Wirzburger Enterprises, c2004, 15cm high.

$25 - $35   **Go Figure Collectables, VIC**

Wizard Toyfare exclusive figure of 'Rowdy Roddy Piper' wearing his infamous panther T-shirt and leather jacket, limited edition of 3000, c2005, 15cm high.

$35 - $45   **Go Figure Collectables, VIC**

'Happy Days' figurines of Fonzie's whole gang including Potsy, Richie and Ralph, still in original unopened packaging, manufactured by Mego, c1976, 20cm high.

$155 - $175   **Kenny's Antiques, VIC**

G1 (Generation One) Transformer 'Blaster', transforms from 'Boombox', 1980's style, to robot with gun. Blaster is the Autobot communications officer, in hard plastic with moving parts, 'rub sticker' and decals, 13cm wide, 22cm high.

$55 - $75   **The Toy Collector, SA**

Six plastic MASH action figures, c1981, 10cm long.

$125 - $145   **P. & N. Johnson, NSW**

Four WWF wrestling action figures, c1987, 20cm high.

$190 - $210   **P. & N. Johnson, NSW**

'Mr T' doll from the TV series 'A Team', all clothing and jewellery attached, c1983, 34cm long, 6cm deep, 14cm wide, 34cm high.

$110 - $130   **Dr Russell's Emporium, WA**

Hard plastic figure of 'Spawn' with movable limbs and body, produced by McFarlane Toys as merchandise to accompany release of the movie titled 'Spawn', c2000, 17cm wide, 26cm high.

$15 - $25   **Chapel Street Bazaar, VIC**

Metro-Goldwyn Mayer Inc. figure 'The Kraken' from the movie 'Clash of the Titans', c1980, 37cm high.

$200 - $240   **Kings Park Antiques & Collectables, SA**

Gabriel 'Lone Ranger' action figure on Silver action horse, clothes and weapons all removable, both figures fully articulated, c1974, 32.5cm long, 40cm

$170 - $190   **The Toy Collector, SA**

Technofix motorcycle with rider, friction driven, c1950, 19cm long.

$430 - $470   **Antique Toy World, VIC**

Oscillating tin toy of a bee on a flower, made in Germany, c1950, 10cm long, 10cm high, 7cm diameter.

$185 - $205   **Dr Russell's Emporium, WA**

Tin toy mixer made by Daya, c1960, 15cm wide, 12cm high.

$70 - $90   **Secondhand Furniture Mart, TAS**

'Mettoy Minor' toy typewriter, c1950, 26cm wide, 6cm high.

$40 - $50   **Western District Antique Centre, VIC**

Boxed tin sky car, c1970, 30cm long, 18cm wide, 19cm high.

$40 - $60   **Cat's Cradle Comics, VIC**

Boxed musical tin tractor, c1970, 30cm long, 18cm wide, 19cm high.

$40 - $60   **Cat's Cradle Comics, VIC**

Metal and plastic toy X-7 space ship, battery operated, c1980, 14cm high, 20cm diameter.

$230 - $270   **Southside Antiques Centre, QLD**

Chinese made 'Rocket Racer' with original box, c1960, 200cm long, 80cm high.

$140 - $160   **Chris' Antiques & Collectables, VIC**

Tin toy rocket marked 'E. Flim Lemez', c1960, 12cm wide, 40cm high.

$175 - $195   **The Junk Company, VIC**

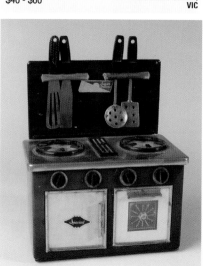

'Super Deluxe' tin toy oven with cooking utensils, 17cm long, 20cm high.

$65 - $85   **Antiques and Collectables - Port Macquarie, NSW**

Australian made tin toy top with wooden handle, made by Ace Australia, c1950, 16cm diameter.

$40 - $60   **Shop 9, Centenary Antique Centre, NSW**

Tin motor bike, friction operated, c1950, 8cm long, 6cm high.

NZ$175 - $195   **Collectamania, New Zealand**

Wind-up tin 'shaking' dog toy, c1950, 15cm long, 8cm deep, 8cm high.

$185 - $205   **Philicia Antiques & Collectables, SA**

Windup toy tin trike with original key, c1960, 12cm long, 10cm high.

$165 - $185   **Maryborough Station Antique Emporium, VIC**

'Mischievous Monkey' by Modern Toys, c1960, 33cm high.

$480 - $520   **Antique Toy World, VIC**

Toy battery operated 'Charlie Weaver' Bartender' made by 'T. N., Japan', c1978, 13cm deep, 13cm wide, 30cm high.

$85 - $105   **The Junk Company, VIC**

A toy battery operated 'Bubble Blowing Monkey', c1960, 13cm deep, 10cm wide, 28cm high.

$185 - $205   **The Junk Company, VIC**

'Blink-A-Gear' robot by Taiyo, battery operated, boxed, c1960, 36cm high.

$1150 - $1350   **Antique Toy World, VIC**

Tri-ang toy crane, c1950, 17cm deep, 14cm wide, 45cm high.

NZ$175 - $195   **Collectamania, New Zealand**

Japanese Tin Toys

There is little or no information available on most of the smaller Japanese toy makers.

There were many in the early 1950's when they took over the toy market, resulting in numerous new companies with very little history.

The 'Alps' Shojo Ltd toy company commenced business in 1948 in Toyko and is still in business today. They were responsible for making specialty toy vehicles and novelties.

Many of these toys were battery operated and the mixed tinplate and tin space toys are among the most popular collectables today.

Battery operated highway patrol bike with light called 'Police Rider', made in Japan by 'ALPS', c1960, 33cm long.

$2300 - $2500   **Wisma Antik, WA**

ACTION FIGURES & AUSTRALIAN TOYS

'Mego' Robin Hood plastic fully poseable figure with fabric clothes and plastic weapons, c1974, 20cm high.

$110 - $130   **The Toy Collector, SA**

'Palitoy' action man British Parachute Regiment, plastic body fully articulated 12 inch figure, all equipment and clothes removable, c1978, 30cm high.

$190 - $210   **The Toy Collector, SA**

Palitoy action man German storm trooper, plastic, fully articulated, 12 inch figure, based on a German WWII soldier, all equipment and clothes removable, c1965, 30cm high.

$190 - $210   **The Toy Collector, SA**

Security action figure, United States Department of State Diplomatic Security Service in full gear, Special Agent 'Patrick McGuinness' life action figure for adult collectors, boxed as new, made by Dragon, c1995, 34cm long, 20cm wide.

$40 - $60   **Alan's Collectables, NSW**

'Boomaroo' toy truck, Australian made, c1950, 350cm long, 140cm wide, 200cm high.

$230 - $270   **Chris' Antiques & Collectables, VIC**

Toy cash register by Australian manufacturer 'Boomaroo', famous for their tinplate toys, c1950, 16cm wide, 18cm high.

$115 - $135   **Chapel Street Bazaar, VIC**

Toy tractor by Boomaroo, c1950, 27cm long, 15cm deep, 15cm high.

$170 - $220   **Patrick Davey Antiques, VIC**

Mechanical toy bear including box, c1950, 11cm deep, 22cm high.

$225 - $265   **Urbanized, VIC**

Boomeroo dump truck, c1930, 55cm long, 13cm wide, 13cm high.

$225 - $265   **Whimsical Notions, NSW**

Original 'Boomaroo' Hyster with original rubber wheels and logos, c1950, 30cm wide, 27cm high.

$480 - $520   **Wisma Antik, WA**

Toycraft Australia double decker bus, c1945.

$45 - $65

Unique & Antique,
VIC

Australian 'Wyn-Toy' tin truck, c1940, 15cm long, 7cm high.

$60 - $70

Sue's Book Nook,
NSW

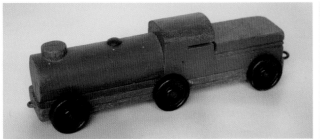

Toycraft Australia locomotive.

$100 - $120

Unique & Antique,
VIC

Toycraft Australia log truck.

$120 - $140

Unique & Antique, VIC

'Wyn-Toy tin dump truck with front loader, c1940, 32cm long, 13cm high.

$140 - $160

Vintage Charm,
SA

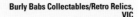

Boxed toy Jeep in original box manufactured by Wyn-Toy, c1950, 26cm long, 14cm high.

$280 - $320

Burly Babs Collectables/Retro Relics,
VIC

Skanson Beanie Kids figure, a mutation from the standard 'Prickles the Echidna' bear, c2005, 7cm deep, 11cm wide, 23cm high.

$5 - $15

Cardtastic Collectables,
VIC

Wyn-Toy tipper truck, c1950, 50cm long, 16cm high.

$75 - $95

Chapel Street Bazaar,
VIC

Wyn-Toy sand and gravel truck, c1950, 30cm long, 11cm high.

$75 - $95

Chapel Street Bazaar,
VIC

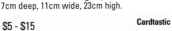

Skansen Beanie Kids figure, 'Cozzie the Aussie' bear, c2005, 7cm deep, 11cm wide, 23cm high.

$5 - $15

Cardtastic Collectables,
VIC

Skansen Beanie Kids figure, 'Santa Paws' the bear, c2004, 7cm deep, 11cm wide, 23cm high.

$10 - $20

Cardtastic Collectables,
VIC

'Beanie Baby' Diana teddy bear wearing tiara and in perspex case, c1985, 18cm high.

$40 - $50   **Marge's Antiques & Collectables, NSW**

'Ezy-Bilt The Master Toy', a South Australian 'Meccano' style set, c1945.

$220 - $260   **Southern Antique Centre, NSW**

Meccano set with box including instruction manual, c1950.

$155 - $175   **Wooden Pew Antiques, VIC**

Boxed Ezy-Bilt set No. 2 by Colton Palmer & Preston, c1960.

$185 - $205   **Kings Park Antiques & Collectables, SA**

'Astro Nits' cereal toys, complete set of 20, c1970.

$140 - $160   **Cat's Cradle Comics, VIC**

Toys collected from packets of cereal, c1980, 3cm high.

$10 - $20   **Chapel Street Bazaar, VIC**

Assorted cereal toys.

$10 - $20   **Gardenvale Collectables, VIC**

Plastic vintage cereal toys, assorted colours and characters, c1960, 5cm high.

$5 - $15   **The Mill Markets, VIC**

Cereal toys still in original cellophane packages, not assembled, c1960, 10cm long, 5cm wide.

$40 - $50   **Chapel Street Bazaar, VIC**

Snap camel train cereal toys.

$50 - $70   **Gardenvale Collectables, VIC**

Clockwork toy cat with original box, marked 'Made in US Zone Germany', makers name 'G.N.K.', 10cm long, 6cm high.

$115 - $135   **Shop 2, Centenary Antique Centre, NSW**

Wind up 'Uncle Sam' toy by Durham Industries, c1950, 10cm wide, 16cm high.

$30 - $40   **Helen's On The Bay, QLD**

Metal enamelled duck on tricycle, key operated, c1970, 50cm wide, 22cm high.

$185 - $205   **Urbanized, VIC**

Clockwork gear robot, marked 'Made in Japan', c1950, 25cm high.

$650 - $750   **Wisma Antik, WA**

Clockwork toy penguin with original key and original box, manufactured by A. Wells & Co. Great Britain, c1950, 12cm high.

$110 - $130   **Shop 9, Centenary Antique Centre, NSW**

Pepsi Cola 'Mack Truck' by Corgi, c1970, 19cm wide, 10cm high.

$60 - $80   **Treats & Treasures, NSW**

Corgi Toys family butcher's 'Smith's Karrier' van, c1960, 9cm long, 4cm wide.

$110 - $130   **The Restorers Barn, VIC**

Limited edition 'Arnott's Thorncroft' delivery van with roof rack, by Corgi, c1970, 19cm wide, 10cm high.

$65 - $85   **Treats & Treasures, NSW**

'Hopping Puppy' wind up toy, c1950, 13cm high.

$75 - $95   **Maryborough Station Antique Emporium, VIC**

Britains Ltd die-cast toy cannon, can fire match heads, c1950, 10cm long, 4.5cm wide.

$30 - $40   **Wooden Pew Antiques, VIC**

Die-cast toy cannon, fires match heads, made by The Crescent Toy Co. in England, c1960, 13cm long, 5.5cm wide.

$40 - $50   **Wooden Pew Antiques, VIC**

Tin cowboy and sherrif badges, c1960, 3cm high.

$5 - $15   **Chapel Street Bazaar, VIC**

Micro Models International tow truck, Australian made.

$75 - $95   **Unique & Antique, VIC**

Diecast 'Mitre 10' FJ Holden panel van 1953, scale 1:25 boxed in Perth, c1990, 17cm long, 6cm wide.

$22 - $32

The Restorers Barn, VIC

Zulu Regiment 1879, five lead Zulu warrior figures, boxed, Imperial Production, 4.5cm long, 6cm high.

$85 - $105

Alan's Collectables, NSW

Matchbox 75 series, boxed and made in England by Lesney, 1:50 scale, boxed as new, c1982, 7cm long, 3.5cm wide, 2cm high.

$40 - $50

Alan's Collectables, NSW

Matchbox Yesteryears 'Foden' breakdown tractor.

$60 - $80

Unique & Antique, VIC

Astra search light, die cast and battery operated, sometimes used in military training, c1950, 9.5cm high, 10.6cm diam.

$90 - $110

Trains Planes & Automobiles, NSW

Cowboy and Indian toy models made by Britains, c1950, 2cm wide, 6cm high.

$200 - $240

Thompsons Country Collectables, NSW

Hollow cast Britain's Lead Knight, hand painted Flag Bearer and Lance Knight, c1954, 11.25cm high.

$330 - $370

The Toy Collector, SA

Crescent Scout boxed car complete with ammo, boxed, c1957, 19.5cm long, 8cm wide, 8cm high.

$140 - $160

Trains Planes & Automobiles, NSW

Matchbox 'Motorway Extension Set', contains no cars, c1970, 42cm long, 26cm high.

$80 - $100

Cat's Cradle Comics, VIC

Matchbox Yesteryears 'Thomas Flyabout'.

$75 - $95

Unique & Antique, VIC

Matchbox Yesteryears 'Lipton Tea' horse drawn coach.

$100 - $120   **Unique & Antique, VIC**

'Matchbox' die cast 1955 FJ Holden panel van with Ronald McDonald House logo, c1996, 10cm long.

$6 - $10   **The Restorers Barn, VIC**

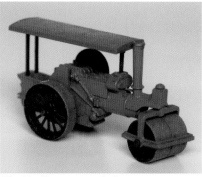

Matchbox Yesteryears road roller.

$85 - $105   **Unique & Antique, VIC**

McDonalds Snoopy give-away toy, made in China, c1990.

$2 - $6   **Chapel Street Bazaar, VIC**

'Cyclops Lightning' pedal car, c1950, 95cm deep, 45cm wide, 48cm high.

$430 - $470   **Lydiard Furniture & Antiques, VIC**

'Cyclops Comet' pedal car, c1954, 77cm long, 46cm high.

$650 - $750   **Town & Country Antiques, NSW**

Cyclops 'Comet' pedal car, no dents, full tread on rear tyres, original paintwork. Horn still attached, c1955, 80cm long, 40cm deep, 50cm high.

$610 - $710   **Habitat Antiques, NSW**

'Push-Me Pull-Me' mechanical cart, made in Melbourne, c1950, 100cm deep, 45cm wide, 45cm high.

$175 - $195   **The Junk Company, VIC**

DC7 Airliner, Japanese, battery operated, c1960, 53.5cm long, 59cm wide, 16.5cm high.

$760 - $860   **Trains Planes & Automobiles, NSW**

Hand made model balsa wood DC3 aeroplane, c1950, 160cm long, 180cm wide.

$5800 - $6200   **The Restorers Barn, VIC**

Pan American tin toy plane 'Clipper Fortuna with a mechanical switch to operates door and passenger windows, c1960, 55cm long, 60cm wide.

$460 - $500

The Restorers Barn, VIC

USAF B-45 tinplate 'Tornado' aeroplane with a friction mechanism, trade mark to the base, c1960, 32cm long, 39cm wide.

$140 - $160

Chapel Street Bazaar, VIC

Tin plate 'Pan American' Clipper Meteor aeroplane by Tomyama, c1960, 34cm long.

$275 - $315

Antiques and Collectables - Port Macquarie, NSW

Vintage 'Snorks' friends from the Smurf era, c1980, 7cm high.

$5 - $10

The Mill Markets, VIC

Assorted Smurfs, Smurfettes, collected from 'BP' petrol stations, made by Schlech, c1980, 8cm high.

$5 - $10

The Mill Markets, VIC

Pretty pink and mauve Smurf house with removable roof, door and windows open, imported from Germany, c1980, 8cm wide, 12cm high.

$35 - $45

Chapel Street Bazaar, VIC

Smurf figures imported from Germany, c1980, 6cm wide, 5cm high.

$15 - $25

Chapel Street Bazaar, VIC

South East Asian water theatre puppet with glass eyes and human hair, c1950, 65cm long.

$190 - $210

Salt's Antiques, QLD

'Mobo' spring suspended rocking horse, c1950, 53cm deep, 98cm wide, 90cm high.

$360 - $400

Coming of Age Antiques, QLD

Wooden rocking horse, c1940, 120cm long, 110cm high.

$1150 - $1350

Shop 19, Centenary Antique Centre, NSW

Scratch built steam engine on wooden base, 25cm long, 16cm wide, 20cm high.

$410 - $450

Barry McKay, NSW

Tin 'Mobo' rocking horse with metal frame, c1950, 100cm long, 59cm high.

$265 - $305

The Restorers Barn, VIC

'Wilesco' West German live steam 'work shop' steam engine, c1978, 46cm wide, 33cm high.

$930 - $1030

Salt's Antiques, QLD

Bakelite and metal bubble pipe marked 'Product of L. G. Pimblett Sydney' with original box, c1945, 39cm long, 5cm deep, 15.5cm high.

$140 - $160

Ross Agnew, NSW

Live steam 'O' gauge Locomotive, c1950, 23cm wide.

$650 - $750

Bank House Antiques, QLD

'Miss Mini Mod' doll furniture, in sealed box, c1968, 40cm long, 25cm wide.

$40 - $50

Cat's Cradle Comics, VIC

Battery operated monkey with clapping symbols, c1950, 17.5cm wide, 26.25cm high.

$110 - $130

Kenny's Antiques, VIC

Western wagon, complete in box, c1970, 21cm long.

$30 - $40

Cat's Cradle Comics, VIC

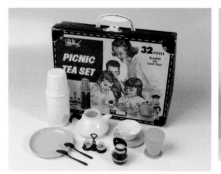

Redbox Deluxe toy picnic and tea set, c1960.

$25 - $35

Chapel Street Bazaar, VIC

Britains 2150 Centurion tank, boxed and complete with all accessories, c1950, 23cm long.

$850 - $950

Antique Toy World, VIC

Hand made shoofly in the form of an elephant, c1950, 72cm long, 39cm wide.

$60 - $80

Step Back Antiques, VIC

Mechanical seal ride from Sea World Australia, c1970.

$650 - $750

Salt's Antiques, QLD

Humorous celluloid figure of a cat in chef's hat and apron holding a carving knife and a rat, c1940, 18cm high.

$205 - $245

Lancaster's Toowoomba Antique Centre, QLD

German 'Bulldog' tinplate toy gun with original paintwork, c1950, 12cm long.

$70 - $90

Kingston Antiques, VIC

Child's cowboy leather holster with fringe, bull's head and flash design, orange, red and black with belt, c1960.

$5 - $15

Savers, VIC

HMAS 'Swan' model battleship built in Williamstown, Victoria, a scale tin model, c1960, 238cm long, 35cm wide, 46cm high.

$1150 - $1350

Tarlo & Graham, VIC

Cow, elephant, swan, made of celluloid, c1950.

$15 - $25

The Mill Markets, VIC

A Fisher Price childrens camera.

$12 - $22

Tyabb Packing House, VIC

Plastic toy mix master, c1960, 20cm high.

$30 - $40

Bill Hayes Antiques, NSW

Boxed twenty two piece original child's tea set with handpainted finish.

$135 - $155

Lancaster's Toowoomba Antique Centre, QLD

Toy 'Super Washer' washing machine, battery operated, made by Nasta Ind Inc New York, c1977, 14cm wide, 19cm high.

$25 - $35

Nicki's Collection, NSW

Battery powered bartender tin toy, with revolving eyes complete with box, c1960, 30cm high.

$200 - $240

The Restorers Barn, VIC

Britains Ltd. 155mm gun used by British and American Armies designed to go with early lead toy soldiers, fires small lead shells, c1957, 27.5cm long, 10cm wide, 10cm high.

$470 - $510

The Toy Collector, SA

Britains 'Swoppet' plastic knights, all parts fully changeable, various colours, c1967, 6.25cm high.

$140 - $160

The Toy Collector, SA

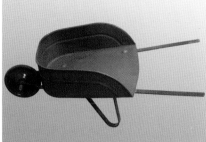

Child's Australian wheelbarrow, c1940, 58cm long, 30cm deep.

$115 - $135

Shaws Antiques, NSW

Louis Marx Fred Flintstone bump and go toy, battery operated, tin and felt body, c1960, 55cm long, 17.5cm wide, 30cm high.

$750 - $850

The Toy Collector, SA

Child's toy, 8mm mini projector.

$45 - $65

Photantiques, NSW

Resin figure of the famous Mad magazine character 'Alfred E. Newan', c1994, 36cm high.

$275 - $315

Chapel Street Bazaar, VIC

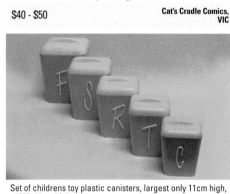

'Western House' cowboy building, boxed, c1970.

$40 - $50

Cat's Cradle Comics, VIC

Black colour half doll from atop a chocolate box manufactured in Germany for sale in Argentina only, c1950, 15cm long.

$600 - $700

Ritzy Bits - ACT, ACT

Set of childrens toy plastic canisters, largest only 11cm high, c1950, 11cm high.

$45 - $65

Olsens Antiques, QLD

Plastic 'Timpo' Crusader Knights figure, c1975, 6.25cm high.

$50 - $70

The Toy Collector, SA

Unopened boy's tool set consisting of axe, pocket knife, dagger and utensils, c1960.

$100 - $120

The Bottom Drawer Antique Centre, VIC

'Indians with Teepee' playset, boxed, c1970.

$15 - $25

Cat's Cradle Comics, VIC

CONTRIBUTING DEALER'S INDEX

ACT

Fyshwick Antique Centre
84 Gladstone Street
Fyshwick ACT 2609
T: 02 6280 4541
F: 02 6239 1025
M: 0422 641 332
fyshwickantiquecentre@fyshwick.com

Nana's Pearls
Canberra Antiques Centre
37 Townsville Street
Fyshwick ACT 2669
T: 02 6251 8008
F: 02 6251 9009
M: 0419 616 689
E: denisebird@bigblue.net.au

Needlewitch
Canberra Antiques Centre
37 Townsville Street
Fyshwick ACT 2609
T: 02 6162 3737
F: 02 6292 3170
M: 0414 453 825
E: needlewitch@ihug.com.au

Ritzy Bits - ACT
PO Box 7099
Kaleen ACT 2617
T: 02 6241 3908
F: 02 6253 8429
M: 0418 623 007
E: ritzybits@homemail.com.au

Rose Cottage Antiques
Canberra Antiques Centre
37 Townsville Street
Fyshwick ACT 2609
T: 02 6293 2507
M: 0411 481 394
E: sales@work.netspeed.com.au

Upwell Antiques
Canberra Antiques Centre
37 Townsville Street
Fyshwick ACT 2609
T: 02 6232 6255
F: 02 6232 6256
E: upwell.antiques@bigpond.com

Vintage Living
Unit 3/6 Weedon Close
Belconnen ACT 2617
T: 6253 2105
M: 0412 160 166
E: rosemac@homemail.com.au

NSW

506070
308 Trafalgar Street
Annandale NSW 2038
T: 02 9566 1430
M: 0413 764 101
E: mike@506070.com.au
www.506070.com.au

Alan's Collectables
Shop 3 William Street Plaza
Gosford NSW 2250
T: 02 4324 6884
F: 02 4324 6884
M: 0408 546 073
E: alatique@bigpond.net.au

Andrew Markerink
Master Clockmaker
PO Box 470, Camden NSW 2570
T: 02 4636 6463
F: 02 4636 6074
M: 0416 288 445
E: markerink.clocks@ozemail.com.au

Antiquariat Fine Books
The Penders, Wingecarribee Street,
Bowral NSW 2576
T: 02 4861 2199
F: 02 4861 2899
E: books@antiquariat.com.au
www.antiquariat.com.au

Antique General Store
Cnr Powderworks & Warraba Roads
North Narrabeen NSW 2101
T: 02 9913 7636
M: 0410 531 108

Antiques & Collectables - Hamilton
60 Beaumont Street
Hamilton NSW 2303
T: 02 4969 3003

**Antiques and Collectables -
Port Macquarie**
39 Lake Innes Drive
Wauchope NSW 2446
T: 02 6585 1017
M: 0417 237 410

Antiques At Birkenhead
Shop 27 Birkenhead Point
Shopping Centre, Roseby Street
Birkenhead Point
Drummoyne NSW 2047
T: 02 9719 1917
F: 02 9719 1930

Antiques Down Under
234 Pacific Highway North
Coffs Harbour NSW 2450
T: 02 6652 5492
F: 02 6652 3462

Antiques On Consignment
117 Old Hume Hwy
Braemar NSW 2575
T: 02 4872 2844
F: 02 4872 3592
M: 0416 251 946
lydie@antiquesonconsignment.com.au
www.antiquesonconsignment.com.au

Austiques Antiques & Collectables
The Antique Department Store
62 Parramatta Rd
Glebe NSW 2037
T: 02 9692 8611
M: 0412 245 715
E: julie@austiques.com.au
www.austiques.com.au

Avoca Beach Antiques
173-175 Avoca Drive
Avoca Beach NSW 2251
T: 02 4382 1149
F: 02 4382 1149

Barry McKay
By Appointment
T: 02 9522 9239

Bill Hayes Antiques
1 Wallace Street
Wauchope NSW 2446
T: 02 6585 2674
F: 02 6585 2674
M: 0427 661 176
E: oldstuff@dodo.com.au

Blackheath Antiques & Jewellery
Victory Theatre Antiques
17 Glovetts Leap Road
Blackheath NSW 2785
T: 02 4787 6126

Blake & Angel
16 Burns Bay Road
Lane Cove NSW 2066
T: 02 9420 8261
F: 02 9428 2248
E: redhillantiques@bigpond.com.au
www.blakandangel.com.au

Bob & Dot's Antiques & Old Wares
394 George Street
Windsor NSW 2756
T: 02 4577 4055

Bowhows
PO Box 7332
Bondi Beach NSW 2026
M: 0433 556 440

Brae-mar Antiques
Shop 50
Southern Antique Centre
243-245 Princess Highway
Kogarah NSW 2217
T: 02 4285 2417
M: 0408 610 112

Buttons Buttons Buttons
Shop 25 Nurse's Walk
The Rocks NSW 2000
T: 02 9252 0833

Centenary Antique Centre
29 Centenary Road
Newcastle NSW 2300
T: 02 4389 1922

Chilton's Antiques & Jewellery
579 The Kingsway
Miranda NSW 2228
T: 02 9524 0360
F: 02 9525 6625
M: 0416 082 278
E: chiltonsmiranda@bigpond.com.au

Coliseum Antiques Centre
118 Maitland Road
Mayfield NSW 2304
T: 02 4967 2088
F: 02 4967 2428
E: coliseum@iinet.net.au

Collector's Cottage Antiques
Shop 7 Centenary Antique Centre
29 Centenary Road
Newcastle NSW 2300
T: 02 4389 1922

Copperfield Antiques - NSW
Shop 24
Gordon Village Arcade
767 Pacific Hwy
Gordon NSW 2072
T: 02 9418 4833
F: 02 9418 4833

Curio Retro
By Appointment
T: 02 9517 3877
www.curioretro.com

Dannykay Antiques
2/26 Bent Street
St Marys NSW 2760
T: 02 9673 6536
F: 02 9864 1039

David Barsby Antiques
By Appointment
T: 02 9460 8026
F: 02 9460 8024
E: david@barsbyantiques.com.au
www.barsbyantiques.com.au

Doug Up On Bourke
901 Bourke Street
Waterloo NSW 2017
T: 02 9690 0962
F: 02 9690 0962
M: 0425 237 391

East West Collectables
Shop 85 Sydney Antique Centre
531 South Dowling Street
Surry Hills NSW 2010
T: 02 9361 3244

Eliza Jane Antiques
34c Taylor Street
Annandale NSW 2038
T: 02 9518 6168
M: 0416 167 151

Elizabeth Antiques
369 Penshurst Street
(cnr Eden Street)
Chatswood NSW 2067
T: 02 9417 6811
F: 02 9417 6811
E: eliant@optusnet.com.au

Four Winds Gallery
28 Cross Street
Double Bay NSW 2028
T: 02 9328 7951
F: 02 9327 6431
E: fourwindsgallery@telstra.com
www.fourwindsgallery.com.au

Galeria del Centro
78 Pudman Street
Boorowa NSW 2586
T: 02 6385 1109
E: glcent@yol.net.au

Gallery Narcisse
Shop 3, Sydney Antique Centre
531 South Dowling Street
Surry Hills NSW 2010
T: 02 9361 5200
M: 0419 220 056
E: narcisse@fl.net.au

Garden Street Bazaar
62 Garden Street
North Narrabeen NSW 2101
T: 02 9970 8855
M: 0414 783 348
E: gary@frontiertech.com.au

Garry Auton Antiques
The Antique Department Store
62 Parramatta Road
Glebe NSW 2073
T: 02 9692 9577

Gaslight Antiques
106 Queen Street
Woollahra NSW 2025
T: 02 9363 2423
F: 02 9327 8357
M: 0419 332 525

Glass Stopper
The Sydney Antique Centre
531 South Dowling St
Surry Hills NSW 2010
T: 02 9150 3305
F: 02 9150 0666
M: 0407 922 291
E: glassstopper@bigpond.com.au

Green Gables Collectables
Shop 3/124 Station Street
Blackheath NSW 2785
T: 02 9997 2879

Gumnut Antiques & Old Wares
296 The Entrance Road
Long Jetty NSW 2261
T: 02 4334 4444
F: 02 4334 4444
M: 0428 257 725
E: gumnut@tac.com.au

Habitat Antiques
101 Newcastle Rd
(New England Hwy)
East Maitland NSW 2323
T: 02 4934 3434
M: 0401 311 323

Heartland Antiques & Art
321 High Street
Maitland NSW 2320
T: 02 4933 9923
M: 0414 012 608

Home Again
121 Midson Road
Epping NSW 2121
T: 02 9876 3322
www.homeagain.com.au

Hunters & Collectors Antiques
681 Military Road
Mosman NSW 2088
T: 02 9968 3099
M: 0414 449 366
E: hacantiques@optusnet.com.au
www.huntersandcollectorsantiques
.com

Isadora's Antiques
Shop2, 53a Manning Street
Taree NSW 2430
T: 02 6551 8333
M: 0416 078 737
E: isadorasantiques@bigpond.com.au

Janet Smith
Newcastle Antique Centre
144 Parry Street
Newcastle West NSW 2302
T: 02 4961 6484
E: ajandaj@hunterlink.net.au

Jennifer Wren Antiques
By Appointment
M: 0412 153 812
E: jenniferwrenantiques@hotmail.com

John Pettit Rare Banknotes
Level 57 MLC Centre
19 Martin Place, Sydney NSW 2000
T: 02 9235 0888   F: 02 9235 0588
M: 0414 426 537
E: jpettit@accsoft.com.au
www.johnpettit.com

Kollectik Pty Ltd
152 Falcon Street
Crows Nest NSW 2065
T: 02 9954 5345
M: 0402 577 272
E: kollectik@iinet.net.au

Marge's Antiques & Collectables
Philip Cross Antiques
548 Old Northern Road
Dural NSW 2158
M: 0411 881 714

Margo Richards Antiques
Shop 27 Nurses Walk
The Rocks NSW 2000
T: 02 9252 2855

Marian's Collection
Shop 1 Sydney Antique Centre
531 South Dowling Street
Surry Hills NSW 2010
T: 02 9368 7822
M: 0418 287 216

McLeods Antiques
378 South Dowling Street
Paddington NSW 2021
T: 02 9361 0602

Michael A Greene Antiques
108 Queen Street
Woollahra NSW 2025
T: 02 9328 1712   F: 02 9327 5166
M: 0400 804 978
E: greeneantiques@bigpond.com
www.michaelgreene.com.au

Mittagong Antiques Centre
85-87 Main Street
Mittagong NSW 2575
T: 02 4872 3198
F: 02 4872 3216
E: mittagongantiques@bigpond.com

Mooney Collectables
PO Box 163
Port Macquarie NSW 2444
T: 02 6584 0249
M: 0407 945 951

Moor-Cliff
Sydney Antique Centre
531 South Dowling Street
Surry Hills NSW 2010
T: 02 9451 1619
F: 02 9452 2034
E: moorcliff@bigpond.com.au

Munro's Mill Antique Centre
175 Peel Street
Tamworth NSW 2340
T: 02 6766 6767

Myriad Art
Shop 44 Antiques & Collectables -
Hamilton NSW
60 Beaumont Street
Hamilton NSW 2303
T: 02 4969 3003

Newcastle Antique Centre
144 Parrt Street
Newcastle West NSW 2302
T: 02 4961 6484

Nicki's Collection
By Appointment
T: 02 9319 0181
M: 0403 551 360

Northumberland Antiques & Restorations
271 (Lot 88) Scenic Highway
Terrigal NSW 2260
T: 02 4384 6464
F: 02 4384 6464
M: 0417 232 893
E: info@ccantiques.com.au
www.ccantiques.com.au

Obsidian Antiques
The Antique Department Store
62 Parramatta Road
Glebe NSW 2037
T: 02 9692 8611

Old Bank Antiques
257 Dowling Street
Dungog NSW 2420
T: 02 4992 3268

Old Bank Corner Collectables
117 Albury Street (Hume Highway),
Holbrook NSW 2644
T: 02 6036 2560
F: 02 6036 2560
M: 0429 190 848
E: obcc@bigpond.net.au

Old King Cole Antiques
321 Concord Road
Concord West NSW 2138
T: 02 9736 2324
M: 0414 229 755

Old Technology
Shop 29, Centenary Antique Centre
29 Centenary Road
Newcastle NSW 2300
F: 02 9638 3132
M: 0427 499 150
E: otaustralia@netscape.net

Old World Antiques (NSW)
57 Evan Street
Sans Souci NSW 2219
T: 02 9529 7782

P. & N. Johnson
Shop 75
Southern Antique Centre
245 Princess Highway
Kogarah NSW 2212
T: 02 4625 7383

Past Connections Antiques & Decorative Arts
530 Military Road
Mosman NSW 2088
T: 02 996 02811
F: 02 9960 3141
M: 0412 404 308
E: pastconn@bigpond.net.au

Pastimes Antiques
212 Parramatta Road
Camperdown NSW 2050
T: 02 9550 5554
M: 0408 210 905
E: barbil@ozemail.com.au
www.antique-art.com.au

Patinations
Shop 13
Centenary Antique Centre
29 Centenary Road
Newcastle NSW 2300
T: 02 4926 4547

Philip Cross Antiques
548 Old Northern Road
Dural NSW 2158
T: 02 9651 4138
M: 0411 881 714
E: pcrossantiques@optusnet.com.au

Photantiques
32 Glenquarry Crescent
Bowral NSW 2576
T: 02 4861 5356
F: 02 4872 3216
M: 0419 614 711
E: photantiques@bigpond.com

Poplar Antiques
By Appointment
M: 0402 549 772

Quaint Collectables
PO Box 503
Moss Vale NSW 2577
T: 02 4868 1338
F: 02 4869 1438
M: 0403 391 326
E: ddp@acenet.com.au

R. Johansson
By Appointment
M: 0438 001 031
E: mson@bigpond.net.au

Reflections
Shop 79, Sydney Antique Centre
531 South Dowling Street
Surry Hills NSW 2010
T: 02 9360 6628
M: 0418 827 779

River Emporium
81 River Street
Woodburn NSW 2472
T: 02 6682 2255
M: 0412 394 315
E: riveremporium@optusnet.com.au

Rosebud Antiques
By Appointment
T: 02 9223 2222
M: 0403 075 793
marie@jackmanconsulting.com

Ross Agnew
By Appointment
M: 0438 641 426

Round Corner Antiques & Gifts
Shop 8/22 Kenthurst Road
Round Corner Dural NSW 2158
T: 02 9651 2870
F: 02 9651 2870
M: 0401 695 975

Seguin's Antiques & Café
Church Hall
120 Johnston Street
Annandale NSW 2038
T: 02 9552 3996
F: 02 9552 3994
M: 0410 647 546
E: seguins@bigpond.net.au

Settlers Store
131 Mortimer Street
Mudgee NSW 2850
T: 02 6372 3612
F: 02 6372 3513
M: 0412 672 913
E: antiques@settlersstore.com.au
www.settlersstore.com.au

Shaws Antiques
4 Boxers Creek Road
Goulburn NSW 2580
T: 02 4829 8100
F: 02 4829 8100
E: antiques@goulburn.net.au

Shipping Office
Shop 11, Coliseum Antiques Centre
118 Maitland Road
Mayfield NSW 2304
T: 02 4967 2088
M: 0411 444 988
E: coliseum@iinet.net.au

Southern Antique Centre
245 Princes Highway
Kogarah NSW 2217
T: 02 9553 7843
F: 02 9553 7845
M: 0410 436 944
E: southernantiques@bigpond.com
www.southernantiques.net.au

Sport Memorabilia
Syndey Antique Centre
531 South Dowling Street
Surry Hills NSW 2010
T: 02 9361 3244   F: 02 9332 2691
M: 0414 977 519

Sue's Book Nook
Southern Antique Centre
243-245 Princess Highway
Kogarah NSW 2217
T: 02 9553 7843

Sydney Antique Centre
531 South Dowling Street
Surry Hills NSW 2010
T: 02 9361 3244
F: 02 9332 2691
www.sydantcent.com.au

The Antique Department Store
62 Parramatta Road
Glebe NSW 2307
T: 02 9692 8611

The Exchange Galleries
327 High Street
Maitland NSW 2320
T: 02 4934 3934
F: 02 4930 6200
M: 0412 780 261

The Glass Stopper
59 The Kingsway
Kingsgrove NSW 2208
T: 02 9150 8305
F: 02 9150 0666
M: 0407 922 291

The Nostalgia Factory
2/162 Moss Vale Road
Kangaroo Valley NSW 2577
T: 02 4465 1022
M: 0413 084 605
nostalgiafactory@bigpond.com

The Rug Shop
11 Byron Street
Bangalow NSW 2479
T: 02 6687 2424
E: rugs@bangalow.com
www.orientalcarpets.com.au

Things 4 U
547 Burke Street
Surry Hills NSW
T: 02 9331 4104

Thompsons Country Collectables
11 New Street
(Rear 265 George St)
Windsor NSW 2756
T: 02 4577 2381
E: dandyprat@hotmail.com

Timeworn Old Wares & Collectables
Centenary Antique Centre
29 Centenary Road
Newcastle NSW 2300
T: 02 4926 4547

Towers Antiques & Collectables
539 King Street
South Newtown NSW 2042
T: 02 9519 6574
F: 02 9799 4691
M: 0419 201 455
towersantiques@optusnet.com.au
www.towersantiques.com.au

Town & Country Antiques
200 Great Western Highway
Hazelbrook NSW 2779
T: 02 4758 6686
F: 02 4758 6686
M: 0418 619 850
E: pegleg80@hotmail.com

Trains Planes & Automobiles
86 Great Western Highway
Mount Victoria NSW 2786
T: 02 4787 1590
F: 02 4787 1117
M: 0410 773 378
E: info@antiquetoys.com.au
www.antiquetoys.com.au

Treats & Treasures
114 Cowabbie Street
Coolamon NSW 2701
T: 02 6927 3422
M: 0428 694 448
grahame@treatsandtreasures.com.au
www.treatsandtreasures.com.au

True Blue Antiques
Shop 3
Southern Antique Centre
245 Princes Hwy
Kogarah NSW 2217
T: 02 4228 7059

Twice Around
Rear 107 Glenroi Avenue
Orange NSW 2800
T: 02 6362 0322
F: 02 9361 3570
M: 0416 277 490
E: info@twicearound.com.au
www.twicearound.com.au

Vampt
268 Cleveland Street
Surry Hills NSW 2010
T: 02 9699 1089
F: 02 9699 1856
M: 0414 806 549
E: info@vamptretrondeco.com
www.vamptretrondeco.com

Victory Theatre Antiques
17 Glovetts Leap Road
Blackheath NSW 2785
T: 02 4787 6002
F: 02 4787 6003
E: victory@pnc.com.au
www.victorytheatre.com.au

Wenlen Antiques
The Antique Department Store
62 Parramatta Road
Glebe NSW 2037
T: 02 9692 8611
M: 0413 021 270
E: wenlen@optusnet.com.au

Whimsical Notions
293 Great Western Highway
Warrimoo NSW 2774
T: 02 4753 7700
F: 02 4753 7700
M: 0411 332 537
E: whimsical1@bigpond.com.au
www.local.com.au/whimsical

Windsor Bridge Antiques
17 Bridge Street
Windsor NSW 2756
T: 02 4587 7788
F: 02 4587 7759

Windsor Cottage Antiques &
Collectables
267 George Street
Windsor NSW 2756
T: 02 4577 4499
windsorcottage@unwired.com.au

Woollahra Decorative Arts Gallery
228 Oxford Street
Bondi Junction NSW 2022
T: 02 9389 8388   F: 02 9389 8399
M: 0414 338 363
E: amathest@ihug.com.au
www.nouveaudeco.com.au

Yesterday's Gems
Shop 1a, Jack Simmons Arcade
13 Vernon Street
Coffs Harbour City Centre NSW 2450
T: 02 6652 5001
www.bmnc.com.au/yesterdaysgems

QLD

20th Century Antiques &
Collectables Market
31-33 McLean Street
Coolangatta QLD 4225
T: 07 5536 8848

Adornments
141 Latrobe Tce
Paddington QLD 4064
T: 07 3369 2033

Angel Cottage
127 Long Road (Gallery Walk)
Eagle Heights
Tamborine Mountain QLD 4271
T: 07 5545 0322   F: 07 5545 0322
M: 0414 732 000
E: angelajbowen@bigpond.com

Antipodes Antiques
Shop 9 Paddington Antique Cnt
167 Latrobe Terrace
Paddington QLD 4064
T: 07 3369 1863
F: 07 3368 1502
M: 0412 451 369
antipodesa@optushome.com.au

Bank House Antiques
25 Cressbrook Street
Toogoolawah QLD 4313
T: 07 4698 2179 A/H
M: 0408 989 032

Baxter's Antiques
2 Lombank Street
Archerfield QLD 4108
T: 07 3216 6146   M: 0418 192 188
E: baxtersantiques@ecn.net.au

Bob Butler's Sentimental Journey
91 Main Street
Lowood QLD 4311
T: 07 5426 3399
F: 07 4638 2203

Bower Bird Art & Antiques
PO Box 230
Mt Molloy QLD 4871
T: 07 4094 2006

Brisbane Antiques Pty Ltd
10 Albion Road
Albion QLD 4010
T: 07 3262 1444
F: 07 3262 1994
M: 0412 012 440
graham@brisbaneantiques.com.au
www.brisbaneantiques.com.au

Brisbane Vintage Watches
Brisbane Arcade, Shop 20-21
Gallery Level, 160 Queen Street
Brisbane QLD 4000
T: 07 3210 6722
F: 07 3210 6766
E: wachtel@dcc.net.au
www.brisbanevintagewatches.com

Chambers & Crosthwaite Antiques
26 Nudgee Rd
Hamilton QLD 4007
T: 07 3268 6778

Chelsea Antiques & Decorative Art
Centre P/L
20 Hudson Road
Albion QLD 4010
T: 07 3862 1768
F: 07 3862 1748
M: 0417 630 706

Collectable Creations
139 Herries Street
Toowoomba QLD 4350
T: 07 4632 0546

Coming of Age Antiques
8506 Warrego Highway
Withcott QLD 4352
T: 07 4630 3227
F: 0414 521 543

Discovery Corner
812 Sandgate Road
Clayfield QLD 4011
T: 07 3862 2155
F: 07 3862 1344
M: 0402 339 643

Eilisha's Shoppe
109 James Street
New Farm QLD 4005
T: 07 3358 1448

H.O.W Gifts & Collectables
95 The Esplanade
Mooloolaba QLD 4557
T: 07 5478 3200
F: 07 5478 3233
M: 0418 792 480
iris@houseofwindsor.com.au

Harrington Antiques
Shop 6/ 20 Hudson Road
Albion QLD 4010
T: 1800 005 650
M: 0414 464 704
mark@harringtonantiques.com
www.harringtonantiques.com

Helen's on Discovery Antiques
& Decor
Shop 11b, 112 Discovery Drive
Helensvale QLD 4212
T: 07 5529 7311

Helen's On The Bay
Shop 8, 128 Lae Drive
(Cnr Oxley Drive & Lae Drive)
Runaway Bay QLD 4212
T: 07 5529 1582
F: 07 5529 1523
M: 0416 085 287
E: helensridge@iprimus.com.au

Hollyhock Antiques
166 Holberton Street
Toowoomba QLD 4350
T: 07 4633 3676

John Summerville Military Antiques
Shop 40 Paddington
Antique Centre
167 Latrobe Tce
Paddington QLD 4064
T: 07 3284 0225
M: 0416 171 249

Laidley Old Wares
149 Patrick St
Laidley QLD 4341
T: 07 5465 1214
laidleyoldwares@bigpond.com

Lancaster's Toowoomba
Antique Centre
3 Railway St
Toowoomba QLD 4350
T: 07 4632 1830
M: 0403 372 054

Northside Secondhand Furniture
76 Loudon Street
Sandgate QLD 4017
T: 07 3269 4490
M: 0403 339 618
E: dmwheildon@aol.com

Olsens Antiques
Behind the National Bank,
Bundaberg CBD QLD 4670
T: 07 4152 5933
F: 07 4152 5933
M: 0407 556 301
E: pikekathy@hotmail.com

Paddington Antique Centre
167 Latrobe Terrace
Paddington QLD 4064
T: 07 3369 8088
F: 07 3368 2171
E: info@pac.antiques.net.au
www.pac.antiques.net.au

Range Antiques
1 Burke Street, Toowoomba QLD 4350
T: 07 4632 6629
M: 0412 644 899
E: rangeantiques@hotmail.com

Rockaway Records
249 Waterworks Road
Ashgrove QLD 4060
T: 07 3366 9555
F: 07 3366 9777
E: sales@rockaway.com.au
www.rockaway.com.au

Roger Hose Antiques
37 Logan Road
Woolloongabba QLD 4102
T: 07 3391 0440
F: 07 3391 3566
M: 0418 871 300
E: antiques@gabbavillage.com
www.gabbavillage.com/antiques

Roundabout Antiques
Old Bank Building at the Roundabout
Bunya Highway
Wondai QLD 4606
T: 07 4169 0111   F: 07 4169 0111
M: 0417 714 105
E: sales@roundaboutantiques.com.au
www.roundaboutantiques.com.au

Salt's Antiques
New England Highway
Crows Nest QLD 4355
T: 07 4698 1266
F: 07 4698 1738
M: 0438 469 812

Sherwood Bazaar
526 Oxley Road
Sherwood QLD 4075
T: 07 3379 7548
F: 07 3379 9807
M: 0418 700 473
E: sbazaar@ozemail.com.au
www.sherwoodbazaar.com

Southside Antiques Centre
484 Ipswich Road
Annerley QLD 4103
T: 07 3892 1299
E: ssac@aol.com

The Goods
(House of Fine Jewellery)
Shop 41-42 Gallery Level
Brisbane Arcade
Queen Street Mall
Brisbane QLD 4000
T: 07 3310 2770
F: 07 3210 2771
M: 0413 834 467
www.thegoods.net.au

The New Farm Antique Centre
85 Commercial Road
Newstead QLD 4006
T: 07 3852 2352
F: 07 3252 9295
M: 0419 786 967
E: newfarmantiques@optusnet.com.au

The Silky Oak Shop
31 Logan Road
Woolloongabba QLD 4102
T: 07 3891 3911
F: 07 3891 3511
M: 0413 657 999
E: lendit@bigpond.net.au
www.thesilkyoakshop.com

The Time Machine
101 Currie St
Nambour QLD 4560
T: 07 5441 2647

Tiffany Dodd Antique &
20th Century Furniture
Shop 31
Paddington Antique Centre
167 La Trobe Terrace
Paddington QLD
T: 07 3876 8117
M: 0414 693 738
www.tiffanydodd.com.au

Titles & Treasures
2/272 Lillian Avenue
Salisbury QLD 4107
T: 07 3216 6995
M: 0407 585 590
E: reilly.john@bigpond.com.au

Toowoomba Antiques Gallery
100 Margaret Street
Toowoomba QLD 4350
T: 07 4639 4989
F: 07 4638 5355
M: 0419 653 434
E: toowoomba.antiques@bigpond.com

Turn O' The Century
377 Oxley Road
Sherwood QLD 4075
T: 07 3379 7311   F: 07 3379 1660
M: 0419 706 875
E: totc@bigpond.net.au

Yande Meannjin Antiques
Shop 13
Paddington Antique Centre
167 Latrobe Terrace
Paddington QLD 4064
T: 07 3886 6037   F: 07 3886 6037
M: 0419 704 714
E: yande@iinet.net.au

SA

All In Good Time Antiques
12a High Street
Strathalbyn SA 5255
T: 08 8536 4449   F: 08 8536 4449
M: 0408 832 757
E: aigt@bigpond.net.au

At The Toss of A Coin
2/219 Unley Road, Malvern SA 5061
T: 08 8373 0170

Cool & Collected
161 Magill Road
Stepney SA 5069
T: 08 8362 5196

Gaslight Collectables and Old Books
20 Market Street
Burra SA 5417
T: 08 8892 3004   F: 08 8892 3003
M: 0407 555 876
E: deeton@bigpond.com

Glenelg Antique Centre
6 Sussex Street
Glenelg SA 5045
T: 08 8376 0450

Joanne Petit de Mange
Cabinet 93
Pedlars Antique Market
205 Magill Road, Maylands SA 5034
T: 08 8297 0076
E: artsplus@senet.com.au

Kings Park Antiques & Collectables
325a Goodwood Road
Kings Park SA 5034
T: 08 8172 0566
F: 08 8276 2539

Mac's Collectables
By Appointment
T: 08 8263 7779
M: 0402 356 010
E: mac151@internode.on.net

Michael Krassovsky
By Appointment
T: 08 9402 0153

Mid Century Modern
129 Magill Road
Stepney SA 5069
T: 08 8363 3413
F: 08 8362 1027
E: pjs@bigpond.net.au
www.midcenturymodern.net.au

Old World Antiques
133 Magill Road
Stepney SA 5069
T: 08 8362 0166
F: 08 8272 9548
E: eamonp@tpg.com.au

Pedlars Antique Market
205 Magill Road
Maylands SA 5069
T: 08 8363 0087
F: 08 8363 0087
E: pedlars@bigpond.net.au

Pendulum Antiques
Main Road
Inglewood SA 5133
T: 08 8380 5414
F: 08 8380 5223
M: 0417 879 868
E: pendulums@internode.com.net

Philicia Antiques & Collectables
317 Goodwood Road
Kings Park SA 5034
T: 08 8357 8177
F: 08 8357 8177
M: 0409 695 234
E: philicia@tpg.com.au
www.philicia.tpg.com.au/home.html

Rare Old Times Antiques &
Collectables
453 Brighton Road
Brighton SA 5048
T: 08 8358 4288
F: 08 8358 4288
E: rareoldtimes@ihug.com.au

Rock N Rustic
187 Magill Road
Maylands SA 5034
T: 08 8363 3446
M: 0408 810 840

Squatters Antiques & Restorations
94 Thomas Street
Murray Bridge SA 5253
T: 08 8532 5087
M: 0418 800 031
E: michelegros@bigpond.com
www.squattersantiques.com

The Toy Collector
Ingle Farm Shopping Centre
Cnr Wakleys & Montague Road
Ingle Farm SA 5098
T: 08 8395 4567
F: 08 8395 4567
M: 0411 700 777
toys@thetoycollector.com.au
www.thetoycollector.com.au

Vintage Charm
26 High Street
Strathalbyn SA 5255
T: 08 8536 4999
M: 0407 870 081

White Park Antiques
3/333 Unley Road
Malvern SA 5061
T: 08 8172 0544
F: 08 8172 0544
M: 0404 495 066
E: whitepark@bigblue.net.au

Woodside Bazaar
43 Main Street
Woodside SA 5244
T: 08 8389 7772
M: 0401 854 753
E: acaldhouse@adam.com.au

TAS

Ancanthe
102 Elizabeth Street
Hobart TAS 7000
T: 03 6236 9026

Antiques On Macquarie
407 Macquarie Street
South Hobart TAS 7004
T: 03 6224 1373
M: 0418 540 126

Archer St Antiques & Gallery
36 Marlborough Street
Longford TAS 7301
T: 03 6391 1011

Archers Antiques
Sorell Antiques Centre
15 Somerville Street
Sorell TAS 7172
T: 03 6265 2246   F: 03 6265 2246
M: 0417 084 685
E: archersantiques@hotmail.com

Eclectica
1567 Channel Highway
Margate TAS 7054
T: 03 6267 2545
F: 03 6267 2545
M: 0417 361 547

J. B. Hawkins Antiques
'Bentley' Mole Creek Road
Chudleigh TAS 7304
T: 03 6363 6131
F: 03 6367 6262
M: 0419 985 965
E: jhawkins@acenet.com.au
jbhawkinsantiques.com

Kookaburra Antiques
113 Hampden Road
Battery Point TAS 7004
T: 03 6223 1019

Leven Antiques
23 King Edward Street
Ulverstone TAS 7315
T: 03 6425 5226
F: 03 6425 7316
M: 0419 509 730
E: cbroadfi@iinet.net.au
www.levenantiques.com

Louisa's Antiques
'The Manse', 1802 Midland Highway
Bagdad TAS 7030
T: 03 6268 6183
M: 0400 565 467

Pieces
Shop 3 The Forum Complex
7 Pendrigh Place
St Helens TAS 7216
T: 03 6376 2000
F: 03 6376 2000

Richmond Antiques
2 Edwards Street
Richmond TAS 7025
T: 03 6260 2601
F: 03 6260 2601
M: 0428 602 601
E: antiquedownunder@aol.com

Secondhand Furniture Mart
160 Cimitiere Street
Launceston TAS 7250
T: 03 6331 5553
F: 03 6331 5553
M: 0419 896 270
E: thay2069@bigpond.net.au

Sorrell Antiques Centre
15 Somerville Street
Sorrell TAS 7172
T: 03 6265 2246
F: 03 6265 2246

The Evandale Tinker
10b Russell Street
Evandale TAS 7212
T: 03 6391 8544
M: 0419 331 821
E: evandale_tinker@yahoo.com.au

The Old General Store - Kempton
86 Main Street
Kempton TAS 7030
T: 03 6259 1296
F: 03 6259 1296
E: sueandtony@southcom.com.au
www.antiqueart/dealer.cfm?thisdealer=Kempton

VIC

44 Brooke Street
44 Brooke Street
Smythesdale VIC 3351
T: 03 5342 8186

Abra Card Abra Roycroft
680 High Street
East Kew VIC 3102
T: 03 9859 4215
F: 03 9589 4215

Affordable Collectables & Antiques
355a Wellington Street
Clifton Hill VIC 3068
T: 03 9481 3342

Ainsley Antiques
2120 Ballan Road
Anakie VIC 3221
T: 03 5284 1371
E: ainsleyball@hotmail.com

Alan Syber's Antiques Antiquarian
Shop 18 Tyabb Packing House
18a Mornington-Tyabb Road
Tyabb VIC 3913
T: 03 5977 3411
M: 0418 552 553
E: syber@bigpond.net.au

Alltime Antiques & Bairnsdale Clocks
704 Princes Highway
Bairnsdale VIC 3875
T: 03 5152 6962
F: 03 5153 0756
info@bairnsdaleclocks.com.au
www.bairnsdaleclocks.com.au

Andrew Price Antiques
331 Koornang Road
Carnegie VIC 3163
T: 03 9578 4117

Angel's Antiques
206a Buckley Street
Essendon VIC 3040
T: 03 9331 0639
M: 0419 307 150
E: earljulie43@hotmail.com

Antique Centre of Stonnington
941-951 High Street
Armadale VIC 3143
T: 03 9822 3700
F: 03 9822 3711
www.antiquescentreonline.com

Antique Effects
108-110 Urquhart Street
Ballarat VIC 3350
T: 03 5331 3119
F: 03 5331 2063
M: 0418 508 011
E: info@antiqueeffects.com.au
www.antiqueeffects.com.au

Antique Prints and Maps
at Full Circle
59 Church Street
Hawthorn VIC 3122
T: 03 9819 4042
F: 03 9819 6460
M: 0409 517 113
E: paul@fullcircle.com.au
www.fullcircle.com.au

Antique Toy World
15 Cookson Street
Camberwell VIC 3124
T: 03 9882 9997
M: 0419 513 290

Antiques & Collectables Centre - Ballarat
9 Humffray Street North
Ballarat VIC 3350
T: 03 5331 7996
F: 03 5331 7996

Antiques, Goods & Chattels
22 Main Road
Ballarat VIC 3350
T: 03 5334 3799
M: 0428 521 714

Arleston Antiques
64 Cook Street
Flinders VIC 3929
T: 03 5989 0602
F: 03 5989 0345
M: 0427 243 300
E: humevale@satlink.com.au

Armadale Antique Centre
1147 High Street
Armadale VIC 3143
T: 03 9822 7788
F: 03 9822 4499
M: 0412 732 590

Australian & New Zealand
Arms Co Pty. Ltd.
424b Station Street
Box Hill VIC 3128
T: 03 9890 1912
F: 03 9897 1100
E: cobbsamurai@ozemail.com.au
www.cobbsamurai.com

b bold - 20th Century Furniture &
Effects
187 Elgin Street
Carlton VIC 3053
T: 03 9349 1166
www.antique-art.com.au/b-bold.htm

B. C. Galleries
1069 High Street
Armadale VIC 3143
T: 03 9804 3785
F: 03 9804 3353
E: B.C.Galleries@bigpond.com.au
www.bcgalleries.com.au

Baimbridge Antiques
64 Thompson Street
Hamilton VIC 3300
T: 03 5572 2516
F: 03 5571 2001
M: 0409 525 329
E: ruth@baimbridgeantiques.com.au
www.baimbridgeantiques.com.au

Bayside Antiques Centre
570 Hampton Street
Hampton VIC 3188
T: 03 9598 0913

Bendigo Antique Centre
57-61 High St
Bendigo VIC 3550
T: 03 5443 8570

Born Frugal
420 Church Street
Richmond VIC 3121
T: 03 9428 5889
M: 0409 979 865

Burly Babs Collectables /
Retro Relics
53 Humffray Street North
Ballarat VIC 3350
T: 03 5331 6236
M: 0408 329 131

C. V. Jones Antiques & Art Gallery
14 Armstrong Street North
Ballarat VIC 3350
T: 03 5331 1472
F: 03 5331 1472
M: 0417 506 981
E: cvjones@netconnect.com.au
www.cvjones.com.au

Calmar Trading
By Appointment
T: 03 9435 5187
M: 0412 336 086
E: pruscuklic@labyrinth.net.au

Camberwell Antique Centre
25-29 Cookson Street
Camberwell VIC 3124
T: 03 9882 2028
F: 03 9882 2028
M: 0418 586 764

Cardtastic Collectables
449 North Road
Ormond VIC 3204
T: 03 9578 5363
E: cardtastic@cardtastic.com.au
www.cardtastic.com.au

Carnegie Collectables
742 North Road, Ormond VIC 3204
T: 03 9597 9147
E: sportmem@optusnet.com.au

Cathcart's Antiques
By Appointment
T: 03 9397 6410
F: 03 9497 6410
E: barrie@cathcartsantiques.com.au
www.cathcartsantiques.com.au

Cat's Cradle Comics
36 Sydney Road
Coburg VIC 3058
T: 03 9386 8885
M: 0425 776 158

Cedar Lodge Antiques
169-175 West Fyans St, Newtown
Geelong VIC 3220
T: 03 5221 3348
F: 03 5221 3348
M: 0418 520 024
E: cedarl@pipeline.com.au
www.pipeline.com.au/users/cedarl

Chapel Street Bazaar
217-233 Chapel Street
Prahran VIC 3181
T: 03 9529 1727
F: 03 9521 3174

Chris' Antiques & Collectables
43 Maroondah Hwy
Healesville VIC 3777
T: 03 5962 6055

Circa Vintage Clothing
Shop 1/102 Gertrude Street
Fitzroy VIC 3065
T: 03 9419 8899
E: enquiries@circa-vintage.com
www.circa-vintage.com

Collectique
By Appointment
T: 03 9592 6256

Colman Antique Clocks
1421 Malvern Road
Malvern VIC 3144
T: 03 9824 8244
F: 03 9824 4230
M: 0402 084 074
E: michaelcolman@optusnet.com.au
www.colmanantiqueclocks.biz

Comics R Us
Level 1/220 Bourke Street
Melbourne VIC 3000
T: 03 9663 9666
E: comicsrus@bigpond.com

Costiff Antiques
By Appointment
T: 03 9751 1574
M: 0407 351 117
E: costiff@ozonline.com.au

Cote Provence
444 Mt Alexander Road
Ascot Vale VIC 3032
T: 03 9370 7444
F: 03 9374 3371
M: 0409 420 847
E: jbarbey@vtown.com.au
www.antique-art.com.au

Days of Olde Antiques &
Collectables
733 Sturt Street
Ballarat VIC 3350
T: 03 5332 7735
M: 0418 352 183

De Bretts Antiques
By Appointment
T: 03 9370 1855

De Mille
7 Crossley Street
Melbourne VIC 3000
T: 03 9663 9666
F: 03 9633 9666
M: 0414 518 123

Debbie Pech
By Appointment
T: 03 5572 4129
M: 0419 116 988

Decades of Fashion
13 Main Road
Ballarat VIC 3350
T: 03 5332 2222
M: 0401 364 953
www.decadesoffashion.com.au

Decodence Collectables
By Appointment
T: 03 9744 6251
M: 0411 141 075

Den of Antiquities
25a Bell Street
Yarra Glen VIC 3775
T: 03 9730 2111
F: 03 9730 2111
M: 0413 454 966

Design Dilemas
Shop 5/17 Irwell Street
St Kilda VIC 3182
M: 0425 718 736

Eagle Antiques
'Tanglewood'
339 Mt Macedon Road
Mt Macedon VIC 3441
T: 03 5426 1561
F: 03 5426 2462

Fat Helen's
78 Chapel Street
Windsor VIC 3181
T: 03 9510 2244
M: 0419 541 902
E: fathelens@optusnet.com.au
www.fathelens.com

Flashback
79 High Street
Northcote VIC 3070
T: 03 9482 1899
M: 0421 345 322
E: vinfab@alphalink.com.au
www.vintagefabric.com.au

Found Objects
Shop 6-7 Irwell Street
St Kilda VIC 3182
M: 0414 855 564

French Heritage Antiques
68-69 Beach Road
Mentone VIC 3194
T: 03 9583 3422
M: 0414 266 914
E: frenchheri@froggy.com.au

Furniture Revisited
209 Sydney Road
Brunswick VIC 3056
T: 03 9387 1867

G & N Miller Antiques
By Appointment
T: 03 9578 1975
M: 0402 288 717

Galerie Montmartre
PO Box 392
Clifton Hill VIC 3068
T: 03 9486 8686
F: 03 9486 8687
M: 0439 899 811
E: posters@galeriemontmartre.com
www.galeriemontmartre.com

Gardenvale Collectables
165 Martin Street
Gardenvale VIC 3186
T: 03 9596 0211

Glenn Stevens Antiques
29 Main Road, Ballarat VIC 3350
M: 0439 311 668

Go Figure Collectables
Shop 3, 116-120 Glenferrie Road
Malvern VIC 3144
T: 03 9576 2213
M: 0416 163 018
E: jeffx@gofigurecollectables.com.au
www.gofigurecollectables.com.au

Gorgeous
85a Chapel Street
Windsor VIC 3181
M: 0416 399 403

Graham & Nancy Miller
By Appointment
T: 03 9578 1975

Granny's Market Pty Ltd
1098 High St, Armadale VIC 3143
T: 03 9509 1314
F: 03 9576 1646
M: 0408 995 867
E: rosies@bluep.com

Grant & Wendy Brookes
By Appointment

Hamilton Street Antiques
181-183 Sunshine Road
Tottenham VIC 3012
T: 03 9314 9559
F: 03 9314 9559
M: 0407 056 960
E: hamant@ozemail.com.au
www.oddspot.com.au

Hermitage Antiques - Geelong
Wintergarden
51 McKillop Street
Geelong VIC 3220
T: 03 5222 3193
F: 03 5222 2240
M: 0409 658 738
metzger@hermitageantiques.com.au
www.hermitageantiques.com.au

Hurnall's Antiques & Decorative
Arts
691 High Street
East Prahran VIC 3181
T: 03 9510 3754
F: 03 9510 3754
M: 0407 831 424
E: marvinhurnall@yahoo.com.au

Image Objex
By Appointment
T: 03 9406 6544
info@thesecondhandshop.com.au
www.thesecondhandshop.com.au

Imogene
Roy's Antiques
410 Queens Pde
Fitzroy North VIC 3068
T: 03 9569 5391
F: 03 9569 5395
M: 0412 195 964
E: imogene@imogene.com.au
www.imogene.com.au

Imperial Antiques
941 High St
Armadale VIC 3143
T: 03 9822 6942
M: 0407 381 1912

Industria
202 Gertrude Street
Fitzroy VIC 3065
T: 03 9417 1117
F: 03 5983 2749
M: 0419 842 198
E: maxwatts@optusnet.com.au

Jennifer Elizabeth Antiques
Tyabb Packing House
14 Mornington-Tyabb Road
Tyabb VIC 3913
T: 03 5977 4414
F: 03 5977 3216
www.tyabbpackinghouseantiques.c
om.au

Jeremy's Australiana
By Appointment, VIC
T: 03 5941 8884
M: 0438 197 193
E: jeremysdifferentstrokes@
  hotmail.com

Kaleidoscope Antiques
943 High Street
Armadale VIC 3143
T: 03 9824 8302
F: 03 9822 4315
M: 0418 300 482
E: antiquescentre@bigpond.com
www.antiquescentreonline.com

Kenny's Antiques
53-55 Pakington Street
Geelong West VIC 3215
T: 03 5278 6110
M: 0409 960 041

Kilbarron Antiques and Collectables
PO Box 5068 Laburnum
Blackburn VIC 3130
T: 03 9878 1321
F: 03 9878 1328
M: 0417 392 110
E: kilbarro@bigpond.net.au
www.kilbarron.com.au

Kingston Antiques
379 St Georges Road
North Fitzroy VIC 3068
T: 03 9481 1307

Le Contraste
83 Chapel Street
Windsor VIC 3181
T: 03 9529 6911
F: 03 9529 6911
M: 0439 732 006
E: contrast@bigpond.net.au

Licorice Pie Records
249A High Street
Prahran VIC 3181
T: 03 9510 4600
E: david@licoricepie.com

Lilydale Antique Centre
24 Main St
Lilydale VIC 3140
T: 03 9739 5477

Lydiard Furniture & Antiques
205 Lydiard Street North
Ballarat VIC 3350
T: 03 5332 6841
M: 0427 348 917

Malvern Antique Market
1008 High Street
Armadale VIC 3143
T: 03 9509 6337
F: 03 9572 2901
M: 0418 144 299

Margaret Sutherland Antiques
By Appointment
T: 03 5335 1973

Marrick's Furniture
36-38 Buckley Street
Footscray VIC 3011
T: 03 9687 0577
M: 0407 183 242
www.antique-art.com.au/marricks.htm\

Martin of Melbourne - Fine Jewels
529 High Street
East Prahran VIC 3181
T: 03 9533 6155
F: 03 9533 6199
E: info@martinofmelbourne.com.au
www.martinofmelbourne.com.au

Mary Titchener Antique Jewels
35 Toorak Road
South Yarra VIC 3141
T: 03 9867 4100
F: 03 9867 4100
E: marytitchener@bigpond.com

Maryborough Station Antique
Emporium
Railway Station
Maryborough VIC 3465
T: 03 5461 4683
F: 03 5460 4988
E: stantiqu@iinet.net.au
www.stationantiques.com

Melbourne Vintage Pens
Armadale Antique Centre
1147 High Street
Armadale VIC 3143
T: 03 9891 6315
F: 03 9855 9671
M: 0419 382 547
E: pford@vintagepens.com.au
www.vintagepens.com.au

Mentone Beach Antiques Centre
68 Beach Road
Mentone VIC 3194
T: 03 9583 3422
M: 0414 166 914
E: frenchheri@froggy.com.au

Miguel Meirelles Antiques
1379 Malvern Road
Malvern VIC 3144
T: 03 9822 6886
F: 03 9822 6825
M: 0419 009 890
www.meirelles.com.au

Mondo Trasho
387 Johnston Street
Abbotsford VIC 3067
T: 03 9486 9595
M: 0438 528 022
E: contact@mondotrasho.com.au
www.mondotrasho.com.au

Moorabool Antique Galleries
16-18 Ryrie Street, Geelong VIC 3220
T: 03 5229 2970
M: 0414 292 970
E: query@moorabool.com
www.moorabool.com

Mt Dandenong Antique Centre
1552 Mt Dandenong Tourist Rd
Olinda VIC 3788
T: 03 9751 1138
F: 03 9751 2037
M: 0425 730 124
E: mdac@alphalink.com.au

Newlyn Antiques
2851 Midland Highway
Newlyn VIC 3364
T: 03 5345 7458
newlynantiques@netconnect.com.au

Newport Temple Antiques
405 Melbourne Road
Newport VIC 3015
T: 03 9391 3381
www.newporttempleantiques.com

Nextonix
162-164 Gertrude Street
Fitzroy VIC 3065
T: 03 9417 1296
M: 0410 251 934

North Sunshine Bazaar
21 Northumberland Road
Sunshine VIC 3020
T: 03 9312 6211

Nostalgia Antiques
118 Maribyrnong Road
Moonee Ponds VIC 3039
T: 03 9370 1109

Old As The Hills
Tyabb Packing House
Shop 1a & 18a Tyabb Road
Tyabb VIC 3913
T: 03 9775 8241
E: trumph65@dodo.com.au

Old Grainstore Antique Market
Cnr Templeton St & Edward St
Maldon Vic VIC 3463
T: 03 5475 2902

Online Antiques
PO Box 387, Kew VIC 3101
T: 0407 321 865
M: 0417 321 865
E: dianne@inlineantiques.com.au
www.onlineantiques.com.au

Patrick Davey Antiques
1377 Malvern Road
Malvern VIC 3144
T: 03 9822 1830
F: 03 9822 1830
M: 0402 035 310
patrickdavey@optusnet.com.au
http://members.optusnet.com.au/~p
atrickdavey

Plasma
2a Cecil Place
Prahran VIC 3181
T: 03 9525 1271
F: 03 9525 1271
M: 0414 339 001
E: dean@plasmafurniture.com.au
www.plasmafurniture.com.au

Prism Original Lighting
By Appointment
T: 03 9885 8762
M: 0417 332 435
E: cturner@bigpond.net.au

Quality Records
263 Glenferrie Road
Malvern VIC 3144
T: 03 9500 9902
F: 03 9500 9902
www.qualityrecords.com.au

Rare Memorabilia Gallery
23 Cookson Street
Camberwell VIC 3124
T: 03 9882 0882
www.rareonline.net

Rathdowne Antiques
310 Rathdowne Street
Carlton North VIC 3054
T: 03 9347 1906

Regent Secondhand
692 High Street
Regent VIC 3073
T: 03 9471 1818
M: 0411 255 776

Resurrection Radio
203 High Street
Ashburton VIC 3147
T: 03 9813 8731
F: 03 9813 8145
E: resradio@ozemail.com.au
www.resurrectionradio.com.au

Retro Active
307 High Street
Northcote VIC 3070
T: 03 9489 4566
M: 0411 096 367
E: retroactive1@optusnet.com.au
www.antique-art.com.au/
gallery/dealers/retroact3

Retro Relics
53 Humffray Street
North Ballarat VIC 3350
M: 0408 329 131

Roys Antiques Pty Ltd
410 Queens Parade
Clifton Hill VIC 3068
T: 03 9489 8467
F: 03 9489 8467
E: mail@roys-antiques.com.au
www.roys-antiques.com.au

Rutherford Fine Jewellery &
Antique Silver
182 Collins St
Melbourne VIC 3000
T: 03 9650 7878
F: 03 9654 1832
M: 0412 357 975
E: info@rford,com.au
www.rford.com.au

Savers
330 Sydney Road
Brunswick VIC 3056
T: 03 9381 2393
F: 03 9381 2595

Scheherazade Antiques
PO Box 2340
Templestowe Heights VIC 3107
T: 03 9850 5623
M: 0408 583 515
E: scherant@optusnet.com.au

Seagull Antiques
By Appointment
T: 03 5254 1044
F: 03 5254 1044
M: 0402 352 489
E: robopage@yahoo.com.au

Seanic Antiques
419 Melbourne Road
Newport VIC 3015
T: 03 9391 6134
F: 03 9391 6134
M: 0418 326 455
E: seanicantiques@ozemail.com.au
www.antique-art.com.au/
seanic.htm

Serendipity - Preston
497 Plenty Road
Preston VIC 3072
T: 03 9471 1430
F: 03 9471 1430
E: serentipity.ctore@optusnet.com

Shag
130 Chapel Street
Windsor VIC 3181
T: 03 9510 8817

Shappere
64 Chapel Street
Windsor VIC 3183
T: 03 9533 2006
F: 03 9882 8548
M: 0409 237 073
E: shappere@yahoo.com.au

Sheridan Brown Antiques
142-144 Burwood Rd
Hawthorn VIC 3122
T: 03 9818 4984
F: 03 9815 1099
wendy@sheridanbrownantiques.com.au

Shirley & Noel Daly Antiques
By Appointment
T: 03 5342 4547
E: nda64907@bigpond.net.au

Step Back Antiques
103 Burwood Road
Hawthorn VIC 3122
T: 03 9815 0635
F: 03 9645 7300
M: 0418 334 475

Stumpy Gully Antiques
1546 Frankston/Flinders Road
Tyabb VIC 3913
T: 03 5977 4169

Sturt Street Antiques & Art
4 Sturt St
Ballarat VIC 3350
T: 03 5333 7408
F: 03 5333 7408
E: antiques@netconnect.com.au

Talking Piece Antiques
478 Woods Point Road
East Warburton VIC 3799
T: 03 5966 5823
E: richardk@foxall.com.au
www.talkingpieceantiques.com.au

Tarlo & Graham
60 Chapel Street
Windsor VIC 3181
T: 03 9521 2221
M: 0414 867 336
E: targra@bigpond.net.au

The Botanic Ark
Copelands Road
Warragul VIC 3820
T: 03 5623 5268

The Bottom Drawer Antique Centre
545 Tyabb Road
Moorooduc VIC 3933
T: 03 5978 8677
E: sales@ thebottomdrawer.com.au
www.thebottomdrawer.com.au

The Junk Company
583 Elizabeth Street
Melbourne VIC 3000
T: 03 9328 8121
M: 0417 032 829
E: thejunkcompany@hotmail.com
www.thejunkcompany.com

The Mill Markets
3 Mackey Street
North Geelong VIC 3215
T: 03 5278 9989
F: 03 5278 9929
E: iballis@ozemail.com.au
www.millmarkets.com.au

The Old Post Office Antiques
185 St Georges Road
North Fitzroy VIC 3065 &
477 Plenty Road
Preston VIC 3072
T: 03 9481 5506
M: 0419 896 193

The Restorers Barn
129-133 Mostyn Street
Castlemaine VIC 3450
T: 03 5470 5669
E: shop@restorersbarn.com.au

The Rustic Rose
38 Victoria Road
Loch Vic 3945
T: 03 5659 4445
M: 0407 594 445
E: therusticrose@ datafast.net.au

The Wool Exchange Geelong
44 Corio Street
Geelong VIC 3550
T: 03 5224 2400

Three Quarters 20th Century
Furnishings
128 Gertrude Street
Fitzroy VIC 3065
T: 03 9419 7736
F: 03 9372 9755
E: geeway@alphalink.com.au

Tony Barons
Camberwell Antique Centre
25 Cookson Street
Camberwell VIC 3124
T: 03 9579 2029

Tooronga Hall Antiques & Caulfield
Antique W'house
8 Sir John Monash Drive
Caulfield East VIC 3145
F: 03 9885 2551
M: 0412 363 176
E: snookc@ocean.com.au
    thallantiques@optusnet.com

Tyabb Hay Shed
14A Mornington/Tyabb Road
Tyabb VIC 3913
T: 03 5977 3533
M: 0419 572 768

Tyabb Packing House
Shop 1a Mornington - Tyabb Rd
Tyabb VIC 3913
T: 03 5977 4414
F: 03 5977 3216
tyabbpackinghouseantiques.com.au

Unique & Antique
Tyabb Packing House
Tyabb Road, Tyabb VIC 3913
F: 03 9766 4394
M: 0415 322 464
E: kyltyler1@optusnet.com.au

Urbanized
837 High Street
Thornbury VIC 3071
T: 03 9495 0469
M: 0421 024 224
E: chrisandalex@primus.com.au

Victorian Railway Workshops Art &
Antiques
82 Chapel Street
Windsor VIC 3181
T: 03 9525 0009
E: skostosk@bigpond.net.au

Vintage Posters Only
1158 High Street
Armadale VIC 3143
T: 03 9509 4562
F: 03 9509 4562
M: 0419 588 423
www.vintageposters.com.au

Virtanen Antiques
933 High Street
Armadale VIC 3143
T: 03 9822 7879
F: 03 9822 9097
M: 0412 125 173
E: sharen.virtanen@bigpond.com
www.virtanen-antiques.com

Western District Antique Centre
64 Thompson Street
Hamilton VIC 3300
T: 03 5572 1499

White Hills Antiques & Collectables
532 Napier Street
White Hills, Bendigo VIC 3550
T: 03 5448 3434
M: 0438 522 788
E: whitehillsantiques@bigpond.com.au

Womango
47 Chapel Street
Windsor VIC 3181
T: 03 9533 6650
M: 0410 750 310

Wooden Pew Antiques
Peacock Road, Tyabb VIC 3913
T: 03 5977 4666
E: sales@woodenpew.com.au
www.woodenpew.com.au

XXXX Antique Complex
The Bond Store
5-9 Elizabeth Street
Castlemaine VIC 3450
T: 03 5470 5989
F: 03 5470 5989
E: sales@xxxxantiques.com.au
www.xxxxantiques.com

Yanda Aboriginal Art Melbourne
731-735 High Street
Armadale VIC 3143
T: 03 9576 1813
F: 03 9576 1913
M: 0412 740 477
E: kit@yandaaboriginalart.com
www.yandaaboriginalart.com

Yarra Valley Antique Centre
8 Bell Street
Yarra Glen VIC 3775
T: 03 9730 1911
M: 0407 689 609

WA

Antiques & Heirlooms
43 London Court
Perth WA 6000
T: 08 9325 4242
F: 08 9244 3657
M: 0408 095 123
E: kuper@hotlinks.net.au

Ardeco Antiques & Collectables
84 Hampton Road
Fremantle WA 6160
T: 08 9433 1015
F: 08 9331 6900
M: 0412 356 966

Bill & Janet White
By Appointment
M: 0409 454 124

Bloomsbury Antiques
222 Onslow Road
Shenton Park WA 6008
T: 08 9381 6541
F: 08 9367 8005
E: brianoh@iinet.net.au

Carillon Antiques
Shop 39a
Carillon City, Hay Street
Perth WA 6000
T: 08 9322 3838
F: 08 9244 3657
M: 0408 095 123
E: kuper@hotlinks.net.au

Cavendish Antiques
PO Box 287
Cottesloe WA 6011
T: 08 9335 9445

Colonial Antiques & Tea House
258 South Terrace
cnr Silver Street
South Fremantle WA 6162
T: 08 9336 1288
F: 08 9331 6900
M: 0412 356 966
E: colonialantiques@iinet.net.au

Deco Down Under
24 Parade Street
Albany WA 6330
T: 08 9842 1974
F: 08 9842 9545
M: 0417 928 210
walters@decodownunder.com
www.decodownunder.com

Dr Russell's Emporium
476 Beaufort Street
Mt Lawley, Highgate WA 6003
T: 08 9328 8857
F: 08 9328 8857
M: 0409 105 270
E: drrussellsemp@hotmail.com

Esmerelda's Curios
PO Box 47
Darlington WA 6070
M: 0419 464 245
E: esmerelda@ozemail.com.au

frhapsody
PO Box 118
Inglewood WA 6932
T: 08 9370 2056
E: frhapsody@upnaway.com
stores.ebay.com.au/frhapsody

Goodwood House Antiques
84-88 Goodwood Parade
Burswood WA 6100
T: 08 9361 6368
F: 08 9470 5364
goodwoodhouse@bigpond.com.au
www.goodwoodhouseantiques.net.au

John Burridge Military Antiques
91 Shenton Road
Swanbourne WA 6010
T: 08 9384 1218
E: john@jbma.com.au
www.jbma.com.au

Shenton Park Antiques
197 Onslow Road
Shenton park WA 6008
T: 08 9382 3180
F: 08 9382 4159
M: 0404 088 945

South Perth Antiques &
Collectables
151 Canning Hwy
South Perth WA 6151
T: 08 9367 7800
F: 08 9367 7800
M: 0419 944 445
E: groberts@iinet.com.au

Steven Sher Antiques
Stall 30 Fremantle Markets
South Terrace, Fremantle WA 6158
T: 08 9433 5441
M: 0414 413 258
E: stevensher@iinet.net.au
www.trocadero.com/hensteeth

The Rare Coin Company
12 Stanford Road
Albany WA 6330
T: 08 9842 5022
F: 08 9842 1702
E: coindeal@bigpond.com
www.coindealers.com.au

Timeless Treasures
222 Scarborough Beach Road
Mount Hawthorn WA 6016
T: 08 9443 8244

Trinity Antiques
Shop 205 Trinity Arcade
72 St George's Terrace
Perth WA 6000
T: 08 9321 8321
F: 08 9321 6545

Well Warne
By Appointment
T: 08 9470 5558
M: 0417 187 196
E: warneout@bigpond.com

Wisma Antik
44 Kathleen Street, Trigg WA 6029
T: 08 9447 3276
F: 08 9447 3276
M: 0422 272 278
E: antiques@wisma.com.au
www.wisma.com.au

New Zealand

Alexandra Antiques
By Appointment
T: 07 871 9625
M: 021 152 0925
E: tony.hodgson@xtra.co.nz

Anthea's Antiques Ltd
333 Remuera Road
Remuera, Auckland New Zealand
T: 64 9 520 1092
F: 64 9 524 7695

Anticus Antiques
8 Cass Street, Russell
Bay of Islands New Zealand 255
T: 09 403 8000
F: 09 403 8000
M: 0256 161 498
E: anticus@slingshot.co.nz
www.anticusantiques.com

Antiques & Curiosities
Shop 4, 176 Great South Road
Remuera, Auckland New Zealand
T: 09 524 2344
F: 09 524 2346
M: 0274 842 122
E: fenellas@extra.co.nz

Antiques Centre of Wellington
60 Vivian Street
Wellington New Zealand
T: 04 802 4001
M: 0274 443 302

Antiques of Epsom
463 Manakau Road
Epsom, Auckland New Zealand 0
T: 09 630 1440
E: ronson@xtra.co.nz

Antiques On Victoria
89a Victoria Street
Cambridge New Zealand 2351
T: 07 823 4501
F: 07 823 4501
M: 0212 118 754

Banks Peninsula Antiques
By Appointment
New Zealand
T: 03 304 7172
F: 03 304 7182
M: 025 372 178
E: erik.russell@xtra.co.nz

Blue Moon Antiques
15 Liardet Street
New Plymouth
New Zealand
T: 06 757 2311

Bulls Antiques & Collectables
High Street
Bulls New Zealand 0
T: 06 322 1518
F: 06 322 1518
M: 0274 428 499
E: bullsant@xtra.co.nz

Camelot Antiques
PO Box 268
Huntyl, Waikato New Zealand
T: 07 828 9914
F: 07 828 9679
M: 0274 933 102
E: alan@huntly.net.nz
www.huntly.net.nz

Casa Manana Antiques &
Collectables
5B Casabella, 307 Barton Street
Hamilton New Zealand
T: 07 839 1440
F: 07 839 1871
E: casamanana@xtra.co.nz

Classy Clutter And Collectables
620 Ferry Road, Woolston Village
Christchurch New Zealand 8004
T: 03 384 1949
M: 0274 149 099
E: classy-clutter@E3.net.nz
www.classy-clutter.co.nz

Collectamania
118 Great South Road
Ohaupo, Waikato NZ 2452
T: 07 823 8225
M: 027 211 9446
E: janedaly@xtra.co.nz

Collector's Choice
By Appointment
T: 03 385 5420

Colonial Antiques
330 Maungatapu Road
Tauranga New Zealand
T: 07 544 3457

Colonial Heritage Antiques Ltd
40 Duke Street
Cambridge New Zealand
T: 07 827 4211
F: 07 827 4024
M: 021 996 919
sheldrick@colonialheritage.co.nz

Country Charm Antiques
State Highway 2, Clareville
Carterton New Zealand
T: 06 379 7929   F: 06 379 7930
M: 0274 456 409
E: cameron@wise.net.nz
www.country-charm.co.nz

Deborah's Antiques
By Appointment
T: 07 828 4626
M: 0272 215 511

Elmwood Antiques
41 Wades Road, Whitford Auckland
New Zealand
T: 09 530 8694

Gregory's of Greerton
143 Greerton Road
Tauranga New Zealand
T: 07 578 9696

Heritage House Antiques
561-3 Manakau Road
Greenwoods Corner
Auckland New Zealand
T: 09 638 6147   F: 09 638 7029

Ikon Antiques
462 Colombo Street, Sydenham
Christchurch New Zealand
T: 03 366 9330
M: 027 220 7844

In Vogue Costumes & Collectables
Vogue Plaza
40 Rosemount Road, Waihi
Waikato New Zealand 2981
T: 07 863 9366   F: 07 863 9362
M: 0211 465 525
E: invogue@clear.net.nz
www.invogue.co.nz

Kelmscott House Antiques
Tirau Antique Centre
7 Hillcrest Street
Tirau New Zealand
T: 07 8719 819   M: 0211 390 377
E: apps@xtra.co.nz

Lord Ponsonby Antiques
86 Ponsonby Road
Auckland New Zealand
T: 09 376 6463   F: 09 376 6463

Maxine's Collectibles
By Appointment
T: 0274 789 877

Memory Lane
356 Tinakori Road
Thorndow, Wellington New Zealand
T: 04 499 2666
E: memory.lane@paradise.net.nz

Moa Extinct Stuff
Right Up My Alley
Volcom Road
Raglan New Zealand 2051
T: 07 825 7004   F: 07 825 7000
E: ruma1@xtra.co.nz
www.ruma.co.nz

Oxford Court Antiques Centre
'Top of The Hill'
1 Hillcrest Street
Tirau New Zealand
T: 07 883 1720
F: 07 833 1721
E: oxfordcourt@msn.com

Peachgrove Antiques
24 Peachgrove Road
Hamilton New Zealand
T: 07 856 9976
M: 025 987 029
E: peach.grove@xtra.co.nz

Right Up My Alley
Volcom Lane
Raglan New Zealand 2051
T: 07 825 7004
F: 07 825 7000
E: ruma1@xtra.co.nz
www.ruma.co.nz

South Auckland
Antiques & Collectables
By Appointment
T: 09 299 8356
M: 021 654 800

Strangely Familiar
348a Tinakori Road
Thorndon
Wellington New Zealand 0
T: 04 472 3400
F: 04 472 3400
M: 0274 504 090
E: rodney.dormer@xtra.co.nz

Tinakori Antiques
291A Tinakori Road
Wellington New Zealand
T: 04 472 7043
F: 04 472 7043
E: jfyson@paradise.net.nz

Tirau Antique Centre
7 Hillcrest Street
Tirau New Zealand
T: 07 871 9819

Waterfords of
Mangaweka Village
By Appointment
New Zealand
T: 06 382 5886

Woodville Mart
53 Vogel St
Woodville New Zealand
T: 06 376 5865
F: 06 376 5584
M: 0212 163 661
E: sales@woodville.co.nz
www.woodville.co.nz

INDEX

A

Action figures 285, 369, 370
Adams
  display figures 20
  plate 137
advertising
  aeronautical 303
  Australian 303
  badges 36, 37
  Bakelite 37
  beer, wine & spirits 18 – 21, 32
  booklet 28
  bottles 35
  box 20
  brochures 35
  calendars 35
  catalogues 28, 325
  ceramics 18 – 21, 32, 35
  clock 36
  coat hanger 36
  Coca-cola 22 – 25, 284, 294, 296, 320, 353
  display card 32
  display figures 19, 21, 23, 26, 36, 37, 305, 306
  ephemera 18, 21, 24, 25, 27 - 29, 31, 35 - 37
  Fanta 23
  jar 37
  labels 29
  magazine adverts 25, 28, 299, 305
  mannequins 35
  mirrors 31
  other 36, 37, 352
  packaged goods 35
  plaque 24
  posters 40 - 43
  radio 20
  salesman's sample 36
  sample cards 37
  signs 21, 24, 30 - 32
  thermometers 36
  tins 33, 34
  trays 36, 18
aeronautical
  Ansett - ANA 34
  badge 303
  bag 303
  headwear 303
  label 29
  letter opener 303
  lighters 303, 312
  photograph 303
  playing card 303
  posters 42, 303
  Qantas 26, 29
  tin 34
  trading cards 303
AFL/VFL
  autograph 292

badges 291, 292, 295, 296
beer 294
board game 293
bottle tops 25, 294
cap 296
cards 291 – 294, 296, 297
cigarette cards 297
clothing 292
decals 295, 296
decanter 294
drinking glasses 294, 297
drinks set 294
ephemera 291
figurines 292, 295
medallions 291
membership tickets 293, 296, 297
memorabilia 292
pennants 294, 295
photograph 293
posters 292, 294, 295
printed material 291
program 292
records 293, 295, 296
tin 292
trophy 295
air horn 307
Albaware 126
alcohol related
  advertising 18 - 21
  bar 198
  bar decoration 252
  bar set 347
  beer 284, 294, 300, 309
  beer pull 347
  bottle opener 290
  bottle stopper 321
  cocktail cabinets 192
  cocktail shaker 230
  corkscrews 288, 304, 307
  decanter set 347
  decanters 18, 19, 53, 72, 73, 131, 133, 211, 212, 222, 223, 230, 283, 294, 347
  display figures 19 - 21
  drinks cabinet 198
  drinks sets 211, 223, 230
  flasks 359
  ice buckets 20, 246 – 249, 347
  jugs 347
  playing cards 21
  port 284
  posters 41, 42
  pourer 347
  pub mirror 21
  signs 21, 32
  soda siphon 246
  stirrers 347
  water jugs 20
  whiskey jugs 20, 21, 131
  whisky label 358
allover floral/chintz

bowl 48
breakfast set 48
cake stand 49
comports 49
cups & saucers 48
cups, saucers & plates 48
honey pots 49
jars 49
Maling 49
plates 49
Royal Winton 49
teapots 49
toast rack 48
trios 48
vase 48
animals
  Australian studio pottery 51
  Bendigo Pottery 126
  Beswick 54 – 63, 65
  Bossons 137
  Bretby 143
  ceramic 19
  Crown Lynn 77, 78
  crystal 231
  Dino Martens 218
  Downing, Brownie 68
  Empire Ware 131
  Goebel 80
  Greddington, Arthur 57, 60 – 63
  Japanese ceramics 314
  Kiwiana 134
  Lladro 141
  McLaren, Betty 129
  McLaren, Gus 128, 129
  MCP Mingay 129, 130
  Murano glass 217, 218, 220, 223 - 225
  Noritake 314, 319
  oriental 314
  plaster 46
  Poole 89
  Potter, Beatrix 65
  Royal Doulton 98, 99, 300
  Royal Doulton - Bunnykins 92 - 95
  Royal Dux 141, 142
  Royal Worcester 115
  Seguso 217
  Sommerso 225
  SylvaC 120
  Venetian glass 217, 218, 223 - 225
  Wade 121
  Wembley 124
  Zsolnay 143
anodised
  canisters 246
  drinking glasses 246
  egg cups 246
  ice bucket 246
  soda siphon 246
  apple peeler 249

apprentice pieces 258, 321
Arabia 135
  door handles 77
  door knocker 258
  garden statues 258
  lighting 271, 279
  model 258
  tile 143
art
  artefacts - Australian
Aboriginal 38
  artefacts - New Guinean 39
  drawing 306
  miniature 267
  paintings 44
  posters 40 – 44, 285, 303
  prints 44, 45
  sculpture 46, 47, 52, 127 – 129, 131, 224
  statuary 46, 47
Art Deco
  biscuit barrel 251
  canisters 247, 251
  clothing 155
  compact 164
  earrings 169
  figurine 145
  furniture 192, 193
  jugs 139, 146
  lamps 275
  lighting 269, 279
  mirror 193
  perfume bottles 165
  platter 52
  ring 267
  smoker's stand 193
  stove 252
  toilette bottles 212
  trolleys 193, 208
  vases 64, 117, 130, 229
Art Nouveau
  belt 165
  clothing 152
  frame 350
  plant stand 200
ashtrays
  Australian ceramics 352
  Australian glass 286
  Australian souvenir ware 287
  Carlton Ware 352
  ceramic 20, 352, 353
  glass 287, 352
  Murano glass 220
  plastic 352
  Royal Doulton 20, 109, 110, 306
  Venetian glass 220
  Wembley 124, 125, 352
Atari 191
Australian Aboriginal artefacts 38
Australian advertising
  aeronautical 303
  Bakelite 37

beer, wine & spirits 18 – 21
booklet 28
bottles 35
brochures 35
calendars 35
ceramics 35
Coca-Cola 22 – 25, 294, 296
display figures 26
ephemera 27, 28, 35, 37
jar 37
labels 29
magazine adverts 27, 28
other 36
packaged goods 35
posters 40, 41, 43
salesman's sample 36
signs 30, 32
tins 33
tray 36
Australian alcohol related
beer 300
port 284
Australian art
drawing 306
posters 40 - 43
prints 44, 45
sculpture 47, 52
Australian ceramics
Albaware 126
Bakewell's 126
Bendigo Pottery 126
Beswick 55
Boyd, Guy 67
Boyd, Kevin 128
Boyd, Martin 67
Boyd, Merric 67
Carlton Ware 69, 70
Delemere 131
Diana Pottery 126, 127, 251,
294, 299
Douglas, Neil 131
Downing, Brownie 68
Ellis Pottery 127
Empire Ware 131
Florenz 127, 128
Glove Pottery 308
Gunda 132
Hoffman 133
Johnson 132
Lowe, Alan 131
McLaren, Betty 128, 129
McLaren, Gus 128, 129
MCP Mingay 129, 130
Memmott, Harry 130
Moon, Milton 130
Moorcroft 86
Noble, Rose 131
other 126, 131 – 133, 286, 294,
307, 352
Pates Pottery 88
Remued 131
Royal Doulton 110, 111
Royal Doulton - Bunnykins 92, 95
Studio Anna 118
studio pottery 50 – 53, 132
SylvaC 120

Wedgwood 123
Wembley 124, 125, 293, 352
Woods & Son 132
Australian clothing 152 – 155,
157, 296
Australian costume jewellery
brooches 169
general 166
Australian dolls 175
Australian doll prams 177
Australian dressing
accessories
handbags 158, 159
shoes 162
Australian Entertainment
albums 185 - 189
automata 26
McCallum 131
movie related 28
Australian ephemera
see Australian printed
material
Australian furniture
bedside cabinet 197
cabinet 206
chairs - dining 196, 197
chairs - pairs 195
chairs - recliner 197
chairs - sets 196
chairs - single 194 – 197
chest of drawers 197
cocktail cabinet 192
dining suites 197
display cabinet 192
dressing table 193
Featherston, Grant 194, 195
Fler 194
kitchen cabinets 192, 209
lounges 194, 197
Lowen, Fred 194
Parker 196
room divider 209
settee 195
sideboards 196, 205
stools 194, 196, 209
tables - coffee 196, 197
tables - dining 196, 197
tables - fondue 197
tables - small 196, 197
Tessa 194
trolley 209
Australian glass
bottles 35
clear 37, 294, 297, 302
jar 37
other 229, 233, 294, 297, 302
perfume bottle 165
Australian jewellery 267
Australian kitchenalia
bowls 251
canisters 127, 249, 251
furniture 192
sieve 36
tea cosy 253
Australian lighting 272, 273,
277, 278

Australian militaria
badges 312
medals 310
Australian photographic
photographs 293, 298, 346
slides 38
Australian printed material
booklets 28
books 298, 302, 322 – 324
brochures 35
calendars 35
certificate 287
chocolate wrappers 27, 28
cigarette cards 297, 298
comics 324, 326
labels 29
magazine adverts 27
magazines 302, 337 – 339
newspaper 298
postcards 302, 342
posters 40 – 43, 292, 294, 295,
303, 340 – 342, 344
program 292
ration card 346
show bags 36, 37
sport - AFL/VFL 293
sporting 295 – 298
sporting cards 291 – 297
trading cards 303, 345
Australian religious items 287
Australian silver
emu egg 286
spoons 287
Australian silver plate 359
Australian smoking related 354
Australian souvenir ware
ashtray 286
boomerang 38
bowls 286
ceramics 286, 287
certificate 287
cup & saucer 286
desk sets 287
emu egg 286
figures 287
flag 286
jug 287
mirror 287
plaques 286, 287
plates 283, 286
salt & pepper shakers 287
serviette ring 287
spoons 287
taxidermy 286
wall hanging 287
Wembley 124
Australian sport
AFL/VFL 25, 291 – 297
basketball 301
cricket 298
fishing 301
golf 23
horse racing 302
motor 301, 302
Olympics 22, 300
rugby league 302

sailing 25
soccer 25
Australian statuary
bust 46
garden 258
Australian studio pottery
animal 51
bowls 50, 51
candelabra 50
candlesticks 50
comport 52
goblets 52
jars 50
jugs 50, 51, 53
plaque 53
plates 132
platters 51, 52
pots 50, 53
tea sets 53
vases 51 – 53, 133
Australian telephones 257
Boomaroo 378
Australian textiles 259
Australian tins
biscuit 33
cake 292
confectionery 34
nuts 34
tea 34, 284
Australian toys
boats 360
Boomaroo 379
Cyclops 383
die cast 382, 383
doll 175
games & puzzles 363
trucks 366
Australian transport
see aeronautical
see motoring
see nautical
see railways
autographs
AFL/VFL 292
militaria 312
movie related 281
music related 281
other 281
sporting 281, 292, 299
television related 281
automata 26
Aynsley 135

B

badges
advertising 36
aeronautical 303
AFL/VFL 291, 292, 295, 296
Coca-cola 23, 25
militaria 310, 312
motoring 305, 308
movie related 309
music related 190, 285
Olympics 300
other 304, 350
presidential 37

royalty 305
  television related 191
Bailey, Lorna 136
Bakelite
  ashtray 307
  bangles 166, 172
  belt buckle 165
  bracelets 166, 169
  brooches 166, 172
  bubble pipe 385
  cake stands 248, 249
  canisters 247
  cups 37
  flasks 247
  furniture handles 249
  lamp 269
  mixer 249
  pendant 170
  picnic set 247
  radios 180 – 183
  salt & pepper shakers 248
  shaving set 248
  telephones 257
Bakewell's 126
Bally posters 41
bangles
  costume jewellery 166, 168, 172, 173
  silver 263
  Lea Stein 173
bank notes 312
bar 198
bar decoration 252
bar set 347
Barbie 175
Barsony 276
Basketball 301
baskets
  Delemere 131
  Diana Pottery 126
  Fenton 229
  Florenz 127
  Maling 85
  Murano glass 220, 225
  other glass 211, 230
  Remued 131
  Royal Winton 113
  timber 321
  Venetian glass 220, 225
  Wood, Arthur 144
battery casing 232
bayonets 311
BCM Nelson Ware 148
bean slicer 243
bedside cabinets
  stainless steel 199
  teak 197, 203
beer 284
beer pull 347
bells
  brass 312
  Goebel - Hummel 84
Belleek 136
belt buckles 157, 305
belts 165
Bendigo Pottery 126

Beswick
  animals 54 – 63, 65
  figurines 63, 65
  Greddington, Arthur 54 –56, 58, 60 – 63, 65
  jars 64
  jug 64
  plates 282, 368
  Potter, Beatrix 65
  tea set 367
  urn 64
  vases 63, 64
Bing & Grondahl 137
Bishop, Rachel 87
biscuit barrels
  Boyd, Guy 67
  Japanese ceramics 314
  other oriental ceramics 314, 317
  Waterford 210
Bisque
  dolls 175
  vase 137
Bjorn Wiinblad
  candlesticks 66
  figurines 66
  plates 66, 282
  print 45
  vases 66
blender 244
blotters 288, 356
blue & white ceramics 137
blue bag 252
bobbins 351
Bohemia crystal 213
Bonzo milk jug 315
book marks 306
bookends
  bronze 46
  Carlton Ware 73
  ceramics - other 147
  Crown Lynn 77
  Florenz 128
  Goebel - Hummel 84
  metal - other 260
  oriental ceramics 317
  timber 321
books 298 – 302, 308, 309, 322 – 325, 345, 367
Boomaroo toys 378
boomerang 38
boots 162
Bossons 47, 137
bottle opener 290
bottle stopper 321
bottle tops 25
bottles
  beer 18
  Coca-cola 22, 284
  cordial 35
  furniture polish 35
  other glass 22, 35, 229
  pharmaceutical 262
  scientific 262
  Venetian glass 218, 220
bowls
  allover floral/chintz 48

Australian Ceramics 126, 286, 307
Australian studio pottery 50, 51
Belleek 136
Boyd, Martin 67
Branksome Ceramics 144
Carlton Ware 69 – 72
carnival glass 229
Clarice Cliff 74
Crown Devon 75
Crown Lynn 76
Daum crystal 212
Downing, Brownie 68
enamel 252
Fenton 229
glass 229 – 232
Goebel 80
Green, T. G. 138
Grimwades 140
Hoffman 133
Holmegaard 214
Kiwiana 288
Kosta 214
Limoges 141
Maling 85
McLaren, Betty 128
McLaren, Gus 129
Moorcroft 86, 87
Murano glass 217, 220 – 222
Orrefors 216
oriental glass 319
Poole 89
Pyrex 253
Royal Albert 90
Royal Copenhagen 91
Royal Doulton 107 – 110
Royal Doulton - Bunnykins 93
Royal Winton 48, 113, 144
Scandinavian glass 215, 216
Shorter & Son 117
silver 358
silver plate 359
Sommerso 218, 221
stainless steel 253
timber 286, 288, 321
Tunstall 142
Upsala Ekeby 144
Venetian glass 217, 218, 220 - 222
Wade 121
Wedgwood 123
Wembley 125
Whitefriars 210
boxes
  ceramic 113
  Kiwiana 288, 289
  other 319
  Royal Winton 113
  timber 113, 122, 140, 289,318
boxing
  book 301
  photograph 301
  poster 301
  trophy 300
Boyd, Guy 67
Boyd, Kevin 128
Boyd, Martin 67

Boyd, Merric 67
bracelets
  amethyst 263
  costume jewellery 166, 168, 169, 171, 172
  enamel 266
  gold 263
  other 263
  silver 263, 266
  silver plate 168
Bradman, Donald 298
Branksome Ceramics 144
brass
  pen holder 307
  beer pull 347
  bell 312
  candlesticks 270
  corkscrews 304, 307
  door knocker 258
  hood ornament 304
  jardiniere 260
  lamps 273, 306
  lighter 354
  porthole 307
  table 193
bread crock 133
breakfast sets
  allover floral/chintz 48
  Kent, James 148
  Royal Winton 48, 114
Breitling watch 238
Bretby animal 143
Broadhurst
  cups, saucers & plates 145
  trios 145
bronze
  animals 46
  bookends 46
  statuary 47
brooches
  butterfly wing 264
  costume jewellery 166 – 173
  enamel 264
  gold 264, 266
  Lea Stein 174
  other 264
  silver 166, 264, 266, 289, 290
building sets 380
Bunnykins
  bowls 93
  figurines 92 – 94
  lamp 93
  mugs 93
  music boxes 93, 94
  plates 93
Burleigh Ware
  condiment set 137
  teapots 137
busts
  alabaster 46
  plaster 19, 46
butcher's block 260
butter churn 260
butter smoother 253

C

cabinets
  rosewood 203
  silver ash 208
  Victorian ash 206
cake decoration 253
cake stands
  allover floral/chintz 49
  Bakelite 248, 249
  Royal Winton 49
calendars 24
  advertising 35
  ephemera 300
  Kiwiana 288
  timber 288
cameras 348, 350
can cooler 18
can opener 244
candelabras
  Australian studio pottery 50
  silver 270
  silver plate 270
candlesticks
  Australian studio pottery 50
  brass 270
  Fenton 229
  Green, T. G. 138
  glass 270
  Murano glass 222
  other ceramics 270
  other Scandinavian glass 215, 216
  other 270
  plaster 270
  Royal Doulton - Bunnykins 93
  silver 270
  Venetian glass 222, 279
  Wedgwood 122
  Wiinblad, Bjorn 66
canisters
  anodised 246
  Bakelite 247
  Diana Pottery 127
  enamel 250
  other ceramics 250
  other 250, 251
  plastic 248, 249, 251
  tin 250
Capodimonte figurine 145
Carlton Ware
  ashtray 352
  bookends 73
  bowls 69 – 72
  cigarette box 71
  coffee set 72
  cruet set 73
  cup & saucer 71, 72
  decanters 72
  jugs 69, 71, 72
  mug 72
  plates 69, 70, 72
  platters 70
  salt & pepper shakers 73
  sauce boat 71
  serviette ring 73
  sugar castor 73

  teapots 72
  toast racks 73
  vases 70
carnival glass 229
casserole dishes 250
CDs
  see albums
centrepieces
  crystal 212
  Murano glass 223
  other glass 210
  Venetian glass 223
  Waterford 300
Ceramics
  see also Australian ceramics
  see also Australian studio pottery
  see also lighting
  Adams 137
  Albaware 126
  allover floral/chintz 48, 49
  Arabia 135
  Australian Ceramics, other 131 – 133
  Aynsley 135
  Bailey, Lorna 136
  BCM Nelson Ware 148
  Belleek 136
  Bendigo Pottery 126
  Beswick 54 – 65, 282, 367, 368
  Bing & Grondahl 137
  Bisque 137
  Blue & White 137
  Bossons 47, 137
  Boyd, Guy 67
  Boyd, Kevin 128
  Boyd, Martin 67
  Boyd, Merric 67
  Branksome 144
  Bretby 143
  Broadhurst 145
  Bunnykins 93 – 95
  Burleigh Ware 137
  Capodimonte 145
  Carlton Ware 69 – 74, 352
  Chinese 315
  Clarice Cliff 74
  Coalport 137
  Corning Ware 252
  Cornishware 138, 253
  Crown Devon 75
  Crown Lynn 76 – 78
  Delemere 131
  Denby 139
  Dennis China 139
  Diana Pottery 19, 126, 127, 131, 294, 299
  Downing, Brownie 68
  Dresden 145
  Ellis Pottery 127
  Empire Ware 131
  Figgjo 147
  Florenz 127, 128
  Fornasetti 147
  Fosters Pottery 284
  German 79

  Gibsons 149
  Glove Pottery 308
  Goebel 80
  Goebel - Hummel 81 – 84
  Goldschneider 139
  Gouda 139
  Green, T. G. 138, 253
  Grimwades 139, 140
  Gustavberg 150
  Hoffman 133
  Hollahaza 145
  Hummel 272
  Imari 316
  James Kent 48, 148
  Japanese 287, 298, 314, 315, 317, 319
  Johnson of Australia 132
  Kalmar 128
  Kiwiana 76 – 78, 134, 290, 352
  Lancaster & Sandland 146
  Lilliput Lane 140
  Limoges 140, 141
  Lladro 141
  Lord Nelson 48, 299
  Lowe, Alan 131
  Maling 49, 85
  Mason's 141
  McCallum 131
  McLaren, Betty 128, 129
  McLaren, Gus 128, 129
  MCP Mingay 129, 130
  Memmott, Harry 130
  Moon, Milton 130
  Moorcroft 86, 87
  Moorland 147
  Moorland 148
  Moulin Des Loups 20
  Noble, Rose 131
  Noritake 314 – 316, 319
  oriental 314, 315, 317
  Paragon 145, 148
  Pates Pottery 88
  Poole 89
  Portmerion 144
  Price Kensingotn 149
  Quimper 148
  Regal China 18, 19
  Remued 131
  Ridgways 141
  Royal Albert 32, 90
  Royal Copenhagen 91, 283
  Royal Couldon 283
  Royal Doulton 20, 26, 92 – 112, 272, 283, 284, 300, 302, 306, 347, 353
  Royal Doulton - Bunnykins 92 – 95
  Royal Doulton - Character Jugs 96, 97
  Royal Dux 141, 142
  Royal Stanley 146
  Royal Winton 48, 49, 113, 114, 140
  Royal Worcester 115
  Salisbury Bone China 148
  series ware 113, 114
  Shelley 48, 116

  Shorter & Son 117
  Spode 299
  Stanley 144
  Stewart Pottery 134
  Stoke on Trent 250
  Studio Anna 118
  Susie Cooper 119
  SylvaC 120
  Te Mata Potteries 134
  Te Rona Potteries 134
  Temuka Ware 134
  Thomas 145
  Troika 149
  Tuffin, Sally 139
  Tunstall 142
  Upsala Ekeby 144
  Villeroy and Boch 143
  Wade 20,21, 121, 283, 299, 368
  Wedgwood 74, 122, 123, 283, 284, 352, 354
  Wembley 124, 125, 292, 293, 352
  Wilkinson's 148
  Wiinblad, Bjorn 66
  Winter, David 147
  Winterling 144
  Wood, Arthur 144
  Woods & Son 132
  Zsolnay 143
cereal toys 380
certificates
  religious 287
  militaria 312
chains
  fob 267
  gold 267
chairs
  children's 206
  dining 196 – 198, 200, 202, 206, 209
  Featherson, Grant 194, 195
  Lowen, Fred 194
  metal 197
  pairs 195, 199, 207
  recliner 197
  rocking 202
  Rodica 198
  sets 196 - 198, 201, 202, 206, 209
  single 194 – 196 , 198, 199, 201, 202, 204 – 208
  Tessa 194
  Up 5 198
chandeliers 271
character jugs
  Bendigo Pottery 126
  Royal Doulton 96, 97, 283, 302
chargers
  Moorcroft 86
  Poole 89
  Studio Anna 118
cheese board 288
cheese dish 114
chess set 351
chests of drawers
  rosewood 202, 208
  teak 202 – 204
chokers 170, 171

Christmas related
  ceramics 92
  decorations 282
  money box 320
  plates 282
  sign 24
chromed
  chairs 199
  cigarette box 353
  coasters 247
  lighting 271
  smoker's stand 193
  table 193
  tray 247
  trolleys 200, 208
cigarette boxes
  Carlton Ware 71
  chromed 353
  gold 353
cigarette cards 297
cigarette holders 353, 354
Clarice Cliff 74
clocks 18, 26, 234, 235, 288, 289
clothing
  headwear 296
  men's 151, 154, 155
  nurse's uniform 35
  oriental 318
  sporting 292
  women's 151, 153 – 156
Coalport
  comport 138
  figurines 138
  plate 138
  vase 137
coasters 247
coat hanger 36
Coca–Cola
  Australian 22
  badge 23
  bottle tops 25, 294
  bottles 22, 284
  calendar 24
  cans 22
  cards 296
  cups/saucers/trios 25
  display figures 23
  Frisbee 23
  ice bucket 25
  lighters 353
  magazine adverts 24, 25
  money box 320
  pins 25
  plaque 24
  radios 22
  salt & pepper shakers 25
  signs 24
  soccer ball 25
  telephone 22
  thermometer 22
  thongs 23
  toy 25
  train 25
  yo-yos 23
cocktail cabinets 192
cocktail platter 254

cocktail shaker 230
coffee grinder 244
coffee machines 243
coffee pots
  Arabia 135
  Bailey, Lorna 136
  Corning Ware 252
  enamel 243
  Maling 85
  Moorcroft 86
  Noritake 315
  other glass 229
  Royal Copenhagen 91
  Shelley 116
coffee sets
  Boyd, Guy 67
  Carlton Ware 72
  other oriental ceramics 315
  Poole 89
  Portmerion 144
  Royal Doulton 110
  Shelley 116
  Winterling 144
coins 312
comics 179, 309, 326 – 336,
339, 369, 370, 371
commemorative
  character jug 283
  decanter 283
  drinking glasses 283
  general 283
  mugs 283
  plates 283
  royalty 283, 351
  sport 283
Commonwealth Games mug 283
compacts 164
compass 312
comports
  allover floral/chintz 49
  Australian studio pottery 52
  Coalport 138
  Maling 49, 85
  Murano glass 222
  other glass 212
  Royal Doulton 109, 110
  Royal Winton 49, 113
  silver 358
  Venetian glass 222
concrete mixer 260
condiment set 137
condoms 261
copper
  Kiwiana souvenir ware 290
  measuring cups 254
  plant stand 200
cordial set 232
Corgi toys 381
corkscrews
  brass 307
  Kiwiana 288
  other 304
  timber 288
Corning Ware 252
Cornishware 138
costumes

see also dressing
accessories
  clothing 151, 152
  headwear 161
  nurse's uniform 35
  scent bottles 212, 230
  thongs 23
  women's 152
costume jewellery
  bangles 166, 168, 172, 173
  bracelets 166, 168, 171, 172
  brooches 166 – 173
  chokers 170, 171
  earrings 169 - 171, 173
  Lea Stein 173, 174
  necklaces 170, 173
  pendants 171
cream pot 244
credenza 203
cricket
  bats 298
  board game 298
  books 298
  Bradman, Donald 298
  cigarette cards 298
  jug 298
  photograph 298
  plate 298
Crown Devon
  bowl 75
  cup & saucer 75
  jug 75
  plate 75
  sugar castor 75
  tea set 75
  vases 75
Crown Lynn
  animals 77, 78
  bookends 77
  bowls 76
  coffee pot 76
  cups & saucers 76, 78
  door handles 77
  egg cup 78
  jugs 76, 78
  lamp 76
  plates 77
  salt & pepper shakers 77
  server 748
  vases 76 - 78
cruet sets
  allover floral/chintz 48
  Carlton Ware 73
  Lord Nelson 48
  Royal Winton 114
  Shorter & Son 117
  timber 307
crystal
  animals 231
  biscuit barrel 210
  bottle 22
  bowls 212
  brooch 167
  candlestick 270
  centrepiece 212
  chandeliers 271

decanters 211, 212
drinking glasses 212, 284
drinks sets 211
figurine 213
Hummel 213
Kosta 214, 215
necklace 170
perfume bottles 164
vases 214, 215
cuff links 266
cupboard 203
cups
  Aynsley 135
  Imari 316
  paper 25
cups & saucers
  allover floral/chintz 48
  Arabia 135
  Boyd, Martin 67
  Carlton Ware 71
  Clarice Cliff 74
  Crown Devon 75
  Crown Lynn 76, 78
  Dresden 145
  Royal Albert 90
  Royal Winton 48, 113
  Shelley 116
  Spode 299
  Stanley 144
  Susie Cooper 119
cups, saucers & plates
  allover floral/chintz 48
  Broadhurst 145
  Glove Pottery 308
  James Kent 48
  Limoges 140
  Royal Albert 90
  Royal Doulton 108, 110
  Royal Winton 48, 113
  Royal Worcester 115
  Shelley 48, 116
  Susie Cooper 119
cutlery
  silver 358
  silver plate 359
  stainless steel 252
Cyclops pedal cars 383

D

Darlington 211
darning mushroom 351
darts 351
Daum crystal bowls 212
day bed 207
decals 295
decanter set 347
decanters
  Australian Ceramics 131, 133,
  294
  Australian studio pottery 53
  Carlton Ware 72, 73
  ceramic 19, 18
  figural 18, 19
  glass 230
  Murano glass 222, 223
  Regal China 18

Royal Doulton 347
Stuart Crystal 211
Venetian glass 222, 223
Venetian glass 223
Wade 283
Waterford 212
Webb & Corbett 211
Delemere basket 131
demijohn 131
demitasse 315
Denby vases 139
Dennis China vases 139
dentistry samples 261
desk accessories
  ashtray 356
  blotters 288, 356
  calendar 288
  desk set 304
  desk sets 287, 319
  pen holder 307
  pencil holder 249
  typewriter 258
desk sets
  Australian souvenir ware 287
  other metal 319
desks
  metal 199
  rosewood 203
Diana Pottery
  animals 19
  basket 126
  canisters 127
  drinks set 294
  mugs 127, 299
  vases 126, 127
Diana Ware bowls 251
didgeridoo 38
dining suites
  metal 200
  rosewood 209
Dinky Toys 362
dinner sets
  Johnson of Australia 132
  Royal Doulton 111
  Shelley 116
  Thomas 145
Dino Martens
  animal 218
  ewer 218
  vases 218
Disneyania
  bag 367
  book 367
  candle 368
  ceramics 63
  comics 329, 330
  doll 367
  drinking glass 367
  figures 368
  figurine 368
  jacket 367
  lamp 367
  other toys 368
  plate 368
  skittles 367
  stuffed toys 368

table cloth 367
tea set 367
telephone 368
tin 367
View Master slides 367
Winnie the Pooh 63
display cabinet walnut 193
display cabinets
  birch 192
  other timber 192
  Queensland walnut 192
DJ desk 190
dolls
  action figures 285
  Barbie 175
  Bisque 175
  celluloid 175
  composition 175
  furniture 177, 385
  house 177
  kewpie 175
  music related 285
  native 39
  oriental 319
  Pedigree 175, 176
  plastic 176, 177
  prams 177
  stuffed toys 178
  teddy bears 178
  wax 177
dominos 351
door handles 77
door knocker 258
Douglas, Neil plate 131
Downing, Brownie
  bowls 68
  figurines 68
  plaque 68
  plates 68
  print 45
  salt & pepper shakers 68
  teapot 68
Dresden cup & saucer 145
dress up set 285
dressing accessories
  belt buckles 157, 165
  belts 165
  boots 162
  compacts 164
  cuff links 353
  handbags 158 - 160
  hat pins 164
  kit bag 164
  make-up case 157
  manicure sets 157
  overnight bag 157
  perfume bottles 164, 165
  purses 158 – 160
  scent bottles 164, 165
  shoes 162
  suitcases 157
  sunglasses 163
  trouser creaser 157
  umbrellas 164
dressing tables
  birch 204

other timber 193
drink stirrers 347
drinking glasses 210
  anodised 246
  Australian glass 294, 297, 302
  crystal 212
  glass 212, 231 – 233, 284, 367
  Kiwiana glass 308
  Murano glass 219, 223
  plastic 247
  Stuart Crystal 212
  Venetian glass 222, 223
  Webb & Corbett 211, 300
  Wedgwood 283, 284
drinks cabinet 198
drinks sets
  ceramics 146
  Diana Pottery 294
  European glass 213
  glass, other 211, 230 – 232
  Murano glass 223
  Venetian glass 224
  Webb & Corbett 211
duplicators 262, 258

E

earrings
  costume jewellery 169 – 173
  diamond 267
  enamel 266, 267
  gold 266, 267
  Lea Stein 173
  silver 266
  silver plate 169
edged weapons
  bayonets 311
  swords 311
egg cups
  anodised 246
  ceramics - Japanese 315
  Crown Lynn 78
  plastic 246
Ellis Pottery
  figure 127
  jug 127
  vases 127
Elvis
  albums 185, 187
  comic 335
  guitar 285
  memorabilia 281
  sheet music 346
Empire Ware animal 131
emu egg 286
enamel ware
  bowls 252
  bread bin 252
  canisters 250, 251
  pot 250
  tea pot 253
entertainment 179, 180
  see also movie related
  see also television related
  albums 184 – 189
  autographs 281
  automata 26

Beatles 184
Elvis 187
gaming systems 191
memorabilia 281
music groups 22
music related 184 – 191, 323, 335, 346
radios 20, 22, 180 – 183, 374
record player 285
records 284
epergnes 229
ephemera
  see printed material
Ericsson telephones 257
Ernest Borel 237
ewer 218
exercise equipment 355
eye bath 261
eye glasses 261

F

fabrics 255
fans 243 – 245
Fanta yo-yos 23
Featherston, Grant
  chairs 194, 195
  settee 195
Fenton
  baskets 229
  bowl 229
  lighting 277
Figgjo tureen 147
figures
  Australian Ceramics 131
  Australian souvenir ware 287
  Bendigo Pottery 126
  Bossons 137
  Ellis Pottery 127
  papier mache 47
  plaster 47
  terracotta 46
figurines
  Beswick 63
  Bing & Grondahl 137
  Bjorn Wiinblad 66
  Bossons 47
  Capodimonte 145
  Clarice Cliff 74
  Coalport 138
  Downing, Brownie 68
  European glass 213
  Goebel 80
  Goebel - Hummel 81 – 84
  Goldschneider 139
  Hollahaza 145
  Hummel 213
  Lladro 141
  Murano glass 217, 223, 224
  oriental ceramics 314
  Paragon 145
  Potter, Beatrix 65, 90
  Rosin, Louredan 219
  Royal Albert 90
  Royal Copenhagen 91
  Royal Doulton 98 - 106, 300
  Royal Doulton - Bunnykins 92 - 95

Royal Dux 141, 142
Seguso 217
Sommerso 219
Venetian glass 223, 224
Wade 121, 368
Wedgwood 74
Wembley 292, 293
  fire tools 290
fishing
  lines 355
  lure 355
  reels 301, 355
flag 286
flambé 272
flasks 247
  other 253
  silver plate 359
Fler chair 194
Florenz
  basket 127
  bookends 128
  vases 127
flour castor
  Cornishware/T. G. Green 138
fondue set 254
Ford magazine advert 305
Fornasetti paper weight 147
Fosters Pottery mug 284
franking machine 308
Frisbee 23
furniture
  American 205
  Art Deco style 192, 193
  Australian 192, 194 – 197, 205,
  206
  bar 198
  bedside cabinets 197, 199, 203
  cabinets 203, 208
  chairs - dining 196 – 198, 200,
  202, 206, 209
  chairs - pairs 195, 199, 207
  chairs - recliner 197
  chairs - rocking 202
  chairs - sets 196, 198, 201,
  202, 206, 209
  chairs - single 194 – 199, 201,
  202, 204 - 208
  chests of drawers 197,
  202 – 204, 208
  children's 206, 207
  cocktail cabinets 192
  commodes 197, 202, 204
  credenza 203
  cupboard 203
  day bed 207
  desks 199, 203
  dining suites 197, 200, 209
  display cabinets 192, 193
  dressing tables 193, 204
  drinks cabinet 198
  English & European 198
  Featherston, Grant 194, 195
  Fler 194
  G Plan 198
  kitchen cabinets 192, 193, 209
  lounges 194, 197, 203

Lowen, Fred 194
  magazine rack 205
  metal, glass & plastic 199, 200
  mirrors - other 193
  mirrors - wall 21, 31, 204
  outdoor 208, 209
  Parker 196
  plant stand 200
  plastic 205
  room divider 209
  Scandinavian designers &
  style 201 – 204
  settee 195
  sideboards 193, 196, 198, 202,
  203, 205, 208
  smoker's stand 193
  sofas 198, 201
  stools 194, 196, 200, 201, 208, 209
  tables - coffee 197, 204
  tables - dining 196 – 198, 200, 209
  tables - fondue 197
  tables - games 200, 204
  tables - small 193, 197, 200,
  201, 204
  tables - sofa 201, 204
  tables - telephone 200
  Tessa 194
  trolleys 193, 200, 208, 209
furniture handles 249

G

G Plan furniture 198
games 363
  AFL/VFL 293
  board 285
  cards 345, 346
  chess set 351
  darts 351
  dominos 351
  gaming token 351
  music related 285
  Pac-Man 239
  sporting 298
gaming systems
  Atari 191
  games 191
  Nintendo 191
  Sega 191
garagenalia
  oil cans 258
  petrol bowsers 258
  taxi meter 258
Georg Jensen
  bowl 358
  cutlery 252, 358
  jewellery 266
German ceramics 79
Gestetner Duplicator 258
Gibsons teapot 149
Glass
  see also lighting
  Australian 229, 233, 286, 294,
  297, 302
  Bohemia 213
  bottles 18, 22
  carnival 229

crystal 164, 210 – 215, 231,
270, 284, 300
  Darlington 211
  Daum crystal 212
  Dino Martens 218
  English 210, 211
  European 212, 213
  Fenton 229, 277
  Holmegaard 214
  Hummel 213
  Kiwiana 230, 308
  Kosta 214, 215
  Lalique 165, 213
  Latticino 219, 225
  Millefiori 213
  Murano 217 – 228, 279, 280
  opalescent 165, 210, 213, 230, 232
  oriental 319
  Orrefors 216
  perfume bottles 164, 165
  Pyrex 232, 253, 254
  Rosin, Louredan 219
  Scandinavian 214 – 216
  sculpture 47
  Seguso 217
  Sommerso 214, 215, 218, 219,
  221, 225, 227, 279
  Stuart Crystal 211, 212, 270
  Venetian 217 – 228, 279, 280
  Vicki Lindstrand 214
  Waterford 210, 212, 300
  Webb & Corbett 211, 300
  Wedgwood 283, 284
  Whitefriars 210
Globes – celestial & terrestrial
261
Glove Pottery 308
goblets
  Australian studio pottery 52
  silver 358
Goebel
  animals 80
  bowl 80
  figurines 80
  jugs 80
  salt & pepper shakers 80
Goebel - Hummel
  bell 84
  bookends 84
  figurines 81 – 84
  plaque 84
  plate 84
  vase 84
Goldschneider figurine 139
golf
  autograph 299
  badge 23
  balls 355
  bookends 299
  ceramics 299
  lighters 299, 353
  magazine advert 299
  memorabilia 299
  money box 320
  paper weight 299
  pill box 299

Gouda
  jug 139
  vases 139
gravy boat 130
Gredington, Arthur 54 – 58, 60 – 63
Green, T. G.
  bowls 138
  canister 138
  flour castor 138
  pie funnel 138
  salt pig 138
Grimwades
  bowl 140
  tobacco jar 139
gun (replica) 311
Gunda vase 132
Gustavberg vase 150

H

hand bags 158, 159
handkerchief 300
harmonica 190
hat pins 164
headwear 157, 161, 296, 303, 311
heaters 243
hedge clippers 260
Hills Hoist 36
Hoffman
  bowl 133
  bread crock 133
Holden playing cards 28
Hollahaza figurine 145
Holmegaard
  bowl 214
  vases 214
Homepride 26
honey pots
  allover floral/chintz 49
  Royal Winton 49
  Shorter & Son 117
hood ornament 304
Hornby trains 364, 365
horology
  clocks 18, 36, 234 – 236, 288,
  289, 308
  watches 179, 237 – 242, 302,
  311, 312
horse racing
  books 302
  drinking glass 302
  magazine 302
  plate 112
household and workshop
  appliances 243 – 245, 249, 252
  architectural 258
  enamel ware 250 – 253
  garagenalia 258
  iron 245
  kitchenalia 26,36, 243 – 254, 260
  plastic 26
  rugs 259
  sauna 243
  scales 252
  soft furnishings 255, 256
  storage containers 26
  telephones 22, 257, 368

tools 260
wallpaper 256
work related 258, 260
humidor 353

I

ice buckets 20
aluminium 347
anodised 246
Limoges 140
other 25
plastic 247, 249
ice cream scoop 253
ice crushers 245
ice pails 147
Imari cup 316
industry, science & technology
eye glasses 261
globes 261
medical 261, 299
nurse's uniform 35
other 258
pharmaceutical 262
scientific 262
taxidermy 262, 286
thermometers 19, 22, 36, 290
viewing devices 261
information boxes
Alexandra Copeland 50
Archimede Seguso 217
Arthur Greddington 62
Atmos clock 236
Australian Women's Weekly 339
Bakelite 247
Barsony 276
buying fabrics 256
collecting Aboriginal
artefacts 38
collecting Beswick figures 57
collecting oceanic artefacts 39
Conway Stewart 357
cruise line memorabilia 306
Dino Martens 218
Featherson, Grant 195
Fred Lowen 194
Fred of Homepride 38
Hummell figures 81
Japanese tin toys 377
Kalmar ceramics 128
Lea Stein 173
Lilliput Lane 140
Lorna Bailey 136
Lucite 158
Martin Sharp 44
Moorcroft Australian
designers 86
Murano glass 226
Oreton 160
Parker 51 357
Pedigree dolls 176
Rachel Bishop 87
Rolex 237
Rosin, Louredan 219
Royal Doulton Bunnykins

figures 92
Royal Doulton figurines 104
Royal Doulton HN numbering
system 100
Sally Tuffin 139
Tessa furniture 194
Tulip chair 201
Venetian glass 226
Wade 121
Bjorn Wiinblad 66
ink block 318
insect sprayer 258
insulator 232
iron 245
ivory
carvings 321
glove stretchers 318
snuff bottle 318

J

Jackson, Michael
doll 285
dress up set 285
James Kent
breakfast set 148
cup, saucer & plate 48
trio 48
jardiniere 260
jars
allover floral/chintz 49
Australian studio pottery 50
Beswick 64
glass 37, 233
Moorcroft 86
Royal Winton 49
jelly moulds 247, 252
jewellery
see also costume jewellery
bangles 263
bracelets 263 – 266, 289, 290
chains 267
cuff links 266
earrings 266, 267
general 266
Georg Jensen 266
locket 267
Masonic 266
miniature 267
necklaces 266, 267
pendants 266, 267
rings 266, 267
stick pin 266
tie clip 290
Johnson of Australia dinner
sets 132
jugs
Arabia 135
Australian Ceramics, other 131
Australian souvenir ware 287
Australian studio pottery 50,
51, 53
Bailey, Lorna 136
Bakewell's 126
Belleek 136
Beswick 64
blue & white ceramics 137

Boyd, Merric 67
Branksome Ceramics 144
Carlton Ware 69, 71, 72
Crown Devon 75
Crown Lynn 76, 78
electric 243
Ellis Pottery 127
German ceramics 79
Goebel 80
Gouda 139
Japanese ceramics 287, 298,
314, 316
Lowe, Alan 131
Mason's 141
McCallum 131
Murano glass 226
Noble, Rose 131
oriental ceramics 315
Pates Pottery 88
Royal Doulton 107, 111, 284
Royal Doulton - Character
Jugs 96, 97
Royal Stanley 146
Royal Winton 113, 114
Shorter & Son 117
stainless steel 253
Studio Anna 118
Tunstall 142
Venetian glass 218, 226, 228
Wade 121
water 20
water 35
Wedgwood 122, 284
whiskey 20, 21
juicer 245

K

Kalmar
plaque 128
vases 128
Kiss
action figures 285
badges 285
board game 285
record player 285
kit bag 164
kitchen cabinets
painted 209
Tasmanian oak 192, 209
kitchenalia
anodised 246
apple peeler 249
appliances 243 – 245, 249, 252
Australian 250, 251, 253
Bakelite 247 – 249
bean slicer 243
bowls 251 – 254, 259
bread bin 252
butcher's block 260
butter churn 260
butter smoother 253
cake decoration 253
cake stands 248, 249
can opener 244
canisters 127, 246 – 250
cocktail platter 254

coffee grinders 244, 253
coffee machines 244
coffee pot 252
colander 254
cooling rack 254
Cornishware 138, 253
cream pot 244
cutlery 252
egg cups 246
enamel ware 250 – 253
flasks 247, 253
fondue set 254
furniture 192, 193, 209
furniture handles 249
ice cream scoop 253
ice crushers 245
jelly moulds 247, 252
jug 253
juicer 245
knives 250
measuring cups 248, 254
mixers 245, 249
nutmeg grater 244
picnic set 247
pie funnel 254
plastic 246 – 249, 251
plates 26, 252
pots 250
rolling pins 253
salt & pepper shakers 26,
248, 254
serving fork 249
serving set 248
sieve 36
slicer 245
stove 252
tea cosies 253, 259
trays 254
urn 245
water fountain 147
weights 252
Kiwiana
album 189
architectural 77
art 47
blotter 288
book 308
books 322, 345
boxes 288, 289
ceramic 140
ceramics 76 – 78, 134, 139,
140, 283, 290, 352
cheese board 288
clocks 288, 289
corkscrew 288
Crown Lynn 76 – 78
desk accessories 288
doll 176
glass 230, 308
jewellery 289, 290
Maori 288 – 290
militaria 76 – 78, 311
money box 320
nautical 307
printed material 308
silver 289, 290

silver plate 290
small wooden items 288, 289, 307
souvenir ware 288 – 290
sport 283
Stewart Pottery 134
Te Mata Potteries 134
Te Rona Potteries 134
Temuka Pottery 134
tins 33, 34
toastrack 288
transport - motoring 308
transport - railways 308
knife rests 147
knives 250
Kosta
  bowl 214
  vases 214, 215

L

labels 29
Lalique
  perfume bottle 165
  plate 213
  vase 213
lamps
  Barsony 276
  Crown Lynn 76
  floor 91, 224, 274, 275, 277, 280, 317
  Kiwiana glass 230
  Maling 85
  Murano glass 224, 225
  other 269
  Poole 89
  Royal Copenhagen 91
  Royal Doulton - Bunnykins 93
  table 93, 225, 269, 272, 274 – 280, 367
  Venetian glass 224, 225, 279
Lancaster & Sandland mug 146
Latticino vases 219, 225
laundry basket 260
Lea Stein
  bangle 173
  brooches 173, 174
  earrings 173
  necklace 173
lead figures 362
letter opener 303
light meter 350
lighters 299, 303, 312
lighting
  Art Deco & modern classics 269
  candelabras 50, 270
  candle 368
  candlesticks 50, 66, 122, 215, 216, 222, 229, 270
  ceiling 271, 279
  chandeliers 271
  lamps - floor 85, 89, 91, 224, 274, 275, 277, 280, 317
  lamps - other 269
  lamps - table 93, 225, 230, 269, 272 – 280, 367
  other 280, 306

Venetian glass 279, 280
  wall 280
Lilliput Lane models 140
Limoges
  bowl 141
  cup, saucer & plate 140
  ice buckets 140
  trinket box 140
  trio 140
  vase 140
linen 255
Lladro 141
locket 267
Lord Nelson
  allover floral/chintz 48
  cruet set 48
  mug 299
Louis Vuition 157
lounges
  Australian 194
  fabric 203
  Lowen, Fred 194
  plywood 197
  Tessa 194
Lowe, Alan jug 131
Lowen, Fred
  chairs 194
  lounges 194
  stool 194
lunch box 191

M

machine gun (replica) 311
magazine racks 205, 248
magazines 281, 302
make-up case 157
Maling
  allover floral/chintz 49
  baskets 85
  bowls 85
  coffee pot 85
  comports 49, 85
  lamp 85
  vases 85
manicure sets 157
mannequins 35, 261
Maori
  art 47
  carvings 288, 289
  souvenir ware 288, 289, 290
map 345
Masonic
  drinking glass 212
  jewellery 266
Mason's
  jug 141
  tureen 141
match striker 143
Matchbox toys 382
McCallum jugs 131
McLaren, Betty
  animal 129
  bowl 128
McLaren, Gus
  animals 128, 129
  bowls 129

salt & pepper shakers 129
sculpture 129
MCP Mingay
  animals 129, 130
  gravy boat 130
  vases 129, 130
measuring cups
  copper 254
  plastic 248
Meccano
  building sets 380
  trains 364, 365
medallions
  AFL/VFL 291
  Australian 312
medals
  life saving 312
  militaria 310
medical
  condoms 261
  dentistry samples 261
  eye bath 261
  eye glasses 261
  mannequin 261
  nurse's uniform 35
  pill box 299
  steriliser 261
  x-ray viewer 261
Memmott, Harry 130
Memorabilia
  see also movie related
  see also music related
  see also sport
  see also television related
  see also transport
  Australian souvenir ware 286
  autographs 281, 292, 299, 312
  Christmas 24, 92, 282, 320
  commemorative 283, 286, 305
  entertainment 281
  other 309
  royalty 284, 286, 305, 351
  souvenir ware 286, 288 – 290
metronome 190
micrometer 260
microphone 191
microscope 262
militaria
  air force 312
  army 310 – 312
  Australian 310 – 312
  badges 310, 312
  bell 312
  ceramics 76 – 78
  certificate 312
  compass 312
  customs 310
  edged weapons 311
  headwear 311
  kit 312
  Kiwiana 3111, 312
  lighter 312
  machine gun (replica) 311
  medals 310
  navy 311, 312
  other 310 – 312

photograph 312
police 310 – 312
uniform 312
watches 241, 311, 312
Millefiori jug 213
miniature 267
Minic Toys car 361
mirrors
  hand 287
  other 193
  wall 21, 31, 204
mixers 245
Mobo 385
models
  house 258
  Lilliput Lane 140
  Wade 121
  Winter, David 147
money boxes 300, 320
Moon, Milton
  pots 130
  vases 130
Moorcroft
  bowls 86, 87
  charger 86
  coffee pot 86
  jar 86
  plate 86
  vases 86, 87
Moorland
  plaque 147
  tea set 148
motoring
  see also motor sport
  Ford 305
  ashtray 352
  badges 304, 305, 308
  belt buckle 305
  bottle 308
  brochure 304, 305
  calendar 35
  corkscrew 304
  desk set 304
  display figure 305
  drum caps 37
  magazine adverts 304, 305
  magazines 339
  mascots 304, 305
  number plates 304, 305, 308
  oil cans 258
  petrol bowsers 258
  picnic set 37
  plaque 304
  playing cards 28
  postcard 305
  signs 30, 32, 304
  taxi meter 258
  tins 33, 305
motor sport
  mug 302
  postcard 301
  shop display 301
  watch 302
Moulin Des Loups 20
Movado watches 238, 240
movie related

album 188
autographs 281
badge 309
booklet 28
can 22
comic 179
figures 179
memorabilia 179, 281
posters 340 – 342, 344
Royal Doulton - Figurines 102
science fiction 281
serving tray 309
Star Trek 281, 334, 335, 340, 371
Star Wars 179, 309, 329, 341,
342, 344, 369, 370,
toys 360 - 375
mugs
Belleek 136
Boyd, Martin 67
Carlton Ware 72
Diana Pottery 127, 299
Fosters Pottery 284
glass 232
Kiwiana ceramics 283
Lancaster & Sandland 146
Lord Nelson 299
oriental ceramics 315
pewter 302, 307
Pyrex 232
Royal Doulton - Bunnykins 93
Royal Doulton 110
silver plate 359
Studio Anna 118
Wade 121, 299
Wedgwood 283
Murano glass
animals 217, 218, 220, 223 – 225
ashtray 220
baskets 220, 225
bowls 217, 220 – 222
candlesticks 222
centrepieces 223
comport 222
decanters 222, 223
drinking glasses 219, 223
drinks set 223
figurines 217, 223, 224
jugs 226
lamps 224, 225, 280
lighting 279
paper weights 226
plates 221
sculpture 224
vases 217, 220, 223, 225 – 228
music related
albums 184 – 189
autographs 281
badges 190
books 323
DJ desk 190
Elvis 185, 187, 281, 285, 335, 346
groups 22, 284
harmonica 190
Kiss 285
magazines 285
memorabilia 281, 285

metronome 190
Michael Jackson 285
music boxes 190
performers 285
poster 285
record needles 190
record players 190, 285
records 184
Royal Doulton - Bunnykins 93, 94
sheet music 346
sound system 191
speaker 191
tape recorder 191
The Beach Boys 285
The Beatles 184, 285

N
nautical
air horn 307
ashtrays 306, 307
Australian 306
book marks 306
buoy 318
ceramics 306, 307
corkscrew 307
counter display 306
cruet set 307
drawing 306
Kiwiana 307
lighting 306
menu 307
mug 307
pen holder 307
plate 112
porthole 307
scrimshaw 321
ship's log 306
souvenir ware 307
toys 361
necklaces
amber 172
costume jewellery 170 – 173
gold 267
Lea Stein 173
pearls 267
pewter 266
silver 266
tourmalines 267
netsuke 318
Nintendo 191
Noble, Rose 131
Noddy 371
Noritake
animals 314, 319
coffee pot 315
salad set 315
tea set 316
vase 316
number plates 304, 305
numismatics & scrip
Australian 312
bank notes 312
coins 312
medal 312
medallions 312
nutmeg grater 244

O
obelisk 217
oil cans 258
Olympics
badge 300
beer 300
bottles 22
calendar 300
ceramics 94, 300
figurines 300
handkerchief 300
money box 300
trophy 300
Omega watches 237 – 242, 302
oriental
buoy 318
boxes 318, 319
bracelet 172
ceramics - Chinese 315
ceramics - Japanese 287,
298, 315 – 317
ceramics - other 314, 315
clothing 318
desk set 319
dolls 319
duster 319
engraving 319
glass 164, 319
glove stretchers 318
ink block 318
ivory 318
lighting 317
netsuke 318
other 318, 319
snuff bottles 318
tin 318
ornament 147
Oreton 160
Orrefors 216
overnight bag 157

P
Pac-Man watch 239
paintings 44
paper weights
Fornasetti 147
Murano glass 226
other glass 211, 231, 232
other 299
Venetian glass 218, 226
Paragon
figurines 145
plates 148
Parker furniture
chairs - dining 196
chairs - single 196
stool 196
table - coffee 196
table - dining 196
Pates Pottery 88
pedal cars 383
Pedigree dolls 175, 176
pen nibs 356
pencil holder 249
pendants

costume jewellery 171
enamel 267
gold 267
Masonic 266
other 267
pearl 267
pewter 266
silver 267
pennants 294, 295, 306
pens 232, 356
perfume bottles 164, 212, 230
periscope 261
petrol bowsers 258
Phantom comics 328
pharmaceutical
bottles 262
weights 262
photographic
badge 350
cameras 348, 349, 386
equipment 350
frames 350
manual 350
photographs 293, 298, 301,
303, 309, 312, 346
slide viewer 350
slides 38
tripod 350
view finder 350
picnic sets 37, 247
pie funnels
Cornishware/T. G. Green 138
other ceramics 254
pill box 299
planes 260
plant stands 200, 321
plaques
aluminium 286, 304
art 45
Australian Ceramics 132, 133
Australian studio pottery 53
Downing, Brownie 68
Goebel - Hummel 84
Kalmar 128
metal 24
Moorland 147
oriental ceramics 317
Royal Albert 32
Studio Anna 118
timber 287
plastic
ashtrays 352
bangles 172
brooches 166, 171
canisters 247 – 251
chairs 199, 205
Christmas decorations 282
container 26
display figures 26
dolls 176, 177
drinking glass 247
earrings 169, 171
egg cups 246
furniture 208
ice buckets 25, 247 – 249
lamps 269, 273–275, 277, 278, 280

letter opener 303
magazine rack 248
measuring cups 248
money boxes 320
necklaces 170, 172
pencil holder 249
picnic set 37
sculpture 47
serving set 248
signs 32
stools 200, 201
tables 197
telephones 257
plates
  Adams 137
  allover floral/chintz 49
  Arabia 135
  Australian Ceramics - other 35, 132, 286
  Australian studio pottery 132
  Aynsley 135
  Beswick 282, 368
  Bjorn Wiinblad 66, 282
  blue & white ceramics 137
  Boyd, Guy 67
  Branksome Ceramics 144
  Carlton Ware 69, 70, 72
  ceramics - Chinese 315
  Ceramics - other 148, 298, 306
  Clarice Cliff 74
  Coalport 138
  Crown Devon 75
  Crown Lynn 77
  Douglas, Neil 131
  Downing, Brownie 68
  Goebel - Hummel 84
  Kiwiana souvenir ware 289
  Lalique 213
  Moorcroft 86
  Murano glass 221
  other 252
  Paragon 148
  Pates Pottery 88
  Poole 89
  Quimper 148
  Ridgways 141
  Royal Albert 90
  Royal Copenhagen 91, 283
  Royal Couldon 283
  Royal Doulton - Bunnykins 93
  Royal Doulton 26, 107 – 112
  Royal Winton 49, 113, 114
  Royal Worcester 115
  Shelley 116
  Spode 299
  Studio Anna 118
  Susie Cooper 119
  Venetian glass 221
  Wedgwood 122, 123, 283
  Woods & Son 132
platters
  Australian Ceramics 132
  Australian studio pottery 51, 52
  Carlton Ware 70
  Shorter & Son 117
  Wedgwood 122

playing cards 18, 21, 28
Poole
  animal 89
  bowl 89
  charger 89
  coffee set 89
  lamp 89
  plates 89
  vases 89
port 284
porthole 307
Portmerion coffee set 144
postcards 301, 302
posters 340
  advertising 40, 41, 43
  aeronautical 303
  art 44
  music related 285
  sporting 292, 294, 295, 301
pot pouri 115
pots
  Australian studio pottery 50, 53
  Boyd, Kevin 128
  Boyd, Martin 67
  enamel 250
  Memmott, Harry 130
  Moon, Milton 130
  Potter, Beatrix 65, 90
pourer 347
pram 259
precious objects
  see also boxes
  see also small wooden items
  apprentice pieces 258, 321
  ivory 321
  money boxes 300, 320
  music boxes 190
  religious items 270, 283, 287
  scrimshaw 321
Price Kensington 149
printed material
  advertising 27
  booklet 28
  books 298, 299, 301, 302, 308, 309, 322, 323, 325, 345, 367
  brochures 35, 304, 305
  calendars 24, 35, 300
  catalogues 28, 325, 345
  certificates 287, 312, 346
  chocolate wrappers 27, 28
  cigarette cards 297, 298, 345
  comics 179, 309, 326 – 336, 339, 369 – 371
  display figure 346
  game cards 346, 345
  labels 29
  magazine adverts 24, 25, 27, 299, 304, 305
  magazines 302, 337 – 339
  manual 350
  map 345
  menu 307
  newspaper 298
  photographs 293, 346
  playing cards 18, 21, 28, 303
  postcards 301, 302, 305, 346

posters 40 – 43, 285, 292, 294, 295, 301, 303, 340 – 344,
programs 292, 301
ration card 346
sample cards 37
sheet music 346
show bags 36
signs 31, 32
sporting 293, 295 – 298
sporting cards 291 – 294, 296, 297
trading cards 303, 345
prints 44
pub mirror 21
purses 158
puzzles 363
Pyrex
  bowls 253, 254
  mugs 232

Q

Qantas
  label 29
  model 26
Quimper plate 148

R

radios 20, 22, 180
Rado watch 241
railways
  books 308, 325
  cabinet 206
  clock 308
  drinking glass 308
  franking machine 308
  oil can 308
  poster 40
  toys 364
  trio 308
ration card 346
record needles 190
record players 190, 285
records
  see albums
recreations & pursuits
  see also alcohol related
  see also desk accessories
  see also photographic
  see also smoking
  see also sport
  see also writing
  games 239, 285, 293, 298, 345, 346, 351
  sewing 351
Regal China decanters 18, 19
religious items
  candlesticks 270
  certificate 287
  plate 283
Remued
  basket 131
  jug 131
  vase 131
retro
  jug 146

prints 44
vases 64, 79, 133
Ridways plate 141
rings
  aquamarine 267
  amethyst 267
  citrine 267
  diamond 267
  gold 267
  lapis lazuli 267
  opal 267
  ruby 267
  silver 266, 267
  turquoise 267
rocking horses 384
Rodica chair 198
Rolex 237 – 242
roller skates 355
rolling pins
  Cornish Ware/T. G. Green 253
  timber 253
room divider 209
Rosin, Louredan
  figurine 219
  Rotary poster 40
Royal Albert
  bowl 90
  cup & saucer 90
  cups, saucers & plates 90
  figurine 90
  plaque 32
  plate 90
  Potter, Beatrix 90
  tea sets 90
  teapot 90
  tray 90
  trios 90
  tureen 90
Royal Copenhagen
  bowl 91
  coffee pot 91
  figurines 91
  lamp 91
  plates 91, 283
  vases 91
Royal Cauldon plate 283
Royal Doulton
  animals 98, 99, 300
  ash bowl 110
  ashtrays 20, 109, 110, 306
  bowls 107 – 110
  Bunnykins 92
  character jugs 96, 97, 283, 302
  coffee sets 110
  comports 109, 110
  cups, saucers & plates 108, 110
  decanter 347
  dinner sets 111
  figurines 98 – 106, 300
  flambé 98, 101, 272
  jugs 107, 111, 284
  lamps 272
  lighter 353
  mug 110
  plates 26, 107 – 112
  series ware 107 – 109

teapot 108
tea set 110
tray 109
trios 108, 110
vases 109, 112
Royal Doulton - Bunnykins
bowls 93
figurines 93 – 95
lamp 93
mugs 93
music boxes 93, 94
plates 93
Royal Dux
animals 141, 142
figurines 141, 142
vase 142
Royal Stanley jug 146
Royal Winton
allover floral/chintz 48, 49
basket 113
bowls 48, 113, 114
breakfast set 48, 114
cake stand 49
cheese dish 114
comports 49, 113
cruet set 114
cups & saucers 48, 113
cups, saucers & plates 48, 113
honey pots 49
jars 49
jugs 113, 114
plates 49, 113, 114
series ware 113, 114
teapots 49, 114
toast racks 48, 114
tray 140
trinket box 113
trios 48, 113
vases 48, 114
Royal Worcester
animals 115
cup, saucer & plate 115
plates 115
pot pouri 115
trio 115
vases 115
royalty
badge 305
beer 284
Coca-cola 284
decanter 283
drinking glass 284
flag 286
jugs 284
memorabilia 284
mug 284
port 284
record 284
teapot 284
thimbles 351
tin 284
trio 284
rugby league
bag 302
postcard 302
rugs 259

S

sailing cup 25
sake set 315
salad set 315
salesman's sample 36
Salisbury Bone China tea set 148
Sally, Tuffin vases 139
salt & pepper shakers
Australian ceramics - other 287
Bailey, Lorna 136
Bakelite 248
Boyd, Martin 67
Carlton Ware 73
ceramics - Japanese 314, 316
Crown Lynn 77
Downing, Brownie 68
Goebel 80
McLaren, Gus 129
metal - other 25
oriental ceramics - other 314, 316
other 254
salt pigs
Cornishware/Green, T. G. 138
salt shaker 316
sauce boats 71
sauna 243
scent bottles 164, 212, 230
scientific
bottles 262
microscope 262
pharmaceutical 262
thermometer 262
scrimshaw 321
sculpture
animals 46
Australian Ceramics - other 131
Australian studio pottery 52
earthenware 47
Ellis Pottery 127
glass 47
Mclaren, Betty 129
McLaren, Gus 128, 129
Murano glass 224
perspex 47
timber 47
Venetian glass 224
Sega 191
Seguso
animals 217
figurines 217
vase 217
Seiko
clock 236
watch 241
series ware
Royal Doulton 107–109, 113, 114
Royal Winton 113, 114
server 78
serviette rings
Carlton Ware 73
mulga wood 287
silver plate 359
serving fork 249
serving sets 148, 248
settee 195
sewing

bobbins 351
darning mushroom 351
machines 351
tape measure 351
thimbles 351
shaving set 248
Shelley
coffee pot 116
coffee set 116
cup & saucer 116
cups, saucers & plates 48, 116
dinner set 116
plates 116
trios 48, 116
ship's log 306
shoes 162
Shorter & Son 117
show bags 36, 37
sideboards
cedar 205
G Plan 198
oak 205
rosewood 203, 208
teak 196, 198, 202, 203
walnut 205
sideboards 193
sieve 36
signs
alcohol related 21
cardboard 31, 32
enamel 24, 30, 32
illuminated 21, 31, 32
iron 32
metal - other 24, 30 – 32
mirrors 21, 31
neon 21
plaster 37
timber 30, 32
tin 21, 24, 31
silver
Australian 286
bangles 263
belt buckle 305
bowls 358
bracelets 263, 266
brooches 166, 264, 266, 289, 290
candelabra 270
candlesticks 270
comport 358
cutlery 358
earrings 266
goblet 358
necklaces 266
pendant 267
photo frames 350
pill box 299
pourer 347
rings 266, 267
spoons 287, 358
stiletto 358
sugar castor 358
tie clip 290
whisky label 358
silver plate
belt 165
bowls 359

bracelet 168
candelabra 270
cutlery 359
earrings 169
fire tools 290
flask 359
mugs 359
serviette rings 359
tankard 359
tea set 359
skittles 367
slicer 245
slide viewer 350
slides 38
small wooden items
basket 321
bookends 321
bottle stopper 321
bowls 286, 321
cruet set 307
Kiwiana 288, 289
magazine rack 205
plant stand 321
smoking
ash bowl 110
ashtrays 20, 109, 110, 125,
220, 224, 286, 287, 306, 307,
352, 353, 356
cigarette boxes 71, 353
cigarette cards 345
cigarette holders 353, 354
hookah 354
humidor 353
lighters 299, 303, 312, 352 – 354
match box dispenser 354
match striker 143
playing card 28
signs 31
smoker's stand 193
tape measure 353
tobacco jars 134, 139
water jug 35
Smurfs 384
snuff bottles 318
soccer
ball 25
character jug 302
soda syphons
anodised 246
Australian glass 229
Kiwiana glass 230
sofas 198, 201
soft furnishings
fabrics 255, 256
linen 255
wall hanging 287
Sommerso
animals 225
bowls 218, 221
figurines 219
lamp 279
vases 214, 215, 219, 227
sound system 191
souvenir ware
Australian 124, 286, 287
Australian Aboriginal 38

doll 175
  Kiwiana 288 – 290
  nautical 307
spelter statuary 47
Spiderman comics 327
Spode
  cup & saucer 299
  plate 299
spoons
  Kiwiana souvenir ware 290
  silver 287, 358
sport
  see AFL/VFL
  see basketball
  see boxing
  see Commonwealth Games
  see fishing
   see golf
  see horse racing
  see motor sport
  see Olympics
  see rugby league
  see soccer
  see tennis
  darts 351
  memorabilia 283
  sailing 25
  wrestling 301
sporting equipment
  exercise equipment 355
  fishing 355
  golf 355
  roller skates 355
  tennis 355
Stanley cup & saucer 144
Star Trek
  autograph 281
  comics 334, 335, 371
  memorabilia 281, 371
  poster 340
  toys 371
Star Wars
  action figures 369, 370
  comics 329, 360, 370
  memorabilia 179, 370
  other toys 369
  posters 341, 342, 344
statuary
  animals 46
  bronze 47
  bust 19, 46
  ceramic 19
  concrete 258
  garden 258
  papier mache 47
  plaster 47
  rubber 19
  spelter 47
  terracotta 46
  timber 47
steam bath 243
steam engines 385
steriliser 261
Stewart Pottery teapot 134
stick pin 266
stiletto 358

Stoke on Trent casserole
dishes 250
stoneware demijohn 131
stools
  Australian 194
  Lowen, Fred 194
  other timber 208, 209
  plastic 200, 201
  Tessa 194
Stuart Crystal
  candlestick 270
  decanters 211
  drinking glasses 212
Studio Anna 118
stuffed toys 178, 368
sugar castors
  Carlton Ware 73
  Crown Devon 75
  silver 358
suitcases 157
sunglasses 163
Susie Cooper 119
swords 311
SylvaC
  animals 120
  vases 120

T

tables
  chromed 193
  coffee 193, 196, 197, 204
  dining 196 – 198, 200, 209
  fondue 197
  games 200, 204
  plastic 197
  small 196, 197, 200, 201, 204
  sofa 201, 204
  telephone 200
tankards
  Kiwiana ceramics 290
  silver plate 359
  Wedgwood 284
tape measures 351, 353
tape recorder 191
taxidermy 262
Te Mata Potteries vase 134
Te Rona Potteries vase 134
tea cosies 253, 259
tea pots
  BCM Nelson Ware 148
  Gibsons 149
tea sets
  Australian studio pottery 53
  Beswick 367
  ceramics - Japanese 316
  Ceramics - other 149
  Crown Devon 75
  glass - other 231
  Moorland 148
  Noritake 316
  oriental ceramics 315
  Royal Albert 90
  Royal Doulton 110
  Salisbury Bone China 148
  silver plate 359
  Susie Cooper 119

tea trolley 193
teapots
  allover floral/chintz 49
  Arabia 135
  Australian Ceramics, other 133
  Bailey, Lorna 136
  Belleek 136
  Burleigh Ware 137
  Carlton Ware 72
  Ceramics, other 149
  Clarice Cliff 74
  Downing, Brownie 68
  Price Kensington 149
  Royal Albert 90
  Royal Doulton 108
  Royal Winton 49, 114
  Stewart Pottery 134
  Susie Cooper 119
  Wedgwood 123
teddy bears 178
telephone box 257
telephones 22, 257, 368
television related
  autograph 281
  badge 191
  beer 309
  lunch box 191
  memorabilia 281
  money box 320
  prop 309
  science fiction 281
  television 191
  toys 371 – 375
  Videoscope 191
Temuka Pottery
  boots 134
  tobacco jar 134
  vase 134
tennis
  autographs 281
  balls 302
  book 302
  memorabilia 281
  racquets 355
Tessa
  chairs 194
  lounges 194
  stool 194
The Beach Boys backstage
passes 285
The Beatles
  albums 184
  figurines 285
  magazines 285
  memorabilia 285
  poster 285
  toys 184
thermometers 19, 22, 290
thimbles 351
Thomas dinner set 145
thongs 23
tie clip 290
tile 143
tins
  Australian 292
  biscuit barrel 251

biscuits 33
cake 292
canisters 250, 251
coffee 33
confectionery 34
ice cream 309
nuts 34
oil 33, 305
other 33, 318, 367, 373
powder 33
tea 34, 284
Tissot watches 240, 241, 243
toasters 243
toast racks
  allover floral/chintz 48
  Carlton Ware 73
  Royal Winton 48, 114
  Shorter & Son 117
  timber 288
tobacco jars 134, 139
tools
  concrete mixer 260
  hedge clippers 260
  micrometer 260
  planes 260
towels 290
toys
  see also dolls
  action figures 285, 372, 375, 378
  aeroplanes 26, 362, 383, 384
  Australian 378, 379, 382, 383, 387
  boats 360, 386
  Britains 366
  building sets 380
  busses 366, 379
  cars 361, 362, 373, 379, 382
  cereal 380
  clockwork 377, 380, 381
  Corgi 381
  Cyclops 383
  die-cast - other 381
  Dinky 362
  Disney 367, 368
  doll furniture 385
  dress up set 285
  Frisbee 23
  games 239, 285, 293, 298, 345, 346, 363
  guitar 285
  Hornby 364
  lead figures 362, 382
  lighting 278
  Matchbox 382, 384
  Meccano 364, 380
  militaria 362, 381, 382, 385, 386
  Minic 361
  Mobo 385
  models 360, 383
  models 386
  movie & television related 369 – 375, 387
  Noddy 371
  promotional 25
  puzzles 363

rocking horses 384, 385
Smurfs 384
Star Trek 371
Star Wars 369, 370
steam engines 385
stuffed toys 373, 374, 379
tea sets 386
television related 179
tinplate 376 – 381, 384
train related 364, 365
trains 25, 364, 365
Tri-ang Minic 366, 377
trucks 362, 366, 373, 379
trucks 378
yo-yos 23
trading cards 345
transport
  see aeronautical
  see motoring
  see nautical
trays
  advertising 36
  chromed 247
  Kiwiana souvenir ware 289
  other trays 254
  Royal Albert 90
  Royal Doulton 109
  Royal Winton 140
  tin 18
  Villeroy and Boch 143
Tri-ang Minic toys 366, 377
tribal
  Australian Aboriginal 38
  New Guinean 39
  Peruvian 267
trios
  allover floral/chintz 48
  Broadhurst 145
  Glove Pottery 308
  James Kent 48
  Limoges 140
  Royal Albert 90
  Royal Doulton 108, 110
  Royal Winton 48, 113
  Royal Worcester 115
  Shelley 48, 116
  Susie Cooper 119
tripod 350
tripod adaptor 350
trishaw 308
Troika vases 149
trolleys
  chromed 200, 208
  Queensland maple 209
  stainless steel 200
trophies
  boxing 300
  Olympics 300
  other 295
trouser creaser 157
Tudor 241, 242
Tulip chair 201
Tunstall
  bowl 142
  jugs 142
tureens

Figgjo 147
Mason's 141
Royal Albert 90
Villeroy and Boch 143
typewriter 258

U

umbrella stand 46
umbrellas 164
Up 5 chair 198
Upsala Ekeby 144
urns
  Beswick 64
  electric 245

V

vases
  Albaware 126
  allover floral/chintz 48
  Australian Ceramics - other 132, 133
  Australian studio pottery 51 – 53, 133
  Bailey, Lorna 136
  Beswick 63, 64
  Bisque 137
  Bjorn Wiinblad 66
  Bohemia 213
  Carlton Ware 70
  ceramic - other 144, 149, 150
  ceramics - Japanese 316
  Clarice Cliff 74
  Coalport 137
  Crown Devon 75
  Crown Lynn 76 – 78
  Darlington 211
  Denby 139
  Dennis China 139
  Diana Pottery 126, 127
  Dino Martens 218
  Ellis Pottery 127
  European glass 213
  Florenz 127
  German ceramics 79
  glass – other 211, 229, 232, 233
  Goebel - Hummel 84
  Gouda 139
  Gunda 132
  Gustavberg 150
  Holmegaard 214
  Japanese ceramics 317
  Kalmar 128
  Kiwiana glass 230
  Kiwiana 134
  Kosta 214, 215
  Lalique 213
  Latticino 219, 225
  Limoges 140
  Maling 85
  MCP Mingay 129, 130
  Moon, Milton 130
  Moorcroft 86, 87
  Murano glass 217, 219, 220, 223, 225 – 228

Noritake 316
oriental glass 319
Orrefors 216
other Australian glass - other 233
Pates Pottery 88
Poole 89
Remued 131
Royal Copenhagen 91
Royal Doulton 109, 112
Royal Dux 142
Royal Winton 48, 114
Royal Worcester 115
Scandinavian glass 215, 216
Seguso 217
Shorter & Son 117
Sommerso 214, 215, 219, 227
Studio Anna 118
SylvaC 120
Te Mata Potteries 134
Te Rona Potteries 134
Temuka Pottery 134
Troika 149
Tuffin, Sally 139
Venetian glass 218 – 220, 223, 225 – 227
Vicki Lindstrand 214
Wedgwood 74, 123
Wembley 125
Whitefriars 210
Vicki Lindstrand vases 214
Videoscope 191
view finder 350
View Master reels 179
Villeroy and Boch 143

W

Wade
  animal 121
  bowl 121
  decanter 283
  figurines 121, 368
  jug 121
  model 121
  mug 299
  water jugs 20
  whiskey jugs 20, 21
wall hanging 287
wallpaper 256
watches
  Breitling 238
  Ernest Borel 237
  militaria 311, 312
  Movado 238, 240
  Omega 237 – 242, 302
  other 237 – 242
  pendant 242
  pocket 237, 241
  Rado 241
  Rolex 237 – 242
  Seiko 241
  Tissot 240, 241
  Tudor 241, 242
  wrist 179, 237 – 242, 302, 312
water bottle 229
water fountain 147
water sets

other glass 231, 232
Venetian glass 224
Waterford
  biscuit barrel 210
  centrepiece 300
  decanter 212
watering can 260
Webb & Corbett
  drinking glass 300
  drinks set 211
Wedgwood
  bowls 123
  candlestick 122
  Clarice Cliff 74
  drinking glasses 283, 284
  figurine 74
  jugs 122, 284
  lighter 354
  plates 122, 123, 283
  platter 122
  tankard 284
  teapot 123
  thimbles 351
  trinket boxes 122
  vases 74, 123
weights 252
Wembley
  animals 124
  ashtrays 124, 125, 352
  bowl 125
  figurines 292, 293
  vases 125
whisky label 358
Whitefriars 210
Wilkinson's serving set 148
Winter, David model 147
Winterling coffee set 144
wire
  cooling rack 254
  furniture 209
  outdoor setting 208
Wood, Arthur basket 144
Woods & Son plate 132
work related
  concrete mixer 260
  duplicator 258
  Gestetner Duplicator 258
wrestling mask 301
writing
  see also desk accessories
  pen holder 307
  pen nibs 356
  pens 232, 356, 357
  typewriter 258

X

x-ray viewer 261

Y

yo-yos 23

Z

Zsolnay animals 143